Struggling to Define a Nation

ROTH FAMILY FOUNDATION

Music in America Imprint

Michael P. Roth
and Sukey Garcetti
have endowed this
imprint to honor the
memory of their parents,
Julia and Harry Roth,
whose deep love of music
they wish to share
with others.

Struggling to Define a Nation

American Music and the Twentieth Century

CHARLES HIROSHI GARRETT

University of California Press

BERKELEY   LOS ANGELES   LONDON

University of California Press, one of the most distinguished university presses in the United States, enriches lives around the world by advancing scholarship in the humanities, social sciences, and natural sciences. Its activities are supported by the UC Press Foundation and by philanthropic contributions from individuals and institutions. For more information, visit www.ucpress.edu.

University of California Press
Berkeley and Los Angeles, California

University of California Press, Ltd.
London, England

Library of Congress Cataloging-in-Publication Data

Garrett, Charles Hiroshi, 1966–
   Struggling to define a nation : American music and the twentieth century / Charles Hiroshi Garrett.
     p.   cm.
   Includes bibliographical references and index.
   ISBN: 978–0–520-25486-2 (cloth : alk. paper)—
ISBN: 978–0–520-25487-9 (pbk. : alk. paper)
    1. Music—United States—20th century—History and criticism.
2. Nationalism in music.   I. Title.

   ML200.5.G37 2008
   780.973'0904—dc22   2008014157

Manufactured in the United States of America

17 16 15 14 13 12 11 10 09 08
10 9 8 7 6 5 4 3 2 1

To my grandparents and their American journeys

What is opposed brings together; the finest harmony is composed of things at variance, and everything comes to be in accordance with strife.

HERACLITUS

Contents

Illustrations

Acknowledgments

When I stepped into Mark Tucker's classroom for the first time, I had no idea that this book might someday be written. But his devotion to jazz history and American music was so inspiring that, seemingly before I knew it, I found myself embarking on my own musical journey. In those years as an undergraduate at Columbia University, I was fortunate to study with many similarly dedicated teachers, including Elaine Sisman, who taught me how to integrate historical sources into my writing; Timothy Taylor, whose example encouraged me to study the intersections of music and politics; and H. Wiley Hitchcock, who fostered my interest in the music of Charles Ives and offered valuable guidance and the best of friendship. Outside the classroom, I will always be thankful to Jeff Eldredge for being the first person to support my budding interest in this field and to Maria Ruvoldt for sharing memorable conversations and wise advice.

My work has profited from countless contributions by the faculty and students affiliated with the Department of Musicology at the University of California, Los Angeles. I benefited from stimulating graduate seminars and conversations that shaped my approach to music history, and I wish to acknowledge everyone who offered helpful advice about various aspects of this project, including Andrew Berish, Philip Brett, Maria Cizmic, Dale Chapman, Francesca Draughon, Amy Frishkey, Raymond Knapp, Elisabeth Le Guin, Erik Leidal, Tamara Levitz, Olivia Mather, Mitchell Morris, Louis Niebur, Stephanie Vander Wel, Jacqueline Warwick, Larry Wayte, and Nadya Zimmerman. I am especially grateful to Glenn Pillsbury for his altruism and his technical help, Kate Bartel for her remarkable kindness, Gordon Haramaki for his boundless warmth, David Ake for his friendship and his exemplary work, Daniel Goldmark for his cheerful outlook and ongoing advice, Loren Kajikawa for sharing new musical finds and memorable meals, and Cecilia Sun for being such a wonderful friend through it all.

Several of the chapters in this book took their initial shape in my dissertation, and I am grateful that the members of my committee, Albert Boime, Robert Fink, and Susan McClary, devoted so much of their time, energy, and expertise to the project. I am especially thankful to Robert Walser, my adviser, for all his efforts to foster my intellectual, professional, and personal growth. Chapter 3 would not have taken shape without his memorable graduate seminar on the music of Louis Armstrong; far more significantly, Rob's thoughtful advice and his concern for my well-being over the years have taught me what it takes to be a great mentor.

My research has been supported by fellowships from the Department of Musicology and the Graduate Division of the University of California, Los Angeles. Additionally, the American Musicological Society provided support for my graduate studies through the Alvin H. Johnson AMS 50 Dissertation Fellowship and the Howard Mayer Brown Fellowship. I also remain indebted to my longtime friend Seth Strumph for his financial assistance at a critical moment of my graduate career.

I could not have asked for a more supportive editor for this project than Mary Francis, whose careful guidance and patience have proven invaluable throughout the writing process. Along with Kalicia Pivirotto, Mary Severance, and other supportive colleagues at UC Press, she helped to enrich many different facets of this book. I am especially indebted to Ann Twombly for her fine editing work.

This project could not have been completed without the assistance of helpful staff at numerous archives. Peggy Alexander, Timothy Edwards, and their colleagues at the UCLA Library Performing Arts Special Collections have been especially generous, as much of my research derives from the sheet music collection held in their Archive of Popular American Music. Charles Reynolds, who heads the Music Library at the University of Michigan, has also gone above and beyond in support of this project. I would also like to thank Bruce Boyd Raeburn and the staff at Tulane University's William Ransom Hogan Archive of New Orleans Jazz for helping me to locate many useful materials related to Jelly Roll Morton.

I have benefited from commentary by audiences who heard earlier drafts of selected material at annual meetings of the Society for American Music, the American Musicological Society, and the International Association for the Study of Popular Music (U.S. branch). A previous version of chapter 4 was published in the *Journal of the American Musicological Society*, and

I am grateful to the journal's editors, Joseph Auner and Catherine Gjerdingen, for giving such thorough attention to my work. W. Anthony Sheppard, Judy Tsou, and Deborah Wong also offered particularly valuable feedback to the initial version of that article.

I wish to thank all the individuals who shared valuable resources or contributed advice as this book developed, including Judith Calvert, James Revell Carr, James Dapogny, Larry Edelstein, Keith Emmons, Daniel Goldmark, Larry Hamberlin, William Howland Kenney, Raymond Knapp, Robert Lang, Jeffrey Magee, Mike Meddings, Malcolm Rockwell, Deane Root, Judy Tsou, and Marshall Wolf. Conversations over the years with Richard Crawford have been particularly helpful in enabling me to better understand the field of American music. I am most grateful to Amy Kuʻuleialoha Stillman for sharing her expertise in Hawaiian music as well as allowing me access to her collection of rare source materials, including various clippings, sound recordings, and early record catalogs. Without her encouragement and advice, my work on Hawaiian music in the United States could not have taken its present shape.

Special thanks go out to Gurminder Bhogal, Elayne Garrett, Roland Garrett, Daniel Goldmark, Brian Harker, William Howland Kenney, David Lasocki, Amy Stillman, Denise Von Glahn, and Travis Winfrey for their illuminating comments on drafts of various chapters and to Michael Pisani and Paul Machlin for their extremely helpful responses to the entire manuscript.

My colleagues at the University of Michigan have lent wholehearted support for my research and scholarship. I thank Dean Christopher Kendall for showing keen interest in my work, Steven Whiting for being such a superb mentor, Louise Stein for her pep talks and kindhearted advice, and Joseph Lam and James Borders for helping to guide my path as a junior faculty member. Stefano Mengozzi, Jason Geary, and Christi-Anne Castro all offered supportive words and camaraderie at just the right moments. And I have been particularly fortunate to share ideas and embark on various adventures involving American music with my friend and colleague Mark Clague, whose boundless energy and buoyant enthusiasm never fail to raise my spirits.

This project would not have been completed without the support and generosity of those dearest to me. It is hard to know how to express sufficient thanks to my brother and my parents, since they have always offered their unconditional support and love. I fear that my parents may end up remembering the many moments when I asked for a last-minute favor or some urgent proofreading advice, but I hope that they will also recognize how the journeys experienced by their families in America helped to shape this book, perhaps in more ways than I will ever know.

My heart and my deepest gratitude are given to Saleema Waraich for her kindness, understanding, love, and support as well as for bringing the warmth and encouragement of her loving family into my life.

Introduction

On the night of 28 April 2006, when the recording "Nuestro Himno" (Our anthem) debuted on hundreds of Spanish-language radio stations across the United States, its premiere confirmed that the act of making music can have important political repercussions. As the first single from a multiartist album entitled *Somos Americanos* (We are Americans), the song attempts to enact in sound an affirmation of group pride. Moving in a slowly majestic tempo, it features ensemble choruses, a familiar hymnlike melody, and Spanish lyrics. Considering that it was concocted by a British producer, Adam Kidron, and features a roster of gifted Afro-Caribbean and Latin American musicians—among them the Haitian performer Wyclef Jean, the Mexican rock singer Gloria Trevi, the Puerto Rican reggaeton artist Ivy Queen, and the Cuban-American rapper Pitbull—some might deem "Nuestro Himno" a modern-day multicultural anthem or an expression of pan-Latin pride. Yet it instead became a musical lightning rod for both harsh criticism and enthusiastic praise. Perhaps this musical premiere would not have set off alarms under different circumstances. But what made "Nuestro Himno" so divisive arose from its historical context as well as the revisionist strategy applied to the material on which the song was based: the national anthem of the United States.

This was certainly not the first time that an unconventional interpretation of "The Star-Spangled Banner" generated public outcry. José Feliciano, Marvin Gaye, and Jimi Hendrix are among the performers who have been charged with taking too many musical liberties or injecting political overtones. But, as its creators freely acknowledged, "Nuestro Himno" is less a literal interpretation than a musical reinterpretation of the anthem. In fact, the introduction to this heavily produced recording initially makes one expect a typical contemporary pop ballad, complete with chanted vocal interjections

1

that issue communal shout-outs and add celebratory flair. Because nearly a dozen artists share the vocals, taking turns to deliver their lines with distinctive timbres, registers, and interpretive approaches, the recording, though retaining much of the anthem's melody, features passages that sound newly composed or improvised. Even more significant for both adherents and critics, however, is the song's treatment of the original lyrics. Rather than presenting a literal Spanish translation, "Nuestro Himno" delivers its own version of the first two verses and chorus of Francis Scott Key's text, preserving much of the original flavor but not the exact content. As a result, the song cuts some lyrical ties and reflects more broadly on the ideals of freedom and the march toward liberty, delivering a message that maps more readily onto any struggle for justice.

Although its altered lyrics were sure to cause a stir, "Nuestro Himno" contains neither explicitly anti-American propaganda nor revolutionary incitement, so there is ample room for discussion of whether the recording embodies a respectful reinterpretation or a desecration of the national anthem. It can be heard as an expression of Latino solidarity throughout the Americas, a multicultural demonstration of U.S. patriotism, or a disloyal act of blasphemy. This song might have elicited a very different response at another historical moment, perhaps being perceived as a sign of solidarity in the wake of a national tragedy or as a musical commemoration of the signing of a treaty between the United States and its neighbors to the south. But the release caused a ruckus in large part because of its arrival in the midst of a national debate—featuring the Bush administration, various factions in Congress, and vocal political action groups—on the status and future legislation of immigrant rights in the United States.

I have not meant to suggest that the uproar that met "Nuestro Himno" was purely accidental. On the contrary, the song's release was timed to act as a prelude to massive rallies that called for more tolerant U.S. government policies on immigration that involve wages, benefits, and citizenship. By opening this discussion without first introducing the debate over immigration rights, my purpose is to emphasize just how vital the climate of cultural conflict proves for understanding the meaning and significance of this song. Seizing on this dispute as a commercial and political opportunity, the Urban Box Office record company promoted the recording as an anthem of solidarity with U.S. immigrants. Moreover, the company's marketing campaign underscored that a portion of the sales proceeds would benefit an immigration rights coalition. Designed as a rallying cry for supporters of liberal immigration rights, the song reflects the power of music to work against the national grain, which suggests how readily a national symbol presents artists with the opportunity for subversion.[1] Responses to "Nuestro Himno" from those on the other side of this debate became extremely heated, as if Spanish-speaking immigrants had invaded the country and wounded one of its cherished icons. Perhaps they recalled the act of rebellion that led to the original anthem, when pro-American lyrics were stamped onto a British song, for their rhetoric suggested that altering its title, language, and lyrics constituted a grave offense, musically analogous to burning the flag.

Although Key's lyrics to "The Star-Spangled Banner" have been published in many languages, including a Spanish version from 1919 prepared by the U.S. Bureau of Education, many of those favoring a crackdown on immigration chose to interpret the act of singing the anthem in Spanish as a display of anti-American sentiment. Like patrolmen of a musical border, they condemned the song and its supporters for misusing "The Star-Spangled Banner" to promote liberal immigration policies. Controversy over "Nuestro Himno" soon led the nation's most prominent politician to weigh in. Asked to comment on the matter, President George W. Bush criticized the song and drew connections among issues of language, immigration, and U.S. citizenship: "I think the national anthem ought to be sung in English, and I think people who want to be a citizen of this country ought to learn English, and they ought to learn to sing the national anthem in English."[2] According to this perspective, speaking or singing in English becomes a means by which to generate and exhibit unity for a nation of immigrants, although it demands a narrow vision of what that unity entails. As part of the political melee that ensued, Bush's critics pointed out that he never raised such objections when Spanish-language versions of the national anthem were performed during his campaign stops in 2000 at Hispanic cultural festivals. Some claimed that he even sang along. One might expect the most patriotic citizens of a multicultural nation, especially a nation so keen on expanding its global influence, to promote the singing of its anthem in all languages. But anti-immigration forces in both houses of Congress responded just as decisively to the contrary by sponsoring Senate Resolution 458 and House Resolution 793. Both called for the national anthem, as well as for all other statements or songs that symbolize national unity, to be recited or sung in English only. Consequently, "Nuestro Himno" ended up fanning the flames of the political battle that initially inspired it.

The furor surrounding the song engages with questions that have always been critical to defining American identity. What is America? Who is American? And who has the right to decide? This striking episode also intersects with many themes vital to the study of American music and culture, including music and national identity, music and politics, and music and social protest. My work enters into each of these debates, while acknowledging how unrealistic it would be to expect to resolve them in the course of a single book. For that matter, regardless of how the dust settles in the current battle over immigration policy, the uproar produced by the sounds of "Nuestro Himno" will never be quelled. The song will live on, perhaps gradually losing some of its original bite, and there will be no political compromise or genuine accord about its true meaning. Whether or not it advances the cause of immigration rights, "Nuestro Himno" will continue to embody the often fierce conflict that permeates discourse on American identity. It is this turbulent interplay between cultural contestation and musical expression—a relationship by which music can reflect, produce, and inspire debate—that forms the primary subject of *Struggling to Define a Nation.*

Highlighting the complex collisions and political dimensions of American music proves especially productive, since the nation's musical history is filled with examples of such clashes, ranging from turn-of-the-century arguments about whether to base concert music on materials related to the land's first inhabitants to the revolutionary politics voiced during the 1990s by the band Rage Against the Machine. Rather than sit idly by or conform to a party line, musicians have always expressed clashing visions of the definition, purpose, and future of the nation. We need only compare Nora Bayes's rendition of "Over There," which rallied the troops during World War I, to the anti–Vietnam War sentiments expressed by Country Joe & the Fish in their "I-Feel-Like-I'm-Fixin'-to-Die Rag" or the jingoistic message of Toby Keith's "Courtesy of the Red, White and Blue (The Angry American)" in the wake of 11 September 2001. If one were to couple Irving Berlin with Madonna, Ethel Merman with Woody Guthrie, Milton Babbitt with Public Enemy, each pair would seem outlandish not simply because of stylistic differences but because of how the artists' music reflects distinctive and divergent visions of national identity.

My approach to studying American music takes its lead from these vivid examples of musical difference, but as I will argue in the following chapters, musical expression does not require explicitly political material at its core for it to be touched by and contribute to contemporary cultural debates. Rather than attempting to reach a unified vision of the meaning of American music, this book explores the ongoing struggles over the definition of national identity that take place in cultural, historiographical, musical, and musicological arenas. It is my contention that by identifying the musical and discursive traditions of contesting American identity, by examining the controversial moments that provoke opposing sides to come into sharp relief, we can distinguish and explore the key debates that have fashioned the nation. Taking this perspective on American music enriches our understanding of the music and the discipline in several respects: by challenging conventional historiographical assumptions; by questioning traditional criteria used to delineate the subject; by embracing the nation's complex musical diversity; and by promoting an analytical stance that is capable of fruitfully addressing many of the major conceptual challenges facing today's music historians. Most compellingly, this approach enables scholars to identify, scrutinize, and gauge the power of musical expression to act as an essential bearer of social, historical, and cultural knowledge.

To explain why placing such emphasis on cultural debate is significant for studying American music, it may be helpful to relate this mode of analysis to the musicological tradition to which this book responds. Academic interest in the music of the United States has increased exponentially over the past four decades. Noteworthy books, dedicated journals, recorded anthologies, course catalogs, and an increasing number of faculty positions all signal what has become a burgeoning scholarly field. What constitutes American music, however, is not always clear and is often left open for discussion. Richard Crawford, the scholar who has written most ardently about the historiographical challenges facing the discipline, made this observation in 1990: "The central problem of American musical historiography has been, and continues to be, to define the range and shape of the subject."[3] Nearly two decades later, solving this problem remains a challenge for a maturing field of inquiry. As one of the struggles to which the title of this book refers, the intellectual debates over how to define a nation's music persist to the present; shifting perspectives and competing answers to this question continually reconstitute the field.

A definition of American music has always been difficult to formulate, owing to the nation's expansionist history as well as its growth through immigration, whether by choice or by force. As a result of land acquisitions, overseas ventures, and shifting immigration policies, the nation's borders and the makeup of its population continue to fluctuate. Questions arise at once. If a musician's country of origin proves vital to defining notions of American music, what are scholars to do with immigrants like Irving Berlin and Carlos Santana? If we demarcate American music by national boundaries, how are we to deal with the transnational musical culture that thrives in the border region between the U.S. and Mexico, or with the music produced in U.S. territories such as Puerto Rico? Irving Lowens draws a useful distinction between (1) music in America, which he understands as music making that occurs within the geographical confines of the United States; and (2) American music, which he relates to the aesthetic attempt begun by late nineteenth-century composers to develop a specifically American style of composition.[4] Yet even this expansive definition fails to encircle influential figures such as Nadia Boulanger and the Beatles, who, despite carrying out most of their activities across the Atlantic, had a striking effect on musical life in the United States. Kyle Gann once proposed the strategy of "finding Americanness by taking the entirety of what American composers have done and subtracting from it the identifiably European, Asian, African, and Latin American elements."[5] But many historians find such an isolationist strategy untenable. In her visionary study of musical modernism in New York during the 1920s, Carol Oja places internationalism alongside nationalism as an equally powerful force. She demonstrates that American composers were as concerned with forming networks with modernists outside the United States as they were with fashioning a distinctly American style of composition.[6] Delineating alternative boundaries around the subject of American music by means of birthplace, citizenship, and geography reveals that each has its own limitations. Indeed, I offer the above examples not as a prelude to defining American music once and for all, as if that were possible for such a dynamic entity, but instead to register the differences of opinion on this subject in musicological discourse.

Perceptions of high and low culture have also served to delimit the field of American music. Following the lead of the German musicological tradition, on which musicology in the United States was originally based, early studies of American music took for granted the authority of concert music to speak for the nation. In this sense, most scholarship before 1950 resembled the work of John Tasker Howard, which concentrated almost exclusively on art music composers.[7] As recently as the 1980s it was still de rigueur for discussions of U.S. nationalism and musical identity to be framed in terms of concert music.[8] But the twentieth century saw crucial changes that have permanently altered perceptions of the nation's musical landscape. Massive immigration, urbanization, the spread of audio recording, and the explosive rise of popular music all have enabled previously excluded voices to be heard and added fresh coordinates to the map of American music. Consequently, a greater spectrum of musical activity—further informed by working-class perspectives, the contributions of women, and the insights of musicians hailing from a wide range of racial and ethnic groups—has conveyed new revelations about the American experience. Scholars have paid increasing attention to these changes, beginning with

Gilbert Chase in his influential book *America's Music* (1955), which tilted the balance away from the concert hall and toward the vibrant worlds of folk and popular music.[9] H. Wiley Hitchcock's *Music in the United States* (1969) features a similarly inclusive strategy, spending equal time tracing what he coined the vernacular and cultivated traditions of American music.[10] Charles Hamm's *Music in the New World* (1983) gives greater weight than his predecessors to popular music, paying added attention to the mass-produced variety.[11] Giving priority to issues of stylistic mixture and acculturation, Hamm adopts a working definition of American music as that which arrived from overseas and underwent significant evolution in the United States. Even as the field has shifted, historians have continued to redefine its scope and range.

In the latest comprehensive history of this subject, *America's Musical Life* (2001), Richard Crawford also advocates an egalitarian perspective, lending as much weight to popular and folk music as to the art music tradition and employing a methodology that takes performance, not composition, as its starting point.[12] Acknowledging the historiographical shift that has overtaken the discipline, Crawford elsewhere asserts that many of today's historians recognize that "the colonial [art music] and the traditional [folk music] spheres have existed on the periphery of the democratic, commercially driven sphere."[13] The steady expansion of the field beyond art music now has reached a point where the extraordinary variety of American music often constitutes sufficient grounds for analysis and celebration. In his preface to a recent edited collection, *The Cambridge History of American Music*, David Nicholls claims: "If there is a single feature which both characterizes and defines American music, it is diversity."[14] Nicholls goes on to explain that this musical diversity, which has been produced by a complex set of actions, interactions, and interrelationships, necessitates a broad range of methodological tactics. Clearly, the discipline has undergone a conspicuous transformation since World War II. There have been decisive gains in coverage, principally in the areas of folk and popular music, as we have come to treasure an enormous range of musical activity. As our histories of American music have become more inclusive, assimilationist narratives have been displaced by multicultural models. Moreover, as Nicholls's comments imply, the discipline has made room for an ever-increasing assortment of scholarly viewpoints that promise both to revisit past debates and to initiate new ones.

And yet, with all that has been accomplished by the efforts of several generations of scholars who have carved out a place for the study of American music and opened up the field to projects such as my own, I am sometimes left uneasy about the path we have traveled toward embracing diversity. By this I am neither arguing for a return to the viewpoint of John Tasker Howard nor suggesting that the doors of inquiry be restricted. What concerns me has nothing to do with the more equivalent balance of representation; rather, it derives from the deficiencies of a historiographical model that prizes diversity without accounting for relations of power. In particular, there has been a marked tendency in American music studies to champion the music in the course of establishing it as a worthy subject within the greater musicological sphere, a tendency that must be seen as necessary for the success of that stage of the endeavor. If celebration outstrips critical engagement, if buoyant enthusiasm ends up hiding internal divisions, however, certain problems inevitably arise. Told from this perspective, the history of American music becomes a sanguine tale of shared achievement, a story that seeks consensus and accomplishment rather than pointed opposition. Much is made of Yankee originality and experimentation, of aesthetic innovation, and sometimes of commercial success, but such treatments downplay the sociocultural tensions that have shaped music making in the United States, the differences of opinion over the direction of American music, and the divergent and contradictory perspectives that constitute the musical nation.

One of the leading voices in the field of American studies, George Lipsitz, suggests that we interrogate what he terms the "cultural politics of pluralism" by examining more closely "the dynamics of oppressive power and of popular resistance to it."[15] In a broad sense, this book can be seen as an attempt to take on this challenge as it applies to the field of American music. To accomplish this, my approach seeks to illustrate the limitations of a pluralistic model by treating music as a crucial site of cultural conflict and by moving the notions of tension and debate from the sidelines to the center. We can fully understand these conflicts only by conceiving of musicological inquiry with respect to intersecting relationships of power. My attention is thus especially drawn to the cultural complexities and contradictions of American music, what Josh Kun identifies as "its clashes and exchanges and convergences and contests, its never-ending play of differences and particularities," and in studying how these clashes shape, inspire, and take form in music.[16] Consequently, *Struggling to Define a Nation* centers on stories that illustrate musical collisions rather than seamless assimilation, that demonstrate the ways in which music can serve the purposes of either inclusion or exclusion, and that distinguish musical efforts that aim to build consensus from those that forge resistance.

Many readers will recognize in this book the underlying influence of Marx, Foucault, Gramsci, and others who have theorized about the relationship of cultural production to power, human agency, and resistance. Among the leading cultural critics to investigate Marx's claim that the economic mode of production determines the form and nature of cultural production was Theodor Adorno, whose work deeply informs mine. Through his compelling analyses of the music of Bach, Beethoven, and other composers, Adorno demonstrated how classical music, often exalted for its pure form and aesthetic beauty, nonetheless reflects the social circumstances in which it was created.[17] Consequently, as one of the musicologists who has drawn on his work writes, "[Adorno] provides the means for understanding how compositions of the tonal repertory are informed by the fundamental social tensions of their time."[18] Not all have been willing to accept certain aspects of Adorno's top-down analysis of cultural production. Richard Hoggart, Stuart Hall, and other postwar British cultural theorists who became known collectively as the Birmingham School came to view popular culture as a terrain of conflict that held the potential for political resistance. Their demonstration of the interpretive force of cultural theory, working-class perspectives, and Marxist politics to illuminate the study of culture has proven extraordinarily influential, spreading through Europe and the United States and helping to spark the cultural studies revolution. Today it is almost impossible to imagine the composition of certain academic disciplines—cultural studies, literary studies, anthropology, history, art history, American studies, queer studies, women's studies, ethnic studies, and more—without access to epistemological models that detect cultural tensions and unpack power relations.

The work of Adorno notwithstanding, it has taken longer for music scholars to embrace these critical approaches. Traditional musicological practice has relied so heavily on treating pieces of music—and especially Western art music—as autonomous works sealed off from the rest of the world, focusing more often on aspects of musical form, style, and aesthetics. The scholars who first embraced cultural theory as a useful tool in the study of music often were not musicologists, and they did not study Western art music; more often than not, they hailed from other disciplines, such as sociology, social history, and media and communication studies, and they were drawn to investigating various manifestations of contemporary popular music. Strongly influenced by the Birmingham School, the resultant branch of popular music studies became known for its politicized slant. Reflecting this line of thinking, a recent primer entitled *Understanding Popular Music* defines its subject as "a site of cultural struggle, with constant attempts to establish dominance, exploit cultural contradictions, and negotiate hegemony."[19]

The historiography of African American music has long followed a similar path, framed in relationship to a history of black America told in terms of oppression, resistance, struggle, and survival. This forceful mode of analysis, blending musical, cultural, and political concerns, is epitomized by LeRoi Jones's (Amiri Baraka's) *Blues People* (1963).[20] Later scholars such as the historian Tricia Rose have applied the wisdom gained from cultural theory to the analysis of black music. Rose's foundational study of rap music, *Black Noise* (1994), explores the internal "tensions and contradictions" of the genre in the course of telling "stories of oppression and creative resistance."[21] In fundamental respects, my work grows out of the traditions of analyzing popular music and African American music as sites of cultural resistance. As much as this politicized body of scholarship has informed my theoretical stance, however, scholarship from disciplines outside musicology is not typically rich in detailed musical analysis. Thus, as inspiring as I find Rose's work, I appreciate her treatment of rap more for its skillful combination of sociohistorical analysis and theoretical savvy than for its musicological content.

Not until the last few decades have the productive insights made possible by cultural theory entered the broader discipline of musicology. Scholars in the field now more readily incorporate aspects of Marxist theory, poststructuralism, literary theory, semiotics, feminist theory, queer theory, and much more. Although these approaches differ greatly, a tenet that many share is encapsulated by an observation from Susan McClary: "Music is always a political activity."[22] In addition to relying on this general principle, I look to recent musicological work that addresses the issues of music and ethnicity, musical appropriation, and racial representation and that analyzes differential relations of power. As cultural theory has filtered into the discipline, an increasing number of musicologists have noticed that "tensions, not tendencies, define historical moments."[23] Numerous studies of individual genres have been constructed in this vein, such as Robert Walser's book *Running with the Devil*, which reveals the world of heavy metal to be an "important site of cultural contestation" and situates these musical practices in "a forthrightly politicized context of cultural struggle over values, power, and legitimacy."[24] Likewise, David Ake structures *Jazz Cultures* around a series of crucial debates that have taken place in jazz history to construct "a historical narrative marked by contestation, contradiction, and plurality."[25] My work is deeply indebted to these two books, which offer models of scholarship that are historically grounded, critically engaged, and anchored firmly in musical analysis. Since placing cultural debate at the center of academic inquiry has become more widespread, what is most distinctive about my approach is perhaps less its methodological framework than its novel application to the broader field of American music. Adopting this analytical strategy serves two key purposes: first, to determine what sorts of understandings a critical stance can reveal about American music that a pluralistic view may obscure; and second, to learn what a broader comparative perspective can reveal that specialized studies fail to discover.

Struggling to Define a Nation traces how composers and performers draw on and manipulate musical materials to construct stories about the nation. I pay particular attention to the ways in which music accrues discursive meanings, for once acquired, these meanings can attach themselves to sounds, provided they are given enough reinforcement within the framework of a shared culture. In other words, though a trumpet fanfare played by Louis Armstrong may not signify much to an infant, beyond its high volume and distinctive sound, it has come to hold a host of connotations for those listeners who are familiar with a set of cultural codes and have heard similar gestures accompany the entrances of kings, leaders, and military parades, to name a few. Although these meanings are not permanently fixed, specific musical gestures, tropes, and even entire genres carry with them connotations that are apparent not only to listeners but also to composers, performers, marketers, and anyone else who depends on the rhetorical capacity of music. By taking advantage of these codes—quoting them, altering them, or otherwise responding to them—musicians can access and transform them to construct new meanings. To account for the power of musical rhetoric, I turn to a dialogic model of music history that comprises a perpetual series of conversations entered into by musicians and listeners. Initially advanced by Mikhail Bakhtin in the field of literary criticism, this model helps illustrate how discursive meanings find their way into musical expression and trace the ongoing musical struggles that construct and transform American identity.[26] If we pay close attention to individual performances and recordings, sound becomes a crucial source of embedded knowledge, demonstrating how music not only reflects and shapes its cultural environment but also conveys information that may not be available in any other form.

While I believe it would be equally rewarding to apply this approach to other stages of U.S. history, I focus primarily on the early twentieth century, which brought a series of crucial transformations to the world of music that continue to reverberate today. Along with massive immigration, internal migration, industrialization, and urbanization came the steady expansion of mass culture and the birth of the modern entertainment industry. Together these developments revolutionized the scope and range of American music, aided by the efforts of Tin Pan Alley publishers and the spread of the commercial recording industry, and sparked the rise of popular music throughout the nation and around the world. By gradually opening doors for new voices, the recording era fostered a greater variety of expression by performers of jazz, blues, pop, gospel, and much more. Consequently, as becomes apparent over the course of this book, such recordings capture points of view that often cut across the grain of conventional narratives of American music. My sustained attention to popular music thus not only mirrors the transformation in music making that persisted throughout the entire twentieth century but also counteracts the tendency of scholars to focus their studies of nationalism on the activities of American concert music composers during this period. At the same time, by bringing popular music and art music into my discussion of Charles Ives, and by addressing a mixture of styles and genres throughout this book, I mean to imply that American music studies would profit by avoiding artificial genre segregation.

Rather than presenting a chronological survey or a thematic overview, the chapters of *Struggling to Define a Nation* are designed as a series of case studies that address key aspects of the struggle to define American music, and to define America through music, which together exemplify how cultural debate lies at the heart of the matter. In addition to what they share in methodological terms, each of the five chapters seeks to illuminate a separate critical question facing historians of American music: (1) What can scholars of American music learn from the expression of cultural debate as it takes form in music? (2) How does a transnational perspective help to improve our understanding of the racial dynamics of American music? (3) How do conceptions of American music change if we look to the music produced and consumed by an ethnic minority community? (4) For what reasons have American songwriters worked to define the nation through a strategy of exclusion? (5) Why must histories of American music gauge the potent effect of musical practices that originated outside the nation's borders? Though answers to these questions outline the book, key individuals and themes reappear periodically to strengthen its overall coherence and to highlight connections between these topics.

To address these questions and to reflect how differently positioned Americans experience America differently, I have chosen a diverse array of subjects—ranging from well-known figures such as Charles Ives, Jelly Roll Morton, and Louis Armstrong to the lesser-known songwriters Jean Schwartz and Sonny Cunha—and music that spans a wide spectrum of genres, including concert music, popular song, ragtime, blues, jazz, and Hawaiian music. Dozens of other prominent figures in the history of American music, among them Bessie Smith, Irving Berlin, Duke Ellington, Jimmie Rodgers, W. C. Handy, Bing Crosby, George M. Cohan, and Mahalia Jackson, also make brief appearances. In addition to examining the roles of specific individuals in defining notions about America, I call attention to the ways in which institutions such as Tin Pan Alley and the recording industry attempt to mold public perceptions about the nation. The expansive scope of topics is a deliberate choice, made to illustrate how thoroughly the theme of contestation permeates musical life and to probe neglected spheres of American music that play critical roles in national self-fashioning. My rationale for choosing these topics aims to transcend the black-and-white racial model often employed in writing about American music and to examine a range of influences on the nation's musical history, including Creole culture, Latin and Afro-Caribbean music, Asian immigration, and America's musical encounter with Hawai'i. Though my choices underscore the multicultural and international roots of American music, this strategy is not intended to add cultural or ethnic diversity for diversity's sake; rather, I aim to recognize varied ways in which the contrast in perspectives and the differences in power distinguish minority communities from mainstream America in the struggle to define the direction of the nation and its music.

The basic outline of my argument is presented in chapter 1, which treats Charles Ives, a composer at the center of the canon of American music, and his relationship to ragtime, the leading popular music at the start of the twentieth century. In his *Four Ragtime Dances,* Ives negotiates the tensions between American and European music, between concert music and popular music, between sacred and secular impulses, and between races. Ives's early experiments with ragtime represent one of his first attempts to create a distinctly American music, a project that occupied Ives and many other composers in the early twentieth century. The outcome of this complicated encounter resembles not a seamless integration of traditions but instead a complex interplay of musical worlds, a sonic expression of the debates that characterized this era's discourse on race, class, and nation. In response to contemporary arguments about ragtime, Ives wrote, "Ragtime has its possibilities. But it does not 'represent the American nation' any more than some fine old senators represent it."[27] What, then, did ragtime represent, and what type, or types, of music did Ives believe best represented America?

Turning away from the realm of the classical concert hall and toward the world of popular music, chapter 2 centers on the jazz pianist, composer, and bandleader Jelly Roll Morton. The multicultural origins of jazz are often compared to a musical gumbo that combines various elements from different communities. In the course of demonstrating how such tensions find expression in Morton's music, this chapter addresses a fundamental epistemological question surrounding the roots of this celebrated American creation. Rather than locating jazz origins solely within the geographical confines of the United States, my work asks how a transnational perspective might enhance our understanding of jazz history. Specifically, I consider what Morton's background, his experiences as a popular musician, his relationship to Latin music and culture, and his creolized musical blend tell us about national identity. Over the course of his itinerant career, which included sojourns in Texas, California, and Mexico, Morton composed or recorded about twenty songs that were clearly marked by what he termed a "Spanish tinge." Tracing the Latin influences proves extremely useful for understanding Morton, who has always been a thorn in the side of conceptions of jazz as black and white, for he did not identify himself as African American but rather displayed immense pride in his Creole heritage. Accordingly, the Spanish tinge offers a stimulating metaphor for the multiracial, transnational, border-crossing nature of American music.

Viewed from this angle, Morton's career points to the significance of international practices on American music, a legacy that can be traced largely to the institution of slavery and to the various waves of immigration that have transformed the nation. Turning to another vital shared journey, chapter 3 considers how American music making has been shaped by internal migration, in particular the Great Migration that brought approximately 1.5 million African Americans to northern cities between the World War I and the start of the Great Depression. My investigation focuses on one of the most celebrated migrants, the jazz performer Louis Armstrong, who left New Orleans and headed to Chicago in 1922. The experience of an urban migrant, attempting to come to grips with the transition from South to North, motivates Armstrong's recording of "Gully Low Blues" (1927), a song that addresses an array of cultural tensions set in motion by migration—regionalism, class, and gender. Viewing the struggle to define American music from the perspective of an ethnic minority community, my approach examines Armstrong's music primarily in terms of the meanings it offered to his fellow African American migrants. What emerges in "Gully Low Blues," in contrast to a piece such as Ives's *Four Ragtime Dances,* is testimony that the sonic negotiation of cultural tensions need not emerge as fractured and conflicted but may instead resonate with the sound of triumph and hope.

National identity is also defined by what it excludes. Demonstrating how nationalism and exoticism are "mutually constitutive," chapter 4 investigates the ways in which musicians and the music industry actively participate in defining a nation.[28] During a patriotic era of emerging U.S. imperialism and mounting concerns about immigration, Tin Pan Alley songwriters produced numerous songs that envisioned a nation demarcated along racial and ethnic lines, including a large body of Asian-themed songs that form the backdrop for this chapter. To illuminate the role that music has played in molding ideas of America, Asia, and Asian America, I trace the history of the song "Chinatown, My Chinatown," offering detailed accounts of its origin, its 1910 Broadway debut, its packaging as sheet music, and its early performance history. By caricaturing local U.S. Chinatowns as foreign, opium-infested districts, the song exemplifies turn-of-the-century musical orientalism as it was directed toward an immigrant community. Yet the popular standard still resonates today in performance, recordings, film, television, cartoons, advertising, and the latest entertainment products. My analysis follows the song's history across diverse performance contexts to the present, showing how the process of defining a nation through musical racialization requires continuous maintenance and is always subject to transformation.

Serving as a companion piece to and a variation on the previous chapter, chapter 5 revisits the project of racial representation and musical nation building during the early twentieth century, but with a crucial twist in context—the colonial encounter between the United States and its recently acquired territory Hawaiʻi. The primary focus is the craze for Hawaiian and Hawaiian-themed music that emerged in the United States during the 1910s and 1920s in the form of sheet music, recordings, touring shows, and instruments such as the ʻukulele and the steel guitar. Considering their treatment of Asian subjects, it is not surprising that Tin Pan Alley songwriters once again banked on the appeal of racial exoticism and cultural stereotypes in the production of Hawaiian-themed songs. What differentiates this encounter, however, stems from the active participation by Hawaiian musicians and performers in these historical developments, which produced an alternative set of musical, political, and economic dynamics. As much as they reveal about mainland efforts to manipulate representations of Hawaiʻi in relationship to the United States, these telling episodes do not represent simple acts of cultural imperialism. For island musicians who achieved artistic goals and reaped financial rewards, music offered greater opportunity for self-representation in the face of American economic and political dominance. Consequently, the multifaceted relationship between the mainland and the Hawaiian Islands reveals how varying processes of cultural collision, cooptation, and crossover play out in the arena of musical culture.

Conceiving of music as a terrain of conflict at first may appear a discouraging task, especially for those of us who depend on music's ability to provide solace in a troubled world. In response to this line of critique, I maintain that factoring in conflict enables historians to develop a more realistic understanding of musical life and to better account for the process of musical change. Identifying the strategies by which musicians struggle to have their voices heard consequently yields a more accurate reflection of the dynamic, contested nature of musical life. Furthermore, though attending to power relationships in the study of music serves to identify the varieties of dominance, this method of inquiry also helps detect and measure currents of potential resistance. The result produces ample opportunity for optimism, especially in situations where stability is restrictive or stifling, for this approach enables us to envision the possibility of change and the promise of social and cultural renewal. It may be a struggle to define a nation, but it can be an exhilarating one.

1. Charles Ives's *Four Ragtime Dances* and "True American Music"

Someone is quoted as saying that "ragtime is the true American music." Anyone will admit that it is one of the many true, natural, and, nowadays, conventional means of expression. It is an idiom, perhaps a "set or series of colloquialisms," similar to those that have added through centuries and through natural means some beauty to all languages. . . . Ragtime has its possibilities. But it does not "represent the American nation" any more than some fine old senators represent it. Perhaps we know it now as an ore before it has been refined into a product. It may be one of nature's ways of giving art raw material. Time will throw its vices away and weld its virtues into the fabric of our music. It has its uses, as the cruet on the boarding-house table has, but to make a meal of tomato ketchup and horse-radish, to plant a whole farm with sunflowers, even to put a sunflower into every bouquet, would be calling nature something worse than a politician.

CHARLES IVES, Essays Before a Sonata

Today, more than a century after its introduction, the music of ragtime is often regarded with nostalgia as a quaint, polite, antiquated music, but when it burst on the national scene in the late 1890s, its catchy melodies and energetic rhythms sparked both delight and controversy. One of the many fruits of African American musical innovation, this style of popular music captivated the nation through the World War I era with its distinctive, syncopated rhythms that enlivened solo piano music, arrangements for bands and orchestras, ballroom numbers, and countless popular songs. Yet the music also drew the attention of critics who attacked it for its rhythmic audacity and of moral guardians who feared the threat that the suggestive, infectious dance music posed to public decency.[1] Contemporary observers entered into a debate about whether ragtime's idiomatic musical language and its widespread appeal embodied "the one true American music."[2] According to Charles Ives (1874–1954), who is hailed by many as the leading art music composer in American history, ragtime did not warrant that lofty standing; however, as we will see, that did not stop him from experimenting with elements of ragtime in his own compositions over the course of his career.

Perhaps such a musical juxtaposition was inevitable in an era that saw Edward MacDowell, Amy Beach, Arthur Farwell, and other prominent composers echo Antonín Dvořák by turning to African American spirituals, Native American music, and traditional American folk songs as bases on which to construct a national style of composition. Though Ives's investigation of ragtime brings to light a similar set of tensions between Western European musical traditions and the development of art music in America, it is especially notable that he chose to explore the possibilities of a modern, urban, commercial popular music rather than folk music. This encounter is further complicated by the racial and class differences between Ives, a privileged white male who grew up in Connecticut and attended Yale University, and the less advantaged African American musicians in the Midwest who pioneered ragtime. Because Ives's relationship with ragtime involved such a variety of cultural tensions—the American struggle to break away from European models, the friction between art music and popular music, and the negotiation of racial and class divides—his ragtime-influenced pieces exemplify how cultural debate over the subject of national identity takes form in musical expression.

During his collegiate career at Yale (1894–98) and in the many years he spent in New York City after graduation, Charles Ives witnessed the ragtime craze everywhere he turned—the music was plunked out by player pianos, presented on the vaudeville stage, performed by theater orchestras, and even published as sheet music in the newspaper from time to time. In addition to hearing ragtime and writing his impressions of it, Ives incorporated various aspects of the music into his own compositions. During the height of the ragtime era, at the start of the twentieth century, Ives composed a series of works he called variously ragtime pieces and ragtime dances. These compositions were clearly important to Ives, for he made frequent attempts to have them performed, and he recycled material from them to create sections of later works, including the First Piano Sonata, A Set of Pieces for Theatre or Chamber Orchestra, the Three-Page Sonata, Three Quarter-tone Pieces, and the Second Orchestral Set. Elements of ragtime also appear in many of his other major compositions, such as the Second Piano Sonata, the Second Violin Sonata, the Third Violin Sonata, *Central Park in the Dark*, *The Celestial Railroad*, the Third Orchestral Set, and the Fourth Symphony. The music held his attention late into his life: his nephew recalled watching Ives at the piano, when suddenly he would "break into one of these ragtime pieces or a march, and he'd do it with such spirit that it was really thrilling."[3]

Even though Ives acknowledged incorporating ragtime elements into his own compositions, the tone of his written commentary about this venture comes across as hesitant, uncertain; his observations mingle praise with condescension and sometimes denigration. Although he considered ragtime a musical idiom capable of adding beauty, he felt that it did not constitute a "refined" product, but rather an "ore" to be mined for use in "art." Such judgments were not unique to Ives or to ragtime; a similar line of discourse would surface when George Gershwin and his contemporaries began to incorporate elements of jazz in their classical compositions. Often one to take contradictory or ambivalent positions, Ives maintained mixed feelings on the subject as he grew older. In comments written in the early 1930s, he recognized that his "early ragtime pieces and marches, most of the *First Piano Sonata*, most of the *Theater Orchestra Set*, etc., seemed to get going 'good and free'—and the hymn-tune sonatas and symphonies less so."[4] Ives scholars have pointed out the significance of ragtime to his development, including a recent biographer who claims that "only when Ives had absorbed and adapted ragtime could he write a true Ivesian allegro."[5] Instead of entirely welcoming this aspect of his musical identity, Ives compared the "shifts and lilting accents" of ragtime to a "bad habit"; but he suggested that "it will naturally start other rhythmic habits, perhaps leading into something of value."[6] In his published writings Ives never fully embraced ragtime.

Why did he hesitate? How could Ives, who found ragtime compelling enough to integrate into so many of his compositions, have expressed such contradictory statements about its intrinsic value and its contributions to his music? Lawrence Kramer suggests that the principal explanation involves race, that the white composer Ives felt extreme ambivalence about embracing the blackness of ragtime.[7] Kramer goes on to characterize Ives's treatment of ragtime in the two scherzo movements of his First Piano Sonata as a musical "continuation of unequal race relations" and a "continuation of blackface minstrelsy."[8] Ives's writings do contain racial assumptions, and I find certain aspects of Kramer's argument to be persuasive, but I do not believe that race or racism alone can account adequately for the complex encounter between Ives and ragtime. Because Ives made use of this music over such a long period and for assorted purposes, understanding this facet of his musical life requires further examination. Indeed, as will become evident, Ives integrated the same ragtime material that he used in the First Piano Sonata in other compositions, but he did not always manipulate it in the same fashion.

Ives's interest in ragtime needs to be understood in relation to his systematic practice of musical borrowing. Examples of compositional borrowing can be traced back for many centuries; what is unusual about Ives, as Peter Burkholder writes, "is not that he borrowed, but the extent to which he borrowed and the innovative ways he found to use existing music."[9] Relying so heavily on this technique that it came to distance him from his compositional forebears, Ives drew not only on European symphonic literature but also on college songs, Protestant hymns, band marches, parlor music, anthems, Stephen Foster tunes, and more. Rather than forever staining his creative reputation, Ives's willingness to incorporate such a wide range of music, especially American vernacular music, and to reimagine it in the context of concert music has helped him such a vital position in the history of American music.

The literature on Ives offers a variety of aesthetic, psychological, and programmatic explanations for this compositional approach, such as Ives's transcendentalist convictions, his antiestablishment stance, his heartfelt embrace of American music, his relationship to his father, and his fondness for the music of his youth. Showing admiration for the expanse of Ives's musical palette, Larry Starr entitled his book on Ives's compositional style *A Union of Diversities.*[10] Taking a similar perspective in the most comprehensive study to date, Peter Burkholder's *All Made of Tunes* demonstrates how Ives incorporated all kinds of music for all sorts of reasons, in varied fashion, and in pursuit of diverse artistic goals. Identifying fourteen separate species of borrowing in Ives's repertoire—including quotation, paraphrase, allusion, collage, and medley—Burkholder systematically documents how borrowing formed the basis for much of Ives's composition. In his otherwise thorough discussion, Burkholder downplays to a certain degree the ethical issues surrounding musical borrowing, the same issues that animate Kramer's work. What was at stake for Ives when he made the choice to investigate ragtime? What do his decisions about borrowing, juxtaposing, and framing this music suggest about his compositional priorities?

I am convinced that a methodological approach that combines elements from Burkholder's analysis and Kramer's cultural critique is ideal for understanding Ives, who often expressed the hope that his music would function as more than an aesthetic object or a display of technical expertise. To investigate these issues, I turn to *Four Ragtime Dances,* Charles Ives's earliest musical exploration of ragtime.[11] Since Ives frequently recycled elements taken from these pieces, tracing their history can help chronicle Ives's changing relationship to ragtime through his career. These dances combine two ostensibly disparate sources: the secular music of ragtime and the sacred hymns of Protestant religious services. Although this pairing may seem highly implausible, even blasphemous, it made sense to an experimentalist like Ives, especially at that point in his life—at the height of the ragtime era and near the end of his decadelong tenure as a church organist. If we consider Ives's racialized understanding of these two musical traditions, which he made clear in his published writings, this uncommon musical blend appears at first to present a moving statement on cultural diversity, whether a union of sacred and secular music or a reconciliation of white and black musical traditions. The compositional structure of the dances tells another story, however; it suggests that the cultural tensions that informed Ives's writings also filtered into his music; indeed, by structuring *Four Ragtime Dances* according to a set of power relations, Ives produced a music full of contestation that, to use his terms, better "represents the American nation."

THE RAGTIME ERA

References to "rag-time" first appeared in sheet music publications in 1896, but the technique of "ragging" a song, or what has been described as infusing music with syncopation to give it a "ragged" feel, was already in circulation. Indeed, Ives himself recalled having seen blackface minstrels employ what he considered to be a ragtime-style technique—"throwing the accent on the off-beat and holding over"—during a visit he took to the Danbury Fair as a teenager around 1892.[12] For a music that emerged in a "separate but equal" era of legalized segregation, ratified by *Plessy v. Ferguson* in 1896, racial factors would play a pivotal role in early ragtime reception. The music's ties with African American culture served alternately as a basis for appreciative curiosity and a reason for bigoted dismissal: audiences learned to associate ragtime with black musical practices because of its originators, such as Scott Joplin and James Scott; marketing practices that packaged ragtime as a black exoticism; and parodies of ragtime performed on the blackface minstrel stage. Even after white composers and publishers, such as Joseph Lamb and John Stark, jumped on the ragtime bandwagon at the turn of the century, rag titles and sheet music covers continued to refer to the music's black origins, advertising the newest "Ethiopian" sensation or the latest "coon song," a genre that took its name from a slur for African Americans and featured stereotypical black dialect, derogatory lyrics, and racist imagery. As Tin Pan Alley composers increasingly embraced the flavor of ragtime, racialized practices endured. Irving Berlin's "Alexander's Ragtime Band" (1911), the hit that helped him gain fame as the "King of Ragtime," refers not only to ragtime syncopation but also to the plantation melodies of Stephen Foster and the comic stock character Alexander, a mainstay of blackface minstrel shows. Consequently, even though ragtime shares some structural and harmonic features with European brass-band music, mainstream discourse of the time stressed its blackness and highlighted those qualities that were out of the ordinary, especially the music's novel approach to rhythm. For most white Americans at the turn of the century, ragtime seemed "massively syncopated, positively shocking in its broken rhythms and shifted accents."[13] Although the popular understanding of ragtime gradually shifted from a black musical exoticism to "white American popular music," ragtime and race remained inseparable, especially for those, like Ives, who lived through the transition.[14]

By the time Ives began to compose *Four Ragtime Dances,* ragtime had gained enormous popularity, its sound filling dance halls, nickelodeons, saloons, theaters, and home parlors across America. What proved most attractive to Ives was its rhythmic sensibility; he later explained how the "shifts and lilting accents" of ragtime seemed "to offer other basic things not used now (or used very little) in music of even beats and accents."[15] For a composer who often prided himself on differentiating between his music and established European models, Ives also distinguished between the techniques of ragtime and the classical canon, albeit with faint praise: "To examine ragtime rhythms and the syncopations of Schumann or of Brahms seems to the writer to show how much alike they are not. Ragtime, as we hear it, is, of course, more (but not much more) than a natural dogma of shifted accents, or a mixture of shifted and minus accents."[16] Ives's response to ragtime was shaped by his attraction to its rhythmic innovations as well as its social function as dance music. In addition to incorporating ragtime in *Four Ragtime Dances* and in dance movements of his concert works, he occasionally used the music for programmatic purposes, as in the ragtime passage that materializes in his song "Walking" at the moment when the tune's wanderers notice a dance going on at a roadhouse.

Given his extensive musical borrowing, Ives's investigation of ragtime hardly seems extraordinary, when in truth it should be considered a radical decision for the time. Other turn-of-the-century American composers attempted to incorporate African American and Native American traditional music in their concert works, but ragtime drew relatively little attention from the same quarters. Ives became one of the first classical composers, and possibly *the* first, to incorporate elements of ragtime in his compositions.[17] His use of ragtime was fairly uncommon for him in comparison with his other borrowings. Over the course of his career Ives rarely drew on contemporary popular music, instead taking most of his quotations from music of earlier eras, especially music that was associated with white American musical traditions.[18] His circumstances help explain Ives's willingness to experiment with ragtime, which was due in large part to his initial exposure to the music at an impressionable age. When he started writing *Four Ragtime Dances*, Ives was in the right place at the right time—living in New York City, a center of the ragtime craze; fresh out of college, away from the watchful eyes of Horatio Parker and his other former professors, who were committed to extending the Western European tradition; and ready to experiment on his own, virtually anonymous, outside the strict confines of the concert music world.

Ives may also have been more willing than some of his contemporaries to experiment with black musical genres as a result of his family history and his personal beliefs. In *Memos*, he writes glowingly of his grandparents' involvement in the abolitionist cause and takes special pride in their virtual adoption of Henry Anderson Brooks, a young ex-slave whom George Ives brought home to Connecticut on his return from serving in the Civil War.[19] With support from the Ives family, Brooks received an education in Danbury and later enrolled at Hampton Institute, a school that Charles Ives's grandmother had helped found.[20] Taking a similar stand in *Essays Before a Sonata*, Ives applauds several examples of brave abolitionist acts, and he also condemns the "evils of race prejudice" in his essay "The Majority."[21] Relatives and coworkers later portrayed Ives as being keenly sensitive to the issue of racial equality. His nephew claimed in 1969 that Ives's "thinking was many years in advance of our own. He was as concerned about the Negro problem twenty-five years ago as we have become about it today."[22] Ives expressed this kind of progressive attitude when he learned that one of his employees had decided to underwrite the company's first insurance policy for an African American client. Ives did not himself initiate this change in company procedure, but the employee who wrote the policy recalled: "When Ives heard about this, he gave me a little tap on the shoulder. 'Good work.' "[23] Although not all commentators would go as far as Ives's biographer Jan Swafford, who states that "making allowances for the language of his time, I do not find Ives making a racist statement anywhere," most depict Ives as a man who was sometimes ahead of his time.[24]

Ives became familiar with popular ragtime songs and piano music, but he did not compose conventional ragtime numbers that could be marketed by Tin Pan Alley publishers. Instead, his first ragtime pieces were intended as compositions for theater orchestra, a type of small ensemble that Ives became involved with during his youth and that powerfully shaped his engagement with ragtime. Supplying the music for variety shows, vaudeville productions, dance performances, and other types of local entertainment, theater orchestras performed music from a very broad repertory, ranging from opera overtures and light intermezzos to waltzes and ragtime numbers.[25] Ives's exposure to theater orchestras began in Danbury, where his father played in a few such groups, and continued in New Haven, in which there were a number of prominent theaters. When Ives was in college, he carried on the family tradition by occasionally sitting in for George Felsburg, the pianist at Poli's vaudeville theater, and trying out his own "ragging" techniques.[26] In his commentary about a later set of compositions written for theater orchestra, Ives explained how these ensembles were put together and why they varied so much in size:

> The make-up of the average theatre orchestra of some years ago, in the towns and smaller cities, in this part of the country was neither arbitrary nor a matter of machinery. It depended somewhat on what players and instruments happened to be around. Its size would run from four to five to fifteen or twenty, and the four or five often had to do the job without getting put out. Sometimes they would give as much support "during the rescue" as the whole town band. Its scores were subject to make-shifts, and were often written with that in mind. There were usually one or two treble Wood-Wind, a Trombone, a Cornet, sometimes a Saxophone, Strings, Piano, and a Drum—often an octave of High Bells or a Xylophone. The pianist usually led—his head or any unemployed limb acting as a kind of Ictusorgan.[27]

The variable size and membership of theater orchestras shaped both the composition and performance history of *Four Ragtime Dances*, and probably explain why Ives later chose to rescore these compositions for many different types of ensembles.

Determining the exact chronology of the composition of *Four Ragtime Dances* is a demanding task; it is just one of the many challenges faced by Ives scholars when dating his works. Ives reworked and repackaged this ragtime material over several decades, and though his commentary appears in numerous sources, these sources offer conflicting testimony.[28] Ives's earliest estimates indicate that he began to write his ragtime pieces in 1899, the year after he graduated from Yale, while he was sketching *Skit for Danbury Fair*. Over the next few years he composed nine brief ragtime pieces, arranged for assorted combinations of instruments, including solo piano.[29] Between 1902 and 1904, according to a passage in *Memos*, he incorporated this material in *Four Ragtime Dances*, for which several fragments and preliminary sketches survive. One sketch suggests that Ives arranged for a run-through of one of his ragtime pieces by New Haven's Hyperion Theater

Orchestra in 1899, whereas a note on a later score mentions a 1902 attempt in New York City, which failed after the conductor pronounced the work "too hard to play."[30] Ives pushed on for several years, revising this material and arranging for additional run-throughs by theater orchestras in New Haven and New York City.

The strength of Ives's commitment to this music can be gauged by his repeated attempts to have these pieces performed as well as his subsequent development of this material. Rather than tossing them aside as youthful indiscretions, Ives continued to rework and expand his ragtime-influenced pieces over the next decade, eventually integrating this material into larger works. He incorporated three of the *Four Ragtime Dances* into the two scherzo movements of the First Piano Sonata, adding to the sonata's fourth movement a newly composed passage packed with particularly intense ragtime-inflected rhythms. He then reorchestrated some of the same material (used in movement IIb of the First Piano Sonata) to produce the second movement ("In the Inn") of A Set of Pieces for Theatre or Chamber Orchestra. The third of the *Four Ragtime Dances*, which Ives did not use in the First Piano Sonata, grew into the second movement ("The Rockstrewn Hills Join in the People's Outdoor Meeting") of the Second Orchestral Set.[31] Ives even considered grouping these two orchestral pieces, "Rockstrewn Hills" and "In the Inn," into a new set called *Three Ragtime Dances*, but instead let them stand in the aforementioned orchestral sets.[32] Despite numerous musical transformations over the years, Ives continued to think of his later pieces as growing out of his early ragtime experiments; for example, he characterized "Rockstrewn Hills" as "but a rehash and combinations of some of the ragtime dances for small orchestra which grew up between 1902 and 1910–11, generally speaking."[33] Nearly a decade later, in the early 1920s, Ives began to rescore the dances once more but gave up this project for reasons he did not explain.[34] Despite his perpetual fascination with this material—or perhaps because of it—Ives never completed a final version of *Four Ragtime Dances*.

FOUR RAGTIME DANCES

The modern revival of *Four Ragtime Dances* can be attributed to the conductor and Ives scholar James Sinclair, who reconstructed the work, premiered several of the dances in the mid-1970s, and published a full edition in 1990, titled *Ragtime Dances: Set of Four Ragtime Dances for Theater Orchestra*. Since only one page of a full score survives, Sinclair fashioned much of his edition from the remaining sketches, most of which were written for piano but contain orchestral indications.[35] In his editorial remarks that accompany the score, Sinclair explains in detail the process by which he interpreted Ives's sketches to resolve key issues, such as deciding on the pitches of certain notes as well as the order of the four dances. Though he relied on many of the same materials on which Lou Harrison based his edition of Ives's First Piano Sonata, Sinclair chose to ignore the revisions Ives made for the sonata, to come closer to Ives's earlier conception of the piece. He did, however, consult some later works, such as "In the Inn" and "Rockstrewn Hills," for ideas about orchestration, dynamics, and texture. Sinclair's contributions to the score of *Four Ragtime Dances* serve as a reminder that a number of Ives's works have been edited and published by other hands. Nevertheless, his approximation of Ives's early encounter with this material, which produces a pared-down treatment of it, helps clarify the influence of both theater orchestras and ragtime on Ives.

Designed as a quartet of pieces for theater orchestra, *Four Ragtime Dances* is meant to be performed consecutively; each dance lasts a few minutes and the entire work totals around eleven minutes. As part of the thematic design that links all four dances, Ives adopted a structural approach that demonstrates the powerful influence of gospel hymns on his compositional thinking. This was music with which he became familiar as a child, heard at outdoor revivals, played as a church organist, and continued to use throughout his career. Rather than modeling *Four Ragtime Dances* after the three or four independent strains of most piano rags, he used the verse-chorus form characteristic of many Protestant hymns. Each dance begins with a long "verse" section, its material based primarily on two hymns, "Bringing in the Sheaves" (George Minor) and "Happy Day" (Edward Rimbault), and concludes with a short "chorus," so titled, based on a third hymn, "I Hear Thy Welcome Voice" (Lewis Hartsough).[36] Since he often quoted and paraphrased well-known hymn tunes in his compositions, in that sense these pieces are not exceptional. But as Dennis Marshall explains in his discussion of Ives's First Piano Sonata, which recycles material from the ragtime dances, Ives created a unified work by taking advantage of the musical similarities of these particular hymns, relying on both their verse-chorus structure and the closing cadential figure (2–1–3–2–1) they share.[37] As Burkholder points out, the hymns' "common elements make it difficult to ascertain which of these tunes is being used at several points, and Ives was clearly interested in exploring the ambiguity between them."[38] Simply put, these hymns were chosen carefully.

As for the other key musical resource, the elements of ragtime present in *Four Ragtime Dances* suggest what most attracted Ives to this music. Like

Example 1. Charles Ives, *Ragtime Dances: Set of Four Ragtime Dances*, ed. James Sinclair (New York: Peer International, 1990), "Ragtime Dance No. 2," piano. mm. 21–23.

much ragtime piano music, each dance begins in $\frac{2}{4}$ meter, but, in typical Ivesian fashion, metrical shifts and tempo changes abound throughout the verses before the dances finally settle on triple meter at the chorus. Fleeting moments evoke the rhythms of ragtime, which Ives accentuates through heavily syncopated patterns in the treble instruments. But his constant use of contrasting motives, irregular phrases, metric changes, shifts in tempo and key, and extended pedal points moves the piece away from the sound of popular ragtime. The opening of "Ragtime Dance No. 2" captures a sense of its frenetic nature: piano drumming (mm. 1–2), a thorny figure played by the clarinet (mm. 3–4), and a characteristic ragtime lick played by the right hand that seems as if it could have been lifted from Scott Joplin (mm. 21–23, example 1). Yet as identifiable as any single motive may appear, when blended together by Ives these dances sound strikingly out-of-joint.

As Judith Tick has shown and these examples illustrate, the most prominent feature of Ives's use of ragtime involves his rhythmic experimentation.[39] Ives confirmed as much in *Memos*, recalling that the ragtime dances "were but working out different combinations or rhythms that these began to suggest. For instance, if, in a few measures in $\frac{2}{4}$ time, the second beat is not struck and the 16th-note before the second beat is accented, other combinations of after-beats and beats and minus-beats etc. suggest themselves."[40] Elsewhere he describes a section of the First Piano Sonata in which "ragging combinations of fives, twos, and sevens are tried out. There are also measures of twos and threes, grouping or phrasing the various parts in different-length phrases—that is, all threes may be grouped in fours accenting the fourth, and the fours may be grouped in fives accenting the fifth."[41] Ives produced a variety of outlandish rhythmic examples in *Four Ragtime Dances* that demonstrate how he "carried certain tendencies in

Example 2. Charles Ives, "Ragtime Dance No. 2," piano.

mm. 25–26

mm. 63–64

popular ragtime to great extremes" (example 2).[42] Rhythm is the element of ragtime to which Ives refers most often in his written recollections, and it is this aspect of the music that made the greatest impression on his compositional style.

Rather than assembling a musical quilt out of fragments of popular ragtime tunes, Ives drew on the percussive, syncopated qualities of ragtime to develop his own ragtime-influenced style within which he could recompose melodies. To produce *Four Ragtime Dances,* Ives "rags" his source material by extracting short motives from the hymns, making substantial rhythmic and melodic alterations, inserting exaggerated syncopations, adding accent marks to highlight displaced beats, and experimenting with polyrhythms. Adopting ragtime as a style, as a set of techniques, allowed Ives to generate endless variations on the hymn tunes that populate the four dances. He thus found numerous ways in which to adapt a motive from the hymn "Happy Day" (example 3) into the second ragtime dance (example 4).[43] Ragging hymns was not entirely unknown, at least in the popular arena: in fact, one of the earliest primers, *Ben Harney's Rag Time Instructor* (1897), includes

Example 3. Edward Rimbault, "Happy Day" (1854).

Example 4. Charles Ives, "Ragtime Dance No. 2," violin, mm. 5–6.

arrangements of "Old Hundred" and "Come Thou Fount of Every Blessing."[44] For that matter, despite having been composed ages earlier, the gospel hymns chosen by Ives do not lend an archaic tone as much as they demonstrate their own brand of popular appeal, as if their sacred messages were accompanied by a familiar secular sound.[45] But it is safe to say that nothing else like this kaleidoscopic piece for theater orchestra existed at the time. In many circles, mingling hymns with ragtime would have been perceived as sacrilegious, an act just as irreverent to the sacred music of the church as experimenting with ragtime would have been to traditionalists in the concert music world. There is a streak of impishness at work in the process of bringing together music from different cultural arenas, but at the same time the creation of a music all made of tunes, a strategy for which Ives is so revered, suggests a more progressive outlook about diversity and the nature of American music. Consequently, it has been suggested that by combining the two types of music, which coexist through the piece, and by ragging the hymns, Ives was "expressing not ridicule, but intense admiration."[46] How we are to interpret this musical encounter—as a product of mischief, an act of musical integration, a symbol of cultural collision—is an issue I raise now but will reserve for discussion later in this chapter, since a full explanation requires a more extended consideration of Ives's writings.

Looking to the orchestration and instrumentation of *Four Ragtime Dances* as a way to understand Ives's compositional thought is more problematic, since many of the individual choices were not spelled out by Ives but instead interpolated by Sinclair. Some of Ives's sketches for *Four Ragtime Dances* as well as his remarks about its performance history mention his experimentation with different instrumental combinations, a reflection of the variable size of theater orchestras. Not having to address that particular challenge, the instrumentation in Sinclair's critical edition suits a well-equipped theater orchestra of around twenty-five to forty musicians, depending on the flexible size of the string section. Likewise, although Ives's sketches mention most of the instruments that Sinclair employs (including piano, viola, cello, bass, flute, violin, tuba, trombone), in certain cases it was up to Sinclair to choose a specific instrument (e.g., clarinet) to play what Ives indicates in general terms (e.g., woodwind). Nevertheless, a few general observations can be made about the scoring of *Four Ragtime Dances*. In comparison to stock arrangements of orchestral ragtime, which usually assigned specific roles to instruments and stuck with them, at least within each strain, the music of *Four Ragtime Dances* changes texture much more abruptly, exchanging themes and distributing responsibilities more widely among members of the orchestra.[47] Even more noticeable, both here and in Ives's subsequent ragtime works, is the prominent role that Ives gives to the pianist. In addition to reflecting his keyboard proficiency, Ives's choice to incorporate the sound of ragtime piano occurred around the time he left his position as a church organist and turned his attention back to the piano.[48] Ives himself recognized the significance of the piano in "Rockstrewn Hills," an orchestral composition that grew out of the third ragtime dance: "It takes a good pianist to play the piano part, and this movement is almost a piano concerto."[49] Though *Four Ragtime Dances* does not make such high demands on the pianist, it was not composed with amateurs in mind.

Nor does the piece reveal the work of an amateur composer. Despite its seeming haphazardness, the piece is precisely organized. The individual details of the ragtime dances may vary, but each proceeds in the same basic fashion. The verses juxtapose motives from the hymns with their rhythmically ragged variants—interrupted by short, punctuated blasts and dramatic changes in texture and tempo—before the ensemble accelerates and soars into each chorus. More significantly, Ives molded the unusual combination of ragtime and hymnody into a singular shape. In fact, the form of *Four Ragtime Dances* is extraordinarily rare in the Ives repertoire, according to Burkholder's study of his compositional technique, by virtue of coupling verse-refrain form with "cumulative setting."[50] *Cumulative setting* means, roughly speaking, that the development comes first, before the statement of the main theme. Among other precedents, this technique probably derived from Ives's experience playing organ preludes, in which themes are often improvised before they are presented in full. As it applies here, this concept refers to Ives's choice to withhold the hymn "Bringing in the Sheaves" until the end of *Four Ragtime Dances*. Though all the dances contain "ragged" fragments of this hymn, which help link the four thematically, in the final dance Ives paraphrases it in longer, increasingly recognizable passages. Toward the end of the last verse, he presents it most conclusively, repeating the hymn's verse several times before stating its refrain (mm. 63–85, 86–93).

In addition to the long-range process of unfurling "Bringing in the Sheaves," Ives manipulates the hymn-based material to produce a sense of accomplishment during each dance. He manages this by reserving the hymn "Welcome Voice" for the chorus of each dance, where its melody appears against the backdrop of a relatively unadorned texture. Following each verse, in which fragments of the other two hymns emerge in fits and starts, the arrival of "Welcome Voice" thus comes to be heard as a concluding statement to each dance. The chorus of the first dance exemplifies Ives's use of this method. The upper winds and strings paraphrase the melody of "Welcome Voice" while the brass and piano play rag-derived rhythms (example 5, mm. 96–99). The texture thins out and the tempo slows, as the violins assume responsibility for completing the hymn, but at the last moment Ives chooses to leave the music unresolved, the melodic descent incomplete, the harmony perched on the dominant (example 5, mm. 100–102). Ives repeats a similar procedure in the second and third dances, attaining the same level of anticipation, and it is not until the final measure of *Four Ragtime Dances* that Ives completes his setting of "Welcome Voice." Listeners are thus rewarded doubly in the fourth dance by the cumulative setting of "Bringing in the Sheaves" as well as the final definitive statement of "Welcome Voice."

As the conclusion of *Four Ragtime Dances,* the final dance is significant for several other reasons. Because the primary sketch on which Sinclair based his editing of the final dance is one of only two complete sketches that exist for the entire work, and because this material was not otherwise scored by Ives for orchestra, the fourth dance offers a rare picture of Ives's early experimentation with ragtime. It is particularly interesting to note how Ives attempts to wrap things up. In addition to concluding the cumulative setting, the final dance is the only one to contain a quotation from "Welcome Voice," otherwise confined to the chorus, as part of its verse section (mm. 7–23). More audibly, Ives lifts a phrase from "Bringing in the Sheaves," previously restricted to the verses, and inserts it into the final chorus, where he joins the two main themes in counterpoint (example 6, mm. 104–5). The establishment of these two links between verse and chorus gives further indication of Ives's pursuit of formal unity. Yet in the final chorus, which is much softer and less climactic than the earlier choruses, he leaves a few musical doors open. As the final measures of the fourth dance present the first complete statement of the 2–1–3–2–1 shared cadence, which he withheld from the previous three

Example 5. Charles Ives, "Ragtime Dance No. 1," mm. 96–102.

dances, Ives adds chromatic inflections to the harmonic accompaniment that tint and deflect the cadence (example 6, mm. 105–7). Likewise, as he later would in the First Piano Sonata, Ives partially obscures the closing harmony with a chromatic neighbor chord, which avoids a firm conclusion and yields a sense of uncertainty (example 6, m. 108).

Example 5. *(continued)*

Example 6. Charles Ives, "Ragtime Dance No. 4," mm. 100–108.

Example 6. *(continued)*

THE POSSIBILITIES OF RAGTIME

Arranging *Four Ragtime Dances* for theater orchestra indicates a move in the direction of popular entertainment, but the use of unusual techniques, such as delaying the theme over the course of its cumulative setting, suggests the contrary. Because of their unique form, as well as their unexpected swings in tempo, meter, rhythm, and texture, these dances do not fit snugly beside popular ragtime pieces, vaudeville numbers, light classical music, and other standard repertory for theater orchestra. Predictably, Ives's contemporaries were unsure what to make of this music. Of a run-through of several dances by a small orchestra at Keith's Theater in Manhattan "somewhere between 1903 and 1906," Ives recalled that only the pianist liked the music, and "at the second afternoon performance, the manager of the theater came out and stopped them, saying it made too much of a disturbance."[51] Years later, Joseph Reutershan, who helped arrange that run-through, laughingly told Ives, "Well, to tell the truth, I didn't blame him. That was the craziest lot of sounds I ever heard."[52] In his recent biography of Ives, Jan Swafford offers a more sympathetic reaction: "This is music evocative of turn-of-the-century vaudeville and saloons, but it is also an Ivesian rhythmic phantasmagoria full of startling cuts and stumbles and shifts of perspective, eventually gathering into a romping, stomping finish."[53] Despite being composed a century ago, *Four Ragtime Dances* still sounds off-kilter, full of unexpected twists and startling turns.

The experimental nature of these dances indicates that, as much as Ives was drawn to the energy of ragtime, he did not intend to compose conventional rags for mainstream circulation. On the contrary, as Peter Burkholder argues, a composition like *Four Ragtime Dances* intentionally establishes a degree of distance from its source material. Such compositions "are no longer simply vernacular pieces but are concert pieces 'about' vernacular styles and vernacular performance, quoting tunes, using familiar ragtime rhythms, and evoking the spirit and atmosphere of performances by amateur musicians."[54] In other words, Ives did not seek to inspire turn-of-the-century dancers to try out their latest steps at a local dance hall, but instead attempted to recapture the desperate exhilaration of an amateur theater orchestra bent on doing just that. Taking this approach necessarily ended up distancing Ives from his source material as well. Rather than assuming the pose of a budding ragtime composer in *Four Ragtime Dances*, Ives positioned himself as an observer of ragtime, less a musical populist than a witness of popular life. As will become clear presently, his written commentary about ragtime also reflects the same sort of spectator's perspective.

Stepping back from his subject did not diminish his commitment to the music. Ives's sustained attention to *Four Ragtime Dances*—arranging for performances, making revisions, and recycling segments in later works—demonstrates how seriously he took this venture. And yet upon reading what Ives wrote about ragtime and his ragtime pieces, one is left in a bit of a quandary, for his statements appear more dismissive toward the music than his actions would indicate. Lawrence Kramer characterizes the relationship between white art music composers and African American music, evidenced by Ives's experience with ragtime, to be "haunted by ambivalence about the musics on which it drew, with which it mingled on terms compounded of pleasure, envy, condescension, anxiety and celebration."[55] While I am not convinced fully by this argument with respect to Ives's actual use of ragtime in *Four Ragtime Dances*, I find Kramer's statements more compelling when applied to Ives's published reflections on ragtime. Even though Ives catalogs his own musical experience with ragtime, he stops short of unconditional praise and instead expresses the contradictory impulses that were not uncommon in his writings. His comments, discussed earlier in this chapter, exhibit an uneasy mixture of enthusiasm and condescension, of praise and disdain. Rather than applauding specific ragtime songs or admiring individual composers, he suggests that "time will throw its vices away and weld its virtues into the fabric of our music."[56] A generous explanation might propose that a humble Ives recognized that his own music did not take full advantage of ragtime's possibilities, that the music offered more than he was able to unearth. What seems more likely, however, is that his comments represent a case in which the older Ives played down his musical debts, asserted his own primacy as a composer, and in the process revealed his own musical priorities.[57]

One way to reconcile his music and his commentary is to note that Ives wrote *Essays Before a Sonata* more than twenty years after his initial exposure to ragtime, *Memos* a dozen years later, and both long after the peak of the ragtime era. Married and retired to the country, Ives was twice as old, not in the best of health, and living a very different sort of life. By this point he was far removed from the original music that fired his imagination, perhaps removed even further as a consequence of his own achievements in rhythmic experimentation. Looking back on his youth, Ives writes of "the old ragtime stuff" and compares the scherzos of the First Piano Sonata to a "boy away sowing his oats in the ragtimes."[58] Ives scholars have documented his mounting distaste for city life and modern technology, including the radio and the phonograph. Though the younger Ives appears to have had more sympathy for those writers who celebrated ragtime as "the perfect expression of the American city, with its restless bustle and motion,"[59] the older Ives sided with ragtime's critics, who associated the music with "the noise, rush and vulgarity of the street."[60] In fact, Ives expressed a similar perspective in one of his songs from this period, "The See'r," which he dated 1920. To accompany the song's lyrics, which concern an old man sitting down for the day and watching odd things going by, Ives depicts the strange goings-on via a series of increasingly frenzied ragtime syncopations.

At this point in his career, Ives's priorities had changed, as he tried to frame his public image, publish his compositions, and locate himself with respect to the musical establishment. Ironically, in the process of subscribing to what Frank Rossiter describes as the "genteel tradition" in American music, Ives turned to the writings of Daniel Gregory Mason, a Columbia professor and composer whose music epitomized the type of musical conservatism against which Ives typically rebelled.[61] As part of a running debate in the 1910s about how best to cultivate a national style, Mason argued against the integration of vernacular sources like ragtime into American classical music and in favor of maintaining closer ties to European music: "From this point of view it will be seen that the enthusiasts of nationalism, in advising our composer to confine himself to Indian, Negro, or ragtime material, in adjuring him not to listen to the siren voice of Europe, are not merely misleading but cheating him. They are asking him to throw away his birthright of wide cosmopolitan influence for a mess of purely parochial pottage."[62] Weighing in on this issue a few years later in *Essays Before a Sonata*, Ives did not take the opportunity to defend the use of ragtime in classical music or to promote his own compositions as counterexamples. Instead, he seconded many of Mason's views and also drew on a metaphor Mason employed to compare ragtime to ketchup. But there was one crucial difference in Ives's commentary. Unlike Mason, Ives resolutely defended the use of American vernacular music—not ragtime, however, but the white Protestant tradition of gospel hymnody that he held dear.

Leafing through *Essays Before a Sonata* helps identify Ives's racialized views on the subject, since several of his key statements on ragtime are positioned just after those that address the use of Negro spirituals, Native American songs, and white Protestant gospel hymns. In the following passage, Ives offers his views on the creation of an "American" music:

> A composer born in America, but who has not been interested in the "cause of the Freedmen," may be so interested in "negro melodies" that he writes a symphony over them. He is conscious (perhaps only subconscious) that he wishes it to be "American music." He tries to forget that

the paternal negro came from Africa. Is his music American or African? That is the great question which keeps him awake! But the sadness of it is that if he had been born in Africa, his music might have been just as American, for there is good authority that an African soul under an X-ray looks identically like an American soul. There is a futility in selecting a certain type to represent a "whole," unless the interest in the spirit of the type coincides with that of the whole. In other words, if this composer isn't as deeply interested in the "cause" as Wendell Phillips was, when he fought his way through that anti-abolitionist crowd at Faneuil Hall, his music is liable to be less American than he wishes.[63]

Both in this excerpt and in his subsequent discussion about using Native American musical material, Ives advises composers to pay closest attention to the "spirit" of a given type of music. Generally speaking, he states that integrating any type of music is permissible as long as the composer "is confident that they have a part in his spiritual consciousness."[64] In other words, as Burkholder writes, "Ives felt strongly that an American music would have to be based not just on American tunes (or even on borrowed American tunes at all) but rather on American experience and American ideals for it to be truly native."[65] Though Ives's commentary implies that a legitimately American music could derive from any of a variety of musical sources, his tone suggests that he personally felt the greatest enthusiasm for Protestant hymns. Drawing on his experience to create music that he hoped would have much greater significance, he goes on to claim that if a composer can capture the spirit of singing hymns at a New England camp meeting, then "he may find there a local color that will do all the world good. If his music can but catch that spirit by being a part with itself, it will come somewhere near his ideal—and it will be American, too—perhaps nearer so than that of the devotee of Indian or Negro melody."[66] His use of "perhaps" leaves some room for debate, but Ives would take an even firmer stance when he revisited these issues a decade later.

In a telling passage from *Memos*, which seems to allude to the kind of personal or critical encounters that led Ives to cement his position, he differentiates between white sacred musical traditions and black spirituals. More closely affiliated with Protestant hymns and the songs of Steven Foster, two types of music that he frequently integrated into his own compositions, Ives places himself in opposition to the foreign-born Dvořák and his *New World* Symphony, a work that was thought to have gained inspiration from African American and Native American music:

Some nice people, whenever they hear the words "Gospel Hymns" or "Stephen Foster," say "Mercy Me!", and a little high-brow smile creeps over their brow—"Can't you get something better than that in a symphony?" The same nice people, when they go to a properly dressed symphony concert under proper auspices, led by a name with foreign hair, and hear Dvorak's *New World Symphony,* in which they are told this famous passage was from a negro spiritual, then think that it must be quite proper, even artistic, and say "How delightful!" But when someone proves to them that the Gospel Hymns are fundamentally responsible for the negro spirituals, they say, "Ain't it awful!"—"You don't really mean that!"[67]

Along the same lines, though Ives commended the performance tradition of black spirituals, he continued to reserve greater praise for its white antecedents:

But it was not, to my mind, these physical techniques as much as the fervor, conviction, and a real human something underneath, that the negroes heard in these Gospel Hymns. . . . But the darkies used these things in their own native way, and made them somewhat different— "more beautiful and more artistic" says Rollo. Yes, and so did some of the Yankees. I'm not trying to say that many of the spirituals, jubilees, etc. aren't in their own way natural, spontaneous, beautiful, and artistic—but some white Congregationalists or Methodists (drunk or sober) already had somepin' also natural, spontaneous, beautiful, and artistic—and that somepin' was to start the negro spirituals.[68]

Once again, Ives calls for white Protestant gospel hymns to be given the same level of respect as black spirituals. Yet, by employing racialized language and sporadic sarcasm—through the voice of Rollo, who personified for Ives much of what he felt was wrong with the music world—he distinguishes between the two and highlights the significance of white Protestant hymnody, which he felt stood at the core of these traditions. While acknowledging that the black spirituals as well as the music they later inspired could be remarkably beautiful and artistic, Ives argued that such music derived from and constituted an off-shoot of the musical tradition to which he was most committed.

In contrast to hymnody, ragtime now occupied a much lower rung on Ives's ladder of priorities, to the extent that he could compare its value, as we saw in this chapter's epigraph, to dinner-table condiments. By this point, after several decades of massive popularity, ragtime was known less as a novel musical sensation and more for its widespread commercial success. Yet for Ives to have produced such flippant commentary about Protestant hymnody is unimaginable. The temptation thus exists to connect the dots between Ives's promotion of white Protestant hymnody and his faint praise of ragtime, an African American creation, but I am not prepared to claim that his relationship to ragtime should be reduced entirely to a racial equation, at least not a simple one. My view inclines toward the commonly held perception of Ives as someone fairly sensitive to issues of racial equality. Unlike other critiques of Ives—say, those decrying his gender politics—attempts to expose Ives as a racist have not flourished.[69] Because he was such a voracious borrower, Ives has been accused of demonstrating some degree of racial bias by generally avoiding certain types of music, including African American musical genres like the blues as well as music written by (Jewish) Tin Pan Alley composers.[70] One explanation for these compositional choices comes from Burkholder, who suggests that Ives used "the music of white Americans, rather than that of Indians or blacks, because it was the flavor of his own people and region that he sought to capture."[71] A second way to answer such accusations would be to call attention to an obvious counterexample—Ives's experiments with the music of ragtime.

Had he wanted to steer clear of black-identified genres, surely Ives would have avoided ragtime altogether. It was not as if he understood the music to be racially unmarked. On the contrary, race powerfully shaped Ives's understanding of the genre, just as it influenced members of his entire generation. As mentioned earlier, he associated the techniques of ragtime with blackface minstrelsy, which he once described as "a form of 'theatricals' that unfortunately has almost disappeared."[72] Moreover, some of his writings contain not-too-veiled racial allusions, such as his comparison of ragtime to "something like wearing a derby hat on the back of the head, a shuffling lilt of a happy soul just let out of a Baptist church in old Alabama."[73] Yet, regardless of any racial connotations he linked to ragtime, and despite the patronizing quality of his later remarks, Ives chose to compose *Four Ragtime Dances*, music in which both Protestant hymns and ragtime play crucial roles. How are we to reconcile what Ives composed with what he wrote about it? Discovering an answer requires turning once more to the music, this time keeping in mind the composer's later written comments about hymnody and ragtime.

Put simply, how do ragtime and gospel hymns fare in *Four Ragtime Dances?* How does their treatment by Ives compare with the tone of his written statements? In his analysis of the First Piano Sonata, Kramer argues that the "debunking here is directed at the hymn tunes, which are mocked and distorted by being ragged," and he describes Ives's rhythmic start of the fourth movement to be a "protracted spell of noisy, grinding, motoric rhythms, a kind of sonoric abyss that eventually spews forth a rag."[74] In contrast to the sonata, Ives's earlier treatment of much of the same musical material in *Four Ragtime Dances* presents a clear alternative. Echoing Ives's commentary on the gospel hymns, this set of pieces works exactly the other way around, slowly unveiling the final hymn through its cumulative setting. Ives's ragtime techniques do end up distorting the hymns, in the course of producing extreme melodic variations and injecting rhythmic propulsion into the quartet of dances, but mockery hardly seems to be at issue, especially considering how things work out. In his description of the dances, Jan Swafford proposes that Ives mixed hymns and ragtime "not to sully the sacred, but . . . to infuse the secular with spiritual joy."[75] Alternatively, one also might say that this process infuses the spiritual with secular joy.

Not all of Kramer's conclusions about the First Piano Sonata hold true when the same analytical approach is extended to *Four Ragtime Dances*, but I find provocative his contention that "whenever a dominant social group [white America] begins to appropriate the expressive idioms [ragtime] of the group it dominates [African Americans], the process of appropriation bears traces of the social circumstances that ground it."[76] Such traces do appear in *Four Ragtime Dances*, and once hymns are added into the mix, it becomes clear that, from a structural standpoint, ragtime occupies a far less prominent position. After all, Ives draws his primary melodic material from the three gospel hymns, and it is their verse-chorus structure that determines the form of each dance. Furthermore, the cumulative settings of each individual dance, and the set as a whole, do not serve to unveil the latest ragtime hit but instead dramatize the gradual emergence of the hymn material, a process that brings with it a palpable sense of accomplishment. By delivering a truly "welcome voice" in the form of a hymn by the same name, each concluding chorus carries an air of triumph. That Ives would give precedence to the Protestant hymns over ragtime in the structure of these pieces should come as little surprise. This is true not only in light of the views Ives later expressed about hymns, but also because at this point in his career Ives was busy writing numerous hymn-based compositions. Admittedly, the choice to rely on a cumulative setting that brings a hymn to light while incorporating the rhythms of ragtime seems more conventional than, say, to base a composition on a ragtime tune and fill it with hymn-style harmonies. Yet, at the same time, Ives's choice in *Four Ragtime Dances* to give more weight to the white gospel hymns than to the black-identified ragtime resonates with Kramer's larger argument that Ives's music mimics the racial power dynamics, or unequal race relations, that characterized turn-of-the-century America.

Without meaning to brush these observations entirely aside, I question whether a broad structural argument is enough to account fully for either the cultural or aesthetic significance of the piece. In the end, Ives chose to call this music the *ragtime* dances, and snippets, echoes, and traces of ragtime surface throughout the entire work. Lacking the influence of ragtime to re-shape the hymns, this music would lose nearly all its idiosyncratic flavor. For as much as *Four Ragtime Dances* shares some of the priorities that Ives expressed in his writings, its existence also shows that in a fundamental respect Ives was looking ahead. One of the first to experiment with ragtime, Ives exhibited a progressive attitude in comparison with his art music contemporaries. Despite the level of cultural debate surrounding ragtime's questionable reputation—stemming variously from its mass popularity, its secular associations, and its black origins—Ives appreciated the music enough to experiment repeatedly with its possibilities. His incorporation of ragtime therefore stands as a remarkably bold act for its time, a controversial move in its cultural context. Although he chose to downplay ragtime's influence in print, as Ives often did with his musical forebears, he was willing to learn from ragtime and eager to revisit his ragtime-influenced pieces. Consequently, Ives's defenders consider his use of ragtime to reveal an attitude of inclusion and acceptance, his interest in these pieces to signal sincere and sustained experimentalism.

Facing such contradictory perspectives about Ives and *Four Ragtime Dances* makes it difficult to choose an interpretive route. Are we to understand this work as a progressive step toward racial understanding or as a perpetuation of unequal race relations? However paradoxical it might appear, I wish to acknowledge both positions, for music often works in ways too complex to allow for simple answers. In so doing, I am not proposing to integrate Kramer's cultural criticism seamlessly with an uncritical celebration of Ives, for effortless unification is not always possible, whether in cultural debates, musical compositions, or musicological endeavors. In other words, rather than magically resolving this predicament, I wish to keep in the foreground the contradictions and tensions that animate this complicated piece. Serving in part to reinforce the same set of race relations that its existence simultaneously works against, the music of *Four Ragtime Dances* deserves to be lauded for its achievements, just as the constraints of those achievements need to be recognized. Likewise, before entirely condemning the piece, one must ask whether it is reasonable to place on Ives the burden of fulfilling the promise of racial parity, a task that subsequent generations have been unable to accomplish.

Acknowledging the opposing impulses and contradictions enacted by *Four Ragtime Dances* also offers another means by which not necessarily to reconcile but at least to come to terms with the incongruity between

Ives's music and his written commentary. Locating a disjunction between a composer's art and life is hardly uncommon, nor is it rare to discover discrepancies between the way a particular piece of music works and what a composer has to say about it. This becomes evident for a composer like Ives, who often adopted notably forceful, sometimes downright belligerent positions in his various writings. Instead of trying to smooth out the rough edges or to explain away any distracting inconsistencies, it becomes more productive in the case of Ives and ragtime to shine a spotlight directly on them. That Ives's writings about his use of ragtime display deep anxiety and ambivalence, as Kramer would frame it, is not a predicament to be overcome but instead a useful reflection of Ives's experience as an art music composer in the ragtime era. That Ives told a very different story in compositions like *Four Ragtime Dances* from the one he detailed in prose may produce an unavoidable contradiction, but it is a fruitful and significant one that indicates how musical compositions and surrounding discourse can work toward very different ends, perhaps especially in an era of heated cultural debate. Indeed, notwithstanding his eventual claims in print, Ives went ahead and experimented with the music of ragtime for decades. Demonstrating the capacity of music to register an alternative social experience, the act of composing seems to have afforded Ives the opportunity to explore ideas that he might have been unwilling or unable to articulate in words. Moreover, perhaps this explains his choice not to publish final versions of these early compositions. Whether or not he recognized it himself, blending the music of ragtime and Protestant hymns enabled Ives to conduct an experiment in musical diversity that he could articulate much more thoroughly in a sonic realm than in the social realm of his era, a point made all too clear by his own published writings.

We may be attracted to music that attempts to produce a sense of multicultural equality or upset by music that serves to encode racial prejudice, but rarely does there exist music so unambiguous and one-dimensional. On the contrary, individual pieces of music, at times whole genres, hold our attention precisely because their efforts to grapple with musical and cultural tensions do not, sometimes cannot, produce clear-cut solutions. Thus, to best account for music ranging from the relatively sympathetic yet undeniably patronizing portrait of black life in Stephen Foster's "Old Folks at Home" to the paradoxical merger of nihilism and empowerment present in early punk rock, it may be more productive to view musical compositions not as an end product but instead as part of an ongoing process of answering a question. Such a perspective becomes especially germane for music that strives to cross identifiable boundaries, whether of genre, class, race, or nation. Indeed, as Kramer's argument implies, mixed-genre creations like *Four Ragtime Dances* cannot help bearing traces of the power relations that characterize the meeting of classical composers with various other worlds of music. By paying attention to these traces and observing the cultural tensions that make this music so compelling, musical scholarship can better respond to the dynamic, contested world we live in.

The music of *Four Ragtime Dances* sounds remarkably confusing and disorderly, less a melting pot than a mishmash, a cluttered jumble. Even when the dances are performed exactly as written, they bring to mind the remarks that Ives made after a particularly uneven performance of his *Three Places in New England:* "Just like a town meeting—every man for himself, wonderful how it came out."[77] To make the most of this piece, I look to the work of scholars such as Josh Kun, who suggests: "When we talk about music in America, and music's role in shaping American identities and American meanings, we should be thinking of music in terms of the differences it contains, the differences it makes audible, not the unities or harmonies it can be used to fabricate."[78] I similarly lean toward what Larry Starr describes as the "rough, effusive, *messy* quality" of Ives's music, its "willingness to risk apparent chaos," rather than Starr's broader metaphor of "a union of diversities."[79] The point, it seems, is not that varied musical practices or genres are meeting on common ground, sharing space equally, and learning to get along perfectly, but that they are crossing over and colliding, bumping up against one another, struggling to be heard above the commotion, even as they participate in the process of trying to work things out. Because it engages with so many sources of musical friction—between traditional European and modern American compositional practices, between the sacred and secular, between classical and popular, between races— *Four Ragtime Dances* presented a major challenge for Ives. In its concluding moments Ives tries to resolve some of the built-up tensions in a way that asserts his personal priorities by avoiding references to ragtime and using "Bringing in the Sheaves" as a countermelody; however, as the chromatic neighbor chord that deflects the final cadence intimates, even he is unable to reach a decisive resolution.

"A RAGTIME WAR"

Ragtime has continued to resonate with composers for the last century, infusing the music of American composers such as John Alden Carpenter and Virgil Thomson and reaching overseas to influence international figures, including Erik Satie, Paul Hindemith, Igor Stravinsky, and Sergei Prokofiev.[80] Like Ives, each of these composers drew on aspects of ragtime—its percussive, syncopated qualities, its formal structure, its infectious dance rhythms, its cultural connotations—as points of departure toward very different ends. Such a wide range of purposes can be gauged by the diverse aims of two ragtime-influenced compositions that appeared around the time Ives composed *Four Ragtime Dances:* Scott Joplin's attempt to expand the music's expressive possibilities by composing a ragtime opera, *Treemonisha* (1911), and John Powell's satirical treatment of ragtime in his piece "Clowns" (1912), the attitude behind which complemented Powell's public speeches against racial miscegenation.[81] Like *Four Ragtime Dances,* these two pieces feature their own articulation of musical lineage, the classical-popular divide, the ethics of appropriation, and racial and class politics. Likewise, they trigger interest and debate in large part because the cultural and musical tensions that permeate them are audible and unresolved.

Charles Ives was keenly aware of the ability of music to register cultural debate, and he drew on this knowledge in his orchestral composition *Central Park in the Dark,* which appears to have been composed in the same period that saw his early ragtime experiments (ca. 1906).[82] As Denise Von Glahn illustrates in her analysis of the piece, Ives attempts in *Central Park* to contrast the timelessness of nature, embodied by the park, with the transitory distractions of contemporary urban life, represented by the encroaching sounds of the city.[83] Looking back, Ives characterized the piece as presenting a "picture-in-sounds of the sounds of nature and of happenings that men would hear some thirty or so years ago (before the combustion engine and radio monopolized the earth and air), when sitting on a bench in Central Park on a hot summer night."[84] To channel the atmosphere of the era, Ives conspicuously quotes the melody of "Hello! Ma Baby," an 1899 ragtime song by Joe Howard and Ida Emerson.[85] The lilting tune may strike twenty-first-century listeners as old-fashioned and nostalgic, even those familiar with the vestiges of racial politics that are present in the original song: the "coon" references in the second verse, the dialect of its black characters, and the two African American figures depicted in the cover art of its sheet music. Instead of serving chiefly as a marker of racial difference or musical nostalgia, ragtime also functions here as a symbol of modern disruption, emblematized by a Tin Pan Alley creation and expressed in the song's insistent refrain, "Hello! ma baby, Hello! ma honey, Hello! ma ragtime gal."

Around two-thirds of the way into *Central Park in the Dark,* during the seventh of ten iterations of a slow-moving atonal ostinato that evokes the park at night, Ives brings in this ragtime song to evoke "pianolas having a ragtime war in the apartment house over the garden wall."[86] Producing a series of sonic interruptions, the melody of "Hello! Ma Baby" appears repeatedly in various forms: quietly distorted at first (m. 67), announced more prominently by the piano (m. 79) and the E-flat clarinet (m. 80), and eventually blasted by the trumpet with support from the percussion (m. 103). Rather than assigning it an unassuming, unmarked role, as an interchangeable musical element feeding into this piece, Ives here calls on ragtime for its unruly and boisterous qualities, its capacity to pierce the New York night and raise a ruckus. Indeed, the quotation of "Hello! Ma Baby," a song that tells of two lovers courting by the recent technological advance of the telephone, contributes its own testimony to Ives's portrait of the intruding modern world. This notable Ivesian moment, featuring different subsets of the ensemble moving at separate tempos, also registers the onset of another aspect of musical modernity. For in the process of quoting ragtime to capture a bygone era, Ives chronicles exactly what had begun to materialize around him at the turn of the twentieth century: the rising influence of African American musical practices on musical life in the United States, the rapid growth of the Tin Pan Alley publishing industry, and the widening reach of popular music in America. Together, these developments, spurred on by the pioneering achievements of the recording era, would bring to prominence a new set of musicians who relied on sharply alternative ways of making music, musicians like the jazz pianist Jelly Roll Morton, the subject of the following chapter, whose music presents a radically different perspective not only on the use of ragtime but also on the nature of American music.

2. Jelly Roll Morton and the Spanish Tinge

One of the most popular jazz compilations of the past few decades, *The Smithsonian Collection of Classic Jazz,* opens with two separate renditions of Scott Joplin's "Maple Leaf Rag" that are intended to introduce listeners to the defining elements of jazz. Joplin's rendition of his piece, preserved on a 1916 piano roll, closely approximates his published score, presenting each sixteen-bar strain as written and taking all marked repeats. Jelly Roll Morton (1890–1941) takes a fundamentally different approach in his 1938 solo piano rendition of "Maple Leaf Rag." Morton alters the structure, tempo, melody, and rhythm of the original tune, modifies and improvises on Joplin's phrases, and introduces fresh, syncopated figures of his own. Instead of replicating Joplin's relatively straight rhythmic approach, Morton swings the eighth notes while joyfully, and audibly, stomping along. At times he lies behind the beat like a dawdling child before abruptly rushing forward with a trombonelike interjection in the left hand, finding delight in creating cross rhythms and changing textures. Morton's unpredictable array of accents and anticipations, his short, sharp blasts and quiet, curlicue phrases, his addition of blue notes and pungent harmonies that Joplin never envisioned—all have come to represent the unique spirit of jazz.

In comparison to Ives's *Four Ragtime Dances,* Morton's performance of "Maple Leaf Rag," in what he described as the style played in New Orleans, offers a very different take on ragtime. In one sense, Morton remains much more faithful to the original material than Ives, for his version retains many of the musical elements of Joplin's composition. He does not extract a few bars of Joplin's music and then experiment with their rhythmic possibilities, nor does he discard the composition's original themes in favor of improvising something completely new. This is not to say that his transformations would have pleased Joplin, who insisted on having his compositions performed as written, but much of Joplin's original composition is still audible despite Morton's across-the-board transformation. Morton achieves a stylistic conversion by experimenting with the entire body of "Maple Leaf Rag," tugging it in new directions and molding it into jazz. Although both Ives and Morton may be seen as using the raw material of ragtime for their own musical ends, their means of alteration remain quite distinct. Ives mines the ragtime genre, extracting small components or musical cells, then adapts and manipulates these components to compose *Four Ragtime Dances*. Morton leaves a substantial amount of Joplin's rag intact, but he remolds this material through a wide variety of jazzy techniques. Where Ives extracts and rebuilds, Morton revamps and renovates.

That Morton and Ives approached ragtime from contrasting angles is to be expected, given two musicians from vastly different backgrounds who held divergent musical priorities. Raised in a privileged white household in Connecticut, Charles Ives was trained in classical music composition at Yale University. By his late teens, Morton, with little formal education of any sort, had already left his Creole household in New Orleans to begin his long and winding career as a popular entertainer. At the time Ives began composing his ragtime dances, he was writing his music as much for himself as for a concert music audience, which only much later materialized to witness his idiosyncratic experimentalism. In contrast, Morton performed in public for much of his career, entertaining audiences who came to appreciate the appeal of jazz. An attempt to understand the history of American music from only one of these two poles necessarily results in a skewed perspective. To counteract the tendency to focus discourse about American identity on concert music, and to avoid framing the story of popular music strictly in terms of its relationship to the concert music world, I shift my attention in this chapter from Ives to Morton, exploring what his musical career tells us about American identity and jazz, the quintessentially American music.

I wish to return to a striking moment in Morton's rendition of "Maple Leaf Rag," when he produces "a hint of the tango."[1] As Morton reaches the tune's fourth and final strain, he briefly plays a new rhythm arranged in a 3+3+2 pattern, a Latin rhythm known as the *tresillo*, which forms part of a typical clave rhythm. Although Morton sprinkles similar rhythmic patterns into other sections of his performance, it is at this moment that one can most readily hear what Alan Lomax has characterized as the "subtle Caribbean beat which throbs in Morton's music."[2] In one sense, Morton was continuing along a path established by ragtime pianists such as Ben Harney, whose *Rag Time Instructor* (1897) stated that "RAG TIME (or Negro Dance Time) originally takes its initiative steps from Spanish music, or rather from Mexico, where it is known under the head and names of Habanara, Danza, Seguidilla."[3] His performance thus might be said also to evoke ragtime numbers like Joplin's "Solace—A Mexican Serenade" (1909). But I am equally interested in these rhythmic patterns for their discontinuity from ragtime, in the sense that they were not part of Joplin's published version of "Maple Leaf Rag." Morton's transformation signals a broader stylistic shift that distinguishes his interpretation of "Maple Leaf Rag" and presents the new way in which he had come to play the tune. Such rhythmic touches also give his demonstration of jazz a slight Latin or Caribbean flavor, what Morton called the Spanish tinge.

The origins of jazz are often likened to a musical gumbo, the product of a creative collision that was centered in the city of New Orleans at the tail end of the nineteenth century and incorporated a variety of musical practices from different communities. In its most simplified form, this story celebrates the musical originators, predominantly from the African American community, who combined musical elements from Europe and Africa to create a distinctly American entity: jazz. That such a hybrid music prospered in an era of systematic racial bias against black Americans makes this achievement all the more remarkable. Without diminishing the significance of these accomplishments, I wish to flesh out two key notions concerning jazz origins by turning to the example of Jelly Roll Morton, whose musical interests and experiences fall outside the conventional narrative. The first of these concerns involves the typical positioning of jazz as a product of American exceptionalism. Although I do not dispute that jazz originated within the borders of the United States, I suggest that framing its development as part of a transnational or global phenomenon may enhance our understanding of jazz history.[4] More specifically, Morton's incorporation of Latin and Caribbean musical influences implies that the international roots of jazz are more complex than the barebones equation involving Europe and Africa would suggest. The second and related concern involves challenging the black-and-white racial model that has often dominated jazz discourse, for Morton did not identify himself as either white or African American; instead, he thought of himself as a Creole, a member of the mixed-race, largely Francophone community that also produced the early jazz pioneers Freddie Keppard and Sidney Bechet.

Jazz historians have begun to reassess the role that Creole musicians played in the creation and development of jazz, especially as their involvement compares with and relates to the participation of African American musicians.[5] Most pertinent to my work is David Ake's compelling treatment of Sidney Bechet's relationship to Creole culture, in which he demonstrates how "lived realities in the jazz world—as in the broader American social and cultural world—are more complex than our simple biracial categories would lead us to believe."[6] Indeed, subscribing to a binary model of race threatens to flatten the more multifaceted reality of Morton's life as a Creole: his cultural background powerfully shaped his musical career even as it forced him to negotiate life as a nonwhite subject in a segregated society. My attention to his Creole heritage derives in part from the emphasis that the folklorist and biographer Alan Lomax places on this issue in *Mister Jelly Roll*—what he quantifies as an "almost insane Creole pride"[7]—and in part from the testimony offered by Morton's contemporaries about this facet of his personality. In one telling encounter, Morton's soft spot for his hometown surfaced during his first meeting with George Guesnon, a Creole guitarist who had just moved from New Orleans to New York City.[8] The instant they met, Morton gave Guesnon the nickname "Creole" and began to quiz him about what was going on in the Crescent City.[9] Once he decided that Guesnon could be trusted, Morton helped him locate an apartment in a rooming house owned by a woman from New Orleans, where Morton was living with Mabel Bertrand, the second of two women with whom he shared long-term relationships. A New Orleans Creole, Bertrand was popular with Morton's friends for her gumbo and her southern hospitality: according to one musician, her "effusive greetings in Creole put New Orleans on the map all over again."[10] Guesnon fondly recalled walking down the hall to rehearse with Morton, enjoy Bertrand's cooking, and sit around reminiscing about New Orleans. Morton's involvement with the Spanish tinge in jazz dovetails neatly with his allegiance to Creole customs.

Though most jazz scholarship has centered on the French aspect of Creole culture, my work here leans toward the clarinetist Barney Bigard's description of his own Creole background as one that was "essentially a mixture of Spanish and French."[11] Bigard's conception was not accepted universally—indeed, Morton would likely have objected to assigning an equal balance—but impressions of Creole culture as Spanish-tinged were by no means uncommon at the start of the twentieth century. "Creole" Guesnon held the same view: "My father was part Negro and French, my mother was Spanish and Negro, so that makes me Creole. Just like jambalaya, all mixed up. They say a Creole is a direct descendant of a Frenchman and a Spaniard, and I speak both languages fluently, as did my grandfather and grandmother."[12] Similar perspectives are shared by scholars today. Gwendolyn Midlo Hall, the renowned historian of Creole culture, offers the following definition: "*Creole* has come to mean the language and the folk culture that was native to the southern part of Louisiana where African,

French, and Spanish influence was most deeply rooted historically and culturally."[13] Recognizing the Spanish-tinged side of Creole New Orleans becomes vital if we are to understand fully Morton's musical background, his exposure to and interest in Latin musical practices, and his conspicuously creolized approach to the creation of American music.

THE SPANISH TINGE

On three occasions in 1938, Jelly Roll Morton met with Alan Lomax for a set of taped interviews and musical demonstrations held at the Library of Congress in Washington, D.C.[14] During this informal mix of conversations and performances, which included several different treatments of "Maple Leaf Rag," Morton described what he termed the Spanish tinge of early jazz. As part of his prefatory comments to his composition "New Orleans Blues," Morton advised Lomax: "Of course you may notice the Spanish tinge in it. This has so much to do with the typical jazz idea. If one can't manage a way to put these tinges of Spanish in these tunes, they'll never be able to get the right season[ing], I may call it, for jazz music."[15] To demonstrate, in his words, "that the tinge is really in there," Morton followed "New Orleans Blues" with a rendition of "La Paloma," which he introduces as "one of the great Spanish tunes."[16] This was no exaggeration, given its role as a signature song of Spain. Composed in 1859 by Sebastián de Iradier, "La Paloma" soon spread through Europe, Latin America, and the United States. It has been recorded thousands of times and has been hailed as "perhaps the most popular Spanish song ever."[17] Morton's performance of "La Paloma" begins with a fairly straight version of the original melody, accentuated by parallel thirds in the treble and underscored by a habanera-style rhythmic pattern struck powerfully in the lower register. Midway through, however, he switches gears to demonstrate an alternative combination of musical elements. As his left hand continues to pound out the habanera bass, Morton's right hand shifts into an aggressively syncopated style, full of rhythmic displacements and blue notes, which combine to produce a polyrhythmic blend of jazz with a Spanish tinge. This segment of his conversation with Lomax contains the majority of Morton's remarks about the Spanish tinge, yet its musical influence can be heard throughout the Library of Congress sessions, most obviously in the Latin rhythms that seep into his demonstration of "Maple Leaf Rag" and that ground pieces like "The Crave" and "Spanish Swat."

The Spanish tinge—or the "Latin tinge," as John Storm Roberts recast the term in 1979 in his influential book of that title—has since come to serve as a catchphrase to describe the broad influence of Spanish, Caribbean, and Latin American musical practices on American music.[18] To acknowledge the historical distinction between these two terms, I employ both in the following discussion, using *Spanish tinge* where Morton's music is concerned and employing *Latin tinge* to designate the wider phenomenon. In the past decade academic interest in this area has seen remarkable growth, as numerous books dedicated to the global spread of Latin music and the history of Latin jazz have appeared.[19] Morton has also proven a very attractive figure, the subject of a steady flow of recording reissues and scholarly publications.[20] It is thus surprising that the role of the Spanish tinge in Morton's music has rarely been treated in detail. This may be explained in part because Morton falls outside the standard historical time line of Latin jazz, which "emerged in New York City when Afro-Cuban rhythms mixed with bebop in the 1940s."[21] By the time that Machito, Chano Pozo, and other Latin jazz pioneers migrated from Cuba to Manhattan, Morton was already nearing the end of his career. In terms of Morton criticism, the Spanish tinge apparently has been overlooked because of the tendency of scholars to extol Morton's innovative composing and arranging for jazz ensemble, whereas this facet of his music turns up more often in his solo recordings and in his piano sheet music. The prime exception is the jazz critic Martin Williams, who stressed on many occasions the importance of the Spanish tinge in Morton's music, and my work attempts to build on and extend his observations. In contrast to Williams, whose writings focus on Morton's recordings for the Library of Congress, I wish to account more fully for the Spanish tinge as it relates to other aspects of Morton's career.[22]

As it is has been applied to Morton, the phrase *Spanish tinge* usually functions as shorthand for certain rhythmic patterns that appear in his compositions and recordings. For example, Mark Tucker's entry on "Jazz" in *Grove Music Online* states, "When Jelly Roll Morton spoke of the 'Spanish tinge' present in jazz, he had in mind rhythmic patterns like the *tresillo*, habanera and *cinquillo* of Cuban and other Caribbean and Latin American dance genres."[23] Of these patterns, the habanera shows up occasionally in Morton's music, but he more often relies on the *tresillo* (example 7). Since these two rhythms share a close relationship, differentiated only by a single tie, they often are grouped under a broader umbrella heading of "tango / habanera" rhythms. Rather than confining the following discussion to the identification of these rhythmic cells, however, I find it more productive to follow the lead of Williams, who characterized the influence of the Spanish tinge on Morton as "both more general and more deep than the fact that he wrote several jazz tangos."[24] Indeed, over the course of his career, Jelly Roll

Example 7.   a) tango/habanera

b) *tresillo*

c) tango/habanera (tied)
   or *tresillo* in cut time

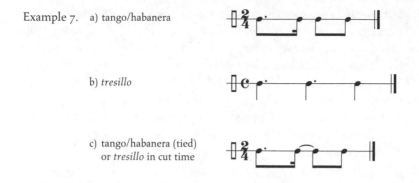

Morton composed or recorded (or both) nearly twenty songs with a discernible Spanish tinge—whether gauged by musical techniques, programmatic references, or geographical origin—a substantial body of material that represents nearly 15 percent of his total compositional output (table 1). Furthermore, Morton's interest in this music was accompanied by a Spanish or Latin tinge that colored numerous aspects of his life, including his ancestral roots, his upbringing in New Orleans, the time he spent in Mexico and California, his association with other musicians, and his personal ties to Creole culture. Morton's encounter with the Spanish tinge was neither a minor flirtation nor a temporary detour; on the contrary, it helped shape his personal biography and occupied his lifelong creative imagination.

Before proceeding to a discussion of Morton's musical background, a few points of clarification are necessary about the provenance of the habanera and its relationship to jazz. The habanera dance is generally seen as the product of an Afro-Cuban transformation of European social dance traditions, which occurred in nineteenth-century Havana, the city from which the term derives. There has been more debate about the actual origins of the habanera rhythm, which has been traced to Cuba, to Africa, to Africa via Cuba, to Africa via Spain, and so on. In a field that often maps the rhythmic roots of jazz directly to Africa, recognizing a measurable degree of Latin influence can have considerable ramifications on one's perspective on jazz. Ernest Borneman once argued, for example, that jazz should be seen as a "mature and developed form of Afro-Latin music," whereas Thomas Fiehrer advanced the claim that the "roots of jazz are actually Afro-Latin-American."[25] In his nuanced treatment of this subject, Christopher Washburne suggests that, given the prevalence of certain rhythms such as the *tresillo* in Cuban and Caribbean musical styles, it may be appropriate to view these rhythms as Afro-Cuban or Afro-Caribbean rhythms when they are found in jazz contexts.[26] Though I recognize the existence of this debate, I will not attempt to resolve it here, for unraveling the rhythmic threads of the already hybrid musical cultures of Africa, Spain, and the Caribbean is far beyond the scope of this project. I am concerned more with jazz practice and jazz discourse, and in particular how certain musical elements were perceived as "Spanish" or "Latin" by early jazz musicians and how subsequent practices and commentary have been framed in the same terms.

Since Morton did not publish his first song until 1915 and did not record until 1923, it is unlikely that his notion of a Spanish tinge was set in stone before he left New Orleans as a teenager. But he was exposed to Latin musical cultures during his childhood in late nineteenth-century New Orleans. Ruled separately by the Spanish and by the French before the United States obtained it as part of the Louisiana Purchase in 1803, the port city had long attracted immigrants from Spain, Mexico, the Caribbean, and beyond. Morton recalled growing up in a multicultural environment: "New Orleans was inhabited with maybe every race on the face of the globe. And of course, we had Spanish people, they had plenty of 'em. And plenty o' French people."[27] Although Morton considered himself one of the "French people," he also recognized how a Spanish tinge colored his personal history: several of his ancestors spoke "only French and a little Spanish," and Morton was christened Ferdinand in tribute to King Ferdinand of Spain.[28] What Morton never acknowledged publicly, and may not have known, was the extent of his own ties to the Caribbean. Thanks to the meticulous research of Lawrence Gushee, we have learned that Morton's ancestors immigrated to the United States from what is now Haiti—formerly colonized by the Spanish and then by the French—and not, as Morton proudly declared, "directly from the shores of France."[29] Some of his forebears followed the path of a large migration that resulted from the late eighteenth-century slave revolt in the French colony of Saint-Domingue, which forced thousands of refugees—French settlers, enslaved Africans, their mixed offspring, and free persons of color—to flee to Cuba and, after France and Spain went to war, head to New Orleans.[30] This exodus more than tripled the size of New Orleans, to nearly twenty-five thousand documented residents, over the first few decades of the nineteenth century, a process that helped establish musical ties between the United States and the Caribbean.

Although he may not have been aware of it, Morton followed in the footsteps of an earlier Creole pianist and composer, Louis Moreau Gottschalk (1829–69), some of whose ancestors moved from Haiti to New Orleans following the slave rebellion. As much as any other American composer of his era, Gottschalk popularized concert music with a Latin flavor by infusing his

TABLE 1. The Spanish tinge in the music of Jelly Roll Morton
(Composed and performed by Morton [solo piano], except where noted)

Year	Title	Label	Notes
1923	"New Orleans Joys"	Gennett	also known as "New Orleans Blues"
	"Kansas City Stomp"	Gennett	
	"The Pearls"	Gennett	
1924	"Mamanita"	Paramount	
	"Mamanita"	Gennett	issued as "Mamamita"
	"Mamanita Blues"	Vocalstyle	piano roll
	"Tia Juana (Tee Wanna)"	Gennett	composed by Gene Rodemich and Larry Conley, 1924
	"Jelly Roll Blues"	Gennett	
1926	"Dead Man Blues"	Imperial	piano roll
	"Soap Suds"	OKeh	*JRM's St. Louis Levee Band*
	"Original Jelly-Roll Blues"	Victor	*JRM's Red Hot Peppers*
1927	"Billy Goat Stomp"	Victor	*JRM's Red Hot Peppers*
1929	"Sweet Anita Mine"	Victor	*JRM and His Orchestra*
1930	"Fickle Fay Creep"	Victor	*JRM and His Red Hot Peppers*
1938	Library of Congress sessions "Creepy Feeling" "The Crave" "Fickle Fay Creep" "Kansas City Stomp" "La Paloma"		composed by Sebastián de Iradier, 1859
	"Lowdown Blues"		"New Orleans Blues" with vocals
	"Maple Leaf Rag"		composed by Scott Joplin, 1899
	"Mama 'Nita"		
	"New Orleans Blues"		

TABLE 1. *(continued)*

Year	Title	Label	Notes
	"Original Jelly Roll Blues"		
	"Panama"		composed by William H. Tyers, 1911
	"The Pearls"		
	"Spanish Swat"		
1938	"Creepy Feeling"	Jazz Man	
1939	"The Crave"	General	*JRM Seven*
1940	"Panama" "Mama's Got a Baby"	General	*JRM Seven*

music with Afro-Caribbean rhythms, basing a number of pieces on Cuban dance forms and employing programmatic titles such as *Souvenir de Porto Rico* and *Souvenirs d'Andalousie*. The music of this celebrated composer circulated in New Orleans for decades and furnished one of the means by which Spanish and Afro-Caribbean influences spread within the city's musical culture. In the latter half of the nineteenth century, New Orleans also hosted a number of touring musical ensembles from Mexico, groups that performed various types of Mexican music and left their mark on the city by helping to popularize the set of Mexican waltzes entitled "Sobre las Olas" (Over the waves).[31] To take advantage of a growing market in the United States, American music publishers began to import sheet music from Mexico and Spain; Junius Hart, a publisher in New Orleans, achieved special renown for his extensive catalog of sheet music by Cuban, Spanish, and Mexican composers. By the turn of the century, Spanish-tinged music also began to reach New Orleans via sheet music from black musical theater productions in New York City.[32] Eventually, sheet music for the most popular Spanish tunes, such as "La Paloma" and "La Golondrina," could be found "in any music store" in the United States.[33]

In addition to hosting traveling musicians and importing foreign sheet music, New Orleans served as the new home for Spanish and Latin American immigrants who contributed to the city's musical life as professional musicians and music teachers. Consequently, Morton took his first music lessons with "a Spanish gentleman in the neighborhood" who taught him to play the guitar.[34] Other Latin immigrants focused on perpetuating their own musical traditions. According to one of Morton's contemporaries, the northeast corner of the French Quarter housed a sizable Spanish-speaking population, which carried on the practice of singing Spanish serenades each night.[35] Whether Morton, who grew up just outside the Quarter, encountered these serenaders is unknown, but he did recall hearing "a lot of Spanish tunes" during his childhood in New Orleans.[36] Consequently, like other members of the early jazz community, he became well acquainted with pieces that had a Spanish, Caribbean, or Mexican flavor, such as "La Paloma," "Panama," and "Sobre las Olas."[37]

Morton was not the only musician of his generation to comment about the Spanish element in early jazz. Another jazz artist to offer corroborating testimony was Warren "Baby" Dodds, who grew up in New Orleans and later recorded with Morton, Louis Armstrong, and other jazz legends. Looking back on his early days, Dodds identified what he felt was a distinctive Creole approach to the blues: "In the downtown district where the Creoles lived, they played blues with a Spanish accent. We fellows that lived Uptown, we didn't even play the Creole numbers like the Frenchmen downtown did—such as *Eh, La Bas*. And just as we changed the Spanish accent of the Creole songs, we played the blues different from them. They lived in the French part of town and we lived uptown, in the Garden district. Our ideas for the blues were different from theirs. They had the French and Spanish style, blended together."[38] Dodds's position as an uptown outsider is of particular significance here, for he later notes that an interest in Spanish rhythms eventually spread from the Creole district throughout New Orleans. Though Dodds intended to characterize a larger community of musicians, his impressions apply to Jelly Roll Morton, a downtown Creole musician who not only integrated Spanish rhythms in his tunes but also produced numerous and varied examples of "blues with a Spanish accent."

BLUES WITH A SPANISH TINGE

A Spanish tinge colors one of Morton's earliest compositions, "New Orleans Blues," in which the blues merge with a Latin rhythm to generate what Martin Williams has termed a "twelve-bar blues-tango."[39] This piece holds a significant place in Morton's career. Not only did he describe it as one of his first compositions, it became one of the first he recorded (as "New Orleans Joys" in 1923) and later published (as "New Orleans Blues" in 1925).[40]

Morton continued to perform the piece for decades and did so for Alan Lomax at the Library of Congress, where he prefaced his rendition by stating: "Of course you got to have these little tinges of Spanish in it . . . in order to play real good jazz. . . . I'll give you an idea what this, the idea of Spanish there is in the blues."[41] Morton's various recordings of the tune mix elements of blues and ragtime with "little tinges of Spanish," and these musical intersections also occur throughout the published sheet music.[42] The construction of "New Orleans Blues" comprises a series of twelve-bar blues choruses, which feature harmonies that follow a typical blues progression. To some degree, Morton's left-hand accompaniment calls to mind ragtime and stride piano by leaping between solo bass notes and chords that fill out the harmonies at a higher register. But what is more striking about the left hand is its reliance on the *tresillo* rhythm. In contrast to a song like W. C. Handy's "St. Louis Blues," which inserts a brief tango interlude into a larger composition, the *tresillo* pattern underpins nearly all of "New Orleans Blues," and it is this steady rhythmic foundation that gives the piece its most audible Spanish tinge (example 8).

After the five-measure introduction that leads into this first blues chorus, it becomes clear that Morton intends to take advantage of various types of musical interplay between his ragtime-blues and the *tresillo*. Over the entire chorus, Morton emphasizes the rhythmic contrast between bass and treble, as the left hand provides a steady *tresillo* bass, while every right-hand entrance begins on a syncopated offbeat. The opening measure of the chorus, repeated twice to settle into the rhythmic groove, illustrates how the hands perform very independently yet combine to work in tandem. At the start the right hand appears to function at odds with the left: every attack occurs on a different sixteenth-note beat until Morton reaches the final quarter note (the thirteenth sixteenth-note) of each of the first three measures. Consequently, at first hearing, the two rhythmic patterns seem to make little sense together, as if Morton's music echoes the cultural and musical collision between blues and the Spanish tinge by establishing an off-kilter rhythmic relationship. By repeating the first few bars, however, Morton's performance begins to suggest how the two rhythms can be heard as interlocking, how they create a polyrhythmic groove, a steady yet dynamic momentum, when sounded together. But Morton is not satisfied with extending this opening vamp. In the fourth bar, he begins to introduce new rhythmic patterns with his right hand, while keeping the *tresillo* firm in his left, which produces different rhythmic combinations in almost every one of the remaining nine bars of the chorus. Such rhythmic flexibility in "New Orleans Blues" thus indicates both the dynamic improvisational possibili-

Example 8. Jelly Roll Morton, "New Orleans Blues," mm. 6–17, renumbered as 1–12 to illustrate blues form. Published by Melrose Brothers Music Company (1925).

ties and the perpetual tension produced by the collision of these different musical impulses. Indeed, because of the distinctive set of rhythmic patterns generated by improvising over a *tresillo* bass, it may be useful to characterize this aspect of the Spanish tinge not only by the presence of a specific rhythmic cell but also by its resulting polyrhythmic character.[43]

In addition to generating rhythmic momentum, Morton relies on the harmonic construction of this particular *tresillo* pattern to yield an ongoing sense of musical tension. The rhythmic pattern of the opening three measures of the first chorus implies a triumphant arrival on every fourth beat, the moment when both hands play together for the first time; however, the Spanish-tinged ostinato produces a sense of instability at the same instant. This sense of unease results from the harmonic motion of the *tresillo* bass, which rocks back and forth between tonic and dominant. To be more specific, if one considers only the bass line of the opening measure, the first dotted quarter note states the B-flat tonic, the second dotted quarter shifts the tonic to its unstable second inversion—edging toward the dominant as a $V \, {}^{6}_{4}$ chord—and the final quarter note drops down to the F dominant. As a result of this chord progression, the fourth beat, rather than standing as a final destination point of rhythmic cooperation, serves as a temporary staging area in which to prepare for the upcoming tonic in the next measure. Moreover, since the right hand sits out during the start of almost every measure, the tonic that arrives on each downbeat oftenrings out alone in the bass register. Yet, despite its clear harmonic function from measure to measure, the use of a *tresillo* bass line does not predetermine the path of "New Orleans Blues." Perhaps this is to be expected, for Morton here uses a Spanish tinge as part of a jazzy twelve-bar blues, not as the foundation for a classic tango. Rather than conforming to the tonic and dominant harmonies of the *tresillo* bass, Morton outlines a typical blues progression and accentuates each crucial harmonic shift along the way: for example, in measure 4 Morton introduces A-flat to form a B♭7 chord, followed by a punctuated series of repeated chords that prepare the way for the E-flat harmony that arrives in measure 5. Morton's right hand also introduces chromatic touches, added sixths, and bluesy inflections that, like each of the syncopated entrances of the right hand, work against what might be expected to occur over the *tresillo* bass.

Why then would Morton choose to combine a *tresillo* bass with the blues, if the resulting concoction produces contradictory rhythmic and harmonic implications at every turn? Most likely for that very reason, at least in the opinion of Gunther Schuller, who praises Morton's 1923 recording of the tune for its "bimetric and birhythmic independence."[44] In "New Orleans Blues," rhythmic patterns in the treble collide with the habanera bass, as the right hand tries to assert a minor bluesiness while the left obstinately maintains its allegiance to a dominant-tonic alternation. This volatile combination at once produces the sensation of rocking between tonic and dominant, swerving between major and minor, and bouncing from one syncopated rhythm to the next. Instead of seamlessly fusing these disparate musical impulses, or blending them in a musical melting pot, Morton juxtaposes jazz and the blues with the Spanish tinge, allowing them to clash with one another, to work in combination yet maintain their mutual independence. To describe "New Orleans Blues" as failing to unify its disparate elements is not intended as a criticism; on the contrary, the piece may be heard as a sonic metaphor for cultural difference and conflict. A similar dynamic later developed between the contrasting musical and cultural impulses of Latin music and jazz in the 1940s. Jairo Moreno describes this often oppositional relationship as "an expressive praxis and cultural locus characterized by dialectic tension, and precisely because of it as a cause for musical celebration."[45] In this sense, Morton's approach in "New Orleans Blues" can be understood as foreshadowing things to come.

In his various recordings of this piece, Morton further brings out its tantalizing rhythmic tension by combining his acute sense of swing in the right hand with the "masterful way he drops behind the beat" with his left.[46] As a result, even though the bass and treble lines intertwine, the two hands never reach a conclusive resolution; they generate a percolating equilibrium of intricate cross rhythms and harmonic misdirection. Such musical interplay has prompted some critics to argue that the Spanish tinge played a foundational role in the creation of jazz. Williams, for instance, asserts that "without a coming-to-terms with the habanera or tango rhythm, with its behind-the-beat syncopations—as contrasted with ragtime's mostly ahead-of-the-beat syncopations—you just don't have jazz."[47] Few early jazz musicians seem to have integrated Latin musical impulses to the same extent as Morton, but Williams's observations certainly resonate when it comes to this aspect of his music. It is the edgy combination of musical elements working at cross-purposes, rather than smooth progress toward a unified goal, that makes his music so compelling. Morton appears to have recognized this quality of perpetual friction as well, since he chose to conclude the piece in a different fashion by dropping the *tresillo* bass from the final chorus and adopting in its place a 4/4 stomp rhythm in the left hand to round out the tune. Just as "New Orleans Blues" requires the presence of the Spanish tinge to create its momentum, so must it disappear before the tune can come to a close.

Displaying his hometown pride, Morton kept this piece in his repertoire until the end of his career. Though its original title, "New Orleans Joys," indicates enthusiasm, the revised title, "New Orleans Blues," should not be interpreted as a major shift in Morton's perspective. After all, he made no significant changes to the piece's melody, harmony, tempo, form, or other key musical characteristics. Instead, the tune appears to have been renamed for the sake of marketability: to advertise the bluesy components of the piece, to latch on to the popularity of the blues, and to call to mind the titles of other city-specific hits, such as "St. Louis Blues." What stands out about this decision, especially for an itinerant musician, is Morton's choice to retain the "New Orleans" portion of the title. In addition to proclaiming the authenticity of his music to northern audiences, many of whom were migrants with southern roots, this decision reflects Morton's impulse to commemorate the city where he composed the tune. By highlighting this connection, Morton also participated in a broader trend, for the Spanish tinge has served on numerous occasions as a musical signifier for New Orleans. As part of his work on the syncretisms that have developed between Hispanic and African American musicians, Peter Narváez has documented how New Orleans blues musicians have "often been inclined to use the Spanish tinge when musically identifying their home city."[48] For a composer who named many of his tunes after places, the connection between "New Orleans Blues" and the Spanish tinge is especially noteworthy, since none of Morton's other compositions with place-specific titles stress Latin rhythms.[49]

Interestingly, Morton chose to incorporate a Spanish tinge into another composition with an explicit autobiographical connection, "Jelly Roll Blues" (1915). In addition to being Morton's first publication for solo piano, it has been suggested that this significant work might even be considered "the first published jazz composition."[50] Before consumers discovered what the music sounded like, however, they would likely have noticed the crowded mix of visual iconography used to market the tune. For that matter, the cover of "Jelly Roll Blues" is so overloaded with musical signifiers that it blurs any clear sense of genre (figure 1). Perhaps its attempt to engage so broadly with cultural tensions surrounding race, ethnicity, and class, as they played out on the musical landscape, explains why the publisher Will Rossiter used the same cover image for multiple sheet music releases by Morton. Though the tune was entitled a "blues" and marketed as a fox-trot—clinging to the coattails of the latest dance craze—the cover art emphasizes the novelty appeal of the tune and its composer by placing two dancing figures atop a jelly roll and against the backdrop of a blue and white tablecloth. Even though the dancers' sophisticated evening attire implies an air of classical elegance, their precarious postures, balanced on the tips of their toes, indicate a fresh spirit of exuberance. Their depiction in silhouette produces similarly mixed signals, evoking traditional European artistic practices while simultaneously carrying racial overtones about music in America. One may read the cover along class lines, as it portrays two formally dressed figures who are inspired to dance and move their bodies freely as soon as they pick up the banjo and guitar, two instruments associated with vernacular musical traditions. Yet the literal blackness of this artistic technique also conjures a racial and musical otherness. Are these two aristocrats who have donned blackface to enter a different musical world, or are they a pair of crudely drawn African American performers enacting a lively combination of sophistication and downhome excitement? Equally telling is the choice of these particular musical instruments. At this historical juncture, the banjo had long been associated with African American musical life, and the guitar often served as a musical signifier of Spain or Latin America, a connection further emphasized here by the tiered skirt of the female figure's dress and the ribbons wrapped around the neck of her guitar. Thus, in addition to its sweeping gesture toward vernacular music, the cover art hinted that the "Jelly Roll Blues" would contain a mixture of African American and Latin musical elements.

The expectations raised by the cover of "Jelly Roll Blues" are met by Morton's music in a manner reminiscent of "New Orleans Blues." This Spanish-tinged blues is also distinguished by a habanera-style section that operates neither as an exotic diversion nor as a short-lived distraction. Indeed, "Jelly Roll Blues" serves as a perfect complement to "New Orleans Blues," arranged in reverse, since it is not until the final chorus that Morton introduces *tresillo* figures (example 9). Instead of mimicking the strategy of "New Orleans Blues" by first establishing and ultimately abandoning the Spanish tinge, Morton tops off the dramatic arc of "Jelly Roll Blues" with a triumphant Spanish-tinged finale. What further differentiates the pieces and propels them along distinct trajectories derives from their separate strategies of rhythmic organization. Each of the entrances by the right hand in the final chorus of "Jelly Roll Blues" occurs on a syncopated offbeat, as in "New Orleans Blues," but the rhythmic interaction between bass and treble is entirely different. Because the right-hand phrases in the opening five bars repeat a fairly simple rhythmic pattern (mm. 45–49), they do not produce the same level of rhythmic tension with the *tresillo* bass. Rather than competing for attention with the left hand, the phrasing in the right hand helps to accentuate the *tresillo*, a rhythmic bond that Morton brings forward with individual accents and dynamic markings. Such a firm commitment to this rhythmic impulse at the opening of the chorus eventually leads Morton to insert a few measures that abandon the *tresillo*, measures that come across as relatively serene patches of rhythmic stasis (mm. 50 and

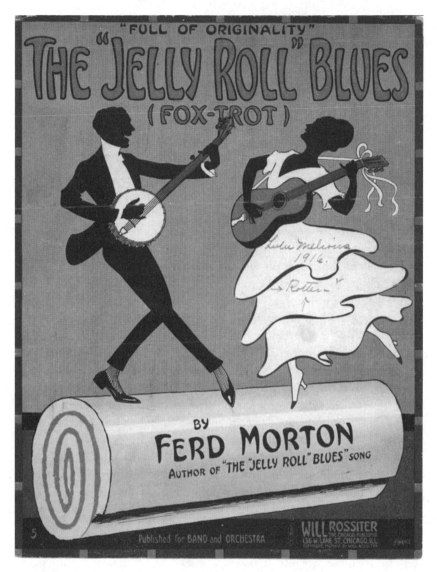

FIGURE 1.   Cover art by Starmer for Ferd Morton, "The 'Jelly Roll' Blues." Published by Will Rossiter (1915).

54). But each time this occurs, the *tresillo* bass returns at once, so that these moments are quickly repositioned as momentary departures from the tune's main rhythmic thrust. Even the first repeat (mm. 55–56), in which the right hand shifts into a running series of accented eighth notes scored in parallel octaves, can be understood as an accentuation of the Spanish tinge, both through its loose evocation of stereotypically Spanish music on top of a repeated *tresillo* pattern and as a result of its dramatic crescendo, which climaxes on the opening measure of the chorus, where the *tresillo* is reasserted once again.

In contrast to the opening chorus of "New Orleans Blues," Morton employs the same phrasing at each structural signpost of the blues in this chorus of "Jelly Roll Blues" (mm. 45, 49, 53). This framework produces a clear statement of the main melodic idea, the requisite harmony, and the *tresillo* rhythm, without introducing any distractions that could diminish these musical elements. Thus, by the time Morton introduces some minor rhythmic variations (mm. 51–52), they are heard in comparison to the already established *tresillo* pattern, understood as slight rhythmic hiccups that are cured quickly in the next measure. The constant process of returning to the *tresillo* pattern occupies "Jelly Roll Blues" until its conclusion. Whereas Morton adopted the Spanish tinge in "New Orleans Blues" as a method of staking out new territory for cross-rhythmic experimentation, in "Jelly Roll Blues" he introduces, establishes, departs from, and returns to the *tresillo* rhythm as a method of organizing and enlivening the conclusion of the piece. By using this strategy in "Jelly Roll Blues," Morton appears more intent on taking advantage of the recognizable flavor of a Spanish tinge than in realizing its potential for suggesting new rhythmic ideas.

If not for his musical background and his experience composing pieces like "New Orleans Blues," Morton's use of the Spanish tinge in "Jelly Roll Blues" might be understood purely in opportunistic terms, as a well-timed attempt to take advantage of America's escalating interest in the tango during the mid-1910s. But it is important to note that "Jelly Roll Blues" developed into an unofficial theme song, a personal favorite that Morton continued to perform for decades after its publication. Indeed, some of his solo piano recordings of the tune milked the Spanish-tinged section for all it was worth. In his 1938 rendition of "Jelly Roll Blues" at the Library of Congress, Morton concludes the piece with four choruses, all grounded by a habanera bass, before he segues into "Lowdown Blues," an alternative version of the same piece, which features vocals as well as a habanera-style chorus of its own. If one were to draw conclusions about the composer strictly from this piece, it could be argued that the Spanish tinge lies at the heart of Jelly Roll Morton's blues.

Morton's relationship with blues and the Spanish tinge shifted once more in his next significant Spanish-tinged composition, "The Crave." Displaying a third strategy for exploring the musical possibilities of a Spanish tinge, this composition maintains the *tresillo* bass as its rhythmic foundation from

Example 9. Ferd Morton, "Jelly Roll Blues," mm. 45–56. Published by Will Rossiter (1915).

start to finish. Originally composed a few years after the initial publication of "Jelly Roll Blues" (1915), this provocatively named composition marks the moment when Morton jumped fully onto the tango bandwagon and suggests his ability to exploit the exotic appeal of the Spanish tinge.[51] At this point in his career, Morton was living in Los Angeles, one of many musicians who had relocated from New Orleans to California during the 1910s. He scored a hit with "The Crave" when it was adopted by a local dance orchestra at the end of World War I and then caught on with the Hollywood crowd.[52] Although he did not publish or record the tune at the time—presumably because of the music industry's reluctance to hire nonwhite jazz performers until the following decade—Morton later returned to "The Crave," performing it for Alan Lomax in 1938 and recording it the following year. By no means a frivolous exercise in nostalgia, Morton's repackaging of "The Crave" earned a great deal of critical admiration. James Dapogny describes it as a "piece of unusual beauty, with elegant long lines, effectively devised and placed textural variety, and a fine, strong ending."[53] In actuality, the phrase *Spanish tinge* seems inadequate to characterize "The Crave," for if all "Spanish" touches were removed, little of the piece would remain. As opposed to its calling on a Spanish tinge to flavor the blues, it would be more accurate to say that "The Crave" incorporates a "blues tinge" to color a Spanish-flavored tune. For starters, the piece is not written in blues form but instead comprises a series of three strains, a compositional structure often used in the music of ragtime.[54] Moreover, unlike the previous examples, the *tresillo* rhythm remains constant throughout, requiring neither transformation nor replacement. In his Library of Congress performance of "The Crave," Morton further highlights the significance of this rhythm by employing the same *tresillo* pattern as a pedal point for an entire strain, thus relieving the left hand of its role in defining a harmonic progression and allowing Morton the opportunity to dig into the rhythmic intensity of the *tresillo*.

Though the *tresillo* bass saturates "The Crave," Morton turns to the blues for the purpose of producing fleeting moments of contrast. I do not mean that the blues are ever wholly absent: blue notes and bluesy harmonies pepper the entire tune. What is novel in comparison to his earlier pieces is Morton's use of the blues as an element of harmonic and structural variation, a means of temporary diversion. This technique is most evident at the start of the second strain, when Morton inserts a pungent two-measure break, an unexpected interjection that Martin Williams calls "one of the delightful strokes in all his music."[55] This bluesy break comes as a surprise in part because its sharp, crunching dissonance follows the sinuous linearity and tamer chromaticism of the first strain, and in part because Morton by now has established so firmly the *tresillo* rhythm. In a move that recalls the strategy of the last chorus of "Jelly Roll Blues" but produces greater dramatic effect, Morton withholds the *tresillo* bass for just a moment, drawing attention to its absence and setting the scene for its return. Indeed, the process by which Morton produces musical tension at this moment—holding back something vital that listeners long to hear, and then delivering it—can be understood as a musical imitation of the piece's title. Displaying an interest in this compositional strategy, which extended beyond "The Crave" and the tango era, Morton later composed several other

Spanish-tinged pieces built entirely around the *tresillo* rhythm, including "Spanish Swat" (1938) and "Creepy Feeling" (1938).

A TIJUANA TINGE

In addition to crossing musical borders, Morton navigated geographic ones over the course of a nomadic career that took him southeast to Florida, northeast to New York City, north to Chicago, northwest to Seattle and Vancouver, and west to Los Angeles and San Francisco. Several years after introducing "The Crave" to Hollywood audiences, Morton drifted farther south and spent the last few months of 1921 in San Diego and Tijuana, Mexico. Tijuana's popularity as an American tourist destination had grown exponentially in response to the onset of Prohibition in 1919, and the Mexican border town featured a host of new casinos, cabarets, and saloons, all of which supplied employment opportunities for U.S. jazz musicians. Morton's experiences in Mexico stamp two of his most famous compositions, "Kansas City Stomp" and "The Pearls." According to Morton, he composed the former title during his time "down on the . . . borders of Mexico, right near the American border, from near the California side, in a little place called Tijuana, Mexico. The tune was named after a saloon that was ran by a friend of mine . . . and his saloon was named the Kansas City Bar."[56] Morton told a related tale about "The Pearls," which he claimed was a tribute to one of the saloon's waitresses, who wore an eye-catching pearl necklace.

Strikingly, these two compositions inspired by his experiences in Mexico do not feature Latin rhythms; in strictly sonic terms, they seem to express as much about the music of New Orleans or Chicago as they do about life in Tijuana. Nevertheless, I think it is useful to acknowledge both pieces as a reflection of Morton's personal history of crossing the U.S.–Mexican border and as a broader symbol of the transnational history of jazz.[57] Morton was not the only major musical figure of this period to venture in this direction. Most famously, W. C. Handy traveled with Mahara's Minstrels in 1899–1900 to Havana, Cuba, where he claimed to have heard the tango rhythm for the first time, more than a decade before he began to use it in his own compositions. A number of Morton's contemporaries also performed jazz in Mexico, including the clarinetist Clem Raymond, who played for several years with Morton's Incomparable New Orleans Jazz Band and landed a job of his own in Tijuana at the Kansas City Bar.[58] Likewise, Norma Mason and Ma Rainey were among the early blues singers whose paths crossed back and forth between Texas and Mexico.[59] In a climate that encouraged geographic border crossing, an experience that often serves as a prelude to musical experimentation, one might expect Morton to have begun a "Spanish" or "Mexican" period at this stage in his career. But that is not what happened. It took three years until Morton recorded his next Spanish-tinged piece, "Mamanita." Although Morton never commented publicly on this matter, it seems likely that the Mexican- or Spanish-tinged music he encountered at this juncture did not strike him as novel or foreign. That is to say, perhaps the music of Tijuana did not inspire Morton to alter his own compositional style because he had heard plenty of Spanish-tinged music before arriving there and had begun years earlier to compose pieces like "The Crave" and "New Orleans Blues."

Interestingly enough, a few years after he returned to the United States and settled in Chicago, Morton recorded "Tia Juana (Tee Wanna)," a song composed by the bandleader Gene Rodemich and trombonist Larry Conley.[60] Morton's 1924 rendition for Gennett Records, for which he had previously recorded the Tijuana-inspired songs "Kansas City Stomp" and "The Pearls," has been interpreted by some critics as a nostalgic gesture toward his time in Mexico. Morton omitted the vocals from his solo piano rendition of "Tia Juana (Tee Wanna)," but his performance nevertheless seems to reflect the dreamy wistfulness painted by the original lyrics. Reading along these lines, Phil Pastras proposes that we may hear Morton's performance "as if he is making a musical statement about the bicultural experience of playing jazz in Tijuana."[61] Pastras goes on to suggest that this personal connection with the material may explain why Morton chose to record a piece of music he did not compose, which was not his usual practice. As much as Morton's performance is a paean to his sojourn in the border town, it also served to promote the aims of his new employers, Melrose Brothers, to exploit America's newfound fascination with Mexico and Latin America. Consequently, this recording by Morton represents another key example of how defining the "Spanish tinge" solely in terms of Latin rhythm patterns proves insufficient. To gain a fuller understanding of his release of "Tia Juana" requires not only paying attention to its musical details but also contextualizing this release in light of the era's practices of musical exoticism.

An entirely distinct song entitled "Tia Juana," which was composed by Florinda Gardner in 1924, provides a snapshot of Tin Pan Alley marketing practices of the time. That two tunes sharing virtually the same title could turn up in the same year also points to the emergence of the Mexican border town in the American popular imagination. Gardner's title and lyrics describe the town as a location known well enough by then that consumers re-

quired no parenthetical advice about its pronunciation. Her portrait of Tijuana envisages a dramatic land full of wealth, freedom, and possibility. To
capitalize on notions of exotic intrigue, Gardner's publisher marketed the
tune by placing on its sheet music cover a stereotypical image of a Mexican
bandit: a shady character sporting a handlebar mustache, smoking a ciga-
rette in the moonlight, and peering out from beneath his sombrero. Taken
as a whole, the music and cover art for Gardner's "Tia Juana" drew on common tropes of musical exoticism, pairing risk and danger with the rewards
of autonomy, wealth, and pleasure. In contrast, the cover art for Rodemich
and Conley's "Tia Juana (Tee Wanna)" proposes a different path, bypassing
the danger and getting right to the milk and honey. It portrays a black-tie
affair in a swanky, spacious ballroom, full of dancers taking advantage of the
free-flowing alcohol that was outlawed in the States at the time. To flaunt
the border town's reputation as a gambler's paradise, the portrait of the
dance hall is framed by a roulette wheel. Despite their differing strategies,
these two publishers clearly tried to fulfill similar American desires and fantasies, for the enticing vision of luxury and excess depicted by the cover art
for Rodemich and Conley's song would have been equally well suited to
Gardner's lyrics.

The couples dancing on the cover of Rodemich and Conley's "Tia Juana
(Tee Wanna)" signal another facet of the song's appeal, which was reinforced by the opening bars of its first verse. Here, Rodemich and Conley re-
fashioned the omnipresent rhythm of the Charleston, a dance sensation introduced by James P. Johnson in 1920. In addition to mapping short phrases
onto a basic Charleston contour, Rodemich and Conley positioned words
with long vowel sounds (e.g., "me," "see," and "be") on each key accent.
Linking a popular dance style to an attractive tourist destination made good
marketing sense, and this combination also conveyed some degree of historical accuracy, since American dance bands helped popularize the
Charleston in Mexican dance halls like the one pictured on the song's cover.
It is important to note that the musical language in this Tin Pan Alley song
uses the latest American dance fashions, rather than specifically Mexican
melodies or Latin rhythms. Though Rodemich and Conley's compositional
strategy thus shares little with Morton's earlier Spanish-tinged pieces, a
rigid distinction should not be drawn between these composers. After all,
Morton incorporated Charleston-style riffs into compositions of his own,
including "The Chant" (1926), and he wrote music that falls somewhere between the Charleston and the *tresillo*, such as the right-hand riffs that punc-
tuate "Soap Suds" (1926). For that matter, Morton may have found "Tia
Juana (Tee Wanna)" attractive in part because of the structural similarity

between the two rhythmic patterns.[62] But Morton was not content with creating his musical rendition out of the Charleston, a point that he made clear through his individualized adaptation of the tune.

Morton's transformation of Rodemich and Conley's "Tia Juana (Tee Wanna)" can be appreciated best in comparison to two other recordings of the song from 1924: one by the Gene Rodemich Orchestra, featuring Rodemich conducting from the piano and Conley on lead trombone; the other by the Wolverine Orchestra, a Chicago band that took its name from Morton's popular piece "Wolverine Blues." Predictably, the Rodemich Orchestra remains faithful to the published sheet music, alternating back and forth between verse and chorus, emphasizing its dance-oriented nature, and adding novelty percussion to accentuate the Charleston beat. The Wolverine Orchestra, featuring the young Bix Beiderbecke on cornet, makes use of this Tin Pan Alley song for a different purpose. Instead of foregrounding the Charleston, the Wolverines perform a more relaxed rendition of the tune that spotlights a series of improvised solos based on its chorus.

In contrast to both of the ensemble versions, Morton's solo piano rendition of "Tia Juana (Tee Wanna)" amplifies the song's programmatic element, infusing the tune with a Spanish tinge with the help of several techniques that occur in neither of the group recordings nor, in some cases, the published sheet music. Morton's recording includes the two sixteen-bar verses that contain the Charleston rhythm, but he focuses equal attention on the thirty-two-bar chorus, to which he adds his own embellishments and countermelodies. Morton seems to have been drawn especially to the repeated four-bar descending phrase in the chorus, which Rodemich and Conley chose to harmonize with a series of parallel thirds in an apparent attempt to evoke the sound of Mexican music. Conley had earlier spent time as a performer in Mexico with several bands, which may have shaped the composition of the song, but he did not carry this experience into the recording studio. In contrast to the Rodemich Orchestra, which recorded the melodic line as written but without accentuating the parallel harmonies, Morton emphasizes this aspect of the piece by toying with the pace of the behind-the-beat line through the use of rubato and by accentuating the doubled thirds, causing them to ring out against the left hand. Consequently, as Phil Pastras describes it, Morton's performance ends up sounding like "pure mariachi."[63] But this was not all. Finally, and most compellingly, Morton decided to change the rhythmic foundation of the song's chorus by substituting a *tresillo* bass, which does not appear in the other recordings or in the sheet music. To complement the mariachi-style melody in the treble, Morton relies on this rhythmic pattern throughout the first full rendition of the chorus, filling it with a level of rhythmic excitement similar to what the Charleston provides for each verse. Recalling the strategy of "New Orleans Blues," he shifts to a stomp rhythm for the final chorus to round out the performance.

It is impossible to pinpoint any single reason for Morton's decision to recast the tune in this fashion, to give his version of "Tia Juana (Tee Wanna)" what has been characterized as a "south-of-the-border" feeling, a musical affect that might have prompted Gennett Records to label the release a "Spanish Fox Trot."[64] Morton made no public comments and left no written indications concerning what he meant to accomplish—whether conjuring the music of New Orleans or his early Spanish-tinged blues; whether revisiting his interest in the tango; whether recalling his time in Tijuana or memories of Mexican mariachi music; or whether displaying his savvy at manufacturing the exotic. What can be said today, however, is that his performance calls to mind all these threads and suggests once more how broadly one must conceive of the Spanish tinge.

A TINGE OF CREOLE NOSTALGIA

As part of the same June 1924 studio session for Gennett Records that produced "Tia Juana (Tee Wanna)," Morton recorded a Spanish-tinged piece of his own entitled "Mamanita," which again features a *tresillo* bass and also employs the device of parallel thirds throughout its second theme.[65] Gennett also attached the label "Spanish Fox Trot" to "Mamanita," but the composition did not originate as a companion piece. Morton had written the tune a few years earlier, during his time on the West Coast, and already had recorded it for Paramount two months earlier. Morton recorded "Mamanita," like several other of his Spanish-tinged tunes, on multiple occasions, producing a 1924 piano roll for Vocalstyle entitled "Mamanita Blues" and later revisiting the piece at the Library of Congress in 1938. Even though he never recorded "Mamanita" with a group, he apparently considered doing so. Omer Simeon recalled auditioning for Morton by playing the clarinet part from an arrangement of the tune.[66] "Mamanita" held additional resonance for Morton, since he named it in tribute to Anita Gonzales, whom he described as the "only woman I ever loved."[67] Decades after watching Morton work on the tune, his bandmate Paul Howard reminisced: "I could almost hum it now. [Morton] put everything he had into that piece, because he sure did love that lady."[68]

To compose a Spanish-tinged tune for a woman named Anita Gonzales might seem an obvious tactic, but Morton's strategy reveals more about the composite nature of the Spanish tinge than first meets the eye. As it happens, the tune's blend of musical and cultural signification is only befitting a woman so complex. Though she spoke "with an accent reflecting her New Orleans heritage," Gonzales' background and her formulation of a hybrid identity were quite complicated.[69] Born in 1883, given the name Bessie Johnson, and raised by her mulatto mother in Biloxi, Mississippi, she originally met Jelly Roll Morton in New Orleans, possibly through her youngest brother, "Dink" (Ollie) Johnson, a drummer who played with Morton. The pair lost contact for a number of years, but reconnected after Morton moved to Los Angeles in the mid-1910s. By this point, Bessie Johnson had changed her name to Anita Gonzales and had begun an effort to pass as Mexican, embracing this new ethnic identity to the extent that her death certificate falsely lists two parents of Mexican descent. Phil Pastras has argued convincingly that even though their love affair lasted for less than a decade, Gonzales' relationship to Morton "touched virtually every aspect of his life."[70] Although conclusive documentation has yet to be found to establish a marriage between the two, Morton often referred to Anita as his wife and to her brothers as brothers-in-law, and he spoke with deep regret about the end of their relationship. In his final months, Morton traveled once more to Los Angeles, where he reestablished contact with Gonzales and ended up naming her the heir to his estate.

What makes Gonzales even more intriguing in terms of a Spanish tinge is that at the same time she chose to pass as Mexican, she also preserved her affiliation with Creole culture, a trait that ran in her family. During her time in Los Angeles, Anita helped finance the Original Creole Orchestra, featuring her brothers Dink and Bill Johnson, which became one of the first groups to introduce New Orleans jazz to audiences in Los Angeles. Anita's brother also opened Dink's Place, a café that specialized in Creole food. These ties proved very attractive to Morton, who maintained a close allegiance to his hometown of New Orleans and to Creole culture, even though, or perhaps because, he lived outside Louisiana for his entire adult life. Morton was unable to preserve every facet of his Creole upbringing. His French grew rusty over the years, and his attendance at Mass was said to be spotty at best. But he was able to hang on to what a fellow musician called "the Louisiana touch," which emerged whether he was cooking red beans and rice, describing to Alan Lomax the finer points of three-card Spanish poker, or engaging in his "Creole manner of joking."[71] Morton's fondness for his hometown continued through his final years, when he and Dink gave performances in which they played old hits and exchanged memories about

New Orleans between numbers.[72] As a final act in recognition of their common heritage, Gonzales arranged for a Catholic funeral service when Morton passed away in 1941. The couple's shared commitment to Creole culture resonates with Narváez's observations regarding Morton's use of the Spanish tinge as an emblem of New Orleans. With this in mind, the Spanish tinge in a piece like "Mamanita" can be understood not only to evoke Gonzales' adopted surname but also to signify her ongoing ties to Creole New Orleans.

The pair returned to similar ground a few years later when they collaborated on the song "Dead Man Blues," for which Morton supplied the music and Gonzales wrote lyrics. Taking its title from this tune, Pastras's book *Dead Man Blues* explores the couple's relationship in detail, explaining how aspects of Morton's biography intertwined with his musical career. His discussion of their collaboration on "Dead Man Blues" again exposes a connection between the Spanish tinge and New Orleans in Morton's music. The best-known version of "Dead Man Blues" is a 1927 ensemble recording that opens with comic patter about a New Orleans funeral. This version makes the most of its programmatic link to cultural practices in Morton's hometown by including tolling bells and a slow dirge, but it contains no obvious references to Latin musical practices. Nor do Gonzales's lyrics contain any obvious allusions to Spanish or Latin culture.[73] One year earlier, however, Morton had produced a Spanish-tinged piano roll of "Dead Man Blues." Without the opportunity to include dialogue or more suggestive instrumentation on a piano roll, Morton instead chose to employ a *tresillo* bass as the accompaniment for one of its strains.[74] In addition to its apparent nod to Gonzales, the Spanish tinge here performs double duty as a musical signifier of New Orleans. Taken collectively, the two versions of "Dead Man Blues" display how connections to the Spanish tinge and to Creole New Orleans continued to circulate in music that Morton associated with Gonzales.

Morton's personal predilections also shaped his professional activities. Simply put, in the words of the clarinetist Albert Nicholas, Morton "wanted New Orleans musicians that could play the music he wanted to hear."[75] Such priorities may be explained to some degree as an inevitable outgrowth of Morton's peripatetic career, for he often had to assemble brand-new groups during the course of his travels. As a result of Morton's commitment to New Orleans–style jazz, he often chose to sidestep local talent in Los Angeles, Chicago, and New York and instead to recruit musicians from his old stomping grounds to join him for northern gigs; it became common knowledge among jazz musicians that "if Jelly had any work he's going to get somebody from New Orleans."[76] Though this practice was not unusual among his contemporaries—most notably Joe Oliver, who enlisted Louis Armstrong and other musicians from New Orleans to join him in Chicago—the blustery Morton also ruffled the feathers of local musicians by "always boasting about how great New Orleans musicians were."[77] Such vocal expressions of favoritism for New Orleans musicians, and particularly Creoles, have helped spawn charges that Morton was prejudiced against black musicians.[78] According to his actions as well as the testimony of many fellow musicians, however, what mattered even more than ethnic or racial background was a close acquaintance with the musical practices of New Orleans. Morton felt especially comfortable around other Creoles socially; however, his favorite clarinetist, Omer Simeon, explained that he "was mighty particular about his music and if the musicians couldn't play real New Orleans, he'd get someone else."[79] Consequently, Morton hired both Creole and African American musicians over the course of his career.

Baby Dodds, an African American drummer who hailed from the uptown section of New Orleans, also felt that it was joint familiarity with certain musical codes that enabled Morton's Red Hot Peppers to play well together in the studio: "On all the jobs with Jelly Roll it was he who picked the men for the session. He went around himself and got the men he wanted to record with him. . . . Sometimes the various men in the band wouldn't see each other for months. But when Jelly Roll gave us a ring we met for rehearsal and we all knew what was expected of us. Of course we all knew each other from New Orleans but those record sessions were the only times we all got together to play music."[80] The Spanish tinge was not, of course, the only musical bond between these musicians, but it is worth noting that Dodds recalled performing "Billy Goat Stomp" with Morton's band "in Spanish rhythm like so many of the numbers used to be played in New Orleans."[81] Given this perception, it is surprising that Morton did not produce more Spanish-tinged group recordings, such as the Red Hot Peppers' "Original Jelly-Roll Blues" (1926), which incorporates guitar and castanets to "give a Spanish style effect."[82] Although Morton rarely took advantage of his fellow musicians' familiarity with Spanish-tinged repertory, much more frequently integrating these touches into his solo piano efforts, he revisited this type of material during his final studio dates in January 1940. For these sessions Morton hired several old hands from New Orleans, including Albert Nicholas and Zutty Singleton. The ensemble focused mainly on Morton's tunes, including the calypso-inspired "Mama's Got a Baby," and also recorded a version of the Spanish-tinged chestnut "Panama" (1911), an old standby composed by William H. Tyers that originally featured a habanera bass.[83]

It is unclear whether Morton's commitment to incorporating the Spanish tinge remained constant in the period between his mid-1920s recordings of "Mamanita" and "Dead Man Blues" and the release of "Panama" in 1940. Morton seldom recorded during the 1930s, an especially challenging decade for the record industry, which makes it hard to determine if he kept Spanish-tinged material fresh in his active repertory. We do know that the musical world changed around him. In fact, were it not for Morton's earlier compositions, it could be claimed that his comments about the Spanish tinge at the Library of Congress were made in response to musical trends of the day. By the time he spoke with Alan Lomax in 1938, the tango had been eclipsed by a national craze for the rumba, sparked by the 1930 hit "El Manisero (The Peanut Vendor)" from the Cuban bandleader Don Azpiazu and spurred on by recordings of that tune by such leading artists as Louis Armstrong and Duke Ellington. Furthermore, the presence of a Latin tinge in the jazz world could be felt not only in the repertoire of Ellington's orchestra but also in its musical style and its personnel, especially after Juan Tizol, a trombonist and composer from Puerto Rico, joined the ensemble in 1929. These developments gave rise to public commentary about Spanish and Afro-Caribbean musical influences from several leading musicians. In an article published in the same year that Morton spoke with Lomax, Ellington also identified a Spanish influence on early jazz: "When I came into the world, Southern Negroes were expressing their feelings in rhythmic 'blues' in which Spanish syncopations had a part."[84] A few years later W. C. Handy published his autobiography, *Father of the Blues* (1941), in which he describes first hearing Latin music and explains how the strong reaction by a crowd of dancers to songs based around habanera-style rhythms convinced him to incorporate them into his blues compositions.[85]

What distinguishes Morton's perspectives from the writings of Ellington and Handy is that he illuminated his commentary at the Library of Congress by performing musical demonstrations. Whether he was inspired most by nostalgia about his own journey, by what he may have seen as a chance to set the record straight, or by the increased presence of Latin-tinged music around him, the opportunity to speak with Alan Lomax clearly rekindled Morton's interest in this facet of his music. In addition to explicitly demonstrating the Spanish tinge by playing "New Orleans Blues" and "La Paloma," Morton performed a variety of other Spanish-tinged pieces: the standard "Panama"; his early tunes "Jelly Roll Blues," "Mamanita," and "The Crave"; and several pieces he first recorded on this occasion, including the dark, deliberate "Spanish Swat" and the sinuous "Creepy Feeling." When the Library of Congress sessions were issued on LP, there was enough material to fill a dedicated album entitled *The Spanish Tinge*. These sides captured the attention of jazz critics—"very sensitive, Spanish-tinged blues piano," wrote Don Locke—and contributed to popularizing the notion of a Spanish tinge.[86] During the last few years of his life, Morton also featured this repertory in his live appearances. The jazz enthusiast Roy Carew was so affected by hearing these pieces at a club in Washington, D.C., that he encouraged Morton "to record some of the smooth running Spanish type of music he had played for me."[87] Morton took this advice and produced studio versions of several pieces he had performed for Lomax, including "Creepy Feeling" (1938) for the Jazzman label and "The Crave" (1939) for General, which was later released on the aptly titled album *New Orleans Memories*.

One of his many sidemen, Walter "Foots" Thomas, characterized Morton's approach to jazz composition in this way: "I always felt his melodies came from New Orleans but that his rhythms came from the Latin countries."[88] Coming from one of his close associates, this is a valuable statement: it suggests that his musical colleagues recognized the significance of Latin rhythms, or what they might have understood as a Spanish tinge, in Morton's music. At the same time it must be underscored that this is the opinion of Thomas, not Morton. For Morton, as I have attempted to demonstrate, does not seem to have drawn a fine line between Latin rhythms and the music of New Orleans; instead, he acknowledged a degree of overlap between the two by identifying how a Spanish tinge colored New Orleans jazz. Moreover, Morton's interest in Spanish music was not limited to the integration of certain rhythms, a point that he clarified in his remarks to Alan Lomax: "I personally didn't believe that the Spanish tunes were really perfected in the tempos, the fact that the tempos wasn't always correct. And I heard a lot of Spanish tunes and I tried to play 'em in correct tempo myself. And I didn't possibly play 'em very correct in tempos. But I wasn't altogether satisfied with some of the melodies. I decided to write some of them myself. I will now try to play one for your approval."[89] Morton's ensuing performance of "Creepy Feeling" displays these multiple aspects of the Spanish tinge. On the one hand, Morton directs the listener's attention toward the melodic qualities of the tune. He begins the first strain of the tune by spinning out a descending melody that unwinds itself or, as its title would imply, creeps its way down until the *tresillo* bass enters, then continues by introducing similar gestures over the *tresillo* rhythm. Playing the chromatically ornamented line slowly enough to allow each note to resound enables him to achieve a balance between unfurling the minor melody and repeating the insistent bass line. The deliberate pace also allows Morton to concentrate on melodic improvisation, which led Martin Williams to dub

"Creepy Feeling" the "inventive *tour de force*" of Morton's Spanish-tinged tunes. "Morton plays on its three themes," Williams writes, "as if his ability to improvise variations is inexhaustible, and they flow out of him as easily and naturally as breathing."[90]

On the other hand, Morton produces the dramatic highpoint in "Creepy Feeling" by establishing, then confounding, his listener's expectations. Once introduced, the *tresillo* pattern functions as Morton's rhythmic foundation, a solid base against which to improvise. But a few minutes into his performance, after playing five sixteen-bar strains grounded on the *tresillo* pattern, Morton begins a new strain by changing keys and sounding a single dissonant F♯ in the upper register. At this moment, his left hand cuts out entirely for nearly two measures, as he clings to the bluesy note with his right hand. After suspending time for a few seconds, he continues by performing a strain that is characterized far more by cross-rhythmic interaction than by the melodic improvisation that occupied the earlier strains. This is an ironic but evocative moment, one that produces a vivid, if droll, sense of musical tension, for it is precisely when Morton suspends the rhythmic pulse, when he calls attention to the Spanish tinge by withholding it, that we are fully able to appreciate its significance.

THE LATIN TINGES OF JAZZ AND AMERICAN MUSIC

In his review of the 1957 Riverside rerelease of Morton's Library of Congress sessions, Richard Hadlock argues that "Morton's concern with 'Spanish' influences is personal and not necessarily a mirror of jazz history. He might as justifiably have selected polkas."[91] Hadlock may have intended his commentary as a tribute to Morton's ability to synthesize various influences into his version of jazz, but I have tried throughout this chapter to demonstrate the significance of Morton's interest in Spanish-tinged music, rather than, say, polkas. In Hadlock's defense, it is true that no other prominent jazz musician of the early jazz era integrated these musical influences to the same extent as Morton. But he was not completely alone, for many of his contemporaries played, published, and recorded Latin-tinged jazz; these included lesser-known New Orleans figures, such as the trombonist Manuel Manetta and the clarinetist Clem Raymond, as well as international jazz icons, such as Louis Armstrong and Duke Ellington. Furthermore, even if Morton's path did not run parallel to those of other early jazz musicians, this aspect of his career may be seen as a harbinger of the later emergence of proponents of Latin jazz, among them Machito, Mario Bauzá, and Chano Pozo.

Although acknowledgment of the Spanish tinge is critical for under-standing the creative musical life of Jelly Roll Morton, the broader meta-phor of a Spanish tinge has much to tell us about the complex, contested, and multicultural history of jazz and American music. Morton's affinity with Creole culture makes it impossible to enclose his experiences within a black-and-white racial model, just as his exposure to various aspects of Latin and Caribbean musical culture complicates the basic notion of jazz origins as melding European and African musical influences. Such historiographic challenges are viewed warily in some circles, and rightly so, for widening the lens of analysis beyond a binary racial model can threaten to dilute the crucial contributions by African American musicians to jazz. I am keenly sensitive to such concerns, especially because the relationship between the Creole community and the black community has been fraught at times; per-haps, however, we can look to the notion of a Spanish tinge as carrying some potential to partially reconcile the two. By focusing on the roles that the Ca-ribbean and Latin America played in Morton's family history and his music, we can view the Spanish tinge as a reminder of the various paths by which Africans reached the Americas and through which black America has been formed. In the process, the notion of a Spanish tinge helps flesh out the experience of what Paul Gilroy calls the "Black Atlantic," which encom-passes the rich and complicated history of the African diaspora on both sides of the Atlantic Ocean.[92] For that reason, as much as my discussion has cen-tered on a single jazz musician from the United States, the Spanish tinge may serve as a symbol for the broad diversity and international pedigree of jazz history.

Exploring how international influences apply to the broader history of music in America, many scholars have traced in fine detail the ways in which European and African musical practices have shaped music in the United States. Yet, over the past century, Latin music also has played a significant role in the musical history of the nation, from tango and rumba to mambo and Cubop to salsa and *rock en español*. As an increasing amount of work has demonstrated, some sort of Latin tinge marks a variety of genres of American music that are not always thought of as Latin, including the blues, boogie-woogie, country, funk, hip-hop, and rock and roll.[93] Though each of these studies has led to a better understanding of the rich history of American music, it is important to emphasize that they do not all reach the same conclusions about the role played by the Latin tinge. For instance, in the case of rockabilly, the influence of Latin music is felt primarily as a set of rhythmic gestures; whereas in the case of salsa, a Latin tinge character-izes virtually all the genre's elements—its Spanish-language lyrics and the cultural background of its originators, its main proponents, and its initial audience. What exactly constitutes the Latin tinge is neither identical from one case to another nor fixed in any specific case; it may leave a minor impression on a single piece of music or register a deep and lasting mark on an entire genre. Consequently, some critics have argued convincingly that the concept of a Latin tinge is not nearly enough, that it does not sufficiently register the effect of Latin influences on specific musical genres.

Indeed, recognizing just a tinge of Spanish or Latin may not be sufficient to address the experiences of Jelly Roll Morton, for Spanish, Caribbean, and Latin American influences touched aspects of his entire musical life. Defined in terms of a broad historical perspective, the Latin tinge helps explain the journey of Morton's ancestors, the development of the city where he was born, and the rationale for the name he was given; viewed in terms of cultural history, the tinge introduced Morton to all the "Spanish tunes" he heard as a child as well as to the guitar that became his first instrument. The tinge can be traced throughout the population of New Orleans, from the immigrant communities that maintained their own musical traditions to the music teachers who trained the city's budding jazz musicians, including the Spanish gentleman who served as Morton's first music teacher. Read as a geographical marker, the tinge serves as a reminder of Morton's sojourn in Tijuana; interpreted as a strategy of musical exoticism, it came to flavor his subsequent recording of "Tia Juana (Tee Wanna)." The notion of a Latin tinge extends beyond the widely acknowledged rhythmic patterns that characterize many of his compositions. It resonates as well in the intentionally "Spanish" melody of Morton's tune "Creepy Feeling," the parallel thirds he accentuates in "Tia Juana (Tee Wanna)," and his choice to feature songs like "La Paloma" and "Panama" in his repertory. Finally, as displayed by tunes like "New Orleans Blues" and "Mamanita," this musical tinge appears to have held special resonance for Morton as a sonic signifier of New Orleans Creole culture.

A Latin tinge clearly played a significant role in Morton's life, and his career vividly illustrates how Latin musical influences are woven into the fabric of American musical history. Yet, as is made evident by the above examples, accounting for the broad scope of these influences also requires stretching the definition of "Latin tinge" in multiple directions to accommodate its various permutations. Thus, even as the resulting perspectives on Morton are meant to indicate the potential this concept possesses for wider application, they also point out one of its primary constraints as a general expression. In other words, although employing the Latin tinge as a broad conceptual device acknowledges the presence of Latin musical influences, relying too heavily on the term can threaten to evacuate its meaning and to obscure the abundant variety of ways in which these influences are felt. One solution to this problem is to define and contextualize the nature of the Latin tinge whenever it arises, which is the main strategy employed in this chapter. For another remedy, we can look to Jelly Roll Morton, whose wide-ranging career suggests that rather than tossing out the phrase altogether, we extend it. Because its nature can vary so extensively, it may prove more productive in future studies to conceive of the Latin tinge not as a single entity but as a multifaceted, variable array of influences, not as a singular tinge but as a collective set of Latin tinges that color the history of American music.

3. Louis Armstrong and the Great Migration

Jelly Roll Morton's sustained interest in Latin-tinged music and his personal history of border crossing not only display the transnational impulse that informed his approach to jazz but also underscore the far-reaching influence of global musical practices brought to the United States as a result of immigration, whether by choice or by force. This chapter revisits the subject of migration from a different angle, focusing on the story of internal migration within U.S. borders, an ongoing process that has profoundly influenced the history of American music. Of primary interest here is the relationship between music and what has been coined the Great Migration, the massive population shift beginning in the mid-1910s and spanning the 1920s that saw more than 10 percent of the total African American population migrate from the South to the North. During this period the city of Chicago emerged as one of the nation's blues and jazz capitals, as local fans, migrant musicians, and music industry agents flocked to the black entertainment district on the city's South Side. My investigation of the development of jazz in the context of migration centers on one of the most celebrated figures to make this trip, Louis Armstrong, who journeyed north from New Orleans in the early 1920s.

Studying this phenomenon from the perspective of a young African American musician, whose recordings gave voice to the experiences, hopes, and strivings of a marginalized community, provides a fresh look at the struggle to define the musical nation at the start of the century. It would be conceivable to frame this inquiry as a history of reception, for early jazz met notably fierce resistance because of divergent musical priorities and racial bias, among other factors, or as an essay on jazz historiography, since jazz has served as a continual site of cultural contestation over the entire course of its history.[1] What intrigues me to a larger extent are the strategies Armstrong employed to craft creative musical responses to a changing world. Since African Americans had just gained greater access to the recording industry, Armstrong was among the earliest black musicians to have an opportunity to participate more fully in America's musical life. To explain how Armstrong fashioned a different vision of America, I look to the ways in which his music, and in particular his song "Gully Low Blues," enacted a set of contemporary sociocultural tensions that held special significance to the African American community. More specifically, I seek to understand Armstrong's music in light of his experience as one of the tens of thousands of southern black migrants adapting to life in Chicago.

One significant aspect of this project involves trying to map the connections between sound and environment, between Armstrong's music and the city. Attempts to theorize the relationship between music and place have increased steadily in the disciplines of musicology, ethnomusicology, jazz studies, and musical geography.[2] These theoretical concerns already have had an influence on the wider field of American music, whether broadening our understanding of the commemorative "place pieces" of Charles Ives or directing our attention to the ways in which today's hip-hop artists express their connections to local communities.[3] The historical diffusion of jazz has led to dozens of local and regional studies that document jazz scenes around the world, ranging from New Orleans, Kansas City, Chicago, Detroit, New York, and Los Angeles to France, Norway, Russia, and Japan. Place-specific methodologies have been applied as well to the music of individual performers, including recent work that explores how Armstrong's early years in New Orleans influenced his musical style, technique, and approach.[4] Of all of this research, I am most indebted to the historical scholarship of William Kenney, whose valuable writings on Chicago jazz bring to life the rich cultural milieu that informed the music Armstrong created there during the 1920s.[5] Though my project shares Kenney's concern with matters of cultural and historical analysis, I am interested as well in pursuing questions about how the environment and the experiences of an urban jazz musician can find their way into musical expression. Consequently, my work overlaps to some extent with that of Andrew Berish, who argues that "music *articulates* place, it joins sounds to real and imaginary places . . . and it also expresses, represents, and embodies place through certain musical structures, musical codes, and musical practices."[6] Is it then possible to hear the sound of Chicago in Armstrong's music of the 1920s?

I believe the answer to be a qualified yes. I concur that Armstrong's experience in Chicago led to his use of certain musical gestures, codes, and practices, which collectively gave voice to the black urban experience during the

Jazz Age, but the complicating factor that differentiates my approach derives from Armstrong's status as a recent migrant. As someone influenced by his experiences growing up in the South, like so many jazz musicians of his era, Armstrong does not articulate or embody a single place through his music. Thus, it becomes necessary to account for the influence not only of his experiences in Chicago but also of his recent migration from New Orleans. I am not intending here to revive the legend that jazz and its practitioners migrated slowly up the Mississippi River to Chicago—a city the river never reaches—but rather to contextualize Armstrong's music within the larger picture of migration in the United States. To understand how these dual experiences influenced his music, I have found invaluable Brian Harker's detailed treatment of Armstrong's early musical development, which identifies specific ways in which Armstrong mixed northern and southern techniques in his music of the 1920s.[7] I have been inspired as well by *Race Music*, Guthrie Ramsey's expansive study of black music since 1940, which includes persuasive commentary about selected tunes in the context of black migrant life in Chicago.[8] By similarly investigating how urban black musicians drew on musical practices associated with both the rural South and the urban North, I seek to apply the notion of what Ramsey calls "the Migrating Blues Muse" to music created during an earlier era of black migration.

Internal migration has long been recognized as essential to the history of African American music, fostering the growth of urban musical communities and providing thematic material for a wide-ranging variety of genres. This link has been especially pertinent for understanding the blues, which has "always been a migratory music."[9] Consequently, blues scholars have produced comprehensive analyses of the intersection of music and migration. For example, Roger House demonstrates how the music of William "Big Bill" Broonzy stems from his experiences alongside fellow southern migrants in Chicago and preserves a "cultural record of their lives in the era of the Great Migration."[10] The significance of the Great Migration to jazz history is also well established. As part of his work on the rise of jazz as an urban phenomenon, Burton Peretti issues this commanding statement: "This migration, more than any other historical event, defined the social and intellectual significance of jazz for African Americans."[11] Unfortunately, many historical accounts of jazz leave unclear the details of how this experience affected individual jazz musicians and left its mark on individual pieces of music.

What I pursue here, following the lead of Harker and Ramsey, is an attempt to identify how migration, along with the various cultural tensions it set in motion, influenced Armstrong and shaped his 1927 recording of "Gully Low Blues." Centering my cultural and musicological analysis on this particular song offers the opportunity to hear the sound of migration finding expression in music and to envisage the reasons why such material would resonate so powerfully at this historical juncture. This investigation must be speculative to a certain degree, for the most conventional sources of reception history, such as contemporaneous reviews or interviews concerning "Gully Low Blues," do not exist or have not been preserved. Nevertheless, a combination of helpful resources—including the content of the song, the musical and cultural context of its creation, autobiographical recollections from Armstrong and members of his band, and commentary from Chicagoans and from musicians around the country—help account for the cultural work performed by a song like "Gully Low Blues." By contextualizing this musical release as part of an era that was so vital to black cultural history, I contend that "Gully Low Blues" would have held special significance for those listeners who shared similar life experiences as recent African American migrants. Attempting to understand this song from the perspective of the community for whom it was originally designed serves several key purposes. Not only does this stance identify the ways in which marginalized musical communities work through cultural tensions that are most germane to their own experiences, thus creating distinct and divergent portraits of life in America, but this approach proves absolutely vital for producing a broader account of the meanings present in this rich musical expression.

THE MIGRATION TO CHICAGO AND THE SPREAD OF RACE RECORDS

The full significance of Armstrong's "Gully Low Blues" can be understood only by recognizing the deteriorating social conditions that initially prompted the Great Migration. In the wake of the failures of Reconstruction, life in the South at the turn of the twentieth century remained extremely difficult for African Americans. Systematic racism in the form of Jim Crow laws limited economic opportunities, living conditions worsened, and the deadly rise of lynching together with the revival of the Ku Klux Klan terrorized the black community. Hopes brightened during World War I, as northern cities began to offer greater economic opportunities for African Americans. Eventually, major increases in wartime production, newly enacted federal immigration restrictions, and rising enlistment in the armed forces combined to create a massive northern labor shortage that helped propel the Great Migration. Consequently, between 1916 and 1930, nearly 1.5 million southern black migrants moved north in search of jobs, better wages, improved housing conditions, and the potential for equal rights. As LeRoi Jones (Amiri Baraka) describes it, "The North suddenly represented a *further* idea of what this country and what a black man's life might be"; this idea prompted migrants to stream into large cities such as Pittsburgh, Philadelphia, New York, Detroit, Cleveland, and, most significant for this episode in jazz history, Chicago.[12]

As perhaps the most fortunate beneficiary of the migration, Chicago saw its black population increase fivefold between 1910 and 1930, from less than fifty thousand to nearly a quarter million, as workers arrived to fill jobs at stockyards, meatpacking plants, steel mills, and rail yards. Such a rapid transformation led Fred Fisher to pen the following line in "Chicago (That Todd'ling Town)" (1922), his famous musical tribute to the city: "more Colored people up in State Street you can see, than you'll see in Louisiana or Tennessee." African Americans in the South came to understand Chicago as a beacon of opportunity in the state where Abraham Lincoln first gained fame. According to the clarinetist Sidney Bechet, expectations in New Orleans multiplied once it became known "they was building a railroad up to Chicago. Back in New Orleans people were hearing a lot of excitement about what was happening up North, and I had this idea in my head that I was to see other places. I wanted to go North and see Chicago and I wanted to see New York. I guess I just about wanted to see all there was."[13] Likewise, Langston Hughes later recalled that as a child he "used to walk down to the Santa Fe station and stare at the railroad tracks, because the railroad tracks ran to Chicago, and Chicago was the biggest town in the world to me, much talked of by the people in Kansas."[14] Like Bechet, Hughes also followed those tracks north, and he later wrote a weekly newspaper column for the *Chicago Defender* from 1942 to 1962.

Hughes's eventual employer, the *Defender*, was originally founded by Robert S. Abbott in 1905, and it quickly grew into the nation's largest African American newspaper, attracting local readers and garnering an even larger national audience. By 1919 nearly two-thirds of its circulation was being shipped to locations outside Chicago, reaching hundreds of thousands of readers each week in more than fifteen hundred towns across the South.[15] Distributed by traveling entertainers, sold by Pullman porters, and made available by U.S. mail, the *Defender* became the "most widely read newspaper in the black South."[16] The project advanced by the *Defender* is significant to understanding this era in American music because the paper continually encouraged rural migration to Chicago through front-page articles, weekly editorials, entertainment listings, and help wanted advertisements, all of which promoted the city as a promised land of opportunity, a "northern mecca."[17] The paper became so effective at encouraging migration that some southern towns outlawed its distribution. Like the recorded blues craze of the 1920s, the *Defender* was not intended to be an elitist endeavor. Interested parties from all walks of life could purchase copies in barber shops, theaters, churches, grocery stores, and train depots, and those who could not read would listen as others read the paper aloud.[18]

The experiences of one impressionable reader give a sense of the paper's influence. Born in 1899 as a sharecropper's son in a small Georgia town, this young musician migrated with his family to Atlanta, a common strategy of rural folk, who would move to a southern city before braving the trip north. In Atlanta he noticed billboards around town advertising northern jobs and also read in the *Defender* about "the great opportunities . . . for my people in the north."[19] Disenchanted with life in the South and eager to break into the world of entertainment, he decided to migrate "to Chicago where I had the opportunity to become a great musician."[20] The budding entertainer ended up doing just that, first making a splash in Chicago's blues world as a performer known as "Georgia Tom" before changing gears in the late 1920s and becoming the leading figure in black gospel music under his given name, Thomas A. Dorsey.

Louis Armstrong later stated: "All in all, the 'twenties in Chicago were some of my finest days. From 1922 to 1929, I spent my youngest and best days there."[21] Indeed, historians of Chicago have characterized the latter half of the 1920s, when Armstrong recorded "Gully Low Blues," as the "most prosperous" years black Chicagoans had yet experienced.[22] New residents had spending money and well-deserved leisure time, and the city developed into a hotbed of black entertainment—what the bassist Milt Hinton described as a "paradise for black folk."[23] Restaurants, social clubs, vaudeville theaters, dance halls, and cinemas contributed to the blossoming nightlife on Chicago's South Side. The pianist Lil Hardin, who arrived from Memphis with her parents in 1918 and became Louis Armstrong's second wife in 1924, described the city as "heaven"—"its beautiful brick and stone buildings, excitement, people moving swiftly, and things happening."[24] The gospel singer Mahalia Jackson, who migrated from New Orleans in the late 1920s, provided an even more enthusiastic account of the neighborhood that became known as the "Black Belt":

> The colored world was in full bloom. Never before had Negroes lived so well or had so much money to spend. I'll never forget what a joy it was to see them driving up and down Southern Parkway and Michigan Boulevard in big, shiny touring cars and strolling in the evening, laughing and

talking and calling out happily to each other. The men wore cream-colored spats and derbies and carried walking sticks. Their women had fur coats and led little dogs on leashes. Many of the houses on Michigan Avenue were mansions and the people that lived there had diamonds and silks and drove Rolls-Royces. They could easily afford them because some Negroes had become millionaires in the real estate and insurance businesses.[25]

An expansive city at the center of a huge railroad network that served as the final stop for many traveling shows, Chicago was especially well positioned to attract scores of talented pianists, jazzmen, and blues singers from points all over the map. Thus, the newcomer Jackson was thrilled by the opportunity to see Bessie Smith perform live on the South Side, and Louis Armstrong later gushed about attending a Chicago performance in 1922 by the entertainer Bill Robinson, "whom I had heard and read about in my early days."[26]

Migrant musicians were encouraged to move to Chicago not only by the *Defender*, but also by relatives, acquaintances, and fellow musicians who preceded them, and the migration of networks of friends and relations ensued. For Jackson, growing up in New Orleans, it was the favorable reports from earlier migrants that gave her a "longing to go up to Chicago and see for myself."[27] Born in Vicksburg, Mississippi, Milt Hinton heard about the plentiful jobs and social freedoms from one of his uncles, who "made Chicago sound like the best place in the world."[28] Over time, his uncle "sent for his other brother, then mother, then aunt, leaving me with my grandmother and their youngest sister"; eventually, "when they had furnished everything, and got everything set up, they sent for the three of us, the last of the family."[29] The twenty-one-year-old Louis Armstrong, who eventually stepped to the front of this musical movement, first reached town by train from New Orleans in response to an invitation from his mentor, Joe "King" Oliver, in the summer of 1922. The final lines of Armstrong's first autobiography capture his excitement: "I had hit the big time. I was up North with the greats. I was playing with my idol, the King, Joe Oliver. My boyhood dream had come true at last."[30]

The interrelated trends of northern migration, new forms of urban amusement, and a growing black audience did not escape the notice of the record industry, which had ignored African American performers for the most part during the opening decades of the recording era. Capitalizing on the success of Mamie Smith's "Crazy Blues" (1920) and the subsequent burst in popularity of recordings of urban female blues singers, a number of record companies, large and small, began to produce recordings featuring

black performers.[31] By the early 1920s, the record industry had systematically categorized and segregated their musical offerings into records intended for mainstream white audiences and records targeted for specific ethnic or racial groups. "Race records," the newly coined industry designation
for recordings intended for black listeners, became one of the few forms of
mass media to feature professional black entertainment that was targeted
for, created by, and made widely available to African American consumers.[32]
According to Clarence Williams, enthusiastic black audiences on the South
Side of Chicago "would form a line twice around the block when the latest
record of Bessie or Ma [Rainey] or Clara [Smith] or Mamie [Smith] come
in. . . . Sometimes these records they was bootlegged, sold in the alley for
four or five dollars apiece."[33] In New Orleans "everybody was buying
phonographs . . . and everybody had records of all the Negro blues singers,"
remembered Mahalia Jackson, who sang along with Bessie Smith's records
while dreaming about life up north.[34] On the East Coast, after first hearing
a record by Armstrong and King Oliver in 1923, Rex Stewart and his friends
played it "until our arms were worn out from working the phonograph han-
dle, the record was worn out and our souls were on fire."[35] Across the nation, race records accounted for approximately 20 percent of all releases during the late 1920s, creating a lucrative business that encompassed
comprehensive marketing efforts, dedicated catalogs, and slick publicity
brochures.[36]

In the Chicago studios of OKeh Records, the New York–based company
that initiated the practice of marketing race records, Louis Armstrong and
His Hot Seven recorded "Gully Low Blues" in 1927.[37] The year turned out
to be enormously profitable for American record companies. National sales
of all recorded music topped one hundred million dollars, each double-sided
78-rpm shellac record selling for seventy-five cents to a dollar. It was also
one of the peak years for the sales of race records. According to some estimates, approximately five million race records were sold in hundreds of locations around the United States, as far north as Buffalo and all the way
south to Biloxi; other scholars place sales at nearly double that figure.[38] Although top-of-the-line phonograph players required considerable sums,
Armstrong's recollections indicate the symbolic significance of owning one
as a point of pride for families able to make such a substantial financial commitment. He remembered playing jazz and operatic recordings in his New
Orleans home on "an upright Victrola we were very proud of."[39]

The memoirs of Garvin Bushell indicate that such attitudes were common in black communities. Growing up in Springfield, Ohio, Bushell describes the family's first Victrola, purchased in 1917:

Back in those days, the phonograph was a sign of some degree of luxury with the slightly less than middle classes, and there was no better time to show off your rating than Sunday afternoon. This was done by setting the machine near a front window or open door in the summer and turning it on full blast. As passers-by looked in they would see this large, morning-glory-shaped horn, painted with all the colors of its floral prototype, protruding through a window or a door. The larger the horn, the more convinced the neighbors were that the "Joneses" were quite successful.[40]

Less expensive models were also available. Portable Artophone phonographs, which sold for approximately fourteen dollars, brought recording technology within the reach of many consumers, and it has been estimated that nearly 30 percent of the households in the Mississippi Delta owned phonograph players by 1930.[41] In a coal-mining town in West Virginia, one fan remembered the excitement that met each new batch of records: "Mama would send us kids down to the store to get the latest blues records. Everybody else we knew would be there too and we'd carry those records home, stacked in our arms. All the Negroes lived together in that 'company' town and you could go from street to street and hear those blues records blasting out from the open doors. I'll never forget it."[42] But to be moved by Armstrong's music did not require purchasing one's own record player. Enjoying jazz recordings on a portable wind-up phonograph was common at parties, indoors and out, a sad irony in Chicago: African American music lovers were able to hear the music of bands whose performances they often were prohibited from attending.

In his vivid depiction of early jazz culture in Chicago, William Kenney describes how OKeh Records worked persistently to develop a black, working-class audience for race records using local distributional channels, posters plastered about town, promotional concerts, and radio airplay.[43] In addition to purchasing their favorite 78s at record stores, fans could find them at locations less familiar to today's CD consumers, such as cigar shops, furniture stores, drugstores, department stores, hairdressing parlors, and delicatessens.[44] Music aficionados outside Chicago could purchase records from Pullman porters, who stocked up on recent hits, or through the mail, a nationwide venture that proved popular with the hundreds of thousands who read the *Defender*.[45] The paper presented advertisements for Armstrong's records, as well as a wealth of other music marketed to black audiences, including recordings by blues singers, string bands, and jubilee quartets. Kid Ory, the trombonist who often played with Armstrong, put it simply: "Times were good, and people had money to buy records."[46]

In 1923 Armstrong began making records, initially as the second cornetist in King Oliver's Creole Jazz Band. After spending fourteen months in New York City, where he served as the lead cornet player for the Fletcher Henderson Orchestra and as an accompanist for Bessie Smith and other classic blues singers, Armstrong returned to Chicago in late 1925 to produce recordings under his own name for the city's burgeoning black population. Considered to be the peak of his career by many jazz purists, Armstrong's studio recordings with the Hot Five and Hot Seven between 1925 and 1928 have received tremendous praise from critics and fans alike. Despite a meager budget, few rehearsals, limited studio time, shifting personnel, and bare-bones recording equipment, these 78-rpm double-sided singles are commonly held up as landmark achievements. Without question, the music from these sessions is marvelous, from Armstrong's gleaming lines that dance on top of stop-time chords in "Potato Head Blues" to his majestic performance on "West End Blues." Collectively, these recordings demonstrate Armstrong's significance to early jazz history and illustrate the emergence in jazz of the virtuosic soloist. Rather than recount their powerful effect on jazz history and historiography, my goal here is to place Armstrong's creative achievement back in its original context, not to deconstruct his accomplishments but rather to explain why his music mattered so much at this moment to his fans in Chicago and around the nation. Of the many dozens of recordings by the Hot Five and Hot Seven, I have chosen to focus on a single release that was recorded around the midpoint of these sessions, "Gully Low Blues." Although one song cannot stand in for Armstrong's entire output from this period, I concentrate on this recording because of how powerfully it enacts in music the cultural tensions—including regionalism, urban versus rural culture, class, and gender—that characterized African American experiences during the Great Migration.

"YOU TREAT ME MEAN, BABY, JUST BECAUSE I'M GULLY LOW"

The trumpet fanfare that opens Louis Armstrong's 1927 recording of "Gully Low Blues" remains striking today, its arresting rhythmic snap compelling audiences then and now to listen up. Such curtain-raisers can be traced to Armstrong's contemporaneous involvement with theater and cabaret orchestras in Chicago, groups that often used punchy flourishes to quiet a room and usher in the next tune. Scholarship by Brian Harker and William Kenney makes clear that the young Armstrong effectively integrated a wide variety of musical techniques that he first encountered in Chicago and New York. To listeners familiar with earlier recordings by the Hot Five, Armstrong's horn in "Gully Low Blues" sounded stronger, clearer than before. He had switched from the cornet to the more powerful trumpet the previous year, and this recording session, held 7–14 May 1927, was the first for which his band took advantage of the very latest advances in recording technology.[47] "ELECTRIC" recording, emblazoned in capital letters on each disc and announced prominently in the promotional campaign of every self-respecting record company, offered the highest sound quality possible. The increase in recording fidelity brought a change in the composition of the group, as it allowed for the inclusion of instruments such as the tuba and drums, so that the Hot Five expanded to "Louis Armstrong and His Hot Seven." Owners of the newest Victor Orthophonic, a swanky electric record player introduced in 1925, were rewarded with increased clarity, a wider range of sound, and a dramatic increase in volume.[48] Those who played electrically recorded 78s on their acoustic players also heard a more prominent Armstrong, for his trumpet's piercing sound and Caruso-like range reproduced quite well on older equipment. To every listener he sounded closer, clearer, louder than ever. Moreover, it is likely that Armstrong's brisk, supple line would have sounded especially brilliant and inspirational to those black listeners who had recently migrated, like Armstrong, to the rapidly growing urban centers in the North, for it symbolized the sound of independence and achievement by a fellow newcomer. Fanning out from the South Side of Chicago to Milwaukee, Cleveland, Buffalo, Omaha, and a dozen other cities where OKeh Records distributed Armstrong's newest releases, black audiences could identify with the confident sound of a migrant musician moving up the ladder and, as we shall see, attempting to come to terms with his new urban surroundings.

Armstrong's opening lick in "Gully Low Blues" propels forward, then settles for a moment on the dominant to create tension, a tension shortly swept aside by the entrance of the entire Hot Seven playing the jaunty sixteen-bar opening chorus. After Armstrong presents the lead melody of his composition, the band performs an up-tempo strain of New Orleans–style polyphony, each of the musicians occupying time-honored roles.[49] The rhythm section pounds out the underlying chords, supplemented by instruments that were new for the band and its audience. Joining Lil Hardin Armstrong's piano and Johnny St. Cyr's banjo are low, belting tuba blasts from Pete Briggs and occasional cymbal crashes and percussive accents from the drummer Warren "Baby" Dodds. To fill out the

TABLE 2. Form of "Gully Low Blues"

Section	Measures	Solos	Soloist
Introduction	4	Trumpet	Armstrong
Chorus 1	16	New Orleans polyphony	Armstrong break
Chorus 2	8	Clarinet (interrupted)	Johnny Dodds
Transition	2	Clarinet (alone)	Dodds
Blues chorus 1	12	Clarinet (high range)	Dodds
Blues chorus 2	12	Vocals	Armstrong
Blues chorus 3	12	Vocals	Armstrong
Blues chorus 4	12	Clarinet (low range)	Dodds
Blues chorus 5	12	Trumpet	Armstrong
Blues chorus 6	12	Entire band	
Coda	2	Entire band	

musical texture, Johnny Dodds, Baby's brother, contributes countermelodies and arpeggiated figures on clarinet, while the trombonist John Thomas pipes in with long, swooping gestures. At first, the musicians recall traditional polyphonic ensemble jazz, rooted in the sound of New Orleans, but audible signs of modern Chicago begin to surface as well. In addition to the fleshed-out texture and more commanding sound, due to the band's full instrumentation and improved audio fidelity, listeners would have noticed the more prominent and flamboyant role played by Armstrong, already evident from his opening fanfare and again spotlighted in his first solo break—the only break in the opening chorus (table 2).

By the time that Johnny Dodds begins his initial solo, however, some contemporary audiences might have been puzzled by the relationship of old and new reflected in the song's title and its musical content. For listeners today, such confusion may hinge on the absence of twelve-bar blues form at the beginning of a tune entitled "Gully Low Blues," but this would not necessarily have surprised record buyers in the 1920s. Attaching *blues* to song titles was extremely common, a testament to the music's commercial appeal, regardless of a song's internal form or lyrical content. And, ultimately, the patience of fans expecting a typical blues is rewarded, for "Gully Low Blues" eventually adopts a twelve-bar blues form. What is more surprising about the title of this song is its use of "gully low." Most African American listeners, and jazz devotees versed in black vernacular language, would have noted the disparity between Armstrong's more polished sound and the connotation of the song's title, since the phrase "gully low" originally derived from a slang term meaning low as a ditch or a gully. In musical terms, this might suggest an earthy authenticity, the kind of down-and-dirty sound associated with a sloppy, growling, plunger-muted trombone.[50] Along these lines, OKeh advertised "Gully Low Blues" in the *Defender* as "another mean and low down number."[51] Furthermore, the phrase signified a "poverty-ridden, unsophisticated lifestyle" and thus could be used as a derogatory term by elite city dwellers to deride rural folk for their lack of refinement, education, and wealth.[52] Armstrong's "Gully Low Blues" draws on each of these meanings.

The introduction and opening chorus of the song prove unsettling because the mixture of new and old, urban and rural, resists categorization as wholly one or the other. How can music featuring a theatrical fanfare, a confident city-dwelling soloist, and the most up-to-date fidelity be "gully low"? This sort of question was not purely academic for Armstrong's audiences, since recordings were often purchased according to the appeal of the title and the reputation of the musical artist. As one illustration of this point, OKeh's American executives determined that the title "Gully Low Blues" would resonate with their target audience; however, for overseas distribution, English record executives, who could not rely on their customers' familiarity with African American vernacular speech, marketed the tune, drawing on the song's lyrics, as "Mama, Why Do You Treat Me So?"[53]

Midway through the opening solo by Johnny Dodds, a musical shock completely changes the affect of "Gully Low Blues." His clarinet line suddenly slows down, perilously spiraling out of tempo and out of his sixteen-bar chorus. At this moment, the accompaniment drops away, further dramatizing his solo freefall. Listeners are thrown as well, and one can imagine a first-time record buyer leaning forward to confirm that the phonograph player was operating properly. Unlike the typical treatment of breaks, stop-time passages, double-time passages, and other interludes in early New Orleans–style jazz, "Gully Low Blues" never returns to the opening melody or the original tempo. Instead, when Dodds and the rhythm section recover their bearings, they stand perched at the start of a slow blues progression. Since Dodds recalibrates his four-bar phrases to match what turns out to be a twelve-bar blues, and because he uses portamento techniques to stress blue notes and high-pitched dominants, listeners may reacclimate long before his new solo ends. The clarinet's forever unfinished chorus and the piece's drastic shift in form, tempo, and affect, however, leave the audience uncertain about what will follow.

The clarinet's dramatic slow dive into a familiar blues form symbolizes a descent into the "gully low" blues, and Armstrong's full set of lyrics, which explain the British choice of an alternative song title, reinforce this interpretation:

Chorus 1:
Now, mama, mama, mama, why do you treat me so?
Ah, mama, mama, mama, why do you treat me so?
[*Spoken in response:*] I know why you treat me so bad.
You treat me mean, baby, just because I'm gully low.

Chorus 2:
Now mama, if you listen baby, I'll tell you something you don't know.
[*Sung in response:*] You don't know.
If you just listen to me honey, I'll tell you something you don't know.
If you just give me a break and take me back, I won't be gully no mo'.
[*Sung in response:*] Gully no mo'.

Armstrong sings the blues because he feels he has been treated badly for being "gully low." If we understand "mama," "baby," and "honey" all to refer to his beloved, the basic meaning of "gully low" can be inferred from its context. For those unfamiliar with the idiom, the phrase represents an undefined, undesirable characteristic that Armstrong promises to change. The song thus calls on the age-old blues theme of trying to rebuild a relationship, to be forgiven or redeemed. Almost any American listener who learned the meaning of "gully low blues" could relate to the song's lyrical message, since waves of migration and immigration at the opening of the century meant that by the 1920s "the average American was someone from the country who had moved to the city for a job and was adjusting to a new social environment."[54] But black audiences who were familiar with the term and its discourse of class and urban-rural tensions had direct access to a more specific, culturally rich interpretation. Recent arrivals to Chicago's South Side would have been acquainted with some sort of gully low blues in their own complicated transition to city life, whereas southerners who had heard stories about the North and were thinking about migrating could imagine finding themselves in Armstrong's shoes. In the closest parallel, young black men who moved from the country to the city during the Great Migration might experience this very situation: meeting an uptown city girl and trying to bridge the chasm created by differences in life experience, cultural knowledge, and class. Armstrong's lyrics also held intrigue for the smaller group of Chicago's young black female sophisticates: how exactly would this new "gully low" man redeem and prove himself?

The same urban-rural tensions that shaped the song's reception are equally relevant to its creation, for "Gully Low Blues" also can be understood in light of the relationship between Armstrong and his wife, Lil

Hardin Armstrong, who plays piano on this recording.[55] Though he expressed great pride about his New Orleans roots, Armstrong's recollections of arriving in Chicago display a marked self-consciousness about his southern background. As noticeable as the trout sandwiches his mother gave him to take on the train to Chicago, "anybody watching me closely could have easily seen that I was a country boy."[56] Such insecurity could lead to serious distress. The blues musician Big Bill Broonzy, who arrived two years before Armstrong, could barely fathom the level of prejudice that met him in Chicago: "If you's from a different State in the USA, if your hair is frizzy and you's real black, all the northern Negroes who have their hair straightened and know the town, instead of trying to show me how to act and do, they'll just laugh and call me a Mississippi Negro."[57] In his study of migration in America, James Gregory explains how such hazing practices were not limited to Chicago: "Making fun of newcomers for acting 'country' or speaking in southern accents remained part of the culture of the northern black community all through the diaspora. The result was a lasting discursive connection between the North and respectability, the South and backwardness."[58] That such entrenched cultural tensions found their way into music of the era thus can hardly come as a revelation.

Armstrong's own concerns about his humble background were not entirely misplaced. When he and Lil announced their plans for marriage to the surprise of fellow members of King Oliver's band, he was criticized along these same lines by Oliver himself: "Just think—here we are a Bunch of 'Hip' (hep) musicians—been up North for years—making a 'play for Lil. And here—AH_Real 'country 'sommitch' come up here, and take her from right under our noses."[59] Clearly, such criticism did not dissuade Armstrong, and he recognized how much he profited from Lil's familiarity with the city, her willingness to act as a guide, and her confidence in his abilities. After their relationship shifted from bandmates to husband and wife, Armstrong continued to praise her urbane sophistication: "She was really *up* on things, the *modern* things, and she had such wonderful *taste*, such as how to furnish the apartment."[60] Nevertheless, he continued to be concerned about the rural-urban dynamic brought forth by their relationship: "But *who was I* to think that a Big High-powered 'Chick like 'Lillian Hardin who came to Chicago from Memphis Tenn—the year of 1917—Right out of 'Fisk University—Valedictorian of her Classes—Who Me?—I thought to myself. I just couldn't conceive the idea."[61] In truth, Hardin's academic career was not as highfalutin as Armstrong believed, but her recollections make plain that her family attempted to instill values held by many in the African American middle class, values that offered little support for her music-making career. Her mother actively appealed to Hardin to avoid jazz, music that family elders must have considered gully low.[62] Heard in this light, the lyrics of the two choruses, sung by Louis over chords played by Lil around the time that their marriage faltered, come across as a personal plea.

The song's acknowledgment of regional, class, and gender tensions and its autobiographical connection seem to have remained acute for Armstrong. Decades after the original release, Armstrong rerecorded "Gully Low Blues" and included it as part of the lavish 1957 Decca box set *Satchmo: A Musical Autobiography of Louis Armstrong.*[63] This performance includes a change that hints at the song's intimate connection to his life. In the opening line of the first chorus, Armstrong sings, "Now, mama, mama, mama, why *did* you treat me so?" The second time around, he apparently catches himself and shifts to the present tense of the original lyrics ("why *do* you treat me so?"). For an artist who became increasingly nostalgic as his career progressed, constantly writing about, singing about, and revisiting his past, it was hard to forget old wounds.

"I WON'T BE GULLY NO MO'"

The plunging, interrupted clarinet solo and Armstrong's vocals appear to symbolize the "gully low"–ness of the blues—the shared troubles and growing pains African American immigrants often faced at the time—but just like the clarion call that introduces the tune, Armstrong perseveres. As long as we do as he asks in the second chorus—"just listen, baby"—I believe we can hear Armstrong striving to prove how he "won't be gully no' mo'." The overarching construction of Armstrong's two vocal choruses in "Gully Low Blues"—the first chorus stating a problem ("you treat me mean"), the second proposing a potential solution ("If you take me back . . .")—implies that redemption will be delayed until the end of Armstrong's second chorus, but it is at the moment when Armstrong begins to sing that hope starts to appear on the horizon. As he did in the opening New Orleans–style chorus that features *his* trumpet break, Armstrong here reasserts himself as the leader of the band. His voice reminds us that at this pivotal point in his career not only was he becoming a showman, he was becoming the show. Brian Harker has mapped in detail how Armstrong moved steadily to the forefront over the course of the Hot Five and Hot Seven recording sessions. Instead of settling for a single break or a brief instrumental solo, Armstrong often occupied center stage multiple times during individual recordings, through spoken banter, breaks, vocal choruses, and extended solos.[64] In

"Gully Low Blues," Armstrong steps into the spotlight on five prominent occasions (table 2).

In his rendition of the two blues choruses, the speechlike timbre of Armstrong's voice combines with his frank delivery to represent both the struggle and the glory present in the blues. His rough, gravelly voice displays a vital brand of black masculinity that was only just beginning to have a wider opportunity to present itself on recordings, yet one that was already known to the black listening public.[65] Though scholars have concentrated primarily on his trumpet playing, vocal contributions by Armstrong and other band members turn up on more than half of the Hot Five and Hot Seven recordings in various forms, including blues numbers, scat interludes, comic interjections, and spoken introductions. Armstrong's flexible voice in "Gully Low Blues" produces a wide range of expressive sensibilities. To indicate the strain and trouble of the blues, he strains his voice at the start of each line, singing at the top of his narrow vocal range in the manner of old blues shouters while identifying himself, by way of his gritty timbre and regional accent, as having southern roots. Yet, by the time he reaches the longer vowels at the end of each line, his vocals have dropped down to the gentler, rounded tones of his chest voice, a more comfortable range at which he can extend softer vocal sounds. Such relief becomes particularly soothing for listeners when Armstrong provides responses to his own phrases, first establishing musical tension, then offering possible resolution. The sensibility presented by the comic vaudeville-style line ("I know why you treat me so bad") also lessens the pent-up tension and switches attention to the performer and away from the sorrow of the blues.

Armstrong's voice sounds unpolished here in comparison to his subsequent "sweeter" vocal style, unrefined in relation to pop songs like "Sweethearts on Parade," and less festive than up-tempo numbers like "Heebie Jeebies." In addition, except for his memorable delivery of syncopated triplets in the second line, his spare vocals contain little of the rhythmic pyrotechnics of his trumpet playing. These blues are neither permanently tortured nor naively optimistic. He instead occupies several positions that sometimes complement and sometimes contradict one another. This appears to be a result primarily of what contemporary blues fans must have noticed in this recording: Armstrong has no respondent besides his own voice throughout the vocal passages of the song and therefore had to vary his delivery to create musical contrast. Unlike the blues women he accompanied, thereby creating a dialogue between their voices and his trumpet, Armstrong's voice provides the melody and occupies nearly all the sonic space for the duration of each vocal chorus in "Gully

Low Blues." Unlike a solo bluesman like Robert Johnson, who alternated between voice and guitar, Armstrong did not have the luxury in the age of single-track recording to move as seamlessly from voice to trumpet and back.[66] On the one hand, since Armstrong's vocal approach in the second chorus of the blues does not radically differ from the first, he seems able only to suggest but not to deliver musical redemption. On the other hand, Armstrong's control, flexibility, and omnipresent voice in these choruses indicate that eventually he will.

After Armstrong finishes singing, Johnny Dodds enters for a second time. In contrast to his earlier chorus and to Armstrong's vocal descents, Dodds and his clarinet mine the deep, gully low range for which he was well regarded. During his solo, listeners remain poised for something dramatic to happen, partly to balance the interruption that disturbed his first solo, and partly because his lower range sounds so striking in comparison to his earlier entrance. Dodds issues tentative flares, melodic lines that sprout upward but never reach the top of his range, but he closes without fully responding to the unpredictable departure that marked his first solo. Listeners remain in the musical land of the gully low blues. It turns out, however, that Dodds has well prepared listeners for the song's climactic chorus.

Following the clarinet's tentative exploration of its low register, Armstrong's piercing solo at the top of the trumpet's range sounds all the more triumphant. Entering a few beats before the new blues stanza begins, Armstrong sounds three proud bursts that herald the arrival of the most dramatic section of "Gully Low Blues." Armstrong solos over the same twelve-bar blues progression, but he plays with ferocious power in a virtuosic display that threatens to redefine its underlying musical form. His celebrated chorus consists of six two-bar phrases, the first five of which begin with the type of sustained note that inspired generations of trumpeters—high C—succeeded by nimble lines that cascade down a couple of octaves (example 10).[67] Not only does Armstrong extend each high note of this slow blues, he accentuates these pitches by "ripping" up to them, employing a rough-edged glissando technique to shoot up quickly to the desired pitch.[68] Once he reaches the summit, Armstrong uses his renowned "shake," which contributes a sirenlike vibrato to accentuate each long note. Thus, in addition to hitting high C, Armstrong raises the intensity of each note. His boisterous calls ring out like an alarm bell, grabbing audiences by the collar. Such grand gestures were even more riveting in live performance, since Armstrong would stand poised and upright at such moments, his fingers flying off the trumpet valves to signal each high blast before visibly shaking his horn. His chorus turns into a series of bravura gestures, which he

Example 10. Louis Armstrong's trumpet solo in "Gully Low Blues."

performs not just once but five times. Apparently unbounded, he pushes higher, stepping up to high D in the course of the third phrase, before spiraling down to more solid ground.

Armstrong's solo draws on earlier sections of "Gully Low Blues" by pulling together the repeated dominants that concluded his opening fanfare, the high C's played by Dodds in his first solo, and the series of descents featured in his vocal choruses. But in stark contrast to his straining vocals, Armstrong's trumpet sounds commanding in his upper register.[69] Such high, beaconing notes, which to many musicians of his day seemed impossible and among his early record-buying public inspired awe, here sound completely in the pocket for Armstrong.[70] He nails every one, holds each for as long as he desires, and then repeats himself again and again. The descending lines that follow supply a sense of relief, and their rhythmic and melodic variety suggests his capability of continuing the entire process indefinitely.[71] One commentator has likened the falling figures to "tails dangling from cats on a rafter," another to "classic blues phrase[s] in the gutbucket tradition," but Armstrong's message in "Gully Low Blues" suggests that a more apt comparison might be made to the streamers dangling from the ceiling of a majestic ballroom on Chicago's South Side.[72] These sparkling moments combine grace—the initial triplet rhythms and leaps bring to mind a dancer confidently skipping down a staircase a few steps at a time—with inevitability, as we learn to expect him to tumble down each time to the bottom of the trumpet's range. It was not as if these musical gestures were born at this moment, as we shall later see in more detail. For that matter, Armstrong would recycle elements of this solo the next year as part of his famous introduction to "West End Blues," which closes with a virtually identical quotation of measure 5 from his solo in "Gully Low Blues."[73] Yet, though other jazz instrumentalists had employed similar gestures, few had done so with such authority.[74] Like the dramatic teleological approach he applied in live performance, this repeating pattern creates a suggestive metaphor for the song, as every resounding high C can be heard as a constant attempt to strive for something more.[75] Just as each sighlike descending figure registers the amount of effort required to surmount the gully low blues, each successive burst displays a firm determination to keep trying.

I suggested earlier that this solo nearly destroys blues form in the process of redefining it. By this I mean that Armstrong's trumpet so powerfully states each two-bar phrase and so forcefully strikes the series of high C's that it begins to obscure the underlying chord progression. Like the prolonged high note in his acclaimed solo on "West End Blues" the following year, his trumpet demands so much attention that listeners begin to lose track of the rhythm section. The band may proceed to the next chord of the twelve-bar blues, dividing the time-honored form into three sections of four bars, but listeners must wait for Armstrong to flesh out its expected harmonies. When he picks up his trumpet, Armstrong asserts his independence by working against standard blues practice. His trumpet call flies above the band and snubs the conventions they follow, stamping its own outline on the blues. Because of its special imprint, Armstrong's solo lingers in memory for the remainder of "Gully Low Blues." No other soloists follow Armstrong as the band nears the limit of available recording time. Undoubtedly, OKeh Records was pleased that their budding star occupied this climactic position, and it is difficult to imagine another soloist wanting to succeed him. To wind down the tune, the ensemble joins together for a final blues chorus, escorted by Armstrong's melodic lead and Dodds's flourishes, then caps the performance with a brief arranged coda of the sort employed by society bands and vaudeville orchestras. The novelty ending has been dismissed by some critics as sounding "corny,"[76] but its polish also reminds listeners of the band's connection to urban cabarets and theater orchestras, prolonging the professionalism that typifies "Gully Low Blues" to the last note.

The glorious uplift of Armstrong's trumpet solo most clearly signals musical deliverance from the depths of the gully low blues. If a musician can play like this, how blue can he possibly be? Asserting a variety of personae and featuring the show-stopping displays he had developed during five years of experience in the North, Armstrong provides sonic evidence of how he won't be "gully no' mo'." For that matter, as we have seen, Armstrong's musical vision was not limited to a single trumpet chorus. His role as ensemble leader and his prominence in the song's creation—as its composer, lyricist, main musician, singer, and trumpet virtuoso—signal the accomplishments that marked his increasing popularity as a jazz soloist. In the process of displaying his crowd-pleasing flair throughout the series of Hot Five and Hot Seven records, whether in the form of brilliant horn solos, rollicking dance numbers, or comic vaudeville send-ups, he displayed independence, leadership, and what the black community then called "race pride." Applications of such praise to jazz musicians in the African American press were admittedly rare at the time. Because of concerns about what constituted the proper public image for the black community, columnists for the *Defender* initially dismissed the contributions of popular blues and jazz artists and reserved their accolades for black achievement in the loftier arenas of European symphonic, operatic, and concert music traditions.[77] And despite the subsequent elevation of jazz, critical perspectives on Armstrong's musical significance have not always highlighted this aspect of his legacy. Late in his career, Armstrong lamented, "I think that I have always done *great* things about *uplifting* my *race* (the Negroes, *of course*) but *wasn't appreciated*."[78] Yet, at the time that his band recorded "Gully Low Blues," here was a young African American man, not yet thirty, who had made the journey north, adjusted rapidly to city life, and launched his entertainment career. He was "the talk of Chicago," according to a trumpet-playing admirer, Walter Fuller, whose family had recently migrated from Tennessee.[79] He played the latest, hottest music—one promotional flyer called him the "Master of Modernism"—and had established a foothold in an extremely competitive industry. And he produced music that not only spoke directly to the concerns of his local community but also had begun to make an impression on the broader American public. Few people in Chicago of the late 1920s better exemplified professionalism, creativity, and race pride than Louis Armstrong.

HERALDS OF THE GREAT MIGRATION

With respect to Armstrong's legacy, Thomas Brothers observes, "Not only is [Armstrong] a witness to the cultural dynamics of the Great Migration, his musical achievement can be understood only as a *product* of this phenomenon."[80] Songs like "Gully Low Blues" further suggest that we may more fully account for the influence of this music by recognizing that the Great Migration was also spurred on by the exploits of Armstrong and his contemporaries. That musicians acted as heralds for the Great Migration emerges from the recollections of those musical migrants quoted earlier, among them Louis and Lil Hardin Armstrong, Milt Hinton, Thomas Dorsey, Mahalia Jackson, and Clarence Williams. In fact, many musicians advanced the Great Migration by taking direct action. According to Sidney Bechet, as soon as New Orleans musicians began to land jobs at the top Chicago clubs during the 1910s, "they was all writing back to New Orleans that work was plentiful, telling the New Orleans musicianers to come up."[81] Buster Bailey, a clarinetist who migrated in 1919, concurred: "All my friends were going. There was better money there, I thought, and there was a little girl who had gone there that I wanted to follow. At the time, everybody from New Orleans and many people east of the Mississippi and as far west as Arkansas were migrating North. The word was there was lots of money in Chicago."[82] Even though Armstrong himself initially felt "afraid to leave home because so many of the boys from home had gone up North and came back in such bad shape," Joe Oliver's triumphs and repeated invitations convinced Armstrong to overcome his fears.[83] All told, hundreds of southern black musicians left for the North, Midwest, or West between 1917 and 1930; in Burton Peretti's estimation, "about 6 of 7 major black jazz musicians born in the South before 1915 migrated to the North in 4 decades."[84]

Prominent artists like Armstrong also inspired listeners around the country through their performances and recordings. Consequently, as William Kenney has demonstrated, Chicago jazz in this era came to possess "a powerful cultural symbolism for southern African-Americans."[85] In his memoirs Danny Barker, a New Orleans guitarist who rode the same Illinois Central line to Chicago, describes the effect of Armstrong's releases in the late 1920s:

> Now of course there was much talk of Chicago, because so many musicians went there seeking fame and fortune. And my greatest inspiration was the regular flow of Armstrong records on OKeh, each to me and the other young musicians a masterpiece in jazz playing. All the alert jazz musicians and local music lovers waited anxiously for each of Louis Armstrong's latest releases, as there was much to learn from these classics. I

went to Dave Karonsky's South Rampart Street record store and listened to records and checked on when Louis's next great record would be released and arrive in New Orleans.[86]

Similarly, Roy Eldridge, who would eventually inherit the mantle of jazz trumpet virtuoso, heard Armstrong's recordings years before watching him perform live. Looking back decades later, Eldridge could still remember the moment in 1927, while he was performing in a traveling show in Omaha, Nebraska, when a visiting musician from Chicago introduced him to the double-sided disc containing "Wild Man Blues" and "Gully Low Blues."[87]

The music lovers mentioned by Barker were part of a larger national black audience, men and women who were eager to learn more about possibilities in the North. Whether on the South Side of Chicago or in rural Mississippi, these listeners were exposed to various aspects of contemporary urban culture through Armstrong's music, a common process that continues today in various musical genres. Fans who were already busy managing the transition to urban life could listen for musical encouragement of their own aspirations. Those farther from the city could learn about unfamiliar places, new activities, and the latest slang terms, or they could daydream about what the urban world held in store. On Armstrong's recordings with the Hot Five and Hot Seven one can hear echoes of 1920s Chicago, inscriptions of cultural memory that capture, in the recent words of Robert O'Meally, "how it felt to be human at the time and place when the language of jazz was being created."[88] Reflections of life in a bustling urban environment are to be found in titles such as "Savoy Blues," which celebrated the opening of a lavish ballroom that served Chicago's black community, and "Sunset Café Stomp," which took its name from a popular South Side club where Armstrong and his colleagues performed. The lively cross rhythms of "Struttin' with Some Barbecue" project urban swagger as they commemorate Armstrong's favorite rib joint at 48th and State, and "A Monday Date" contains a reference to Mrs. Searcy, a well-known Windy City bootlegger, which serves as a reminder that all the Hot Five and Hot Seven records were made during Prohibition.[89] After Armstrong reshuffled the membership of his studio band to incorporate musicians with whom he was playing live, his groups also recorded songs they were performing together at Chicago nightclubs, a decision that integrated additional urban touches into the music.[90] The arrival of a new Armstrong release, every six or eight weeks, thus brought the latest word from Chicago, delivering news beyond the latest display of jazz techniques.

Just as the *Defender* editorial staff contributed to the Great Migration with its version of Chicago cheerleading, so too did the northern-based record industry work to market urban glamour. Often both types of boost-erism operated side by side, for by the time the Hot Seven recorded "Gully Low Blues," the *Defender* was running frequent advertisements and occa-sional weekly inserts for the latest race records.[91] Readers learned of Arm-strong's performances and musical activities through the paper's weekly music column. As Armstrong developed into "a cultural hero among black folk," adoring fans copied his approach to the trumpet, his singing, his hair-style, and his flair for fashion.[92] Rex Stewart, who took over as lead trum-pet in the Fletcher Henderson Orchestra upon Armstrong's return to Chi-cago, became enraptured: "I tried to walk like him, talk like him. I bought shoes and a suit like the 'Great One' wore."[93] Aspiring trumpeters copied his recorded solos note for note and pored through published collections of his trumpet breaks. "A musician in Chicago in the early twenties," recalled Armstrong of this star-making atmosphere, "[was] treated and respected just like—some kind of a God."[94] Accordingly, OKeh's promotional mate-rials portrayed Armstrong's band in formal attire, Lil Hardin in a fancy dress and the men wearing "wing-collared shirts, butterfly bow ties, sharply tailored tuxedos, gilets, and patent leather shoes."[95] Kid Ory recalled that photos of Armstrong were so popular at the time that "for a while the OKeh people gave away a picture of Louis to everyone that bought one of the rec-ords."[96] These early publicity shots still retain their appeal. The same pho-tograph of a nattily dressed Armstrong used in the *Defender* to promote the release of "Gully Low Blues" now adorns the cover of the 2000 Columbia box set, *Louis Armstrong: The Complete Hot Five and Hot Seven Record-ings*.[97] The rapidly growing media and entertainment industries ensured that audiences far and wide saw images of this successful young man, who was gradually making a larger name for himself.

Considered within this historical framework, the recording of "Gully Low Blues" symbolized African American achievement in an arena of American popular culture just opening up to black performers. I do not claim that "Gully Low Blues" held the same meanings for every listener, es-pecially those who wished to distance themselves from jazz or from this song's thematic material, but the recording was well suited to resonate with a large audience of fellow migrants and to rouse them with its representa-tion of upward mobility. Though its incorporation of the blues and New Or-leans polyphony appealed to those familiar with these earlier traditions, the dramatic structure of "Gully Low Blues" and its integration of urban mu-sical techniques indicated that Armstrong and his colleagues could prosper in their new surroundings. Armstrong's bold assertion of black masculinity displayed a type of power that was so often unavailable to members of his community. As Krin Gabbard has remarked on the symbolic weight of Armstrong's trumpet, "Jazz provided its practitioners with wide latitude for expressing masculinity while avoiding the less mediated assertions of phallic power that were regularly punished by white culture."[98] It was as if his confident sound implied that better opportunities awaited in the North. For new residents on Chicago's South Side—in particular, men like Armstrong holding well-paying jobs for the first time—such cultural messages offered aural reinforcement in a new environment. All told, Armstrong's musical leadership, his constant presence throughout the tune, and his dazzling trumpet playing produced a steadfast self-assurance that listeners could hold on to during a turbulent era of transition.

In her influential study of twentieth-century black fiction, Farah Griffin identifies key "African-American migration narratives," in which literary characters depart from rural or southern towns, make their way to the cosmopolitan city, adapt to their new surroundings, and balance their ongoing relationship between their urban present and rural past.[99] If we apply Griffin's framework to Armstrong's music, "Gully Low Blues" may be understood as presenting a densely compressed migration narrative that brims with hope and confidence. Indeed, one of the most noticeable achievements of this recording is that it deals directly with a set of deep-rooted cultural tensions, yet it demonstrates how the musical expression of cultural contestation need not sound like a fractured struggle. By crafting its narrative of empowerment, "Gully Low Blues" supports Robert O'Meally's contention that the music created by Armstrong with the Hot Five and Hot Seven provides "not merely a reflection of the modern world" but also "an encoded strategy for *surviving* modern times."[100] In this way "Gully Low Blues" can be heard as supplying an optimistic soundtrack, albeit a partial one, for the experiences of the Great Migration. Armstrong was by no means alone in carrying out this task, for much of the recorded blues during the 1920s and 1930s "came to Delta dwellers as the sound of hope and promise, of faraway cities with good jobs and a more liberal racial climate."[101] At the same time, however, Griffin's framework does not imply that all migration narratives will end happily. On the contrary, the complex and often difficult process of migration prompted musicians of the time to create many different sorts of narratives that addressed a broader range of experiences than those "Gully Low Blues" expresses.

Alternative narratives were needed to signify the wider cultural debate prompted by migration, for once southern migrants reached the big city, what they found did not always meet their expectations. In 1928, the year following the release of "Gully Low Blues," Fred Smith arrived in Chicago with the highest of hopes, which were dampened by a sudden dose of reality: "My family had heard so many things about the big city with the bright lights, and they all wanted to see those lights. But when I came to Chicago, things were not all roses and candy. There were hard times, what with finding an apartment that I could afford with the pay that I was getting and then bringing my family here, and that also meant buying new furniture, clothing."[102] For unprepared migrants, and perhaps especially those who had been won over by *Defender* editorials or summoned by the call of a jazz musician's horn, adapting to the city meant experiencing growing pains that were to be expected for newcomers to a large urban environment: feeling isolated in an impersonal metropolis; being overwhelmed by the large crowds and the fast pace of life; worrying about higher rates of violence and crime; attempting to stay ahead of the higher cost of living; and becoming homesick for old friends and family.

Chicago presented extra challenges for southern migrants, including its bitterly cold winters and its systematically segregated and overcrowded housing. Recalling his first trip to the South Side in the summer of 1918, Langston Hughes declared, "For neither love nor money could you find a decent place to live."[103] That a "promised land" would flaunt its racial hostility in the form of economic discrimination proved even more disheartening. Although greater employment possibilities were available in Chicago, African Americans nevertheless were pushed toward factory jobs and domestic labor and prevented from pursuing most professional careers. Having fled the South, recent migrants still found themselves excluded from certain recreational venues, amusement parks, swimming pools, and many of the celebrated theaters that featured black entertainers. It was in Chicago, after all, where *Amos 'n' Andy* premiered, a year before the release of "Gully Low Blues," and this modern-day minstrel show went on to become one of the most popular radio programs in U.S. history. For newcomers who were unable to benefit from the possibilities available in the North and those who missed the southern way of life, migration could be terribly disorienting and disappointing. To deal with the bumps and bruises that took their toll on new city dwellers and to acknowledge the sorrows and struggles faced by migrants consequently required capturing a broader panorama of their experiences, including many oppositional responses.

It was the classic blues queens of the 1920s, most prominently, who first registered their apprehensions and concerns about urban life in recordings such as Monette Moore's "House Rent Blues" and Mamie Smith's "Lost Opportunity Blues." The most famous of these artists, Bessie Smith, produced songs about the class divide ("Poor Man's Blues"), the cost of housing

("Baby, Won't You Please Come Home"), and the emotional and physical costs of domestic labor ("Washwoman's Blues"). Male blues singers joined in to file their grievances as well; Big Bill Broonzy cut right to the chase in "Starvation Blues." As a result, listeners received conflicting messages about migration from different musical sources. Just as the energetic train whistle that introduces Earl Hines's "Chicago Rhythm" beckoned migrants to board the Illinois Central, Ida Cox's "I've Got the Blues for Rampart Street" suggested that passengers might want to hop right back off. Some listeners could be stirred by songs that championed liberty and freedom, such as "Jim Crow Blues" (1929), in which Cow Cow Davenport proclaims his departure from the land of Jim Crow and heads for Chicago. But for others, the challenges of the big city and the feeling of homesickness proved too great. Acknowledging the nostalgic desire that prompted some migrants to turn back for home, Bessie Smith was one of several to record "Dixie Flyer Blues," "Florida Bound Blues," and "Gulf Coast Blues," all three of which concern departure from the cold, impersonal North for sunnier climes down South.

Musical expressions that grow out of pivotal historical moments and reflect deep-seated cultural tensions are bound to be complex and contradictory. Furthermore, as Jacqueline Stewart points out in her study of African American cinema at the start of the twentieth century, "migration narratives . . . do not necessarily follow a straight path toward empowerment or disillusionment."[104] Perhaps, then, it is unsurprising that in the blues song that most directly addresses the subject of migration to Chicago, the city ends up functioning simultaneously as a site of ultimate desire, grave anguish, and utmost sorrow. The narrative of "Chicago Bound Blues (Famous Migration Blues)," composed in 1923 by Lovie Austin and recorded first by Ida Cox and soon after by Bessie Smith, describes a southern woman's desperation to join her man in Chicago. At first the city stands as the ultimate symbol of hope, the prospective site of the couple's reconciliation. The pain of being apart, however, becomes so unbearable that in the final stanza the female protagonist envisions the tragic headline that will run in the next day's issue of the *Defender*, telling of her death from separation. The multiple perspectives offered by this song correspond to the varied range of migrant experiences and, unlike "Gully Low Blues," present a vivid example of how cultural debate in this era also took musical shape in the form of conflicted agony. As Hazel Carby has pointed out in her analysis of classic women's blues, the experience of migration often produced contentious experiences for black men and women, especially when men departed and women were left behind. Full of buoyancy and freedom, clashes and quarrels, overwhelming delight and profound sadness, this rich body of music thus "embodied the social relations and contradictions of black displacement: of rural migration and the urban flux."[105]

By the time he recorded "Gully Low Blues," Armstrong himself was already very familiar with a diverse set of migration narratives and had contributed his performance skills to many other blues-based recordings. As an accompanist for a number of blues singers, Armstrong had played the cornet on "Pratt City Blues," in which Bertha "Chippie" Hall sings about leaving the city for her hometown, and had teamed with Fletcher Henderson to accompany Maggie Jones's rendition of "Poor House Blues." Indeed, one of his most celebrated performances during his time in New York City involved accompanying Bessie Smith on her recording of "St. Louis Blues," the song by W. C. Handy that tells in its second verse of a woman losing her man to an urban "St. Louis woman" with "her powder and her store-bought hair." Not surprisingly, Armstrong's "Gully Low Blues" does not epitomize the only type of migration narrative in his repertoire. In addition to depicting different sides of Chicago life, his songs with the Hot Five and Hot Seven occasionally touch on the melancholy experienced by fellow migrants, such as the forlorn protagonist of "Lonesome Blues," who implores a long-distance beloved to send a letter. But instead of focusing on the despair of urban existence, a musical strategy with which he was clearly familiar, Armstrong's music in this period, as well as later in his career, often drew on his legendarily cheerful outlook, a quality that also infused his public persona. What is distinctive about his performance in "Gully Low Blues," as compared to so many of the blues tunes discussed above, is that he treats the challenge of adapting to the North as a necessary fact of life. Rather than cast doubt on the decision to migrate, as if that option were no longer negotiable, this recording displays greater concern with learning how to cope with, and flourish in, one's new urban surroundings.

"A SON OF THE SOUTH"

Perhaps the most efficient strategy for adapting quickly to urban life in the North would have been to cut all ties with the South and pretend the past had never existed. Indeed, for the Nobel Prize–winning author Toni Morrison, looking back on this era after the passing of several generations, the Great Migration came to represent the loss of and departure from southern cultural traditions, an experience that symbolized for her what one literary scholar describes as a "radical discontinuity in black history."[106] Such a divide may have grown over successive decades of urbanization, but Armstrong's attitude toward this issue is distinctive for how steadfastly he aimed to maintain a sense of continuity with his southern roots long after his own migration. Rather than distancing himself from the past, Armstrong shared the sentiments expressed by the novelist Richard Wright, a fellow migrant who arrived in Chicago in 1927, at the conclusion of his autobiography: "I was not leaving the South to forget the South. . . . Yet, deep down, I knew that I could not really leave the South, for my feelings had already been formed by the South, for there had been slowly instilled into my personality and consciousness, black though I was, the culture of the South. So, in leaving, I was taking a part of the South to transplant in alien soil."[107] Though delighted by his success in the North, Armstrong remained openly proud of his southern heritage. He incorporated southern imagery and allusions in his recordings of the 1920s, ranging from "Southern Stomps," which he recorded as part of King Oliver's Creole Jazz Band, to his vocal duet with May Alix, "Big Butter and Egg Man," in which he portrays a big spender from down South.[108] Migration thus helps us to understand Armstrong's career from the perspective of Farah Griffin's theoretical framework, since he continued steadily to produce musical migration narratives that tried to balance his urban present with his southern past.

More specifically, Armstrong drew on the music from his formative years in New Orleans, evidenced by his commitment to the blues, collective polyphony, and traditional repertory as well as his ideas for song titles, lyrical content, and spoken passages on individual recordings.[109] Expressing the deep feelings he had for the city, Armstrong recorded many tunes associated with New Orleans, among them "When the Saints Go Marching In," "Way Down Yonder in New Orleans," and "Do You Know What It Means to Miss New Orleans?" in which he at once commemorates the city and laments his self-imposed exile. According to William Kenney, Armstrong adopted this nostalgic strategy as soon as he departed the Crescent City. It was his initial experience as a riverboat musician traveling up and down the Mississippi that "set into motion a lifetime of exile from his southern home, forcing him to translate for new audiences the music he had pioneered back in New Orleans."[110] After he reached Chicago, Armstrong maintained this nostalgic stance on recordings with King Oliver such as "Canal Street Blues" and "New Orleans Stomp." Armstrong subsequently paid his own musical tribute by recording tunes with the Hot Five that he had first heard in his hometown, including "Ory's Creole Trombone" and "Basin Street Blues," and he coined the title "Yes, I'm in the Barrel" after a common saying "from the good old days in New Orleans."[111] In his public interviews and published writings Armstrong revealed that he also tried to conjure up memories of his early days while performing individual tunes onstage and in the studio: "I'm doing something different all the time, but I always think of them fine old cats way down in New Orleans . . . and when I play my music, that's what I'm listening to."[112] When he recorded "Potato Head Blues" with the Hot Seven, Armstrong recalled, he felt it was if he were looking "direct into the Pelican Dance Hall, at Gravier and Rampart Streets in New Orleans, during the days of the First World War."[113] How much of an influence such practices had on individual performances is difficult to quantify, of course, but what can be said is that Armstrong's music of the 1920s not only captured certain trials and triumphs of the Great Migration but also exhibited the shared bonds to southern culture that he and fellow migrants continued to nurture.

Alongside Alberta Hunter, King Oliver, and all the other northern migrants whose music integrated southern techniques and themes, Armstrong participated in a much larger venture that occupied blues and jazz musicians in the 1920s. Since individual artists and the music industry paid close attention to matters of local and regional identity, blues fans could choose from recordings set in a wide range of southern locations, including Ida Cox's "Blue Kentucky Blues," her companion piece "Kentucky Man Blues," and Bessie Smith's "Louisiana Low Down Blues." Likewise, homesick migrants or listeners filled with local pride could search for recordings by regionally identified performers such as Memphis Slim, the team of Georgia Tom and Tampa Red, or Sippie Wallace, who was known as "the Texas Nightingale." Armstrong took frequent advantage of this strategy. By the time he formed the Hot Five, he had already recorded "Alabamy Bound" and "Memphis Bound" with the Fletcher Henderson Orchestra and accompanied Bessie Smith on "Nashville Woman's Blues" and Alberta Hunter on "Texas Moaner Blues." Likewise, over the course of a few months in early 1926, Armstrong recorded "Georgia Man" with the blues singer Bertha "Chippie" Hill, "Georgia Grind" with the Hot Five, and "Georgia Bo Bo" with Lil's Hot Shots. The composite nature of Armstrong's listening audience explains why such recordings were produced. A tune like "Georgia Grind" could appeal at once to consumers who were old enough to be familiar with the original 1915 composition by Spencer Williams and to new fans of recorded blues who appreciated Lil and Louis delivering its suggestive lyrics about doing the "dirty Georgia grind." The title also could be marketed to anyone who had previously purchased Armstrong's Hot Five records, to recent northern migrants with ties to Georgia, and to listeners who were still living in the Peach State.

That regionally specific titles were released alongside songs with generalized titles that evoked rural Southern life, such as "Down Home Blues,"

"Down South Blues," and "Gully Low Blues," testifies to how firmly many African American migrants attempted to retain ties to the South. Since northbound migration inevitably produced dislocation and loss, black migrants attempted to build communities that "took on looks and sounds and institutions that had been marked as southern."[114] They reproduced the same kinds of churches, clubs, and social organizations and preserved familiar customs by "continuing to sing, sell, eat, and dress as they had 'back home.'"[115] Because of Chicago's strictly segregated housing and the tendency of family and friends to congregate in the same neighborhood, migrants from particular regions often lived close by one another upon reaching the city. When Milt Hinton arrived in Chicago, he felt as if he had not left the South, since "just about all the people I grew up with came from small towns in Mississippi."[116] Some newcomers chose to retain close connections to their original homes, making the trip to Chicago a temporary sojourn, whereas those with the means traveled back and forth whenever they could, including Big Bill Broonzy, who "would go back [home] every time I got enough money to get a ticket."[117]

Mirroring the cultural climate in which he lived, Armstrong's music in this era arose from the interaction of what Guthrie Ramsey has termed "southernisms," or transported southern cultural practices, with the established urban culture he encountered in the North.[118] As an emerging star within the commercial music industry, he appealed to the latest sensibilities by integrating urban influences in his music—including careful arrangements, cabaret-style gestures, new repertory, relevant lyrical themes, harmonic advances, and more—but he did so without turning his back completely on southern culture and his New Orleans roots.[119] By navigating these cultural and musical divides in songs like "Gully Low Blues," and by producing what has been described by Brian Harker as "New Orleans style in chic Northern clothing," the recordings by Armstrong and the Hot Five and Hot Seven illustrate how southern musical traditions, rather than being supplanted on account of migration, became vital for manufacturing northern black urban culture.[120] Instead of segregating the rural South from the urban North, jazz became a site where musical practices from both regions collided in productive musical tension, exemplifying another key avenue by which cultural contestation has shaped the history of American music.

The musical and cultural negotiations necessitated by the Great Migration also hold the potential to reframe our understanding of Armstrong's musical life. Because of the complexities of migration, I do not claim that "Gully Low Blues" is symptomatic of all Armstrong performances, or of all his recordings with the Hot Five and Hot Seven; however, I believe that migration can provide a valuable lens for reconsidering later developments in his career. What more might we learn, for instance, about Armstrong's recording of "West End Blues" (1928), once we acknowledge its New Orleans lineage as a piece composed by Armstrong's mentor, King Oliver, and named after a popular African American resort on the shores of Lake Pontchartrain? Indeed, this Hot Five version of a southern-inspired tune integrates touches of the urban and urbane with traditional jazz and blues elements, from Earl Hines's rollicking Harlem stride chords to his elegant, classically inspired runs, from Armstrong's show-stopping trumpet cadenza to his memorably scatted responses to the calls of the clarinetist Jimmy Strong. Are we to understand the elements shared by Armstrong's opening solo in "West End Blues" and his earlier solo in "Gully Low Blues" as being motivated purely by musical reasons—recycling a favorite, preconceived, or familiar trumpet gesture—or by shared cultural resonance? Likewise, what meanings are to be discovered by approaching "Chicago Breakdown" (1927) as a byproduct of migration, since it was composed by Jelly Roll Morton and recorded by the Carroll Dickerson Orchestra, which featured Armstrong, Hines, and other migrant musicians who performed at the Sunset Café? One may look for guidance in William Kenney's suggestive analyses of what he calls Armstrong's "river recordings," tracks released by Victor Records in the early 1930s that touch on themes concerning life on the Mississippi River, among them "Mississippi Basin," Mighty River," and "Dusky Stevedore." Interpreting this set of recordings in light of Armstrong's northern migration, Kenney understands "He's a Son of the South" (1931) not simply as an expression of southern pride but as a musical statement that "turns the Great Migration into a seemingly effortless but stylish strut."[121] Likewise, another of these recordings, "When It's Sleepy Time Down South" (1931), features a spoken introduction that addresses northern migration, as the city-dwelling Armstrong bumps into another recent migrant and they acknowledge a shared longing for their former home.

Armstrong's continuing negotiation of the cultural tensions surrounding music and migration also may explain his shifting reception by African American listeners during subsequent stages of his career. As much as the river recordings register some measure of thematic continuity, a significant twist in Armstrong's musical path occurred at the end of the 1920s, a change in direction that has been subject to heated controversy among jazz scholars. Over the years, Armstrong has been criticized sharply for changing his musical priorities following the Hot Five and Hot Seven sessions, stepping away from his role as a virtuosic instrumentalist on his jazz and blues numbers of the 1920s and turning into more of a popular showman who specialized in delivering personalized renditions of Tin Pan Alley songs during the 1930s. This debate is typically couched in terms of art versus entertainment: Armstrong traded in an aesthetic strategy that prized risk-taking innovation in favor of a more conservative musical approach that led to greater economic rewards. During this period it is undeniable that Armstrong attracted a larger audience, which he maintained for the rest of his career, but this musical transformation was related also to the economic devastation wrought by the Great Depression. Wretched conditions in the early 1930s turned Chicago's South Side into what Mahalia Jackson lamented as "a place of broken hopes and dreams" and helped spread the gospel music of Thomas Dorsey, which presented a newly articulated expression of spiritual hope.[122] In the world of popular entertainment, the Depression prompted an increased demand for escapism, fantasy, and nostalgia. Consequently, it may be argued that Armstrong's lighter fare of the 1930s supplied a new type of musical sustenance for his faithful listeners, just as it attracted additional fans who appreciated his more broadly appealing message.

Without dismissing the musical aspects of Armstrong's direction entering the 1930s, what I propose was just as significant was his changing relationship to the community of African American migrants in Chicago. By producing distinctive interpretations of popular tunes of the day, Armstrong remained an icon of successful migration: adapting to the cultural transformations around him, advancing his mounting stardom, and gaining entry into cinema, radio, and other aspects of the entertainment world. But in the process of courting a national and international following that crossed racial and ethnic lines, Armstrong and his music gradually lost contact with urban life on Chicago's South Side. A creative turn away from producing migration narratives may be inevitable for any migrant musician who becomes acclimated to new surroundings. And perhaps this was unavoidable for someone like Armstrong, whose touring opportunities took him elsewhere in the States and overseas to Europe for several years. Whatever the causes of this change of direction, Armstrong's embracing a more conventional repertory of American popular song meant that his music increasingly fell outside the realm of traditional migration narratives and of Armstrong's experience in black Chicago. Rather than signifying simply a divide between artist and entertainer, Armstrong's transition in the early 1930s signals his changing relationship to his cultural surroundings and his adopted South Side community.

Paradoxically, this transformation resulted from both Armstrong's further migration, which took him beyond the Windy City, and the strength of his bonds with his original hometown. Armstrong eventually left Chicago behind, living his last several decades either touring or at home in Queens, New York, but his love for New Orleans and the South never faded. Over time, the intensity of Armstrong's nostalgia for the South in which he was raised, a nostalgia that helped him identify with other urban migrants during the Jazz Age, eventually led succeeding generations to view him as being behind the times. In particular, Armstrong's fondness for songs like "When It's Sleepy Time Down South," which became his signature piece as well as the one he recorded more than any other, initially helped broaden his fan base but ultimately contributed to a decline in his popularity among African American audiences. On the one hand, "Sleepy Time" directly acknowledges the community, experiences, and concerns of black migrants through both its introductory dialogue and its unabashed glorification of the mythical South. On the other hand, the song's lyrics, which include tributes to a southern mammy and the sound of banjos, rely on plantation-style imagery that evoked the practice of blackface minstrelsy. Over the course of his career, Armstrong also turned "Shine" into an early showpiece, recorded Stephen Foster's "Old Folks at Home," and released a version of "Dixie," the minstrel tune originally penned by Dan Emmett and later adopted as the Confederate national anthem. Such practices were so commonplace in the popular music world of the 1920s and 1930s that black audiences initially stuck by Armstrong. To those in the postwar period who sought more rapid gains in the fight for civil rights and racial equality, however, Armstrong appeared increasingly out of touch. He continued to draw on minstrelsy-derived stage behavior and to perform minstrel tunes and coon songs, "long after such tunes were in vogue and when they could have been excised from his repertoire in homage to his black audience's dislike of them."[123] By continuing to revisit nostalgic themes about the old South and failing to speak directly to the contemporary black experience, Armstrong eventually lost his symbolic position as a beacon of modern progress. In one respect, his wider visibility enabled him to make a greater mark on the American musical landscape, but this musical struggle to define a nation, originally framed by the concerns and experiences of local black communities, was recalibrated to address a different set of cultural tensions as he entered his latter decades.

As this shift in musical generations was taking place, the early accomplishments of Armstrong, and the blues queens who preceded him, pointed the way to the music that accompanied the next crucial phase of African

American migration occurring during and after World War II. Black migrants once more flocked to American cities to land jobs in wartime industries, and Chicago again became one of their primary destinations. Clothed in a new guise, the music of the blues accompanied this journey, too, as the voice of Jimmy Rushing, backed by the hard-swinging Count Basie Orchestra, would declare in the band's 1941 recording of "Going to Chicago." In the late 1940s and through the 1950s, musical themes of migration reclaimed their hold on the city's musical imagination and contributed anew to the formation of the nation's music. When Muddy Waters, Willie Dixon, Buddy Guy, and dozens of like-minded black migrants traveled from the rural South and developed the genre of the "Chicago blues"—an extremely influential combination of blues-based music, electric instruments, and rural-urban themes—the music of migration proved once again to be a vital and flexible wellspring from which to address contemporary encounters with northern urban life.

THE REDISCOVERY OF "GULLY LOW BLUES"

As this second significant phase of urban migration began to take shape, "Gully Low Blues" again took on new life. In 1940, more than a decade after its original release, a search by George Akavian of the OKeh archives, which had been purchased by Columbia Records, revealed that the original recording was in many respects a second take of a song that Armstrong and the Hot Seven had recorded the day before. Since alternative takes were normally wiped clean, "Gully Low Blues" is an extremely rare example of Armstrong's early approach to studio recording, and one that raises thorny issues concerning the intersection of jazz with improvisation, commerce, and off-color humor. The main question is why Armstrong rerecorded the same song the next day, using similar music but substituting a new title and different lyrics. The tune that surfaced in 1940 was subsequently released as "S. O. L. Blues," or "shit-out-of-luck blues," which leads to speculation that it was originally shelved because its content might have caused offense to either OKeh executives or the public.[124] According to Kid Ory, who played trombone on many of the original sessions, OKeh management typically kept its distance during the recording process, affording the artists free rein in the studio, but would step in to deliver a final verdict about whether a given track was acceptable for release.[125]

Several factors, however, argue against interpreting this episode as an attempt by a nervous corporation to avoid controversy. First, in contradiction to the coarse title of the re-release, the lyrical content of "S. O. L. Blues" contains nothing profane or lewd. In comparison, for example, to Armstrong's "Tight Like This" (1928), a risqué response to the popular bawdy blues tune "It's Tight Like That," the lyrics of "S. O. L. Blues" were in fact entirely clean, neither containing profanity nor quoting the song's title. In its single chorus Armstrong pledges to stay true to his woman as long as she is flush with money; as soon as the cash runs out, however, she will be plain out of luck. If OKeh executives were troubled by the song's title, it is more conceivable that they would have asked Armstrong to come up with a new one or gone ahead and changed it themselves to "Out of Luck Blues," "Out of Bucks Blues," or the like. After all, record executives had no qualms about releasing the song that Armstrong recorded the following day under the various titles of "Gully Low Blues" and "Mama, Why Do You Treat Me So?" Since Armstrong was not granted full authority over his music at that point in his career, it would have been highly implausible for him to insist that the original recording be given the title "S. O. L. Blues." If anything, he had extra incentive to release the original tune under any title chosen by OKeh, since his band's compensation consisted of a shared payment in the neighborhood of $100–$150 for each finished master disc. Like most of their musical contemporaries in this era, Armstrong and his colleagues sold the rights to their recordings outright and earned no royalties.

What seems more feasible is that OKeh executives desired a polished product that would improve on the entertainment value of the original recording, for a comparison between "S. O. L. Blues" and "Gully Low Blues" reveals differing musical priorities. The blueprint of "Gully Low Blues" mimics "S. O. L. Blues" in many significant ways, from its opening fanfare to the order of soloists to the final coda; the two new choruses on "Gully Low Blues" constitute the primary distinction. Whether a specific request was made, OKeh certainly would have preferred the extra vocal chorus of "Gully Low Blues," which provided greater opportunity to market the voice that had popularized "Heebie Jeebies" the previous year. Aesthetically, Armstrong's vocal delivery in "Gully Low Blues" is also better served by the new lyrics, especially by the extended vowel sounds that end each line and enable him to take further vocal liberties. In contrast, each line of "S. O. L. Blues" finishes very abruptly, and the harsh consonant sounds at the end of lines (e.g., "bucks") make it extremely awkward for Armstrong to credibly flesh out the remaining bars of each phrase.

The final coda of "S. O. L. Blues" highlights an additional concern for OKeh executives, since Armstrong and his band totally flub the ending. Unable to manage a convincing finish together, they fail to achieve the precision they demonstrated the following day on the rerehearsed conclusion of "Gully Low Blues." This passage may be less significant for jazz scholars who have homed in on Armstrong's trumpet solo, but early audiences who played a single disc at a time surely would have been distracted. As a result, the previous day's finale on "S. O. L. Blues" did not live up to the professionalism otherwise presented by Armstrong and the Hot Seven. This brings us to the issue that critics have had the most difficulty reconciling about "S. O. L. Blues" and "Gully Low Blues": their close musical similarities. The two songs share the same structure, and certain individual passages, including the fanfare and the coda, sound virtually alike. Armstrong also retained almost all the material for his trumpet solos from one day to the next. Both feature a series of five resounding high C's followed by Armstrong's careening descents, several of which are nearly identical. Likewise, the group remains faithful to the basic form, key, harmony, texture, tempo, and instrumental roles, which indicates how many of the most critical musical aspects of "Gully Low Blues" were designed in advance and not improvised on the spot.

In terms of the overarching interpretation I have posited, the survival of both recordings, and Armstrong's apparent pasting of alternative lyrics into an existing musical framework, seems to argue against a preconceived plan by the Hot Seven to make an overt musical statement on black migration; however, it would be unproductive to characterize this fertile cultural creation as the result of pure serendipity. Though configured much differently, the lyrics of both songs, after all, address the cultural tensions of class and gender that would have been understood by Armstrong's listeners. It is equally obvious that, just as he would have acknowledged that his band needed to practice the failed coda on "S. O. L. Blues," Armstrong understood how well the lyrics for "Gully Low Blues" fit into this musical narrative. For that matter, his own experiences and his future performances of *this* song, and not of "S. O. L. Blues," indicate how the lyrics and the recording came to hold personal meaning for him. Finally, this last-minute snag, which required extra time in the studio, displays Armstrong once more to have been a sophisticated professional, a leader able to craft new solutions for the musical problems at hand. In this way, the origin of "Gully Low Blues," just like its musical message and the final 78-rpm product, also signified how Armstrong was making a mark in Chicago.

Instead of designating this as a case of corporate censorship, I suggest that it was the opposing set of values represented by these two recordings that informed OKeh's decision to release "Gully Low Blues" and to bury "S. O. L. Blues" in the company archives. In choosing between the two songs, OKeh's promotional staff would have recognized how appropriately

"Gully Low Blues" evoked the image of Armstrong they were attempting to bring before the public. The recording contains fewer errors, features more of Armstrong's voice, and retains his equally powerful trumpet solo. Perhaps more pertinent to OKeh, and to their intended customers, is the lyrical message of "Gully Low Blues." The two otherwise similar songs construct distinct versions of masculinity and deliver strikingly divergent messages. While arguably a comic figure, the protagonist of "S. O. L. Blues" comes across as selfish and lazy, unable to fend for himself. He proclaims that he will move on to another woman the instant his current partner's money runs out. Armstrong's trumpet solo, though just as magnificent, sounds arrogant and aloof in this context. In contrast, the presentation of a confident masculinity in "Gully Low Blues" is framed within a more pleasing story that held wider appeal. Armstrong sings of cultural tensions involving region, class, and gender that were relevant to so many of his listeners, but instead of threatening to leave a problematic relationship, he asks for the chance to help put things back together. Indeed, his musical optimism accounts for much of the song's continuing appeal across time and beyond its original context. Capable and assured, Armstrong assumes the kind of responsibility so many of his fellow migrants were taking for themselves. Instead of relying on someone else, or running away from the task at hand, Armstrong promises to hoist himself to a higher level, to climb out and soar above the gully low blues.

4. Chinatown, Whose Chinatown?

Defining America's Borders with Musical Orientalism

Louis Armstrong played it hot, and it was a hit all over.

JEAN SCHWARTZ on "Chinatown, My Chinatown"

On 7 April 1894 the Hyperion Theater in New Haven, Connecticut, presented a performance of one of the era's most popular musical comedies, *A Trip to Chinatown*. Having made its debut in New York in 1891, the show already had established the record for longest-running Broadway musical, a mark it held for nearly three decades. It is unknown whether the nineteen-year-old Charles Ives attended the performance. He had arrived in New Haven the previous spring to attend Hopkins Grammar School in preparation for matriculating at Yale, and, as discussed in chapter 1, he subsequently tried to arrange for run-throughs of his ragtime dances by members of the Hyperion Theater orchestra. We do know that Ives became acquainted with "After the Ball," the celebrated song by Charles Harris that was featured in *A Trip to Chinatown*, for he later included a melodic phrase from the tune in one of the ragtime-influenced pieces he composed for theater orchestra. His quotation of "After the Ball" appears in the second movement of A Set of Pieces for Theater or Chamber Orchestra (ca. 1914), where it evokes the memory of hearing popular music emanating from a lively inn.

"After the Ball" was a fitting selection for this purpose, and especially so for a composer who did not often integrate contemporary popular music, other than ragtime, in his own compositions. Published in 1892, the sentimental ballad blends melodramatic nostalgia with a catchy hook, a combination that resonated with American consumers, sold millions of copies of sheet music, and became the music publishing industry's biggest hit to that date. "After the Ball" became ubiquitous: Ives may have heard it during his trip to the 1893 World's Columbian Exposition in Chicago, where John Philip Sousa's orchestra played it; as part of the Hyperion Theater performance of *A Trip to Chinatown;* or at a high school function, a local tavern, or a home parlor. Since Harris subsequently formed his own publishing company and relocated to New York City, the song remains an emblem of the rise of the centralized institution of Tin Pan Alley and its assembly-line approach to mass-producing popular songs, an industrial model for creating music that remained in place for more than fifty years. "After the Ball" reflects the emergence of a commercial popular music industry so pervasive that American consumers, including concert music composers like Ives, could scarcely avoid its reach. Like the previous two, this chapter continues to focus on the struggle to define a nation as it took shape in the world of popular music, addressing the roles played by Tin Pan Alley songwriters, from Irving Berlin to George Gershwin, as well as by individual performers, from Louis Armstrong to Bob Hope, in shaping conceptions of American national identity.

That a musical titled *A Trip to Chinatown* could become so acclaimed at the end of the nineteenth century is intriguing in its own right. In part, Charles Hoyt's decision to produce a play on this subject reflects the growing attraction of American Chinatowns as potential tourist destinations.[1] Likewise, its success as a musical in New York and on the yearlong nationwide tour that preceded its Broadway opening indicates widespread curiosity about America's Chinese immigrant population. Although Hoyt's cast never makes it to Chinatown—a proposed trip to the district functions as a decoy to hide the characters' plans to attend a masquerade ball—the production features a minor character named May Wing, a splashy "Chinese specialty" number by one of the leads, and recurring dialogue about visiting Chinatown. In the opening decades of the twentieth century, Tin Pan Alley songwriters continually revisited similar material, producing numerous songs on the subject of Chinatown and the presence of the Chinese in the United States. A remarkable phenomenon, considering how rarely such topics are treated by pop stars, this body of music responded to America's mounting concerns about the effects of massive immigration by constructing a vision of America demarcated along ethnic and racial lines. Yet, though this music can be understood as a product of its time, the lasting appeal of some of these songs suggests that the cultural tensions they register have endured through successive generations.

At the heart of this chapter is "Chinatown, My Chinatown," a Chinese-themed song that premiered on Broadway in 1910 and became one of the most successful of its kind. To give a sense of its lasting popularity, I begin this story at a celebration held three decades later by the American Society of Composers, Authors, and Publishers (ASCAP). Marking the silver anniversary of the organization, ASCAP staged two concerts in San Francisco on 24 September 1940 under the title "A Cavalcade of Music: Those Who Make America's Music."[2] Nearly twenty-five thousand people made the weekday trek to the Golden Gate International Exposition on Treasure Island to attend the afternoon outdoor concert, featuring music by Howard Hanson, Deems Taylor, William Grant Still, and other prominent American art music composers, many of whom conducted their own works. An even larger gathering took place that night, staged indoors at the California Coliseum and broadcast to an overflow crowd of spectators in nearby Festival Hall. Devoted entirely to popular music, the evening concert presented an array of American musical luminaries, including Jerome Kern, Judy Garland, Carrie Jacobs Bond, Hoagy Carmichael, W. C. Handy, Johnny Mercer, George M. Cohan, and Irving Berlin. The front-page review in the *San Francisco Chronicle* declared: "Such a musical day . . . has scarcely been seen or heard ever before in America."[3]

Toward the end of the evening performance, Gene Buck, the reigning ASCAP president and acting emcee, brought to the stage "one of the greatest melody writers America has ever developed."[4] The recipient of this praise, the composer Jean Schwartz (1878–1956), had earned respect through decades of songwriting success on Broadway and in Hollywood, along with his contributions to ASCAP as one of its twelve founding members. For this special event, Schwartz performed his signature tune, "Chinatown, My Chinatown," cowritten with his longtime collaborator, the lyricist William Jerome (1865–1932). This composition was an obvious choice, owing in part to its suitability for entertaining a Bay Area audience familiar with San Francisco's Chinatown but even more to its popularity as a sheet music hit, recording favorite, and jazz standard.[5] By this time, dozens of artists—including Billy Murray, Fletcher Henderson, Louis Armstrong, Lionel Hampton, and Tommy Dorsey—had released recordings of "Chinatown, My Chinatown," lending credence to Buck's description of the song as one of the "truly great American song hits."

The Bay Area audience was clearly fond of the familiar old tune, presented on this occasion as a leisurely instrumental that began with Schwartz performing alone at the piano. As soon as he finished the opening verse and reached the chorus for the first time, the crowd broke into applause and then began to sing along, joined by the orchestra the second time through the chorus. Like the rest of the evening's program, Schwartz's performance gave fans the opportunity to celebrate a beloved song and its composer. Yet just what constituted a cause for celebration becomes less clear once we recall Jerome's lyrics for the song's chorus:

> Chinatown, my Chinatown,
> Where the lights are low,
> Hearts that know no other land,

Drifting to and fro,
Dreamy, dreamy Chinatown,
Almond eyes of brown,
Hearts seem light and life seems bright
In dreamy Chinatown.

At first glance, the chorus appears fairly innocuous, inoffensive, and somewhat sympathetic toward Chinatown; even Jerome's remark concerning "almond eyes of brown" might be interpreted as a well-intentioned, if racialized, compliment. Chinatown stands for a thrice-dreamy place where "hearts seem light and life seems bright," a site for possible romance where people drift to and fro under low lights.[6] Indeed, the apparent lighthearted innocence of the chorus is one reason modern artists continue to record this song, whereas tunes that treat similar themes with more blatantly racist lyrics have dropped out of the repertoire. But as a closer examination of the song reveals, the dreaminess of this Chinatown springs not from romance but from opium. For, as it was initially conceived, the hearts drifting under low lights were meant to represent drugged-out nocturnal denizens of Chinatown, a district built on illusions where hearts "seem" light and life "seems" bright.

This chapter traces the many lives of "Chinatown, My Chinatown," starting with its 1910 Broadway premiere, in which the song accompanied a staged portrait of New York's Chinese population as primitive, exotic, opium-crazed foreigners. To explain why such a song would be written by a Tin Pan Alley songwriting team in the first place, I begin with the historical, cultural, and musical influences that led to its composition, its presentation onstage, and its production as sheet music. This early history of "Chinatown, My Chinatown" illuminates how and why theatrical practices, cover art, lyrics, and music participated in the formation of a racialized vision of America that excluded Asians and Asian Americans. I am not, however, suggesting that the song's exclusionary potential has always been realized to the same degree. In the hands of different performers and in distinct performance contexts, a song like "Chinatown, My Chinatown" may serve a variety of cultural purposes, as indicated, for example, by the considerable distance between the song's debut on Broadway and its commemorative function at the ASCAP concert. Moreover, though the song achieved its greatest fame during the 1930s, new recordings continued to appear over the next few decades by a diverse roster of prominent musicians, including Chet Atkins, Bing Crosby, Al Jolson, Spike Jones, and Sarah Vaughan (table 3). In fact, the perennial standard continues to resonate today, almost one hundred years after its first appearance, through live performances, modern recordings, documentaries, film, television, advertising, and the latest entertainment products. To account for the song's ongoing cultural significance, the latter section of this chapter brings the story of "Chinatown, My Chinatown" to the present by offering readings of its varied modes of presentation and paying close attention to the ways in which later performers have negotiated the song's original connotations.

By mapping the history of "Chinatown, My Chinatown," I seek to contribute in several respects to the recent growth of scholarship on race and musical representation.[7] The first relates to my subject of inquiry. The music of Tin Pan Alley has proven an extremely rich source for investigations of race, ethnicity, and identity in America, helping illuminate our understanding both of the European American immigrant experience, principally with respect to Jewish American identity making, and of the cultural history of black-white racial relations.[8] Yet the existence of many Tin Pan Alley songs featuring Asian themes suggests that we may have overlooked other important trajectories involving the construction of American ethnic and racial identity, as well as the ways in which music has shaped discourse about Asia and Asian America. The anti-Chinese sentiments of the songs at the center of this chapter represent neither the initial nor the predominant manifestation of racism in American musical culture. Reflecting a wider phenomenon, these songs bear some resemblance to coon songs, which is not surprising since songwriters like Jerome and Schwartz composed both types. But the singular qualities of Chinese-themed songs are equally significant. Instead of demonstrating a generic strategy of ethnic demonization, a song such as "Chinatown, My Chinatown" registered a distinctive set of cultural attitudes held toward a specific immigrant community at a particular historical moment.

The second contribution I wish to make involves my theoretical stance toward this repertoire. As part of the study of racialized music, musicologists first became interested in the subject of musical orientalism in Western art music, where musical representations of the "Oriental other" abound.[9] Recently scholars also have begun to pay more attention to such issues in the world of popular music, from Tin Pan Alley to the present day.[10] Such a flurry of activity indicates that music historians have finally begun to give the amount of attention afforded to representations of Asia and Asian America in other areas of American culture.[11] Focusing on this repertoire lends an important twist to the study of musical orientalism, for not all "Orientals" of the time lived in remote or mythical lands; some were landing on America's shores. In many respects, songs like "Chinatown, My Chinatown" were products of and participants in what Ronald Radano and Philip Bohlman have described as the "racial imagination," but

TABLE 3. Selected recordings of "Chinatown, My Chinatown"

Year	Performer(s)	Label / Issue
1915	Grace Kerns and John Barnes Wells	Columbia 1624
1915	American Quartet (featuring Billy Murray)	Victor 17684
1915	Prince's Orchestra	Columbia 5674
1916	Royal Military Band	Coliseum 947
1928	Art Gillham	Columbia 1619–D
1929	Red Nichols and His Five Pennies	Brunswick 4363
1930	Fletcher Henderson and His Orchestra	Columbia 2329–D
1931	Louis Armstrong and His Orchestra	OKeh 41534
1932	Roane's Pennsylvanians	Victor 22919
1932	Mills Brothers	Brunswick 6305
1933	Harry Roy and His Orchestra	Parlophone R–1554
1934	Casa Loma Orchestra	Decca 199
1934	Jay Wilbur and His Band (in "Eastern Medley")	Rex 8313
1935	Ray Noble and His Orchestra	Victor LPV–536
1935	Louis Prima and His New Orleans Gang	Brunswick 7456
1937	Lionel Hampton (as "China Stomp")	Victor 25586
1938	Slim [Gaillard] and Slam [Stewart]	Vocalion 4021
1938	Tommy Dorsey and His Orchestra	Victor 26023
1949	Al Jolson	Decca DL–5006
1952	Chet Atkins	RCA Victor 47–4896
1955	Bob Hope, *The Seven Little Foys* (soundtrack)	RCA Victor LPM 3275
1955	The Hi-Lo's, *Under Glass*	Starlite ST–7005
1957	Jackie Gleason, *Velvet Brass*	Capitol SW–859
1957	Bing Crosby, *New Tricks*	Decca DL–8575
1978	Gerard Schwarz and His Dance Orchestra, *Come and Trip It: Instrumental Dance Music, 1780s–1920s*	New World NW 293
1990	Canadian Brass, *Basin Street*	Sony/CBS MK–42367
1995	*Oriental Illusions* (perf. Roane's Pennsylvanians, 1932)	Memphis Archives 7018
1997	*Carousel of American Music* (perf. Jean Schwartz, 1940)	Music & Arts CD–4971
1998	Hot Club of Cowtown, *Swingin' Stampede*	Hightone HCDS094

TABLE 3. (*continued*)

Year	Performer(s)	Label / Issue
1998	Andrew Bird's Bowl of Fire, *Thrills*	Rykodisc 10397
2003	Dixieland Ramblers, *Live & Lighting It Up in New Orleans*	Summit 350

Milton Brown, Benny Carter, Eddie Condon, Roy Eldridge, Benny Goodman, Stéphane Grappelli, Spike Jones, Mickey Katz, Kid Ory, Clyde McPhatter, Mitch Miller, Django Reinhardt, Art Tatum, Jack Teagarden, Sarah Vaughan, and Teddy Wilson are among the other musicians who have recorded "Chinatown, My Chinatown."

such imaginary constructions that mark racial difference often develop in response to real historical circumstances.[12] Instead of constructing an imaginary, foreign, distant Other, Tin Pan Alley composers produced this body of orientalist music largely in response to the growth of Asian immigrant communities. Judy Tsou's study of American popular sheet music of the era supports this claim, revealing a broad pattern of "demasculinization, exoticism and dehumanization" in visual and musical representations of Chinese and Chinese Americans.[13] Building on her valuable overview, my analysis of "Chinatown, My Chinatown" identifies similar representational techniques, which reveal how such musical fantasies bear important marks, however partial, of the lives, experiences, and treatment of the Chinese in America. Broadly speaking, the song partakes in a larger cultural process of Asian racialization in the United States and epitomizes what Michael Omi and Howard Winant have termed "racial formation," the social practices by which America constructs its racial meanings.[14] More specifically, Jerome and Schwartz's song, which portrays local Chinatowns as foreign entities within U.S. borders, participated in an American brand of internal orientalism through which the music industry helped construct national identity, defining what America was by identifying what it was not.

By tracing the "social life of sounds" through a tune-centered approach that chronicles "Chinatown, My Chinatown" over the course of the century and across a broad range of musical genres and performance contexts, I aim to show how the persistence of musical orientalism requires continuous maintenance and reinscription.[15] Countless stage performers, recording artists, and amateur musicians have reinforced the song's orientalist message, a message that it retains to a significant degree today. That such meanings are continually being reconstructed, and occasionally contested, is evident in performances of "Chinatown, My Chinatown" in a wide variety of forms, many of which have altered the song's lyrics, music, and staging. Approaches to and uses of the song have changed in response to various cultural and technological factors—including new social dances, the influence of jazz, constraints of audio recording, and the development of sound film—and to broader historical shifts involving American foreign policy and immigration law. As a result, the orientalist work of "Chinatown, My Chinatown" must be understood not only with respect to Jerome and Schwartz's original conception around the turn of the twentieth century, but in relation to later moments at which performers have been newly drawn to this music, either reenacting or revising its racialized message. When performance is viewed as an integral part of the song's complex history of race and representation, musical orientalism turns out to be neither static nor stable, but dynamic and mutable—born in the past and surviving to the present, but changing over time.

STAGING CHINATOWN

For a song entitled "Chinatown, My Chinatown" to gain such prominence in the early twentieth century is surprising, considering that a musical composition on this subject would not have made sense to American audiences a few generations earlier, before the formation of Chinatowns in America. Consequently, the origin of the song and its early reception need to be positioned in relationship to a precise moment in the history of the Chinese in America. In fact, as the following historical sketch makes clear, the same factors that led to the growth of Chinatowns also shaped popular conventions for representing Chinese subjects.

The first Chinese immigrants to America did not immediately settle together in urban Chinatowns; instead, when workers from China began arriving by the tens of thousands in the middle of the nineteenth century, they joined the California Gold Rush, worked on farms, and helped build the transcontinental railroad. Though U.S. manufacturers appreciated cheap Chinese labor, America's established working class felt threatened by the wave of Chinese immigration, which kindled fear of the "Yellow Peril." Anti-Chinese feelings became most intense on the West Coast, where the majority of the Chinese settled, and competition between ethnic groups over labor and land grew heated. In short order, a coalition of xenophobic, prowhite interest groups—including labor unions, agricultural concerns, politicians, and organizations such as the Asiatic Exclusion League—joined forces to push for immigration restrictions. Their efforts culminated in the Chinese Exclusion Act of 1882, the first law to bar immigrants on the basis of race, nationality, and class, legislation that remained largely in effect for eighty years and effectively halted the growth of the Chinese immigrant population.[16] Such hostility during an era of legalized segregation also prompted discriminatory laws regarding land ownership as well as frequent outbreaks of racially motivated violence in rural areas. Consequently, after the Gold Rush and the completion of the railroad, Chinese immigrants began to congregate in urban communities. By the turn of the century San Francisco boasted the nation's largest Chinatown; however, in part because of the 1906 earthquake that leveled the San Francisco district, sizable Chinatowns also grew in Los Angeles, Chicago, Boston, and New York.

In response to the influx of immigrants, literary, theatrical, and musical representations of Chinese subjects began to appear more regularly in the late nineteenth century, which helped identify and neutralize any perceived threats posed by the new arrivals.[17] In one renowned case, Bret Harte collaborated with Mark Twain to stage *Ah Sin* (1877), a play based on Harte's earlier poem "The Heathen Chinee" (1870). The epitome of onstage Chinese characters, the servant Ah Sin functioned as an embodiment of inferiority and difference that were illustrated by his physical traits, attire, race, religion, culture, language, politics, and ethics. Not only did the white actor portraying Ah Sin appear in yellowface makeup, don a Chinese coolie costume, wear his hair in a braid, use stock performance gestures, and speak in pidgin English, but his fellow characters proclaimed Ah Sin to be a "moral cancer," "slant eyed son of the yellow jaunders," a member of "that godless race," "jabbering idiot," and an "unsolvable political problem."[18] This fictional creation resonated with the American public, and both "Ah Sin" and "the heathen Chinee" became catchphrases used to bash the Chinese for decades to follow. Later productions such as Henry Grimm's play *The Chinese Must Go* (1879) presented comparably unfavorable depictions. As scholars of American literature, drama, and the visual arts have documented, similar stereotypes permeated late nineteenth-century culture and were incorporated in emerging twentieth-century cultural forms.[19] For instance, starting in the 1920s, Hollywood released a series of movies featuring Fu Manchu, the sinister Chinese villain, as well as dozens of films set in Chinatown or in London's Limehouse District, as its Chinese neighborhood was known. The most popular works crossed genre boundaries as well as the Atlantic Ocean. The British author Thomas Burke's collection *Limehouse Nights* (1917) inspired *Broken Blossoms* (1919), a silent Hollywood film by D. W. Griffith, and spawned the song "Limehouse Nights" (1920), with music composed by George Gershwin. Such Chinese-themed songs became a regular Tin Pan Alley fixture, and, as Judy Tsou has demonstrated, this music continually recycled caricatures of the Chinese that emphasized their heathen otherness, strange appearance, alien rituals, and mysterious customs.

As a result, Chinatown came to signify "the embodiment of the exotic Orient," the neighborhood effectively serving to stand for what was "non-American."[20] Once negative perceptions of the Chinese intersected with the bleak reality of their economic prospects, Chinatown also became synonymous with poverty, filth, vice, and, most relevant for the present discussion, opium. Written the year before "Chinatown, My Chinatown" premiered on Broadway, an exposé in *Munsey's Magazine* offers a typical view of New York's Chinatown: "But the bulbs do not shine with the brilliancy that they have up-town. A bluish haze enshrouds them. It is the same everywhere in Chinatown. Its lights, like its life, must be seen through this haze of punk [Chinese incense] and opium, and the noisome outpourings of its greasy chop-suey joints and its swarming tenements. That sickening, dominating peanut odor is the smell of opium."[21] Although opium arrived in America long before the first surge of Chinese immigration, and U.S. companies had shipped opium into China since the early nineteenth century, its evils were linked in the public imagination to China and Chinese America.[22] This perception had some basis in reality, since the drug provided legal recreation to Chinese "bachelor" communities before the Harrison Narcotics Act of 1914. The stereotype remained in force, despite an increasingly white clientele and the growth of opium dens outside Chinatown. Linking the local Chinese with opium smoking performed a variety of cultural functions. In addition to recycling a long-standing trope of Asian decadence, this stigma served as a marker of racial difference and immorality. Moreover, since addiction was seen as a sign of weakness, outside observers could view the Chinese, like the poor elsewhere, as victims of their own lifestyle. Recognizing this constellation of negative perceptions about Chinatown proves essential for understanding the cultural background and aesthetic rationale for Jerome and Schwartz's composition.

Chinatown's lurid reputation may have frightened some Americans away, but it beckoned many others, transforming over time "from vice district to tourist attraction."[23] At the turn of the century, a national rise in tourism accompanied the emergence of American Chinatowns as attractive destinations for middle- to upper-class white Americans, who began to visit these districts in search of vicarious thrills. Shepherded by charismatic, self-promoting tour guides such as Chuck Connors, who billed himself as the

"Mayor of Chinatown," curiosity seekers in Manhattan toured old crime scenes, drug dens, and gambling parlors, many of which were manufactured for the occasion. Even the gods recognized Chinatown as a budding tourist destination, if we believe the conceit of *Up and Down Broadway*, a musical comedy that opened at New York's Casino Theater on 18 July 1910 and featured songs by Jean Schwartz and William Jerome, including the Broadway premiere of "Chinatown, My Chinatown."[24] According to the show's slim plot, drawn from contemporaneous debates about the popular stage, a group of immortals descend from Mt. Olympus and tour Manhattan with the intention of reforming Broadway. Eddie Foy, a veteran comic actor who received above-the-title billing, led the heavenly visitors on a tour of New York City sights, including the Polo Grounds, Herald Square, the Opera House, and, midway through the second act, Chinatown.

The musical, in addition to reflecting a typical agenda for a New York tourist of the time, included in that scene the number "In Chinatown," which provided a ready excuse for exotic spectacle.[25] Written by the longtime Broadway dramaturge Edgar Smith, the scene features seven female "Chinatown visitors" who tour the district under the protection of Officer Casey, an Irish policeman. The tour group encounters several Chinatown denizens bearing comic names—"Sing Hi, a chink," "Chu Gum, a chop suey dispenser," and "Fan Tan, a Chinese maiden"—and witnesses the kitchen-sink exoticism of the "Dope Fiend," who performed what the *New York Times* described as an "Apache Chinese" dance, set to a "very clever hop [opium] song."[26] The theater critic for the *New York Clipper* characterized the number in like fashion: "[Martin Brown] had a great make-up as a dope-crazed Chinaman, in a sort of Mongolian Apache that he and Melissa Ten Eyke danced, and the two executed some [r]evolutions in this number that brought them out for several bows."[27] Most New York journalists reacted enthusiastically to the yellowface depiction of an opium-infested Chinatown, the *Dramatic Mirror* admiring the number for its "fervidness" and the *New York World* calling it a "feature of the production."[28] It was at this point in the show that Broadway audiences first heard "Chinatown, My Chinatown," which was interpolated into this scene after the production opened.[29] Sung by Ernest Hare, playing Officer Casey, the tune extended the tradition of staged orientalism by incorporating a visit to Chinatown as a plot device to pinpoint the district's foreign nature and its notoriety for opium use.

As I indicated at the start of this chapter, a number of residual traces of the opium-laden context for "Chinatown, My Chinatown" can be found throughout the song, less conspicuously in the lyrics of the chorus but far more obviously in its two verses:

Verse 1:
When the town is fast asleep,
And it's midnight in the sky,
That's the time the festive Chink
Starts to wink his other eye,
Starts to wink his dreamy eye,
Lazily you'll hear him sigh.

Verse 2:
Strangers taking in the sights,
Pigtails flying here and there;
See that broken Wall Street sport
Still thinks he's a millionaire,
Still thinks he's a millionaire,
Pipe dreams banish ev'ry care.

Jerome's lyrics lay bare the origin of Chinatown's dreams, painting a darker picture of an opium-laced district that operates on its own after-hours schedule. Like the reference in the chorus to almond eyes, the verses accentuate Chinese difference, first by using a pejorative slur and then by referring to the queues worn by Chinese men as "pigtails flying here and there." More significantly, illicit drugs represent the primary attraction of what the chorus calls "dreamy, dreamy Chinatown," for both characters mentioned in the verses are opium smokers. Jerome's first verse employs slang of the day to characterize opium's effects—"dreamy" eyes that "wink"—on a sighing "festive Chink."[30] Likewise, his second verse depicts a Wall Street businessman, who apparently either has been ruined because of an addiction to opium or has turned to the drug as a means of escape, since opium "pipe dreams banish ev'ry care." Whenever the chorus returns, these drug addicts also reappear as two of the "hearts that know no other land," drifting through a smoky opium haze in Chinatown.

Although the tradition of musically representing the Chinese in America had long been established, writing songs about Chinatown was a fairly recent development. In contrast to earlier depictions of individual Chinese figures—lone men such as the miner's servant in the popular song adaptation of Harte's "The Heathen Chinee" (1870) and the title character of another tune, "The Chinee Laundryman" (1880)—Tin Pan Alley lyrics began to register the growth of U.S. Chinatowns. Not only did this development correspond to the broad shift at the end of the nineteenth century toward urban settings in American popular song, but the change in subject matter also signaled the parallel growth of the Chinatown tourist trade. In fact, Jerome is one of the few lyricists to acknowledge the presence of outsiders in Chinatown: here, "strangers take in the sights" and, along with the audience, gaze on the sensation. Ethnic novelty songs of this era often feature verses sung in the third person to set the scene and switch in the chorus to "dialect" written in the first person, which enables the singer to occupy and caricature an ethnic role. But in this song, Jerome's lyrics make little distinction in point of view between verse and chorus, and they never switch to quasi-Chinese.[31] Rather than positioning the narrator as a Chinatown resident, the word *My* in the song's title offers possession of Chinatown, as well as control over its representation, not to locals but to an external narrating voice, a virtual Tin Pan Alley tour guide. Thus, even though some staged incarnations have included putative residents of Chinatown, the song has primarily functioned as a third-person narrative, as in the case of the policeman who sings it in *Up and Down Broadway*.

To construct Chinatown through music, the meandering melody of Schwartz's chorus drifts to and fro like Jerome's inhabitants, the pitches floating up and down in four-bar phrases that at first vaguely conjure the pentatonicism often used to signify Asia before they firmly establish a C-major tonality (example 11). Its simple rhythmic design and singable, lingering melody symbolize how Schwartz's tune subtly gestures toward the "Orient" yet remains firmly grounded in the musical vocabulary of Tin Pan Alley, thus combining topical novelty with ample musical comfort, as if it were ready-made to be adopted as a nostalgic standard. Generally speaking, Schwartz avoids bizarre harmonies, exotic scales, and other stereotypical tropes of musical orientalism.[32] Instead, "Chinatown, My Chinatown" relies on standard musical devices of the era: a short piano introduction and vamp; two verses and a chorus constructed with two- and four-bar phrases; and a syllabic, diatonic melody set to triadic harmonies and following tonal procedures.[33] A significant exception, however, occurs in the song's opening bars. Schwartz pulls open the curtain on Chinatown with a singsong rhythmic pattern, which offers pentatonic hints underscored by repeated parallel fourths (example 12). Such musical tropes have long been used to represent the exotic, and they continue to populate the music scene today. Thus, as clearly as the song's title captures its subject, the opening moments of "Chinatown, My Chinatown" inform listeners that the song aims to fashion Asian difference.

The relative absence of decorative orientalist touches throughout the rest of the song should not divert attention from the song's intent. On the contrary, Schwartz amplifies the foreignness of Chinatown with standard Tin Pan Alley maneuvers: sliding down to the relative minor on the words "other land" to reinforce the melody's deepest plunge and adding off-beat

Example 11. William Jerome (lyrics) and Jean Schwartz (music), "Chinatown, My Chinatown," mm. 31–62. Published by Jerome H. Remick and Company (1910).

chromaticism when the melody reaches its peak on "almond eyes of brown" (example 13). Similarly, he associates "Chinatown" with "other land" by setting both to the song's most memorable motive, a basic but distinctive short-short-long rhythmic pattern, echoed here by the piano accompaniment (examples 11 and 13). In this light, the choice to bypass stereotypically Asian-sounding music does not indicate a more inclusive embrace of Chinatown but instead reflects Schwartz's strategy of incor-

Example 12. "Chinatown, My Chinatown," mm. 1–4.

porating tried-and-true musical support for the song's lyrical message and of composing appropriately unmarked musical accompaniment for Jerome's tourist. Commenting on its homogeneity, Jean Schwartz later admitted, "I still wouldn't give you a nickel for the tune."[34] Notwithstanding his modesty about the lilting melody and catchy rhythm that would appeal to millions of consumers, Schwartz's conventional setting seems quite well suited to its subject. Working in tandem with Jerome's touristic commentary, which evokes yet neutralizes the district's dangers, Schwartz constructs a musical Chinatown that sounds faintly exotic, yet safe, familiar, and ultimately knowable.

Evaluated from this perspective, songs like "Chinatown, My Chinatown" offer the potential to sharpen our understanding of Tin Pan Alley with respect to issues involving ethnicity and national identity. Summarizing the rationale behind ethnic novelty songs in this period, Charles Hamm outlines various cultural functions performed by this music. America's established citizens could point to these songs as proof of their superiority, yet the songs also introduced, however unfairly, recent immigrant groups to native-born Americans. For new immigrants, experiencing musical ridicule could be a form of hazing: to be critiqued could be a step toward recognition and possible acceptance, as those being mocked were forced to build their self-esteem. As Hamm suggests, members of marginalized groups who joined the music industry—such as the Jewish Schwartz and the Irish Jerome—could learn to survive in America by competing with (and musically representing) other immigrants, "like tomcats tied in a sack, trying to claw their way out."[35] In the course of doing so, Hamm shows, American musicians formed bonds by sharing in the process of transforming everyday experiences and grievances into the realm of popular entertainment. In this light, Jerome's lyrics, as performed by the stereotypically Irish Officer Casey, can be seen as another salvo in

Example 13. "Chinatown, My Chinatown," mm. 39–42 and 51–54.

mm. 39–42

mm. 51–54

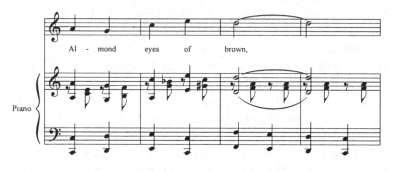

the struggle between Irish and Chinese immigrants that began in the nineteenth century, when the groups competed for railroad and factory jobs and were set against one another in labor disputes.[36] Indeed, Hamm's characterizations apply well to those immigrant groups whose members attended Broadway musicals, patronized vaudeville theaters, and eventually gained access to creating Tin Pan Alley songs.[37] But however accurately this characterization of Tin Pan Alley ethnic songs applies to the careers of songwriters like Jerome and Schwartz, such a model assumes an equal opportunity to enjoy and create these songs. It does not apply as productively to groups like the Chinese, who were not the target audience, were barred from many musical venues, and were almost never hired to offer their own musical perspectives. As cultural outsiders, Chinese immigrants shouldered most of the disadvantages and received few of the benefits available to other audience members and song producers.

Another complication for understanding issues of race and representation involving Tin Pan Alley arises from the content of this particular repertoire. As was true of blackface minstrelsy and staged performances of ethnic novelty songs, much of the appeal of orientalist songs derived from the performance options made available by musical yellowface, including caricature, parody, comic impersonation, and masked social critique. Yet the explanation for the popularity of "Chinatown, My Chinatown," especially in its sheet music form, must rest elsewhere, for the song's narrator neither dons a mask nor attempts to speak as if he or she were Chinese. Rather than assuming a different ethnic identity to voice concerns that might not be otherwise expressible, Jerome's protagonist takes on the narrative role of flaneur or tourist, pointing out certain dangers of Chinatown but also offering reassurance that America could cope with and control its Chinese residents. In this respect the song offers a clear illustration of how music, according to Georgina Born and David Hesmondhalgh, can work "to *reproduce,* reinforce, actualize, or memorialize *extant* sociocultural identities, in some cases also forcefully *repressing* both transformation and alternatives."[38] Tin Pan Alley tunes proved to be an especially effective medium for achieving these ends because of the variety of musical forms they generated: staged, filmed, and recorded versions that audiences could appreciate, as well as sheet music they could play for themselves. Whether presented on stage or played at home, "Chinatown, My Chinatown" allows performers to rearticulate notions of racial and cultural difference—to reproduce extant relations—by describing how Chinese people in America are best confined to Chinatown, knowing no other land. The song mirrors an era when Asian immigrants were being racialized as nonwhites by immigration policies and Chinatowns were developing into "internal colonies."[39] No matter how many times the chorus comes around, Chinatown's residents never depart their opium-filled dreamland.

At the same time, however, it is unclear whether life in this imaginary district would be entirely unpleasant. Reflecting the paradoxical coupling of revulsion and enticement that typically characterizes discourse surrounding the exotic and the primitive, Jerome and Schwartz's Chinatown seems to embody a dream as much as a nightmare. Broadly speaking, curiosity about Chinatown demonstrated the latest instance of American interest in the allure of Asia, its lens focused on a local immigrant community. More pointedly, by placing the spotlight on opium smoking in "Chinatown, My Chinatown" when the U.S. government began to criminalize the use of narcotics, Jerome and Schwartz offer listeners a taste of illicit pleasure, an arena for vicarious thrills, and a shelter from the modern world. To some extent, the song delivers a cautionary tale, warning audience members that they too could end up just like the "broken Wall Street sport," succumbing to opium, losing track of their outside responsibilities, and joining those whose "hearts . . . know no other land." But Schwartz's music makes such an experience sound extremely pleasant, suggesting that opium can lighten hearts and brighten lives. Rather than launching a full-blown attack against drug abusers, the song reveals a desire for the freedoms promised by opium. The district becomes, rather than a danger zone populated by pushers and predators, a dreamy drug paradise where both locals and visitors can forget their cares. Thus, even as it signified foreignness, irrationality, and difference, this version of Chinatown presented an escape hatch to America's growing white middle class, which was increasingly confined to an industrial world. In this fashion the tourist gaze constructed by "Chinatown, My Chinatown" attempted to contain the effects of immigration, while simultaneously recasting Chinatown as a safety valve to help relieve the nation's deep cultural anxieties. Like the contradictory nature of American tourism, which was fostered by the forces of modernization yet functioned largely to introduce consumers to its alternatives, Chinatowns were depicted as bounded, self-contained, foreign districts, yet proposed as sites that granted outsiders limitless freedom.

PICTURING CHINATOWN

The simultaneously dreamy and nightmarish depiction of "Chinatown, My Chinatown" did not resonate at once with U.S. audiences; on the contrary, the song's roundabout path to prominence calls attention to the integral roles played by performers and marketers in the generation of popular hits. This was nothing new for the American music industry. Tin Pan Alley publishers often relied on star performers in splashy theatrical productions to stimulate sales of sheet music, the primary medium by which popular music entered most American homes at the time. And by the turn of the century, American music promoters already had begun to exploit the power of eye-catching imagery to advertise songs on posters and billboards, in newspapers, magazines, and trade journals, and on the covers of sheet music. Yet, in the case of "Chinatown, My Chinatown," recent developments in the music industry bolstered its cause. First, advances in printing technology, which made the reproduction of full-color imagery on the covers of sheet music affordable, offered music publishers a new advertising tool. Second, what made the song's road to success somewhat unusual for its time was that, rather than gaining its fame through a glorious stage run, the song received a critical boost from the fledging recording industry.

Without an intervention by early recording artists, it is doubtful that "Chinatown, My Chinatown" would enjoy its present status, since *Up and Down Broadway* failed to become a hit at the box office.[40] Like the *Times* critic, who pronounced the show "a riot of color, girls, songs, and specialties," most reviewers offered mildly favorable commentary, deeming it an enjoyable, if mindless, summer trifle.[41] The *New York World* printed what turned out to be the most prescient remarks: "While [the production] sparkles with humor in spots it does not carry with it the sustaining interest of a successful summer show."[42] The musical closed after seventy-two performances; it staged a moderately successful post-Broadway tour that included stops in Philadelphia, Baltimore, and Chicago before it closed in Albany. Even though thousands of audience members witnessed the staging of "Chinatown, My Chinatown" in *Up and Down Broadway,* its failure to catch on right away perhaps can be attributed to the show's brief run and the song's assignment to a bit player. It was not until several years later, during an upswing of American isolationism and xenophobia in response to the outbreak of World War I, that the song gained nationwide popularity.[43] Spurred by the release of three recordings, including a rendition by the American Quartet featuring the tenor Billy Murray, "Chinatown, My Chinatown" emerged as one of the top hits of 1915.[44] It became so popular that the small number of Chinese and Chinese American performers on the vaudeville stage also began entertaining audiences with renditions of the tune sung in both Cantonese and English.[45] Around this time, the Jerome H. Remick publishing house brought out a striking new edition of the sheet music, which advanced and capitalized on the song's revival (figure 2).[46] The rerelease of "Chinatown, My Chinatown" proved to be a triumph, quickly selling hundreds of thousands of copies, with later estimates reaching several million.[47]

To design a suitable cover for "Chinatown, My Chinatown," Remick hired Florence Cooney (1888–1950), a young artist from Canada who had relocated to Manhattan after training at the Art Institute of Chicago.[48] Since freelance cover artists usually labored in anonymity, earning around twenty-five dollars per title, it is noteworthy to find Cooney's signature on the cover, an apparent sign of the pride she took in her work. Incorporating a palette of bright red-orange, light brown, sky blue, black, and white, Cooney's poster-style cover for this large-format ($10\frac{1}{2}$ by 13 inches) sheet music was tailored to take advantage of the latest color printing technology. Cooney portrays a young woman sitting on a small boxy stool, holding a long-necked stringed instrument, casually crossing her right leg over her

FIGURE 2.   Cover art by Florence Cooney for William Jerome (lyrics) and Jean Schwartz (music), "Chinatown, My Chinatown." Published by Jerome H. Remick and Company (ca. 1914). Archive of Popular American Music, UCLA Library Performing Arts Special Collections, UCLA Library.

left knee. As the sole representative of Chinatown, she appears to be of Asian descent, with slanted eyes, dark, pulled-back hair, and an outfit resembling traditional Chinese dress. Although she faces prospective consumers, it is difficult to interpret her mood because of her blank facial expression. Even so, her oval face, her gently draped clothing, the open door over her shoulder, and the phallic evocation of the musical instrument all suggest that this exotic beauty might be more available than a typical American girl. Though Cooney's depiction is not overtly sexualized, the figure draws on the exoticism and allure that had long characterized stereotypes of Asian women. Indeed, the decision to use a female to stand in for Chinatown was purely aesthetic, for few Chinese women lived in the United States at the time. Because of Chinese immigration patterns, federal immigration restrictions, and state laws prohibiting miscegenation, America's Chinese population in 1910 was 94 percent male.[49] Unconcerned with demographics, Cooney draws on this stereotype to channel both the exotic, feminized East and the unattainable other, a choice that Chinatown residents would have found cruelly ironic.

Placing her musician in an idyllic setting, Cooney manufactures a fantasy Chinatown, an imaginary place where people look, dress, and act in non-American ways. Her portrait includes a few trees painted in a quasi-Chinese style, several paper lanterns with stylized designs, and a Japanese-influenced bamboo dwelling, topped by a thatched roof with curving edges. The goal of producing Asian difference also informed Cooney's choice of lettering style. Larger than any other component, the song's title runs like a banner across the top of the page, balanced on two pieces of bamboo that represent eaves but also recall a set of chopsticks. Set against a dark background, each of the title's white letters consists of several jagged strokes that allude to the brushstrokes used to form characters in various Asian scripts. The dramatic lettering contrasts sharply with that used for the songwriters' names, Jerome and Schwartz, and their publisher, Jerome H. Remick, which features recognizably whole characters—softened by darker coloring and rounded edges—more characteristic of American advertising of the day. With this simple design choice, Cooney neatly distinguishes between the song's creators and their creation.

The musical instrument on the cover widens the racial divide. Respectable young American women of this era were expected to take piano lessons, which enabled them to provide household entertainment using the latest sheet music, but Cooney's figure plucks a stringed instrument of the sort that upstanding girls seldom played. Drawn with only two tuning pegs, the instrument otherwise resembles the three-stringed sanxian, a fretless Chinese lute, which also became known as the shamisen upon its introduction to Japan around the fifteenth century. By choosing this instrument, Cooney adopted an established strategy for representing either China or Japan. A generation earlier, American sheet music produced for *The Mikado*, the popular Gilbert and Sullivan operetta set in Japan, depicted the American actress Louise Paullin wearing a kimono and holding a shamisen. Another source for such imagery was Puccini's tragic opera *Madama Butterfly* (1904). Publicity shots for both the opera's American premiere in New York City (1906) and for the silent film *Madame Butterfly* (1915), starring Mary Pickford in the title role, depict Butterfly playing the shamisen.[50] Like other commonly recurring imagery—including the kimono, paper lantern, and Asian-style lettering—the shamisen came to function as an all-purpose signifier of Asia. Consequently, the lyrics of "Sing Song Man" (1922) describe the title character as hailing from China, but the sheet music cover art presents two kimono-clad females, the shamisen-playing title character, and cherry blossoms, all set against the backdrop of Japan's Mount Fuji. As Judy Tsou's analysis of the era's representational practices makes clear, by juxtaposing Asian symbols in indiscriminate fashion, the U.S. music industry relied on, and fostered, the inability of American consumers to distinguish among various Asian countries.

In this case, however, Cooney's exposure to Japanese art lends greater significance to her use of the shamisen. Today's audiences are more familiar with the shamisen through its use in traditional Japanese theater, but the instrument also shares an intimate association with geisha, the female courtesans of Japan. In fact, the history of Japanese woodblock prints spills over with depictions of geisha and their shamisens: tuning the instrument, plucking its strings with a plectrum, or carrying their instrument cases on outdoor walks. As a measure of the strength of this bond, it is possible to identify anonymous female figures in traditional Japanese prints *as geisha* solely by their shamisen or black-lacquered shamisen cases.[51] Cooney was especially well positioned to take advantage of this suggestive association, since American interest in Japanese art, design, architecture, fashion, textiles, and decorative arts had blossomed at the close of the nineteenth century, and Japanese color prints were in vogue in Manhattan during the 1910s.[52] She gained further exposure to Asian artistic techniques by studying with William Merritt Chase, an influential painter who was among the first Americans to incorporate artistic techniques from Japan.[53] Familiarity with Japanese prints colors not only Cooney's use of pan-Asian imagery, including her evocation of a geisha, but also her technique, which features similar decorative touches and recalls their flat, two-dimensional quality, most clearly in the placement of the house and trees against a blue background. It should be underscored, however, that she harnessed these techniques not to recreate a scene from ancient Japan but instead to add a patina of Asian antiquity to this portrayal of a modern American Chinatown.

The cover for "Chinatown, My Chinatown" demonstrates how early twentieth-century American artists grabbed whatever signs could be read as representing Asian difference and deployed them to manufacture the exotic. That visual imagery of the time drew on such disparate sources was a predictable result of America's rising international clout and its parallel growth in consumption and trade. Yet, even though the cover art for "Chinatown, My Chinatown" in some respects signals greater familiarity with Asian cultures, this motley image also betrays a fundamental lack of understanding, an inability to distinguish between separate countries and cultures. Not only do the arts (and people) of China and Japan look alike, Cooney's drawing suggests, but customers were not expected to know the difference. Like Schwartz's music, Cooney's portrait depicts a friendlier, safer, knowable Chinatown that resonated with American consumers, but its advertising hook relies on viewers to map an imagined Asia, its exoticism and sexual allure, directly onto a contemporary American community. Unlike Jerome's lyrics, which mix harsh stereotypes with faint touches of reality (e.g., the strangers taking in the sights), her vision of Chinatown lives almost completely in the realm of artistic imagination.

MANUFACTURING CHINATOWN

By creating difference along racial lines, Cooney's cover art demonstrates how American national identity is also produced in relationship to what it excludes. But for this sort of representational strategy to have an effect, frequent reinforcement is required. Not only did the sheet music industry in this period consistently portray the Chinese and Chinese Americans as foreigners, but individual composers often repackaged their own material, perpetuating the same stereotypical images over and over again. It is thus significant to point out that "Chinatown, My Chinatown" was not a one-hit wonder, but instead the product of a songwriting team that specialized in ethnic novelties and composed a number of Chinese-themed songs. Moreover, as we shall see, the songs of Jerome and Schwartz inspired many subsequent lyricists and composers to follow their lead.

The musical lives of Jerome and Schwartz exemplify how composers learned and transmitted these representational practices to subsequent generations of musicians. Early in their respective careers, both songwriters began to hone the skills that would enable them to produce Chinese-themed songs. After leaving home as a teenager, William Jerome Flannery adopted the professional name Billy Jerome and achieved fame as an actor and a song-and-dance man, joining Barlow Wilson's minstrel troupe and headlining at Tony Pastor's Fourteenth Street Theater.[54] The third-generation Irish immigrant thus dealt with the racial politics of late nineteenth-century America: masking his identity with a stage name to avoid anti-Irish prejudice, donning blackface to perform caricatures of African American life, and polishing a repertoire built around ethnic and racial stereotypes. His experience performing songs that mocked American minority groups shaped his later career as a lyricist, then publisher, under the more adult-sounding name William Jerome. Known as a versatile lyricist with a special knack for comedy, Jerome's work with various composers resulted in frequent hits; one contemporary called him "without a doubt, the peer of all stage song writers."[55] In comparison, Schwartz's background suggests that he might have been more sensitive to the experience of recent immigrants. At the age of ten, he emigrated with his family from Budapest, Hungary, and settled on Manhattan's Lower East Side. After a series of odd jobs, Schwartz decided to pursue a career in popular music, landing a position as a song demonstrator at Siegel-Cooper, the first New York department store with its own sheet music department, then joining the Shapiro-Bernstein music publishing firm as a staff pianist and song plugger. But as soon as he entered Tin Pan Alley, Schwartz, like Jerome, followed the trends of the time by composing songs with racial overtones. His first published song, "Dusky Dudes" (1899), imitates the cakewalk, a popular black music genre, and caricatures African American men through its title and its cover portrait of two dandies out for a stroll.

After meeting in 1901, the experienced Jerome and the young Schwartz performed together on the vaudeville circuit and composed songs that addressed racial and ethnic themes; they produced blackface minstrel tunes for Broadway shows, including *The Ham Tree* (1905) and *In Hayti* (1909), and contributed songs to *A Chinese Honeymoon* (1902), an extremely successful show that projected what James Moy identifies as an ongoing "Anglo-American desire to define Americanness by noting difference."[56] The pair's biggest hit from *A Chinese Honeymoon*, which played for nearly a year at the Casino Theater, was "Mr. Dooley," a comic song full of Irish dialect. Their talent for meeting the demand for ethnic songs led to a succession of hits, including "Herman" (1907), a rollicking tune about a portly German brewer. To set Jerome's lyrics about wooing an Irish girl in "Bedelia" (1903), Schwartz combined Irish-derived melodic material with the characteristic

rhythms of coon songs. This tune, subtitled "The Irish Coon Song Serenade," sold an estimated three million copies. Displaying pride in their ancestry, Jerome and Schwartz produced songs that asserted the right of Irish
and Jewish immigrants to be treated as full-fledged citizens. "They're All
Good American Names" (1911) begins by honoring the "brawny sons of
Uncle Sam with good old Yankee names" who worship the "Red, White, and
Blue," but the song's third verse confounds expectations by delivering a roll
call of Jewish and Irish surnames meeting this criteria, including Rosen-
stein, Rosenheimer, O'Toole, and Brady. Their follow-up, "If It Wasn't for
the Irish and the Jews" (1912), applauds the contributions of both groups to
America. Jerome and Schwartz recognized the power of music to combat
negative stereotypes and to revise customary notions about America, and
they made admirable efforts to elevate certain communities.

Residents of Chinatown, however, did not receive the same treatment.
Following "Chinatown, My Chinatown," Jerome and Schwartz continued to
manufacture unflattering portraits of China and Chinese America, producing "The Chop-stick Rag" (1912) with the assistance of the lyricist Grant
Clarke. Written for another Eddie Foy stage vehicle and printed by the newly
incorporated Jerome and Schwartz Publishing Company, this song equates
racial and musical difference by claiming that Chinese people possess a de-
formed version of ragtime. Jerome's lyrics describe a "poor old Chink," an
aged laundryman who plays "the chopstick rag in an oriental key." Gathering around to listen to him "dope, dope, dopey-um, just like opium" are the
usual Chinatown suspects: a "pigtail crowd" and a "hop-fiend girl called
Poppy Pearl." To bring out the song's "dopee strain and weird refrain,"
Schwartz resorts to standard orientalist tropes, such as a vamp built on parallel fourths as well as exaggerated chromatic runs to score its "imitation of
that funny syncopation / As played by the yellow nation." Although the theatrical presentation of "The Chop-stick Rag" presumably offered equal help-
ings of spectacle and stereotype, the song's contrived account did not strike a
chord with consumers, and the two songwriters moved away from Chinese-
themed material for several years. Upon the revival of "Chinatown, My Chinatown" in 1915, however, the pair quickly returned to the subject of the Chinese in America and composed "In Blinky, Winky, Chinky Chinatown."
Irving Berlin's publishing firm promoted this tune as "Jerome & Schwartz
New Chinatown Song," the name of its predecessor rendered on the sheet
music cover in an inviting, nearly elegant script (figure 3).

Even though a billowing curtain frames the scene, the entrance to Chinatown depicted by Al Barbelle's cover art appears much less inviting than
Cooney's vision. In keeping with its demeaning title, his artwork relies pre-

FIGURE 3.   Cover art by Al Barbelle for William Jerome (lyrics) and Jean Schwartz
(music), "In Blinky, Winky, Chinky Chinatown." Published by Waterson, Berlin
and Snyder Company (1915). Archive of Popular American Music, UCLA Library
Performing Arts Special Collections, UCLA Library.

dominantly on a yellow color scheme, ripe with racial connotations. Like Cooney, he draws on conventional Asian imagery, including a lantern and a bamboo border; his lettering is menacing; he forms the title's adjectives with black scrawls and sharpens each letter in "Chinatown" to a fine point. The free mixing of Japanese and Chinese imagery persists, as the female figure on the cover wears a blue kimono-style top and a hairstyle derived from traditional Japanese prints. But what is more disturbing about his depiction is that, judging from the eyelashes, the woman's eyes are open but contain no pupils. Like caricatures that substitute slits for eyes, this empty ghostliness strips the figure of an essential human quality. In light of this visual presentation, it comes as little surprise that Jerome's lyrics also construct a harsher portrait of Chinatown, which now constitutes a "land of no return":

Verse 1:
Lights of blinky, winky Chinatown
They brightly burn for those who yearn
Sunshine in that land of no return
What a great big lesson you can learn
See that girl with dreamy, dreamy eye
Hear her sigh as she goes passing by.

Chorus:
Take me down to blinky, winky, Chinky Chinatown,
Where the lights are burning when the sun goes down.
Down where dreamy dreamers dream sweet dreams
In that land of gladness
Picking little poppies there among the hoppies.
There's no tomorrow, sorrow, grief and care.
Oriental angels whisper, "Take me there."
Ah Sing with his little pigtail wears no frown
Down in blinky, winky, Chinky Chinatown

Verse 2:
See that sallow, shallow looking youth
With no regrets but lots of debts.
Life to him is merely cigarettes,
What he used to be he just forgets.
On the corner see this son of Hop
Wink his eye and whisper to the cop.

In this sequel to "Chinatown, My Chinatown," William Jerome recycles several of the earlier song's orientalist metaphors and names one of its characters "Ah Sing" as an evocation of Harte and Twain's "Ah Sin." Rather than identifying a "festive Chink," this song's protagonist spies a "girl with dreamy, dreamy eye / Hear her sigh as she goes passing by"; likewise, the millionaire has been replaced by a "sallow, shallow looking youth / With no regrets but lots of debts." The chorus paints a similar scene, which Jerome exaggerates by providing more explicit descriptions: "Where the lights are low" expands to "Where the lights are burning when the sun goes down," and dreamy Chinatown becomes a place "where dreamy dreamers dream sweet dreams." Jerome also calls greater attention to the tune's reference to opium ("picking little poppies") by moving it directly into the chorus and amplifies his commentary on the racial difference of Chinese American hair ("Ah Sing with his little pigtail") and eyes ("blinky, winky"). To create an appropriate musical setting, Schwartz contributes to this last point by underscoring "blinky, winky, Chinky" with a clichéd series of repeated, alternating notes that form a singsong phrase to signify Asia.

In an attempt to reproduce the success of its predecessor with a cruder hand, the lyrics, music, and cover art of "In Blinky, Winky, Chinky Chinatown" present inflated versions of the orientalist stereotypes found in "Chinatown, My Chinatown." Although this follow-up tune did not prove as commercially successful—later performers have also shied away from it—its failure did not signal a decline in the appeal or production of these sorts of songs. On the contrary, it was largely because of their effective peddling of such material that Jerome and Schwartz became far more revered and influential in their time than is generally recognized today.[57] Schwartz's reputation has since faded, but several of his contemporaries characterized his accomplishments as "spectacular."[58] Similarly, Jerome's peers considered him to be among the "best verse writers" as well as "one of the most beloved characters in the profession."[59] In short order, the representational strategies used by these "star song writers of the time" influenced their fellow songwriters, who continued to produce orientalist depictions of China and Chinese America for years to come.[60]

Many later Tin Pan Alley songs make reference to Jerome's lyrics. Lovers court when "the lights are burning low" in "My Dreamy China Lady" (1916), and in "Fast Asleep in Poppyland" (1919) a Chinese maiden slumbers where "lights burn low."[61] With less shame, Joe Meyer and George P. Hulten recall three of Jerome's phrases within two lines of their chorus for "Down in Chinatown" (1920): "When the lights burn low, pretty lanterns glow, down in Chinatown / Pretty almond eyes, fill you with surprise, as they wander to and fro." In "Chin-Chin Chinaman" (1917), Joe Goodwin and Ballard MacDonald apparently felt the longer the rhyme, the better the song: their title character sings "in his dinky, winky, blinky, chinky Chin-Chin Chinaman way."[62] Along the same lines, Jack Caddigan and Chick

Story combined lyrical and rhyming elements from both of Jerome's efforts in "Blinky Winky" (1922). Set in "dreamy Chinatown," this song tells of a "dreary, lonely little Chinky" living in "the little Hinky Dinky land of Blinky Winky." Perhaps the most conspicuous example of musical homage arrived from the lyricist Frank Davis and composer Win Brookhouse, who paid tribute to Jerome and Schwartz in "All Aboard for Chinatown" (1915). The song's second verse duplicates Jerome's line "He thinks he's a million-aire," and its chorus welcomes listeners to "Dreamy, dreamy Chinatown," where we chance upon a Chinese musician: "Funny, funny Chinaman / Play-ing, playing music grand / Hear that familiar tune, / It's 'Chinatown, my Chinatown' / So all aboard for fascinating, dreamy Chinatown." Cementing the allusion, Brookhouse sets Davis' lyrics to Schwartz's original tune and supports them with a firm pedal on the tonic harmony, accompanied by a steady barrage of sharply accented open fifths (example 14). Jerome and Schwartz's construction of Chinatown thus forms the foundation for a re-peat performance of the same cultural project. Rarely is the self-referential discourse of musical orientalism so apparent as at this moment—when a member of the group being stereotyped, a "funny Chinaman," is made to sing an earlier orientalist song.

Composing songs about Chinese immigrants in America does not nec-essarily call for such a prejudiced approach. In her art song "Chinaman, Laundryman" (1932), the modernist composer Ruth Crawford addresses the oppressive conditions and exploitation faced by a Chinese immigrant and fashions what Ellie Hisama describes as "a musical statement of com-passion, and of hope."[63] But Tin Pan Alley tunesmiths, following the ex-ample of Jerome and Schwartz, continued to propagate the image of Chi-natown as a mysterious opium den: for instance, the main character in "Ching Chong" (1917) becomes the king of Chinatown because "when the time is ripe / He'll fill your little pipe," and the lyrics and cover art of "Pipe Dream Blues" (1918) portray opium smokers on Chinatown's crooked streets. Songwriters relied on similar metaphors for tunes set in China, in-cluding "Shanghai Dream" (1923), "China Dreams" (1917), and "Shang-hai Dream Man" (1927).[64] Regardless of where the Chinese lived—in America, in China, or in a fantasy dreamland—many of America's popu-lar songwriters characterized each place as a center of vice. Such lyrical tropes surface even in the recording that set off the craze for classic urban blues. In the last verse of "Crazy Blues" (1920), Mamie Smith sings: "I'm going to do like a Chinaman, go and get some hops / Get myself a gun and shoot myself a cop." These musical conventions became fixed to such an ex-tent that they were discussed in contemporary songwriting guides. For ex-

Example 14. Frank Davis (lyrics) and Win Brookhouse (music), "All Aboard for Chinatown," mm. 51–57. Published by Shapiro, Bernstein and Company (1915).

ample, Abel Green compliments Philip Braham and Douglas Furber's arrangement of "Limehouse Blues" (1922) for being "as eerie and menacing as possible, in keeping with the underworld, Chinese-smuggling, opium trafficking locale of Limehouse."[65] Resources for budding songwriters thus inscribed orientalist musical practices, training amateurs even before they reached Tin Pan Alley.

Such techniques were further reinforced once songwriters arrived in New York, as George Gershwin's experiences suggest. In 1914 the fifteen-year-old Gershwin landed a job with Jerome H. Remick as a song demonstrator for shop customers. For three years he helped popularize Remick tunes, including "Chinatown, My Chinatown," "My Dreamy China Lady," "Chin-Chin Fox Trot," and "In Japan with Mi-Mo-San." Although he did not land a full-time position with Remick, he gained plenty of exposure to orientalist techniques. Describing how they met in 1920, James P. Johnson, the stride pianist, recalled that Gershwin was "cutting 'oriental' numbers" at the time, by which he apparently meant Gershwin's piano rolls for "Idle Dreams," "Just Snap Your Fingers at Care," and "Limehouse Nights."[66]

Gershwin also cut a piano roll for the opium-related tune "Chinese Blues" (1915) and composed music for "Idle Dreams" (1917), "In the Heart of a Geisha" (1921), "Beneath the Eastern Moon" (1923), and "In the Mandarin's Orchid Garden" (1930).[67]

Jerome and Schwartz's musical legacy can also be gauged by tracing the integration of "Chinatown, My Chinatown" in other cultural domains. On the opposite coast, Hollywood's reliance on analogous representational practices prompted the song's adoption for film soundtracks. In his encyclopedic 1925 manual for professional silent film accompanists, Erno Rapée compiled lengthy lists of compositions, arranged by the country, or countries, the music was thought to evoke. Lumping together China and Japan as a single entity, Rapée categorized "Chinatown, My Chinatown" as appropriate for accompanying any onscreen characters or scenes from Japan or China.[68] His choice registered not only the durability of the song but also the film industry's views concerning the interchangeability of Asian America and Asia. Since the introduction of sound film, the song has surfaced throughout the history of cinema and television, from the film *Bright Lights* (First National, 1935) to the NBC series *Crossing Jordan* (2001–   ), which featured Louis Armstrong's rendition in an episode during its first season. The tune also has made its mark in animated shorts, a genre that depends on music's ability to signify at breakneck speed, first inspiring a 1929 cartoon entitled *Chinatown My Chinatown*. Directed by Dave Fleischer, this Paramount Screen Song cartoon uses the song to score a comic brawl between two Chinese men, stereotypically drawn, who wield their queues like sabers. Similarly, as Daniel Goldmark has documented, Carl Stalling, the genre's most revered composer, frequently depicted "any aspect of Oriental culture" with stereotypical pentatonic melodies, and he incorporated "Chinatown, My Chinatown" in scores for half a dozen cartoons.[69] Stalling's use of the song also worked in the best interests of one of his employers, Warner Bros., which purchased the Jerome Remick firm in 1929 to supply music for its films.

Although a full catalog of the appearances of "Chinatown, My Chinatown" throughout American culture threatens to dull the senses—and the above summary is far from complete—we should not forget that the combined weight of this type of stereotyped representation had real consequences on American consumers. In his frank recollections of life in New Orleans, the jazz guitarist Danny Barker recalls films of the 1920s that featured "Chinese people [white actors in yellowface], who were always villains," plotting with their henchmen, who "wore pigtails, black oriental costumes, [and] pill-box caps," against innocent white victims.[70] These movies were extremely popular with children and adults alike: "We kids would sit on the edges of our seats at the Ivy Theater when the Chinese were handing out all this brutality. They were never shown favorably, and we were all anti-Chinese. We would leave the theater praying that next week the white star would kill all the Chinese in China—especially a female Chinese actress who was real nasty (the older colored folks leaving the Ivy Theater called her Tomato Nose), and the women all wished and prayed that they would love to get their hands on Tomato Nose."[71] Following along the same lines in a semi-autobiographical novel, the writer Robert Lawson describes growing up at the start of the twentieth century, believing the Chinese to be the most heathen foreigners, since they "smoked opium incessantly" and "lived entirely on a horrible dish called 'chopsooey,' which was composed of rats, mice, cats and puppy-dogs."[72] Though these writers look back with remorse about their earlier attitudes—Lawson ponders what he missed out on by not having Chinese friends—their recollections suggest the pervasiveness of negative perceptions of the Chinese during Tin Pan Alley's heyday.

PERFORMING CHINATOWN

I have highlighted the variety of ways and the multiple spheres in which the influence of "Chinatown, My Chinatown" has been felt; yet to conclude the chronicle at this point would be not only disheartening but imbalanced. That is to say, focusing solely on the early life of Jerome and Schwartz's song— its staging, its dissemination as sheet music, its influence on later songwriters, and its initial appropriations—gives the false impression that the song's meaning has remained static. On the contrary, like the shifting views held by Barker and Lawson, the cultural representations constructed through performances of the song have moved in new directions in response to the changing face of American music and to various performers who have recast the tune. Many musicians have chosen to maintain, or even exaggerate, the song's orientalist message, but others have adopted alternative strategies that have resulted in subverting, at least partially, its original intentions.

Although no recordings of the 1910 production of *Up and Down Broadway* exist, one facet of Jean Schwartz's initial conception of "Chinatown, My Chinatown" remains evident in his 1940 ASCAP performance. This does not involve form or orchestration, for Schwartz chose that night to present the tune as a piano instrumental—which suited an audience so familiar with its melody—and played only one verse, followed by two choruses. But one thing stands out about his rendition in contrast with the vast majority of other recorded performances: its unhurried tempo. In comparison to lively jazz renditions, Schwartz's execution requires nearly double the time to proceed through each chorus. He plays the tune slowly, as if it were a serenade, methodically alternating between his left and right hands, not to stress offbeat accents but instead, ostensibly, to make sure every note can be heard. The deliberate pace of Schwartz's reverential treatment served to memorialize the old melody, yet it also suggested just how well a slow tempo suited the dreamy, smoke-filled Chinatown setting in *Up and Down Broadway*. Few musicians, however, have stayed faithful to Schwartz's initial conception and, a few years after the show closed, performers and recording artists adopted a new approach to the song in response to fashions of the day. This broad shift in performance practice took place during a national craze for dancing the one-step and the fox-trot (ca. 1913–14), which resulted in speeding up the tune and fueling its aforementioned revival in 1915.[73] From that point forward, in addition to hearing quicker versions at dance halls or on 78-rpm records, anyone who purchased the Remick sheet music with Cooney's cover art encountered a brand-new tempo marking of *allegro moderato*.

The earliest recording of the song, which features this faster tempo, also exhibits how performers began to introduce extra musical touches to substitute for what earlier had been supplied by staged orientalism. This 1915 release by the aptly named American Quartet calls attention to the foreign character of Chinatown with a variety of techniques. Following the published edition, the vocal quartet presents the song's narrative in complete form, including both verses and two renditions of the chorus. But to create a more "Chinese" atmosphere, their arrangement introduces a brief but memorable passage—featuring a chorus of male singers who shout "Now!" immediately before a percussionist strikes a gong-like cymbal—which is repeated twice in quick succession to mark the start of each verse. Likewise, once Billy Murray begins to sing the opening verse, the sound of a flute (actually an organ using a flute stop) doubles his vocal line at the octave to accentuate Schwartz's quasi-pentatonic melody, and his cronies add choral interjections that either repeat his lines ("midnight up in the sky") or supply comic relief ("Eye-eye, eye-eye-eye-eye"). At the end of the verse, the entire quartet joins in, slowing dramatically to extend the dominant harmony before proceeding with a collective, triumphant presentation of the chorus. As a final gesture that once again reinforces Jerome's message, everyone drops out to spotlight the solo baritone singing "hearts that know no other land" in his deep register.

By presenting the entire text and amplifying its message with orientalist musical tropes, the American Quartet's adaptation of "Chinatown, My Chinatown" repackaged the original theatrical production for home consumption, and its slightly faster, danceable tempo offered listeners further options for enjoyment. Their rendition is invaluable for gauging early performance practice, and many subsequent artists have followed their example of musically underscoring the song's orientalist qualities; in most other respects, however, their approach to performing the song has not endured. On the contrary, as a result of new musical aesthetics and, more recently, changing sensibilities toward racial representation, audiences have become accustomed to hearing only the chorus of the song. In addition to a shift in songwriting practices that began to promote choruses over verses, the advent of jazz has introduced performances that commonly feature musicians taking turns to present the chorus, usually skipping the verses and often bypassing the lyrics altogether.

This key transformation occurred during the Swing Era, when novel approaches to the song prompted a renaissance of "Chinatown, My Chinatown." Big-band arrangers played a crucial role in reshaping performance practice, starting with John Nesbitt, whose arrangement for Fletcher Henderson jettisoned the song's verses and revved up the tempo of the chorus. To entertain white dancers at the Roseland Ballroom, Henderson's orchestra often played music with "Eastern" themes—including "Nagasaki," "Limehouse Blues," and "Shanghai Shuffle"—but "Chinatown, My Chinatown" became especially renowned for its blistering pace. Rex Stewart recalled it as "a spectacular, out-of-this-world swinger, and we tore into that music with such a vengeance that, wherever we played, dancers screamed for more."[74] In comparison to the fifty seconds Jean Schwartz took to stroll through the song's chorus, Henderson's orchestra flew through it in just over half the time, jamming an introduction and six choruses into their 1930 recording. Gunther Schuller describes how their combination of "fast saxophone ensemble runs, snappy brass riffs, hot lightning-fast eighth-note solos, and a relentlessly charging rhythm section" came to embody the model "flag-waver," which quickly entered the standard big-band repertoire.[75] Flashy arrangements of the tune also sparked competition between rival bands. According to the trombonist Sandy Williams, the Chick Webb Orchestra often finished their sets with "Chinatown, My Chinatown," ending jubilantly on a trumpet's high note. But one evening at the Savoy Ballroom, to Williams's chagrin, the Casa Loma Orchestra "came in when we finished, playing the same tune, but their trumpet man started where we left off, and went on up. And then they started swinging. That was a big letdown that night."[76] As a sign of the extent to which the song's identity became coupled with its use as a flag-waver, W. C. Handy later pronounced it his "favorite fast tune for [the past] three decades."[77]

Stripped of its theatrical staging and its lyrics, and without the addition of any expressly "oriental" passages or exotic instrumentation, Henderson's rendition of "Chinatown, My Chinatown" also expanded the range of potential meanings on which audiences could draw, creating possibilities for reception unforeseen by Jerome and Schwartz. Without explicit, audible markers of difference—aside from the associations carried by the original song and its title—listeners are as likely to focus on tapping their feet to the band's bustling rhythm, enjoying the band's infectious riffs, and appreciating Nesbitt's creative variations. Those audience members unfamiliar with the original tune could associate Henderson's "Chinatown" with the thrill of dancing to the latest swing music, of hearing the day's star players, and of witnessing a polished performance by a professional black jazz orchestra. That said, however, other swing bands of the time hired singers who more directly relayed its message of Chinese difference. Like the American Quartet, many arrangers added new "Asian" touches to the song, channeling the exotic with the crash of a gong, sinuous chromatic passages, or whole-tone riffs, techniques that mimicked in music what yellowface makeup previously had enacted onstage. In a similar vein, the music industry packaged the song on the flip side of tunes such as "Limehouse Blues" or, in the case of Jay Wilbur, as part of an "Eastern Medley," beside "Hindustan," "Japanese Sandman," and "The Sheik of Araby." Since bands in this era remained segregated, non-Chinese musicians continued to assume the primary responsibility for representing Chinatown. The singer and bandleader Cab Calloway built a name through his musical portraits of Chinatown, which told of the exploits of Minnie the Moocher, her partner, Smoky Joe, and their fellow opium addicts.

Once "Chinatown, My Chinatown" became a showpiece for big-band virtuosity, it did not take long for the star performer Louis Armstrong to try his hand. Armstrong's studio recording from November 1931 hangs suspended somewhere between the original song and its arrangement as a jazz instrumental, since he drops the verses and also places the chorus in jeopardy. Attempting to outdo Henderson, Armstrong packs eight choruses into slightly over three minutes, forcing his rhythm section to move so quickly that, according to one recent observer, "it sounds like they're nervous."[78] Even more conspicuous is Armstrong's revisionist attitude toward the song. As the band plays a few choruses in the background, Armstrong delivers a long, spoken introduction that makes no mention of Chinatown but instead promotes the band's upcoming musical display. Armstrong does sing one rendition of the chorus, then begins to deconstruct it. His vocals leave intact a few phrases— "Chinatown, my Chinatown" and "drifting to and fro"—but most of

Jerome's lyrics dissolve into expressions and scat syllables of Armstrong's own design. Depending on how we wish to hear this, Armstrong's Chinatown either remains as dreamy as ever, a place where words and pitches no longer matter, or is revealed to have been a dream all along, a flimsy construct that breaks apart and floats away. Armstrong's extended trumpet solo treats Schwartz's melody in the same impertinent fashion. Instead of relying on the original tune or playing it in full, Armstrong quotes snippets from other songs, building onto Schwartz's harmonic foundation something radically different. He concludes without returning to the original vocals, without a final chorus, and without recapping the original tune. Rather than suggesting closure or a return to the familiar, his dramatic solo fashions a narrative of individual achievement by repeatedly leaping up to high C, then D, and, on the song's final note, all the way up to F.

By stressing how widely Armstrong's rendition diverges from the yellowface, opium-filled staging in *Up and Down Broadway* and the exaggerated orientalism of the American Quartet, I do not mean to suggest that he consciously intended a political statement about Asian American representation; after all, he introduced this rendition of the tune as a musical novelty for his listening audience.[79] But intentional or not, the jazz aesthetic began to place the song in a new context, shifting the spotlight away from Jerome and Schwartz's composition and toward individualized reworkings of the tune.[80] Paradoxically, even though Armstrong's performance remains grounded in and reliant on familiarity with the original song, his rendition also starts to register its partial disintegration, illustrating how jazz practices began to revise, to transcend to a degree, some of the song's initial connotations. This set of contradictions points out the difficulty in attempting to reconstruct the range of potential racial representations in any artistic creation. On the one hand, Armstrong's musical conception of "Chinatown" sounds not like a languorous dreamland, but instead like a vibrant place, full of joy and bustling energy, a desirable place to be. On the other hand, Armstrong pumped life into the song, keeping the title, tune, lyrics, theme, and sheet music in circulation: indeed, Jean Schwartz later commented that it was not until Armstrong recorded it that the song became "a hit all over."[81] Subsequently, "Chinatown, My Chinatown" emerged as a jazz standard, leading to recordings in the 1930s by artists as diverse as the Mills Brothers, Stéphane Grappelli, Louis Prima, Spike Jones, and Tommy Dorsey, many of whom allude to Armstrong's recording in their performances.[82]

As Armstrong cultivated a wider following during the early 1930s, "Chinatown, My Chinatown" became one of his show-stoppers, a special favorite of musicians.[83] Roy Eldridge, who first saw Armstrong's orchestra play live as part of a double bill that also featured a Charlie Chan movie, later described how Armstrong's treatment of the song influenced his own playing:

> In 1932, I first caught Louis at the Lafayette Theatre in New York, and he finally upset me. I was a young cat, and I was very fast, but I wasn't telling no kind of story. Well, I sat through the first show, and I didn't think Louis was so extraordinary. But in the second show, he played *Chinatown*. He started out like a new book, building and building, chorus after chorus, and finally reaching a full climax, ending on his high F. It was a real climax, right, clean, clear. The rhythm was rocking, and he had that sound going along with it. Everybody was standing up, including me. He was building the thing all the time instead of just playing it in a straight line.
>
> I've been digging him ever since. I started to feel that if I could combine speed with melodic development while continuing to build, to tell a story, I could create something musical of my own that the people would like.[84]

Armstrong's trumpet protégés began to rehearse the solo note for note, playing it for auditions and making it part of the standard repertoire, while competitors like Eldridge upped the tempo and raised the high notes even higher.[85] During the same period, the tune was still considered appropriate for exploring novelty effects, as demonstrated by Lionel Hampton's 1937 rendition. Transferring his vibraphone skills to the piano, Hampton in his idiosyncratic approach makes use of a few fingers on each hand to hit the piano keys like mallets, producing a swift and constant stream of notes, full of stepwise motion, trills, and other traces of his percussionist background. The racial overtones of "Chinatown, My Chinatown" remained intact as well; indeed, some renditions scaled new heights of stereotyping, such as the 1938 version by Slim and Slam, a popular comic duo who sought laughs by performing several choruses in a mock-Chinese, singsong dialect. In the same vein, but with less overt racial hostility, the song's novelty appeal continued to inspire madcap performances, including a frantic gong-heavy rendition by the Hi-Lo's, a klezmer rendition by Mickey Katz, and an all-harmonica treatment by Borrah Minevitch and His Harmonica Rascals.

In addition to jazz renditions, popular vocalists continued to record the "hardy perennial" and over time an increasing part of its appeal began to derive from nostalgia.[86] As one sign of this shift, which accelerated after World War II, Jerome Remick packaged the sheet music for "Chinatown, My Chinatown" in compilations of "greatest hits" and "old favorites."[87] And the music industry capitalized on postwar American desire for the familiar by releasing old-fashioned renditions from established entertainers such as Bing Crosby (1957) and Bob Hope, whose performance accompanied his film portrayal of Eddie Foy in *The Seven Little Foys* (Paramount, 1955). This blending of musical nostalgia and racial difference proved to be the perfect project for Al Jolson, whose career began in blackface before World War I. In 1949 the sixty-two-year-old Jolson recorded the tune for the score of *Jolson Sings Again* (Columbia), a biographical film starring Larry Parks as Jolson. By this point, Jolson had sung Schwartz's music for four decades, starting with "Rum Tum Tiddle" (1911) and continuing with the hits "Hello Central! Give Me No Man's Land" and "Rock-a-Bye Your Baby with a Dixie Melody." A montage in the film depicts Jolson entertaining U.S. military troops with standbys like "Chinatown, My Chinatown," reminding them, and the film's expected audience, of an earlier era when the challenges posed by American minority groups appeared to be more under control. In this context, Jolson's melodramatic conclusion seemingly attempts to reinforce the message of Chinese and Chinese American difference as he sings of "dreamy dreamy China, dreamy dreamy China, China, Chinatown."

Crowds gathered to hear Jolson plug the film; for a publicity tour of New York City movie theaters, Jolson tailored each of his personal appearances according to neighborhood. In Little Italy, for example, he delivered a Caruso imitation, and for a Chinatown audience, Jolson performed two songs: "Chinatown, My Chinatown" and "My Yellow Jacket Girl," which he had sung first in *The Honeymoon Express* (1913), a show featuring music by Jean Schwartz and lyrics by Harold Atteridge.[88] The latter song concerns a man who attends a Chinese play and then attempts to court a girl in appropriately "Chinese" fashion. The first verse mentions chopsticks, drugs, and a Chinese "mandolin" (i.e., shamisen), which Schwartz mimics with a liberal sprinkling of grace notes. Pledging himself to the woman he loves "more than tea," Atteridge's suitor promises to do anything—start a Chinese laundry, eat chop suey, or act like Ching-a-ling Fou, the title character from an earlier Chinese-themed song—if only his beloved will "be my yellow jacket girl." By performing two songs that feature orientalist subjects and possessive titles, "*My* Yellow Jacket Girl" and "Chinatown, *My* Chinatown," Jolson enacted once more the role of a privileged observer of Chinatown, trying again to represent and control its inhabitants.

It is nevertheless likely that some residents of New York's Chinatown appreciated Jolson's performance, not necessarily for all it signified, but for its promoting the neighborhood. By the middle of the twentieth century, the district had become known more for its restaurants, bazaars, and foreign merchandise than for its vice traffic. Along the way, local merchants had learned how to exploit Chinatown's Chineseness, to package and profit from the exotic; tourists now marveled at pagoda-style architecture, enjoyed sensational nightclub acts, feasted on unique cuisine, and purchased exotic curios and cheap trinkets. Thus, even though Chinese Americans were not in charge of their own musical representation, certain community members could applaud Al Jolson's exoticizing nostalgia as readily as they earlier might have appreciated Louis Armstrong's exuberance. The collective sympathies of later generations of Asian Americans, however, have not been as fully supportive of such musical messages, for the politics of representation has shifted dramatically in response to historical and cultural trends in the wake of the civil rights era and to radical transformations in U.S. immigration law.

CHINATOWN TODAY

Over the last forty years, changes to immigration policy and civil rights legislation have altered the face of America and the realities of America's Chinatowns. In the 2000 U.S. census, ten million Americans, approximately 4 percent of the nation's population, identified themselves as having Asian ancestry, Chinese Americans constituting the largest subgroup; moreover, demographers predict sustained growth of the Asian American population.[89] New immigrants and American-born Chinese have settled not only in traditionally Chinese neighborhoods of San Francisco, New York, and Los Angeles but in ethnically diverse areas of these cities and in towns across the nation. Because of differing class backgrounds, today's Chinese immigrants are as likely to congregate in suburbia as in the inner city. As a result of the population increase of Chinese Americans, three Southern Californian suburbs—Monterey Park, Cerritos, and Walnut—all featured Asian majorities in 2000. These demographic shifts have prompted fresh reexaminations of Chinese American life by contemporary scholars working across a wide range of disciplines, including history, sociology, and Asian American studies. Titles of recent publications signal a revisionist turn—*Chinatown No More, Reconstructing Chinatown,* and *Claiming America*—that reflects a broader move to place the concerns and actions of their subjects at the center of their work, offering trans-Pacific alternatives to trans-Atlantic narratives about the nation, and identifying what America has meant for Chinese Americans.[90] Sociocultural changes in America have also nourished the artistic careers of Chinese Americans and Chinese nationals in residence, such as the writer Amy Tan, composer Tan Dun, and filmmaker Wayne

Wang, all of whom have shared alternative perspectives about the immigrant experience. In response to increasing participation in cultural production, today's academics are as likely to focus on Asian American self-representation as on the representation of Asian Americans by others.[91] The process of documenting Asian American musical life also has shown signs of growth. Since Ronald Riddle published his 1983 monograph on the music of Chinese San Francisco, numerous scholars have designed projects that focus on Chinese American music, musicians, and perspectives.[92] Their valuable work is beginning to recover the complex, multifaceted musical histories óf the residents of Chinatown.

Images of Chinatown that circulate in contemporary culture, however, often resemble the sinister backdrop of *Chinatown* (Paramount, 1974), the acclaimed film directed by Roman Polanski and starring Jack Nicholson, where the district functions as the site of terrible, unexplained mysteries in the past and as the setting for deadly violence at the film's conclusion. Popular musicians continue to recycle age-old representational strategies as well: witness the construction of modern-day "China Girls" by 1980s pop stars.[93] Such imagery makes it less surprising to learn that Harte and Twain's *Ah Sin* was revived in Los Angeles in 1962, a few years before the start of a new wave of Asian immigration that would later generate protests against such representation.[94] Yet, even if we can designate Ah Sin as a marker of a past era, albeit a not too distant one, it is more difficult to account for the 2001 attempt to revive D. W. Griffith's *Broken Blossoms* as an exotic musical, exhibiting no detectable traces of irony and introducing a batch of brand-new songs, including "Limehouse Nights," "The Chinaman Song," and "Opium Dreams," the last tune sung by the "Dragon Lady" and a "chorus of whores."[95]

In light of these examples, it remains vital for Asian Americanists to continue examining cultural spheres that include few Asian American participants—such as Tin Pan Alley, Hollywood, and Broadway—for scholarship too can work either to reinforce or to bring into question such representational practices. For example, dubious approaches to American music that detach aesthetics from history can result in reference works that characterize "Chinatown, My Chinatown" as a "durable song favorite . . . that *salutes* New York City's Chinatown district."[96] I rely on my above discussion to address the nature of this salutation, but it is true that the song's durability can hardly be questioned. Its popularity as sheet music, its role in accompanying films, cartoons, and television shows, and its distinction as a recording standard in jazz and popular music all testify to the cultural influence of "Chinatown, My Chinatown." In recent years the well-known director Woody Allen has used the song in several films, including *Everyone Says I Love You* (Miramax, 1996), where it accompanies a trio of children made up in yellowface.[97] Even today's state-of-the-art entertainment products incorporate the tune, delivering its message to a new generation of consumers. When the protagonist of the popular video game *Mafia: The City of Lost Heaven* (2002) enters a violent scenario in 1930s Chinatown, players hear a recording by the Mills Brothers over and over until the scene ends.[98]

Almost a century old, the song endures through dozens upon dozens of recordings that are available today.[99] Many are vintage performances from the 1920s through the 1950s, as suggested by table 3; however, modern compilations frequently repackage older versions, and brand-new recordings of the tune continue to emerge. In their 1998 performance, the Hot Club of Cowtown, a Western swing band based in Austin, Texas, skips the song's verses and concentrates on the chorus, presenting several vocal renditions and using it as a platform for instrumental solos.[100] In keeping with the nature of the tune, the trio produces a tone of warm, nostalgic dreaminess through the singer's behind-the-beat drawl, the twangs of a guitar, and the lilting sweep of the violin. Since the group's musical language contains no extra orientalist touches, however, their foot-tapping rendition seems to inform listeners more about their reverence for Milton Brown and other musical pioneers who incorporated the song into the Western swing tradition than about a conscious desire to propagate the song's original message. Modern sensibilities also influence the group's presentation of the chorus. Apparently uneasy with Jerome's original lyrics, the group's lead singer replaces "almond eyes of brown" with "hair and eyes are brown," a phrase still racialized in the context of the chorus but presumably intended to be less offensive. In addition, for the line "hearts seem light and life seems bright," the Hot Club substitutes "hearts are light and lights are bright," a change that suggests that hearts truly are light, as opposed to "seeming" so from the effects of opium. In spite of these updates, which give the tune a more acceptable spin, the song's lyrical fashioning of Chinese difference remains fairly intact. Although this performance does not embellish the song's orientalist qualities, as a result of treating the song so respectfully, singing the rest of the chorus, and evoking the tune's extensive history, even their modernized version cannot fully shed its original connotations.

Although the apparent self-consciousness shown by the Hot Club of Cowtown suggests an attempt to balance portraying how things used to be with how things have changed, the producers of the CD compilation *Oriental Illusions* display a remarkably cavalier attitude toward U.S. history.[101]

Despite the accuracy of the disc's title—the collection includes such songs as "Chinatown, My Chinatown," "Sing Song Girl," and "China Girl"—its packaging flaunts the sort of revisionism in which the original songwriters might take pride: "America's fascination with the Orient at the start of the 20th century fostered the beginning of Chinamania. The average American knew very little about the mysterious far east, but that was about to change. Songwriters began to pen songs about China and this continued well into the 1930's. This compilation contains historical performances that show the influence China had on Western music. Travel with us back in time and enjoy 'Oriental Illusions.'" Undoubtedly, the music of Tin Pan Alley did help introduce notions about China and the Orient to American audiences; but the producers of this collection imply that these songs, which they hope will entertain today's audiences, function as authentic bearers of Chinese culture. In other words, their logic conflates musical influence and attempts at cross-cultural understanding with musical exoticism and racial fabrication. This approach, as troubling as it is to discover on the back cover of a CD released in 1995, confirms a primary thread woven through this chapter: that popular songs like "Chinatown, My Chinatown" created history of their own by molding impressions of China, Chinatown, Chinese Americans, and all Americans of Asian descent.

According to K. Scott Wong, another consequence of America's production of orientalist imagery is that it places contemporary artists in the awkward position of having to define what Chinatown is *not*, rather than to start anew and define what Chinatown is.[102] Though certainly regrettable, this position is by no means unique to the Asian American community, and musical performers throughout the ages have variously incorporated, critiqued, and responded to existing music to formulate their own perspectives. As Krystyn Moon has documented, this process began on the American vaudeville stage at the start of the twentieth century, when Chinese and Chinese American performers began "to promote the appreciation of their heritage, question racism, and gain control over images generated on the stage."[103] Future performers, like today's music scholars, are also afforded the opportunity to play a revisionist role of their own. Perhaps the most extreme stance one could adopt would be to neglect songs like "Chinatown, My Chinatown," to refuse to sing or write about them in hopes that they would float off on their own accord. And, like several of Jerome and Schwartz's other Chinatown efforts, some songs do fade away. But choosing to ignore a popular standard does not mean that other performers will do the same—nor have they—and addressing the issues at stake in this body of songs may require more active engagement.

I have yet to discover a recorded performance of "Chinatown, My Chinatown" that manages to detach itself completely from the song's original intentions, that reconfigures or reconstructs the song into something altogether different. A self-aware performer might do so by echoing the strategy used by the Chinatown History Museum, which reframed the past on its own terms by renaming itself the Museum of Chinese in the Americas. A vivid example of such radical revisionism in contemporary musical culture recently took place when the playwright David Henry Hwang recast Broadway's most famous (and only full-length) depiction of Chinese America, Rodgers and Hammerstein's musical *Flower Drum Song* (1958). Hwang's intent was to "write the book that Hammerstein might have written had he been Asian-American"; his 2001 revival involved a thorough rewrite, in which nearly every line was updated, and the show frames Rodgers's songs in new settings, in terms of scenery, plot, characters, and staging.[104] Following in these footsteps, by rewriting the lyrics or restaging the presentation of "Chinatown, My Chinatown," present-day musicians could latch on to the cultural significance of the tune while reinventing the meanings of its familiar melody, giving voice to the formerly voiceless.

Still, artists might well be cautioned in advance that some of the old expectations for visiting Chinatown remain active in contemporary critical circles. Writing about the revival of *Flower Drum Song* for the *New York Times*, Ben Brantley bemoaned the novel uses to which Hwang put the old songs, entitling his review "New Coat of Paint for Old Pagoda" and stating his preferences for the "cute and cozy ethnic types" of the original production over Hwang's "set of positive Asian role models."[105] Before we toss aside the gains of the past century and replicate the gushing reception that met the Chinatown scene in *Up and Down Broadway*, it should be emphasized that the more diverse set of voices constituting today's critical establishment also can offer support for musical reconsiderations. In the face of what he called a "gauntlet of critics suddenly quite protective of a musical they never much liked in the first place," *Time's* Richard Zoglin deemed Hwang's update to be a success, neither condescending nor preaching to its audience but instead entertaining the crowd with a "richer, more nuanced exploration of the immigrant experience."[106] Attending a performance of *Flower Drum Song* as part of a multiethnic, multigenerational audience during its sold-out run in Los Angeles, I was struck by the sight of so many Asian American performers onstage in an American musical. Like Zoglin, I did not find the show entirely satisfying—perhaps more because of its reliance on certain Broadway conventions than its departures from tradition—but I left the theater with a desire to discuss its triumphs and failures, to commend or carp about the performers, and to debate the ideas the show raised, the images it evoked, and the music it reimagined.

For historians of American music, it might seem tempting to dismiss songs like "Chinatown, My Chinatown" as ethnic novelties, characteristic of and confined to an earlier, less well-informed age; however, because of their continual manufacture, their reproduction through decades of performances and recordings, and the participation of such canonical figures, this repertoire must be regarded as central to Tin Pan Alley, vital to the development of American music. Indeed, since America's music industry continues to rehash age-old Asian stereotypes for contemporary audiences, albeit to address differently configured cultural tensions, the issues brought forth by "Chinatown, My Chinatown" remain salient in the twenty-first century. By gaining a better understanding of how America's music industry envisioned and reproduced the nation a century ago, and by acknowledging the role that music has played in shaping perceptions about Asia and Asian America, we can begin to untangle the roots of musical and social practices that persist today.

5. Sounds of Paradise

Hawai'i and the American Musical Imagination

Before they began composing music about the Chinese in America, the songwriting team of William Jerome and Jean Schwartz published "My Hula Lula Girl" (1903), one of their first songs. Given such a title, one might expect its lyrics to address Hawaiian themes in a tropical setting; however, the song takes place at a "midway by the sea," a popular carnival of attractions likely inspired by Brooklyn's Coney Island, where the song's male narrator travels to gaze at the dancer "Hula Lula." Jerome's lyrics appear to highlight primitivist imagery when it is revealed that Lula, who also dances the "Bungaloo," is an island princess sent to the States by her father, King Mataboola. Jerome also draws on common tropes for the exotic female by spotlighting the entrancing eyes, the unusual beauty, and the sensuous dancing of this "oriental pearl." The notion of a mysterious, orientalized beauty is further pronounced by the sheet music cover art for "My Hula Lula Girl," which features an image of a woman's face partially obscured behind a veil. Such a surplus of signs delivers a confusing message, however, for though it is possible to understand these varied images as deriving from similar impulses to market the primitive and the exotic—whether from Hawai'i, Africa, or the Orient—they are quite difficult to reconcile with one another. Despite the name of the song's title character, Jerome's lyrics make no specific references to Hawai'i and no mention of steel guitars, 'ukuleles, palm trees, pineapples, surfing, grass skirts, or any of the other stereotypical icons that have since been used as shorthand for Hawaiian culture. Consequently, one might say that "My Hula Lula Girl" fails to meet the standard conventions for a Tin Pan Alley Hawaiian-themed song. At the very least, the song indicates how the visual and musical shorthand for Hawaiian culture had not yet been codified by American songwriters at the beginning of the twentieth century.

165

What is even more idiosyncratic about "My Hula Lula Girl," considering that it was created by a pair of songwriters who became so invested in producing ethnic novelty songs of all stripes, is the song's denouement. Though the first verse contributes a slight air of uncertainty about Hula Lula's roots, noting "that's the way they advertise it on the bills," the final chorus pulls open the curtain on this theatrical artifice:

> She is my Hula Lula girl
> She is an oriental pearl
> Eyes that are dreamy, form divine,
> Her father's name is Pat O'Brien
> Back in the good old days of yore
> She measured tape in Macy's store
> On Fourteenth Street, I used to meet
> My dainty Hula Lula girl

In what becomes a self-aware tale that pokes fun at the American taste for the exotic, revealing it to be a fabricated homegrown invention, Hula Lula turns out to be a local Irish American girl who used to work in Manhattan at Macy's department store. To his credit, Jerome's lyrics reflect keen awareness of the elaborate simulation necessitated by this style of commercial entertainment. Perhaps this should come as no surprise, for songs that relied on musical exoticism to portray racial difference, minus the final ironic twist, helped sustain Jerome and Schwartz during their partnership. Indeed, the song's unconventional strategy and its lack of commercial success may explain why the songwriting pair later adopted a less adventurous and more lucrative approach to manufacturing ethnic novelties. Songs of this era rarely chose to imitate the strategy of "My Hula Lula Girl" by exposing the machinery behind musical exoticism.[1] On the contrary, it did not take long for Tin Pan Alley songwriters to figure out how to harness the commercial demand for exoticism and apply it to the production of Hawaiian-themed popular music.

A dozen years later, Jean Schwartz took part in what became a national craze for Hawaiian music that spread across the United States. In 1915, the same year that featured his contribution to In "Blinky, Winky, Chinky Chinatown," Schwartz composed music for a song that registers the prominent place that the territory of Hawai'i had come to assume in the American consciousness, "Hello, Hawaii, How Are You?" The song's lyrics by Edgar Leslie and Bert Kalmar describe the longing of a U.S. military officer, Captain Jinks, for his island sweetheart, Honolulu Lou. Rather than mourning shared heartache, the tune's mostly comic premise, told entirely from the perspective of the captain, involves his exaggerated efforts to contact his beloved by telephone. In doing so, the song marks the recent debut of the Marconi wireless telephone while poking fun at its exorbitant cost, for the captain ends up spending a month's pay on a long-distance call to ask for a "kiss by wireless." Ultimately, however, his time runs out before he ever gets to hear her voice, yet the captain remains just as smitten.

Though "Hello, Hawaii, How Are You?" plays this situation for laughs, the song could work as comedy only for audiences who understood Hawai'i to be a potential site of such desire. Although trans-Pacific calls were not yet possible, despite the embellished claims made by this song, American consumers had become more familiar with the islands as a tropical tourist destination, as the subject of countless contemporary popular songs and recordings, and as a U.S. military outpost, symbolized here by the captain's presence. Increased acquaintance with stereotypical Hawaiian imagery is equally evident in its sheet music cover art, which depicts his Hawaiian lover, wearing a grass skirt, standing next to a hut on a sandy beach, and surrounded by palm trees and seagulls. To appeal to a mainstream U.S. audience, Schwartz follows typical Tin Pan Alley song form, using a piano introduction, a vamp, two verses, and a sing-along chorus with repeats. Although the song does not contain overt references to indigenous Hawaiian music, Schwartz brings out the comic elements of the narrative by evoking the falsetto technique often used in Hawaiian vocal delivery through increasingly syncopated leaps that enliven the song's title phrase and highlight the name Honolulu Lou. He also draws attention to the captain's insistent request for a kiss with repeated rhythmic triplets while reserving an animated series of dotted rhythms for the climax of the chorus, when he bemoans having "to pawn ev'ry little thing I own" to pay for the call. What accounts for the broad shift in representational practices between the creation of "Hula Lula" and "Honolulu Lou"? In what forms did Hawaiian musical sounds and visual imagery come to occupy the American musical imagination? And how and why did America's fascination with Hawaiian music take shape in this era?

HAWAIIAN MUSIC AND HAPA HAOLE SONGS

This chapter traces the significant ways in which Hawaiian musicians and musical practices contributed to the history of American music during the opening decades of the twentieth century, an era during which a craze swept the United States for Hawaiian and Hawaiian-themed music in the form of live entertainment, sheet music publications, phonograph recordings, and imported instruments such as the 'ukulele and the Hawaiian steel guitar. Since most scholarly attention on Hawaiian music has been devoted to indigenous practices, my concentration on the interplay between Hawai'i and the United States in the commercial arena of popular music is meant to address a sizeable gap in the literature. This series of events also resonates with key themes, introduced in my earlier discussion of Jelly Roll Morton and the Spanish tinge, regarding the evolution of American music. In particular, since the popularity of Hawaiian music began nearly half a century before Hawai'i became a state, this musical encounter again reveals the influence of musical practices that originated outside the nation's borders and calls attention to the international, ethnically diverse, and multicultural roots of American music. Of special significance here are the political and cultural clashes that emerged between America and Hawai'i in this era. Nations may try to define themselves unilaterally, but inevitably self-perception is forged in relationship to others. Examining the multifaceted relationship between the United States and a small collection of islands that was annexed as a U.S. territory in 1898 is thus especially fruitful, for it demonstrates how differential power relationships are played out in the arena of musical culture through varying processes of cultural collision, cooptation, and contestation.

This musical encounter was determined to a great extent by inequities of power: between a small set of islands and a nation trying on new imperial garb; between local island firms struggling in vain to keep pace with American mass production and distribution; between the desires of island consumers and the demands of the American mainstream market. The clash of cultures, as one would expect, found expression in music throughout this period, whether in songs composed by Hawaiian musicians that combined elements from both Hawaiian sources and American popular genres or in Hawaiian-themed songs written by Tin Pan Alley composers that perpetuated cultural and racial stereotypes of Hawaiians. Because of the gusto with which American publishers, recording companies, and performers jumped on the Hawaiian bandwagon, music became a site of struggle over representations of Hawai'i and control of Hawaiian music. Alarmed Hawaiians consequently worried that the future of Hawaiian music would not be determined by musicians and composers on the islands but by those affiliated with the American music industry. Though in the short term certain of these fears were realized, over the course of the century Hawaiians eventually would regain a measure of power and influence.

A brief explanation of terminology is necessary, for it is difficult to reach agreement on a single or simple definition of Hawaiian music. Should such a definition focus on indigenous musical practices, on the creative output of individual Hawaiian musicians, or on all music making that occurs in the is-lands?[2] This dilemma derives from many factors, including the wide range of ethnic musical practices on the Hawaiian Islands, the high degree of in-teraction between indigenous and foreign musical traditions—initially from Europe and America—and the considerable efforts by the U.S. music industry to produce Hawaiian-themed music. Various overlaps between the worlds of popular music and indigenous Hawaiian music have created even more complications, as a result of the circulation throughout the Hawaiian Islands of Westernized performance practices and repertory as well as the participation of numerous Hawaiian musicians who created, recorded, and popularized these songs.[3]

Responding to the ongoing debate over defining Hawaiian music, like that about American music, I employ two separate but intimately related meanings of this term. In most cases, *Hawaiian music* here embraces any music making in Hawai'i or music created by Hawaiian musicians, regard-less of its degree of connection to indigenous practices. To understand American perceptions of Hawaiian music in this period, however, it is also necessary to account for the many hundreds of Hawaiian-themed songs created by non-Hawaiian songwriters and marketed by Tin Pan Alley pub-lishers.[4] These American-made songs have often been denounced as "pseudo-Hawaiian" by those who recognize their shallow and misleading representations of Hawaiian music and culture. Indeed, as one leading scholar has demonstrated, "commonly-held stereotypes of Hawaiian music bear little resemblance to the ethnic musical traditions which thrive in Hawai'i."[5] Tin Pan Alley thus helped to propagate many false impressions—whether based on race, gender, or cultural difference—at the time of their creation, but these songs contributed powerfully to what "Hawaiian music" signified to many American listeners. By keeping these opposing definitions in view, while attempting to clarify each usage within the appropriate context, I wish to capture a sense of the conflict between Hawaiian and American perceptions over the meaning, direction, and own-ership of Hawaiian music.[6] As necessary, I will also employ more specific terms to distinguish between individual musical traditions and genres, such as modern Hawaiian hulas, *hapa haole* songs, and Hawaiian-themed Tin Pan Alley songs. I do not claim to present a full history of Hawaiian music as told from island perspectives. Despite the dispossession of various histo-riographic resources, alternative histories that focus on indigenous per-spectives are being written; one may turn, for example, to the inspiring work of music scholars such as Amy Ku'uleialoha Stillman for accounts of

Hawaiian cultural agency, resilience, and resistance.[7] Centering primarily on external perspectives of Hawaiian music that took shape in the United States, my inquiry attempts to demystify the processes of cultural representation. Although our methods differ, I believe that our scholarship shares certain broad aims, seeking to understand how the colonizing project works as well as to dislodge colonial narratives.

The Hawaiian craze that swept Tin Pan Alley bears some resemblance to the concurrent production of orientalist songs discussed in chapter 4. Both types of songs explore racial and cultural differences, experiment with various modes of racial representation, and attempt to differentiate between supposedly primitive and advanced civilizations. Songwriters who settled their gaze on the South Seas may have called on similar musical strategies; however, the rationale behind Hawaiian exoticism was differently configured. In his work on Western opera of this period, Gilles de Van describes exoticism as the "attraction for a civilization—manners, climate, social behavior, clothing—foreign to our own, far from us in time or space."[8] This notion does not really apply to Tin Pan Alley songs about Chinatown, which emphasized the foreignness of local Chinese neighborhoods in an attempt to distance them from the nation; de Van's conception of exoticism, however, better captures the essence of America's initial fascination with Hawai'i. Small, sparsely populated, and distant, the islands did not pose a threat of aggression, nor did islanders add to what some Americans saw as the burden of immigration. After the territory was subdued from a military and political perspective, Hawai'i's image as a sun-swept paradise afforded American consumers much more freedom to indulge in their exotic fantasies, desires that could be fulfilled by Hawaiian-themed Tin Pan Alley songs.

What distinguishes the Hawaiian craze even further from the music composed on Chinese subjects involves the active participation of Hawaiian musicians in shaping some of these developments. Unlike residents of Chinatown—strangers in the nation's midst who had few opportunities to participate in mainstream American musical life—musicians from the islands ended up touring America, performing for enormous crowds, making studio recordings, and sometimes gaining international fame. This is not to say that Hawaiian musicians typically achieved full control over their musical careers; if anything, their success in the United States required continuous negotiation with American impresarios, booking agents, and recording studio executives—situations in which power was seldom theirs. But their well-honed skills and inimitable approaches to music making enabled Hawaiian musicians to gain a foothold in the industry and to achieve some measure of self-representation. Not only do many of their recordings survive, but the musical instruments they popularized and the performance techniques they pioneered remain embedded in contemporary American musical life.

It is perhaps not surprising, in light of its central position as part of indigenous Hawaiian culture, that the dissemination of music became a key channel through which American consumers were introduced to Hawai'i.[9] This brand of cultural diplomacy was promoted by the efforts of one of several musically inclined members of the Hawaiian royalty, Queen Lili'uokalani, an enthusiastic musician who composed hundreds of songs over the course of her long life.[10] Her song "Nani Na Pua Ko'olau" became one of the first Hawaiian songs to be circulated in the United States when Oliver Ditson, a Boston publisher, began printing copies in 1869. Fifteen years later Ditson published Lili'uokalani's best-known composition, the celebrated Hawaiian song "Aloha 'Oe," which she wrote while still a princess in 1878. Introduced to mainland audiences by Henry Berger and the Royal Hawaiian Band during their visit to San Francisco in August 1883, "Aloha 'Oe" has since become synonymous with Hawai'i in the American musical imagination, which demonstrates just how effective Hawaiians became at popularizing their music, and how early they did so.[11] The song's renown grew in the wake of political developments, for Americans became more familiar with Lili'uokalani after she was crowned queen in 1891, then ousted in 1893 by a small group of American planters and businessmen who toppled the Hawaiian monarchy.

In an era when white settlers constituted less than 10 percent of the population of Hawai'i, the events leading from the 1893 coup to Hawai'i's formal annexation by the United States five years later supplied absorbing tropical news, marking the first time in which Americans planned and executed the overthrow of a foreign government.[12] Supporters of annexation convinced the U.S. government that turning Hawai'i into a virtual colony would help bolster American naval defenses, expand Pacific-based trading opportunities, and increase the flow of sugar, pineapple, and other Hawaiian exports. The entire affair delivered a boost to America's imperialist ambitions when Hawai'i was designated an American territory, run by a U.S.-appointed governor and a cadre of U.S.-friendly business interests that controlled the island's agricultural, transportation, financial, retail, and service industries. Consequently, intrigue about Hawai'i rose among Americans, who now felt a closer bond to this still exotic but less distant land. Some dreamed about a South Seas idyll far away from an increasingly industrialized America, while others with the means began to plan island vacations.

In conjunction with topical reports about Hawai'i around the time of its annexation, American songwriters took the genre of the coon song for a brief Hawaiian spin, publishing titles such as "Ma Honolulu Queen" (1896), "My Gal from Honolulu" (1899), "Ginger Lou" (1899), and "The Belle of Honolulu" (1902). These pieces retained the typical characteristics of coon songs—including minstrel stereotypes, ragtime-style rhythms, and comic imitations of African American dialect—and sprinkled in references to Hawai'i and Hawaiian characters. Offering a sense of the genre confusion that ensued, the cover of Lee Johnson's "Ma Honolulu Man" (1899) proclaims itself an "Oriental coon song" that contained a "Ragtime Chorus" and an instrumental "Hawaiian cake walk." Despite what their titles imply, these songs contain no audible traces of Hawaiian music and only scant awareness of Hawaiian culture. Examples such as Johnson's "My Honolulu Lady" (1898), in which the hero exchanges his "Alabama gal for Honolulu Lou," mention Hawaiian female characters solely to evoke the fantasy of an island romance. It is as if the allure of a South Seas beauty was channeled simply in hopes of outshining the relatively mundane figure of a southern belle. For American composers around the turn of the century, Hawai'i functioned as an emblem of the novel and exotic, even though it was not very well understood.

Things began to change as Americans became more familiar with Hawai'i. American tourists had begun visiting the islands in the 1880s, and by the following decade, shipping lines were selling $125 tickets for round-trip travel between San Francisco and Hawai'i. Local business efforts to promote the islands as a tourist paradise and a hub for Pacific trade picked up more steam after annexation. Hawai'i's first systematic promotional campaign began with the founding of the Hawaiian Promotion Committee in 1903, which has been succeeded by a variety of related organizations, including the Hawai'i Tourist Bureau (1919), the Hawai'i Visitors Bureau (1946), and the Hawai'i Visitors and Convention Bureau (1996), an organization that continues to promote tourism in the islands today. During the first few decades of the twentieth century, Americans who could not afford a trip were able to experience Hawaiian music without making the ocean voyage. Displaying a knack for self-promotion, numerous troupes of Hawaiian musicians and dancers mounted tours to the United States, where they variously joined the vaudeville circuit, toured small theaters, and performed at local, state, and international expositions.[13] For many Americans, such visits provided initial exposure to talented Hawaiian performers, including Toots Paka, Irene West, Sonny Cunha, and Joseph Kekuku.

By this time, the U.S. record industry also had begun to tap into the market for Hawaiian musical performances, as a result of a recording enterprise that combined ethnographic, aesthetic, and commercial impulses. The first American firm to record Hawaiian music was the San Francisco outlet of the Thomas Edison Company, which recorded the Hawaiian Quartet on cylinders in 1899; unfortunately, the master recordings were destroyed in the earthquake and fire of 1906, and no existing copies have surfaced.[14] In 1904 the Victor Recording Company issued the first major release of Hawaiian music in the States in the form of a set of fifty-three single-sided discs.[15] Shortly thereafter, in late 1904 or early 1905, the American Record Company followed with a set containing several dozen Hawaiian performances.[16] Over the following decade, several American record companies either visited Hawai'i to record local talent or brought touring Hawaiian musicians into their studios during their trips to the States. Consequently, a handful of years before the Hawaiian music craze arrived in earnest, U.S. consumers could already purchase recordings by emerging island performers. Rather than spotlighting Hawaiian-themed songs written by Tin Pan Alley composers, many of the earliest recordings concentrated on instrumentals and songs written by Hawaiian composers. Thus, at this early stage, island musicians were able to carve out a niche for Hawaiian-produced music within the competitive U.S. music industry.

This is not to say, however, that these artists recorded traditional indigenous repertoire, for the violent encounter between Hawaiians and foreigners had already introduced Western musical scales, harmonies, instruments, and forms into certain areas of Hawaiian musical culture. One larger effect of this cultural collision brought the Hawaiian phrase *hapa haole* into circulation. *Hapa haole*, which translates as "half-foreign" but historically has implied "half-white," refers to a person of mixed descent, the result of miscegenation between native Hawaiians and foreigners. As island musicians were exposed to European and American musical genres in the late nineteenth century, this phrase was subsequently applied to hybrid musical combinations that intermingled island traditions with outside elements, especially those taken from American popular music. In this context, *hapa haole* has been used to refer to various cross-cultural musical encounters: songs that incorporate Hawaiian and English lyrics; indigenous songs recast with English lyrics; pieces that mix elements of Hawaiian music with non-Hawaiian genres, such as ragtime, blues, jazz, and rock; and, according to the broadest definition, English-language songs with lyrics that address Hawaiian themes.

Albert R. "Sonny" Cunha (1879–1933), a composer, arranger, and performer, gained his title as the "father of *hapa haole* songs" as a result of his penchant for intermingling elements of American popular music with Hawaiian melodies.[17] Though he may have first heard American music through recordings and sheet music imported to Hawai'i, Cunha experienced the sounds of ragtime more directly during his time as a student in the United States. In fact, he arrived at Yale Law School in 1898, the year that Charles Ives was completing his undergraduate studies.[18] Rather than choosing to pursue a career in law, however, Cunha returned to Honolulu and began what would be a very successful run as a composer, pianist, arranger, and bandleader. By the time he was in his early forties, his musical achievements and the reputation of his well-known Honolulu family enabled him to gain several prominent posts as a Hawaiian politician.

In 1903 Bergstrom Music, a local Honolulu firm, published Cunha's first *hapa haole* song, "My Waikiki Mermaid," which preceded the U.S. vogue for Hawaiian music by nearly a decade. Written in $\frac{2}{4}$ time, like much ragtime, but taken at a slower pace marked expressively as *"Tempo di Hula,"* this carefree tune outlines the stereotypical attributes of an island girl: affectionate, alluring, attentive, sweet, and beautiful. Following a piano introduction, Cunha relies mainly on English-language lyrics, but he repeats the same Hawaiian-language tag at the close of each of the four couplets that this brief piece comprises. This linguistic mix functions as a significant cultural symbol in two opposing respects. On the one hand, Cunha's lyrics reflect the steady rise of English as the principal language in Hawai'i, a process that began when U.S. settlers arrived en masse in the late nineteenth century and was later enforced by an 1896 law that made English-language instruction mandatory for schools seeking government certification. On the other hand, his decision to include Hawaiian phrases as part of these *hapa haole* songs indicates native pride and acknowledges Honolulu's cultural blend; Cunha himself was a *hapa haole* of Portuguese and Hawaiian descent.

Cunha continued to produce similar depictions of Hawaiian life, including "My Honolulu Hula Girl" (1909), about an impish delight who will "surely make you giggle . . . with her naughty little wiggle," and the more sexually suggestive "My Honolulu Tomboy" (1905), which includes this passage: "And when I take her out for an automobile ride in the moonlight / Sits on my lap all night holds on so tight you bet she's right." The sheet music cover art for these songs, featuring photographs of native beauties adorned with flowers, also foreshadows some of the marketing practices on which the mainland Hawaiian craze would rely. Cunha's compositional style in "My Honolulu

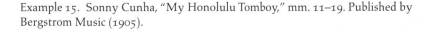

Example 15. Sonny Cunha, "My Honolulu Tomboy," mm. 11–19. Published by Bergstrom Music (1905).

Tomboy" incorporates certain Hawaiian musical characteristics within the setting of this *hapa haole* tune that have been identified by George Kanahele, including large melodic leaps, repeated or sequential patterns, a clear tonic-dominant relationship, and a casual intermingling of English and Hawaiian (example 15).[19] The song derives its basic strophic form from the *hula ku'i* pattern by setting each of its four stanzas, arranged as couplets, to the same melody and separating them by very brief instrumental interludes.[20] Cunha's early songs therefore can be seen as attempting to hold on to elements of Hawaiian music while incorporating new lyrical and musical influences from contemporary American popular genres.[21]

Four years later, Cunha embraced a more distinctively American style for writing *hapa haole* songs in "My Honolulu Hula Girl," which comprises a four-bar introduction that leads into Tin Pan Alley verse-chorus form and relies exclusively on English-language lyrics. Cunha also takes advantage of ragtime techniques by setting the tune in $\frac{2}{4}$ tempo, invigorating its lively chorus with a raglike bass, adding continuous piano syncopations, and topping things off with hemiola-style rhythmic effects for the

Example 16. Sonny Cunha, "My Honolulu Hula Girl," mm. 21–23. Published by
Bergstrom Music (1909).

vocals (example 16). Because of such a heavy reliance on the musical language of American popular music, it is difficult to pinpoint characteristics,
aside from the song's lyrical content and the composer's background, that
connect this tune to Hawaiian musical culture. Fittingly, in this light, the
song took on new life in the 1920s when Cunha made minor lyrical mod-
ifications and repackaged the song under a new title, "Hapa Haole Hula
Girl." Through the early 1930s, Cunha continued to compose tunes on the
subject of desirable Hawaiian women, releasing titles such as "My Hawaiian Maid" and "Hawaiian Girl o' Mine." His musical stature grew as a result of his popular arrangement of "On the Beach at Waikiki" (1915) and
his later mentorship of Johnny Noble and other *hapa haole* composers. In
these ways Cunha's career served as both a prelude and an accompaniment
to the vogue of Hawaiian music that overtook the United States in the mid-
1910s. As much as his *hapa haole* songs foreshadowed the Hawaiian-
themed hits crafted by Tin Pan Alley songwriters, his career also demonstrates how musical ideas were not flowing in a single direction from
Hawai'i to the mainland, but rather were circulating back and forth across
the Pacific. Consequently, once the craze for Hawaiian music took hold on
the continent, it was neither a case of authentic imports finally reaching the
States nor a matter of U.S. songwriters producing imitations of indigenous
Hawaiian music. The truth of this complex cultural exchange lay somewhere in between, and it developed further when an American theatrical
impresario hired five Hawaiian musicians to perform on the Broadway
stage.

THE BIRD OF PARADISE

Plays may come and plays may go but "The Bird of Paradise,"
Richard Walton Tully's delightful story of life in the Hawaiian
Islands, seems destined to go on forever.

Washington Post (1916)

Before the early 1910s, music aficionados in the United States might encounter Hawaiian music at occasional live performances, on a limited number of recordings, and as published sheet music, but it was a theatrical production, *The Bird of Paradise* (1911), that "introduced the vogue of Hawaiian music to the American public."[22] Although it was not the first show to be set in Hawai'i, this Broadway stage play established itself as by far the most successful of its kind. In a recent essay that traces its commodification of Hawai'i and its subsequent influence on American culture, Christopher Balme describes the production as a Polynesian variation on Giacomo Puccini's *Madama Butterfly* (1904).[23] Echoing the basic outline of the opera, *The Bird of Paradise* tells the story of an ill-fated cross-cultural romance between a white American male, Paul Wilson, and a native Hawaiian girl, Luana, who readies herself to leap into a burning volcano at show's end. The resemblance was not coincidental, for the playwright Richard Walton Tully had previously worked with David Belasco, and it was Belasco's earlier melodrama that had inspired Puccini to compose his opera. Tully addresses similar issues of race, nation, and gender in his exploration of the conflicted relationship between East and West. In addition to its floral reference to the tropical bird of paradise, Tully's vision repackages the Japanese butterfly as a Hawaiian "bird" and transforms Japan into "the Paradise of the Pacific," as the islands had become known in the late nineteenth century. Critics also noticed the play's resemblance to Puccini's opera, which had premiered in New York five years earlier, the *Washington Post* dubbing it the "'Madame Butterfly' of the Hawaiian Islands."[24]

The stage representation of Hawai'i delivered by *The Bird of Paradise* suited a nation coming to terms with its recent military and territorial conquests. Set in the early 1890s, just before annexation, the play stages the colonial encounter between American settlers and indigenous natives, between a budding imperial power and a largely preindustrial civilization. Presenting its clash of civilizations in a distant land, like *Madama Butterfly*, also allowed for the playing out of American anxieties concerning racial difference and miscegenation. Equally important for the show's commercial prospects was the voluptuous South Seas setting, which provided the rationale for a spectacular display of tropical escapism. Guided by Tully's interest in Hawai'i, the production attempted to reproduce aspects of Hawaiian culture by importing artifacts, costumes, stage props, and, most notably, a quintet of Hawaiian musicians.[25] As one critic observed of the Broadway premiere, "Native superstitions, native dialect, native dances and native music are ever present."[26] Tully adopted a similarly expansive strategy, expanding his plot beyond the tragic love story and recounting conflicts between foreign and indigenous factions on the island that involved missionaries, beachcombers, fishermen, and sugar planters.

The dramatic and commercial possibilities of this work were not lost on Oliver Morosco, a Los Angeles–based theatrical impresario to whom Tully took his script.[27] Tully's goal of presenting a wide-ranging view of Hawaiian culture dovetailed with Morosco's objective of creating a crowd-pleasing show, and together their efforts generated a sensational theatrical event. Because of the expected costs of the elaborate staging and imported props, the pair sought other investors, including the future U.S. senator James D. Phelan, who purchased a one-quarter stake in the show. Phelan had been responsible, during his earlier years as mayor of San Francisco, for leading the charge to protect America's borders by excluding Asian immigrants, and he welcomed the chance to invest in a play that highlighted themes involving racial difference and miscegenation. Thanks in part to his support, the lavish production featured impressive sets, including a magnificent cave, a thatch of grass huts on a lava-encrusted beach, and a bubbling volcanic crater, but perhaps to Phelan's chagrin, the play ended up popularizing live Hawaiian performers to audiences far and wide.

The Bird of Paradise premiered on 11 September 1911 at the Belasco Theater in Los Angeles, where it performed well enough to land a spot on Broadway several months later. After a warm-up engagement in Rochester, New York, the show opened in New York City at Daly's Theater on 8 January 1912 before moving to Maxine Elliott's for the balance of its run. While it did not become a Broadway hit, closing after 112 performances, *The Bird of Paradise* gained widespread fame as a result of extensive touring through the United States and Canada over the next dozen years as well as productions in England, Australia, India, and beyond. In cities such as Los Angeles, which hosted the show for thirteen successive seasons, *The Bird of Paradise* earned a reputation as "one of the greater successes ever known on the stage."[28] Even upon its ninth visit, one critic could still gush: "The permeating charm of the romance of Hawaii, and its princess, and its people hardly seems to vary, or lose aught of its reality."[29] As a result of these road shows, the play reportedly netted more than a million dollars in profits. Some critics were not as enthusiastic about its success. Looking back a quarter century after its

Broadway premiere, J. C. Furnas despaired that the play "ineradicably imbed-
ded the Hawaii-*cum*-South-Seas tradition in the mass-mind of America"
and ended up inflicting "a nation-wide plague of Hawaiian acts."[30] In truth,
the play spawned numerous spin-offs: Hawaiian-themed numbers in revues
such as the 1916 *Ziegfeld Follies;* full-fledged tropical productions like *My
Honolulu Girl* (1919), *Tangerine* (1921), and *Aloma of the South Seas*
(1925); a revival in the form of a musical comedy entitled *Luana* (1930); and
two full-length films that shared the play's title and setting (1932, directed
by King Vidor; 1951, directed by Delmer Daves), if not an identical plot.

Like the *New York Times* columnist who admired the "scenic beauty" of
The Bird of Paradise, most critics appreciated the production's impressive
staging.[31] The inclusion of native Hawaiian musicians proved equally critical to the show's success, and their music became a key selling point. Re-
viewing its premiere, the *Los Angeles Times* singled out the "really beautiful Hawaiian music given by native players."[32] For Broadway theatergoers,
apparently less familiar with Hawaiian culture than their West Coast counterparts, *The Bird of Paradise* marked "the introduction of the weirdly sensuous music of the island people."[33] The source of this fascination was the
group of five Hawaiian musicians—W. K. Kolomoku, B. Waiwaiole, S. M.
Kaiawe, A. Kiwaia, and W. B. Aeko—who performed onstage and received
full credit in the program. Using Hawaiian techniques for performing the
'ukulele, steel guitar, and *ipu* (an indigenous double-gourd percussion instrument), the quintet supplied "an almost continuous undercurrent of the
sweetly plaintive Hawaiian airs and harmony," performing instrumentals
and songs as well as accompanying songs and dances performed by other
characters in the show.[34] Their performances were so novel and striking that
the *New York World* complimented the group before commenting on any
of the actors, and the *New York Clipper* praised the musicians for supplying
"additional interest and charm."[35] Enthusiastic reviewers of the musicians
and the music of *The Bird of Paradise* commended "the native musicians
who make the haunting musical interpolations of their own land" and drew
attention to the distinctive "threnody of the ukulele and the haunting,
yearning cry of steel pressed against the strings of the guitar."[36]

Although Tully's original script for *The Bird of Paradise* contains neither
music nor lyrics for any individual songs, the "appealing lure of the Hawaiian music interpreted by native singers" played an increasing role in touring productions to establish a tropical mood, to deliver brief musical interludes, and to give onstage dancers a chance to perform the hula.[37] For this
reason, Tully and Morosco recruited talented island musicians, including
Tandy MacKenzie, the most prominent opera star that Hawai'i has yet to

produce, who began his professional singing career by touring for several years with a road company of *The Bird of Paradise*. As a result of their efforts, the *Washington Post* praised the music as being "more effective in the establishment of the languorous, alluring, hypnotic atmosphere which the author describes than all the costumes, native faces, odd properties, and elaborate scenery combined."[38] Won over by the "Hawaiian atmosphere and charm" of a touring production, the *Los Angeles Times* similarly emphasized the role played by the musicians: "The Hawaiian singers are the ones who were at the Belasco before and their music is redolent with the flavor of their enchanting islands. The Hula dance by Kolamoku [*sic*], himself a native, is both striking and to Americans entirely original."[39] Within a few years of the play's crisscrossing the nation, critics from all corners hailed the show. "The haunting strains of the Hawaiian music," according to one report, "have made Mr. Tully's South Sea idyl a classic of the modern stage."[40]

The show's popularity also sparked further interest in Hawaiian music recordings. Early in 1912 Columbia introduced a large set of Hawaiian double-sided discs recorded in a newly constructed studio in Honolulu, featuring the music of island composers and performed by local glee clubs, singers, and instrumental soloists.[41] The musicians who took part in *The Bird of Paradise* also found themselves in high demand, spending time in the recording studio before heading out on the road with the show. The Hawaiian Quintette released nearly two dozen recordings for Victor, including "Aloha 'Oe," "My Honolulu Tomboy," and other songs of Hawaiian origin that had been incorporated into early stagings of the production.[42] Another Hawaiian instrumentalist to benefit from the show's success was Joseph Kekuku, a virtuoso musician who is thought to have originated the method of playing Hawaiian steel guitar. This primarily melodic approach involves placing the guitar flat across the lap and changing pitches by sliding a steel bar up and down the finger board without pressing down behind the frets to form chords. Building on the phenomenal drawing power of Tully and Morosco's extravaganza, Kekuku sailed across the Atlantic in 1919, performing as the steel guitarist in a *Bird of Paradise* troupe that toured Europe for eight years. Traveling productions also shaped the creative lives of some individual audience members. After seeing a performance of the show in the Midwest, Don Blanding was inspired to move from Oklahoma to Hawai'i, where he established a career as an author, song lyricist, poet, and illustrator. In addition to publishing books such as *The Virgin of Waikiki* and *Hula Moons*, Blanding helped to sustain the craze by producing sheet music cover art and penning lyrics for dozens of Hawaiian-themed songs.

To spruce up what became annual productions of *The Bird of Paradise,* Morosco and Tully interpolated Hawaiian musical selections, many of which were marketed in the form of sheet music and commercial recordings. The music derived from a variety of sources, including Hawaiian instrumentals that were given new show-specific titles, such as "The Luana Waltz"; Hawaiian songs to which English lyrics were added, including "Forget Me Not (Mai Poina Oe)" and "Burning Love (Ahi Wela)"; and established Hawaiian *hapa haole* songs, including Cunha's "My Honolulu Hula Girl" and "One-Two-Three-Four" by S. Kalama and Jack Alau. The show became so popular that even the most celebrated Hawaiian melody took a backseat to its celebrity. When Seidel Music published their 1915 edition of "Aloha 'Oe," which included the original Hawaiian lyrics alongside an English translation written by Noble L. Sissle, the sheet music cover pitched the tune as "The Beautiful Melody from *The Bird of Paradise.*" To capitalize on the success of the stage production, publishers also placed photographs of Laurette Taylor, Lenore Ulric, and other actresses who played Luana on the cover of each song sheet. Dressed in Broadway's version of Hawaiian costume, which entailed an abundance of beaded necklaces, a floral headband, and a grass skirt, visual mementos of Luana served as an effective cross-marketing device (figure 4). Sheet music for songs used in various productions of the show enabled consumers to relive their theatrical experience by playing the music at home.

As the key Hawaiian role in the production, and the female embodiment of exoticism, erotic appeal, and island charm, the character of Luana drew considerable attention from the onset. New York critics were enchanted by Laurette Taylor's sensual performance of the hula, a Hawaiian dance that she helped turn into a national sensation. Although her hula performance was taken by some American critics to be an authentic reproduction, Taylor confessed her lack of familiarity with Hawai'i and Hawaiian culture: "I hate to disabuse the public, but I don't know anything at all about Hawaii. I have never been there; I never met any Hawaiians until I began to study the role of Luana, and I'm sure I don't know whether the dialect I used in the play is real or not." Taylor learned her version of the hula from Tully, with coaching from the Hawaiian musicians hired for the show.[43] That did not prevent numerous songwriters from composing titles in her honor. "Sweet Luana," "Luana: My Hawaiian Queen," "By the Sad Luana Shore," and "Luana Lou" all appeared in 1916 alone. Similarly, the phrase "bird of paradise" became synonymous with a desirable Hawaiian girl, which led to a number of knockoff songs that rode the coattails of the show. Billed as a "Hawaiian love song," Ed Madden and Max Hoffman's "Bird of Paradise" (1912) involves the relationships between a sailor and a girl in each port, including the "Hula

FIGURE 4.   Cover art by Gene Buck for W. A. Aeko (arranger) and Arthur Denvir (English lyrics), "Forget Me Not." Published by the John Franklin Music Company (1912). Archive of Popular American Music, UCLA Library Performing Arts Special Collections, UCLA Library.

maid" who waits for him; Phil De Angelis's lyrics for "Beautiful Bird of Paradise" (1913) trace one man's yearning for the "dusky maiden who I call my bird of Paradise." Thus, just as Puccini prompted Tin Pan Alley publishers to release songs based on the title character of *Madama Butterfly*, so too did Tully inspire songwriters to compose Hawaiian-themed songs based on *The Bird of Paradise*.[44] These two musical streams converged in the hit song "Hawaiian Butterfly" (1917), which describes an American male sending pledges to his self-sacrificing, distant love, "beautiful Hulu." Before the show opened, Tin Pan Alley songs published on Hawaiian themes rarely emphasized stock Hawaiian imagery, but once *The Bird of Paradise* became a sensation, virtually all of the hundreds of Tin Pan Alley songs that appeared during and shortly after its long run recycled the same Hawaiian tropes. Indeed, the cultural influence of *The Bird of Paradise* can be gauged in part by how powerfully this set of racialized and gendered dynamics, revolving around images of Hawai'i and Hawaiian women in particular, took hold in the world of American popular music.[45]

The character of Luana and the propagation of her image on- and off-stage offer support for Jane Desmond's argument in *Staging Tourism*, which analyzes the role of tourism in the formation of Hawai'i over the last century.[46] Desmond discusses how this process proceeded hand in hand with the evolution of hula iconography and the image of the hula girl, an eroticized and exoticized female figure who was made less threatening in part through her playing music, dancing, and frolicking in the surf and sand.[47] As a result in part of the dissemination of the hula girl image, Desmond suggests, the islands came to function as an "arena of sensuous play for white mainlanders, a place of mental escape which seized the national imagination."[48] Yet American consumers did not have to settle for Luana's Americanized version of the hula in *The Bird of Paradise* or for the drawings on the covers of Hawaiian-themed sheet music. As Adria Imada has documented, Hawaiian musical ensembles and hula dancers had been appearing regularly in the United States since the late nineteenth century.[49] Indeed, it was a long-term engagement by a quartet of Hawaiian musicians performing in San Francisco that would help stimulate the next major advance in the popularity of Hawaiian music in America.

"EVERYBODY'S CRAZY ABOUT HAWAII"

Hawaiian musicians had previously appeared on vaudeville stages and performed at international expositions, including the 1893 Chicago World's

Fair, but it was not until 1915, when the Panama-Pacific International Exposition took place in San Francisco, that Hawaiian music became firmly ingrained in America's musical consciousness. Held in celebration of the completion of the Panama Canal and the expansion of trade routes to Asia, the exposition also marked the symbolic return of the city of San Francisco after the earthquake and fire of 1906. The fair's various exhibitions, performances, and amusement rides drew massive crowds, attracting an estimated nineteen million visitors over a seven-month run. Since the 1893 Chicago fair, more than two decades earlier, American perceptions of Hawai'i had changed dramatically. Now firmly established as a U.S. territory, the islands had become known as a naval outpost, a more accessible tourist destination, and the subject of an enormously popular traveling show. Viewing this West Coast event as a choice opportunity to promote the islands further, the U.S.-friendly business and agricultural interests that controlled the Hawaiian legislature appropriated $100,000 for the construction of a Hawaiian pavilion at the fair. "The whole idea of Hawaiian representation at the Exposition," explained one of its proponents, "was to gain more publicity for the islands, publicity which would attract the traveler, make the islands better known, and better understood, and cause them to become the tourist mecca of the travel world."[50] According to the official history of the fair, this effective strategy increased the number of visitors to Hawai'i by more than 50 percent the following winter.[51]

Although diminutive in comparison to the lavish buildings constructed by wealthy U.S. states, the Territory of Hawai'i building profited from an excellent location near the Fine Arts Palace and the California building. According to one contemporary study of the fair, the Hawaiian Pavilion proved to be "one of the most popular" destinations.[52] The building itself was designed by an Oakland-based architect, C. W. Dickey, who followed a French Renaissance style, and Hawaiian exhibitors filled its small space to capacity by decorating the interior with painted tiles, native flowers, a statue of surfers, and frieze panels inscribed with text from native legends.[53] For a taste of Hawai'i, visitors could enter an adjoining room to view moving pictures and lantern slides of lush island landscapes; alternatively, they could visit the Hawaiian Gardens in the fair's Horticultural Building to sample pineapple, which was served by *hapa haole* women hired by the Hawai'i Pineapple Growers Association.[54] The day after the fair opened, the *San Francisco Chronicle* praised the Hawaiian exhibit for two special features: "a tropical garden, showing the wonderful foliage of Hawai'i, and an aquarium such as never before seen here," consisting of a dramatic series of backlit tanks that contained thousands of colorful fish.[55]

To draw crowds to this bountiful display, organizers hit upon the idea of using Hawaiian music as a "lure which will bring the thousands of exposition visitors."[56] A contest was held in Honolulu, and the Royal Hawaiian Quartette emerged victorious. Led by George E. K. Awai on acoustic steel guitar, who was joined by Ben Zablan on eight-string 'ukulele, Bill Kaina on 'ukulele, and Henry Komomua on guitar and vocals, the quartet performed twice daily for the duration of the exposition.[57] On a raised platform, surrounded by island palms and ferns, and attired in dashing white outfits, red sashes, and Hawaiian leis, the group performed traditional songs as well as *hapa haole* songs, including many numbers featured in *The Bird of Paradise*. Joining them were occasional guest performers from Hawai'i, such as the steel guitarists Frank Ferera and Joseph Kekuku. According to one enthusiastic commentator, "the Hawaii building was a colossus in popularity, for the strum of ukuleles and the tinkle of guitars gently touching passers-by, compelled entrance to the building."[58] This experience also led to further opportunities for musicians such as Awai, who remained in San Francisco after the fair closed and worked for Sherman, Clay, a local music store and publisher, where he taught 'ukulele and steel guitar and also published his own steel guitar instructional manuals.

To revitalize interest in the pavilion around the midpoint of the exposition, the Hawaiian contingent staged a special daylong celebration on 11 June 1915. Coinciding with an island holiday that commemorates the birth of King Kamehameha, the affair included a formal ceremony, a lavish banquet, and an elaborate production staged at the Fine Arts Palace lagoon. A speech by Lucius Eugene Pinkham, the U.S.-appointed governor of Hawai'i, highlighted the critical role played by the islands in America's national defense, but if we are to judge by the press coverage, the entertainment made a much bigger impression. Despite being programmed against a John Philip Sousa concert, the "Night in Hawaii" attracted an estimated twenty-five thousand visitors. With a nod to the history of Hawaiian royalty and a bow to the Broadway stage, the event was designed in large part to attract the attention of the U.S. motion picture industry; in fact, the show was repeated the next afternoon for motion picture operators who missed the evening festivities. The splashy production presented an honorary pageant queen, sitting in a giant, jewel-encrusted shell and surrounded by five princesses who gazed down on the proceedings. Chanting Hawaiian men wearing native costume paddled outrigger canoes across the lagoon, and they were joined by decorative floats covered with palm fronds and Hawaiian flags. A full program of music by the Hawaiian Quartette, with assistance from other Hawaiian musicians as well as the Philippine Constabulary Band, helped tie the production together. The groups also supplied music for dancing before the evening closed with a round of fireworks. According to the *San Francisco Chronicle*, this "spectacle outrivaled anything of its kind held at the exposition."[59] Likewise, the official historian of the exposition, which featured more than two thousand musical events, later described it as "the most enchanting and beautiful of the night scenes."[60]

The musical programming for the "Night in Hawaii" revealed a dual impulse of remaining faithful to certain Hawaiian practices while responding to the widening appeal of *hapa haole* songs. Thus, in addition to renditions of older Hawaiian-language ballads, such as "Aloha 'Oe" and "Ua Like No a Like," the Hawaiian ensemble performed numerous *hapa haole* songs, including Henry Clark's "Ona Ona," Harry Kahanamu's "Mauna Kea," Ben Jones's "Wiliwili Wai," Frank Kemma's "Ihole Manu," Jack Heleluke's "Fair Hawaii," and William Lincoln's "Winds Form over the Sea." Given a boost from repeated performances by the Hawaiian Quartette, several tunes emerged as hits over the course of the fair, including "On the Beach at Waikiki" (1915), a song with lyrics by Dr. G. H. Stover, music by Henry Kailimai, and an arrangement by Sonny Cunha. Composed by Hawaiian songwriters, published by a Honolulu firm, and publicized by Hawaiian musicians, this *hapa haole* tune aimed to entertain mainstream U.S. audiences while supporting the cause of Hawaiian self-promotion, an objective also advanced by the photograph of Waikiki Beach on its sheet music cover. In subsequent years, many would attribute the sudden increase in popularity of Hawaiian music directly to the exposition, such as the observer who held it "more responsible for the craze for our music and instruments that is now sweeping the country than any other agency."[61] But it may be more accurate to characterize the exposition as one of many factors—including increased American familiarity with Hawai'i, frequent tours by Hawaiian performers, greater availability of recorded Hawaiian music, the continual stagings of *The Bird of Paradise*, then in its fourth year, and the widening popularity of a pleasing musical form of entertainment from the Pacific that acted as a distraction from the war in Europe—all of which combined to form a tipping point that eventually spilled over into the nationwide craze for Hawaiian and Hawaiian-themed music.

Tin Pan Alley's interest in producing Hawaiian songs had little to do with the pursuit of musical authenticity or the quest for cross-cultural understanding; rather, this venture demonstrates clearly how the politics of representation can play into the formation of American national identity. Creating products that combined hula girl iconography and tropical exoticism, the music industry not only supported the American colonial project but also tapped into America's growing fascination with Hawaiian tourist destinations. In an attempt to duplicate the sensation of "On the Beach at Waikiki," Tin Pan Alley firms released dozens of titles that make reference to Waikiki ("My Waikiki Ukulele Girl," "My Rose of Waikiki," "Waikiki Blues"), Honolulu ("Honolulu Honey," "Honolou," "My Honey Lou"), or both ("Waiki-Ki-Ki Lou"). The lyrics for "On the Beach at Waikiki" offer a partial explanation for why so many songwriters integrated a comic brand of stereotypical lyrics in Hawaiian-themed songs. In addition to its use of "Waikiki" in the title, the repeated hook of this *hapa haole* song describes a "sweet brown maiden" who declares "Honi kaua, wikiwiki" ("let us kiss quickly").[62] The use and repetition of short syllabic sounds was understood by non-Hawaiians to be playful, primitive, and redolent of the exotic allure of the islands. By exaggerating the lilting cadence of the Hawaiian language and the sensuality of this particular phrase, Tin Pan Alley songwriters transformed genuine Hawaiian terms like "Waikiki" and "wikiwiki" into a mishmash of nonsensical lyrics and comic song titles. Relying on this approach the year after the exposition, Stanley Murphy, Charles McCarron, and Albert Von Tilzer released "Oh, How She Could Yacki Hacki Wicki Wacki Woo (That's Love in Honolu)" (1916), the chorus of which opens with several lines of rhythmically active gibberish: "She had a Hula, Hula, Hicki, Boola Boola in her walk / She had a Ukalele Wicki Wicki Waili in her talk."

Like those of many Tin Pan Alley compositions that followed over the next few years, the lyrics of "On the Beach at Waikiki" concern the desire of a male visitor to Hawai'i for a local Hawaiian girl. By repackaging the thematic material common to this song and the plot of *The Bird of Paradise*, American publishers began churning out sheet music about the fascination of white males for exotic Hawaiian females, among them "My Honolulu Bride," "I Lost My Heart in Honolulu," "Dreamy Hawaii," and "My Honolulu Lulu" (figure 5). Though the visual imagery that accompanied these songs relied heavily on cultural and gendered stereotyping, certain song lyrics also underscored racial difference, as they used phrases such as "brown-skinned hula girl" or "my little brown Hawaiian maid" or "brown skin babies." What pushes these songs further into the realm of escapist fantasy, in contrast to the cautionary tragedy enacted by *The Bird of Paradise*, is their tendency to downplay the idea of a Hawaiian femme fatale and instead to feature happy endings in which the lovers unite or, much more frequently, to depict a lasting, long-distance love between the male narrator and the hula girl far away. Consequently, as Larry Hamberlin comments in reference to the proliferation of songs based on *Madama Butterfly*, "nostalgic reminiscence became the dominant mood, allowing white audiences

FIGURE 5.   Cover art by Walter Dunk for Arthur F. Holt (lyrics) and William T. Pierson (music), "My Honolulu Lulu." Published by W. T. Pierson (1916). Courtesy of the Music Library, University of Michigan, Ann Arbor.

to indulge in fantasies of interracial romances that would bear no inconvenient consequences."[63] Many of Cunha's early *hapa haole* songs contain a similar set of gender dynamics, told from the perspective of a male who fetishizes Hawaiian beauties. What differentiates most Hawaiian-themed Tin Pan Alley songs is that they accentuate not only the gendered but also the racialized dynamics of this encounter, suppressing the Hawaiian female perspective and focusing on the experiences of a white American male protagonist.

According to Sigmund Spaeth, a contemporary observer who later published a detailed history of Tin Pan Alley, America's fascination with Hawaiian-themed songs "assumed the proportions of an organized publicity campaign . . . and nearly every songwriter tried his hand at something Hawaiian."[64] One songwriter to try his hand was Irving Berlin, who composed four Hawaiian-themed songs in this period.[65] Having already written dozens of ethnic novelty songs during his early career, Berlin turned his attention to writing about the exotic South Seas. Never one to miss a marketing opportunity, he titled his first Hawaiian song "My Bird of Paradise" (1915), the lyrics of which contain distant echoes of the stage production's plot. Like other Hawaiian-themed Tin Pan Alley tunes, Berlin's "My Bird of Paradise" features a slower tempo—here marked *moderato*—and includes a few musical touches meant to evoke Hawaiian music, such as a quick sequence of running eighth notes that accompanies the line "I hear a Ukalele strumming gaily." In addition, like most of his fellow songwriters, Berlin chose to omit the tragic final chapter of the stage production in favor of the promise of a future reunion. The verses of Berlin's song describe the longing of a "Honolulu Girl" for the return of her "Hawaiian lover" from overseas. While the text is somewhat ambiguous—"Hawaiian" might refer to her lover's birthplace—the broader context for these songs and the song's lyrics suggest that "Hawaiian lover" refers instead to the place where the two lovers met. "Wait for me / My Honolulu Girl / My hula-hula girl / I'm coming back to you" promise the opening lines of his long epistolary reply, which eventually concludes with this pledge: "I'll be coming back again / To you, my Bird of Paradise." Berlin accentuates the dramatic arc of the song by employing minor mode for the drawn-out phrases about nostalgic longing and major mode for the quicker dotted rhythms that signify the Honolulu girl before turning to E-flat major once and for all by the end of the chorus.

Berlin adopted different strategies for the Hawaiian-themed songs he contributed to *Stop! Look! Listen!* by Harry B. Smith, which opened on Broadway on Christmas Day 1915. As part of a plot that revolves around the

Example 17. Irving Berlin, "That Hula Hula," mm. 12–19. Published by Irving Berlin (1915).

search for a suitably exotic female to star in a Broadway production, the show's second act takes place in Hawai'i, shifting scenes between Honolulu and Waikiki Beach. Following the lead of *The Bird of Paradise,* the producers hired a Hawaiian octet, comprising primarily Hawaiian musicians, which played *hapa haole* tunes, including "One-Two-Three-Four" and "On the Beach at Waikiki." The ensemble also performed two Hawaiian songs composed by Berlin to accompany members of a cast that included the popular entertainer Blossom Seeley in the role of "A Hula-Hula Girl." Sharing the optimism of Berlin's previous Hawaiian effort, the first song, "Oh, What a Place Is Dreamy Honolulu," depicts an island paradise full of gentle breezes, happy smiles, dancing, and romance. In contrast, Berlin's second song from *Stop! Look! Listen!* takes on an air of parody. In the verses of "That Hula Hula," Berlin pokes fun at the conventions of plaintive romance that already had begun to permeate Tin Pan Alley's Hawaiian-themed songs by setting its lyrical exaggerations to equally inflated musical phrases with a large helping of chromaticism (example 17). Following the sinuous melody and minor tonality of the verse, Berlin's song plunges into a comic rhyming refrain about doing "the Hula in Honolula." Employing a musical technique that became widespread, Berlin constructs its chorus using a series of rhyming two-bar phrases that repeatedly land on the long "oo" sound of "Hula." Taken collectively, these songs display how Berlin simultaneously perpetuated and parodied the craze for all things Hawaiian.

In his final Hawaiian song, "I'm Down in Honolulu (Looking Them Over)" (1916), Berlin adopts a similarly knowing stance toward clichéd tropes about native sexuality. This larger-than-life comic tale revolves around the opportunistic Uncle Jeremiah, who has moved to Hawai'i to look over all of the scantily clad girls in hopes that they will teach him to "say wicky wicky." Recalling the lyrical catchphrase of "On the Beach at Waikiki," Berlin's protagonist seems to have stood for any American consumer who longed to spend time meeting native Hawaiian beauties. By creating a figure that could provoke either envy or censure, Berlin thus tried to profit from and lampoon the lengths American consumers might go to satisfy their Hawaiian appetite. Perhaps in part because of the ironic distance Berlin adopted with respect to his Hawaiian material, these tongue-in-cheek songs did not prove to be what the public wanted—none of the four songs became a major commercial hit. Instead, Berlin made his greatest mark during the Hawaiian music craze by publishing more than a dozen Hawaiian songs through his joint publishing venture with Ted Snyder and Henry Waterson. In addition to his own songs, Berlin's firm published two of the most popular tunes of the era: the aforementioned "Hello, Hawaii, How Are You?" with music by Jean Schwartz, and an even more successful novelty hit, "Yaaka Hula Hickey Dula" (1916).

Composed by E. Ray Goetz, Joe Young, and Pete Wendling, performed by Al Jolson in the Broadway show *Robinson Crusoe, Jr.*, and published by Waterson, Berlin, and Snyder, "Yaaka Hula Hickey Dula" makes several references to Hawaiian culture, each with an ostensibly humorous twist. Though the song reuses a common lyrical theme, tracing one man's attraction to a

Hawaiian maiden named Hula Lou, any serious sentiments of longing are supplanted here by the pursuit of laughs, a slant that Jolson played up on-stage by performing a comic imitation of the hula dance. Along these lines, the song's title pokes fun at the Hawaiian language, enclosing a reference to the hula within a series of nonsense syllables. Relying on repetition to complete this effect, the song contains eighteen separate instances of either the title phrase or a slight variant ("Yaaka hula hickey du"), accentuating the long "oo" sound by extending its duration and often placing it at phrase endings. Literally and figuratively upending Hawaiian music in more obvious terms, the chorus of "Yaaka Hula Hickey Dula" draws its opening vocal phrase directly from "Aloha 'Oe" by presenting an inverted and slightly distorted version of Queen Lili'uokalani's original melody (example 18).[66] The song's infectious combination of willful parody, comic repetition, and tropical exoticism proved extremely popular with U.S. audiences, and consumers could choose the sheet music, Jolson's original recorded version, or any of the other eight recordings of the song that appeared in 1916.[67] Tin Pan Alley's knack for imitating success prompted a litany of similarly fanciful songs, ranging from quick knockoffs like "Yaddie Kaddie Kiddie Kaddie Koo" (1916), "The Honolulu Hicki Boola Boo" (1916), and the onomatopoeic "Doo Wacka Doo" (1924). In "Yaddie Kaddie," also released by Berlin's publishing firm, Albert von Tilzer returned the melody from "Aloha 'Oe" to its upright position, but he delivered lyrics carrying an equally satiric message: "Please tell me, why do they sing that silly thing?"

By 1916 the phenomenon could not be ignored. "Everybody Hula," proclaimed the title of Sonny Cunha's newest *hapa haole* release; on the mainland the *New York Times* took note of "the countless Hawaiian songs of the day."[68] The San Francisco publishing firm of Sherman, Clay pronounced themselves to be the "headquarters for everything in Hawaiian music"; *Variety* readers on the opposite coast opened the weekly trade journal to discover full-page advertisements for Schwartz's "Hello, Hawaii, How Are You?" urging Broadway producers and singers to adopt this "stage number that will never wear out."[69] Around the nation, subscribers to general interest magazines such as *Cosmopolitan* and the *Saturday Evening Post* found advertisements for Hawaiian-themed sheet music beside regular features, stories, and columns. Daily newspapers, street posters, window displays, and the advertising space on the inside leaves and back cover of each song sheet all helped to market the latest Hawaiian hits, which could be purchased in the form of Edison cylinders, phonograph records, and piano rolls, or experienced live as part of theatrical revues, cabaret shows, and vaudeville performances.[70] As the music entered the mainstream, providing a South

Example 18. E. Ray Goetz, Joe Young, and Pete Wendling, "Yaaka Hula Hickey Dula," mm. 49–53. Published by Waterson, Berlin, and Snyder (1916).

Seas diversion from the Great War, it began to fill all sorts of venues, from grand hotels to corner cafés, urban dance halls to beachside resorts; widespread interest in Hawaiian music and the hula also led to the development of tropical-style clubs, decorated with palm trees and grass huts, which specialized in island entertainment.

American curiosity about everything Hawaiian inspired numerous Tin Pan Alley songwriters to compose self-referential songs about the musical fad itself. Some of these compositions deliver straightforward, affirmative messages. In "Honolulu, America Loves You" (1916), the lyricists Grant Clarke and Eddie Cox catalog the elements of Hawaiian culture making a mark in the United States—including the 'ukulele, the hula, and Hawaiian melodies—and then issue a simple thanks: "You, home of beautiful music o'er the ocean blue / You made America happy, and we're much obliged to you." More enthusiastic songs like Percy Wenrich's "Everybody Do the Hula!" (1917) register the influence of Hawai'i on the United States by suggesting how fashionable dancers should drop the fox-trot in favor of the hula and join the party described in its chorus: "Ev'rybody do the Hula / while the ukeleles play / Come on and be Hawaiian / Ev'rybody's tryin' something new today." If we are to believe the comic exaggerations of these songs, not only were people going mad for Hawaiian music but they also discarded other musical customs in the process. For instance, the Irish families in Bert Kalmar's "Since Maggie Dooley Learned the Hooley Hooley" (1916) are said to have "sold their shillelaghs and bought ukuleles to play." "Since They're Playin' Hawaiian Tunes in Dixie" (1917) and "Hawaiian Night in Dixieland" (1922) both maintain that the Hawaiian craze spread through the black South, causing stereotypical minstrel characters like Old Black Joe to put down their banjos and pick up 'ukuleles while dancing the hula. The fad also motivated enterprising songwriters to invent Hawaiian-related updates to earlier songs. The notorious character of Bill Bailey, introduced by Hughie Cannon in 1902, consequently resurfaced in Honolulu in "When Old Bill Bailey Plays the Ukalele" (1915). The songwriter Jack Frost took further inspiration from the craze in "At That Cabaret in Honolulu Town" (1917) by basing the song's lyrics on the titles of other popular Hawaiian-themed songs. This song catalogs fifteen individual song titles by name, from "My Bird of Paradise" to "Luana Lu"; it also makes side references to characters from like-minded songs, such as Irving Berlin's invention Uncle Jeremiah.

Predictably, perhaps, a mild backlash to the entire fad emerged in a few songs containing anti-Hawaiian lyrics, such as another tune by Bert Kalmar entitled "The More I See of Hawaii, the More I Like New York" (1917), which includes this anti-Jolson gripe: "I'm sick and tired of hearing / That crazy Yacki Hula talk / The one who started raving about Hawaii." For Kalmar, however, these sentiments constituted opportunistic posturing, as he also contributed lyrics for numerous Hawaiian-themed hits. Harold Weeks similarly joined in yet simultaneously bemoaned the Hawaiian craze in his song "Everybody's Crazy 'bout Hawaii" (1917). Upon observing that "ev'rybody's crazy 'bout the lazy Honolulu loos / Ev'ry one is sighing for Hawaiian wicki wacki woos," Weeks questions "why this big land should sing a foreign song 'bout a Banyan tree / Or the maidens on the beach at Waikiki." Issuing this protectionist lament in the same year in which the United States would enter the war, Weeks's lyrics propose instead that Samuel Smith's 1823 ballad "America (My Country, 'tis of Thee)" should be sung throughout the land. Unlike the rash of exclusionary Chinatown songs, however, such sentiments barely registered on Tin Pan Alley. Because of the distance between Hawai'i and the United States and the lack of any large-scale history of immigration, the Hawaiian people did not pose a tangible threat to everyday Americans, nor did they prompt calls for confinement or assimilation. In contrast to ethnic novelty songs that demonized mainland U.S. immigrant groups, such as the Chinese, Hawaiian-themed songs fashioned a different set of stereotypes, typically portraying Hawaiians as primitive yet not frightening, sensually alluring yet safe, questioned for their island ways yet envied for living in paradise. Consequently, although these two bodies of song engage with some of the same anxieties—involving life in a modernizing society as well as the fear of miscegenation—Hawaiian-themed songs articulated a different set of perspectives on exoticism, tourism, gender dynamics, and racial distinctions. For that matter, perhaps to the chagrin of Harold Weeks, these Tin Pan Alley songs were already helping define and celebrate the nation. Without resorting to quoting "My Country, 'tis of Thee," each Hawaiian-themed publication could be heard as a reminder of America's expansion into the Pacific. Making an equally powerful argument against Weeks's position, tens of thousands of Americans by this time had begun to attempt making music of their own on instruments imported from Hawai'i.

"I CAN HEAR THE UKULELES CALLING ME"

The popularity of Hawaiian music fanned the demand for imported musical instruments, as American consumers learned to play the Hawaiian method of steel guitar and, in far greater numbers, the 'ukulele. Although the 'ukulele is not indigenous to Hawai'i, after it was brought to the islands by Madeiran immigrants in the late 1870s, the instrument was soon adopted by and has since been closely linked to Hawaiian musical culture.[71] American tourists encountered the 'ukulele on visits to Hawai'i, and Hawaiian musicians further popularized the instrument on their tours of the States. When American retailers began to market 'ukuleles during the first decade of the twentieth century, the instrument required some explanation. A 1907 advertisement contained supplementary details—"most charming of all the Hawaiian musical instruments," "shaped like a guitar, but much smaller," and "easily mastered."[72] Perceptions began to change in the wake of *The Bird of Paradise*, according to the optimistic copy of a 1913 notice: "the sweet, tinkling Music of these quaint Hawaiian instruments has captivated the country."[73] In addition to its exotic appeal and its ability to produce what became known as a characteristically Hawaiian strumming sound, the 'ukulele proved especially popular with American consumers because of its many practical advantages. The relative ease of learning, tuning, and playing the small, four-string 'ukulele, its role as an accompanying instrument for vocals, and its low cost and portability made it a favorite of tourists and novice musicians alike. It soon gained a place beside other stringed instruments such as the mandolin and guitar. Retailers began stocking a wider selection, ranging from cheap knockoffs through top-of-the-line models, and consumers around the country also could order affordable varieties from the Sears, Roebuck catalog.[74] To stay ahead in this market, a Los Angeles music store began offering daily 'ukulele demonstrations along with lessons by Ernest Kaai, the renowned Hawaiian musician who published several 'ukulele instruction manuals that circulated in the mid- to late 1910s.[75]

The 'ukulele was not completely familiar to mainstream American audiences in 1915, if we are to judge from the variety of spellings of the term ("ukulele," "ukelele," "ukalele") as well as the pronunciation note ("You-ka-la-ly") and definition ("Hawaiian guitar") that were included on the published sheet music of Irving Berlin's "My Bird of Paradise." But the increasing popularity of Hawaiian music that accompanied the Panama-Pacific Exposition prompted such a demand that several large U.S. guitar manufacturers began to produce 'ukuleles. This development prompted a decidedly split response from islanders. On the one hand, commentators praised the tiny instrument as a remarkable source of publicity: "The *ukulele* has been responsible for creating a great deal of interest in the Islands, and also has popularized our music to a great extent."[76] On the other hand, the sudden demand for 'ukuleles caused a great deal of frustration for Hawaiian instrument manufacturers. Despite upping their production to around 1,600 'ukuleles per month by 1916, small Hawaiian companies found it impossible to keep up with Gibson, Harmony, and other American manufacturers that were capable of mass-producing tens of thousands of 'ukuleles monthly.[77] What made things worse about the cheapest, machine-made, low-end American 'ukuleles was that some U.S. manufacturers dishonestly marketed them as Hawaiian-made products, thus simultaneously undercutting the prices and damaging the reputation of Hawaiian imports handmade of native koa wood. This practice became prevalent enough that Hawaiian manufacturers were forced to lobby for and eventually secure legislation that prevented American manufacturers from stamping "Made in Hawaii" on 'ukuleles that had been made in the United States.[78] Although they were unable to maximize their profits as a result of these unfair business practices, Hawaiian 'ukulele manufacturers nevertheless had reason to be encouraged by the continual influx of new customers.

"I Can Hear the Ukuleles Calling Me," claimed the title of a 1916 Tin Pan Alley song, and at that moment it seemed as if the entire nation were answering. Drawn on sheet music covers and mentioned by the lyrics of dozens and dozens of Hawaiian-themed songs, the 'ukulele assumed iconic status, functioning as virtual shorthand for the Hawaiian craze. Popular with high school kids, the college crowd, and young adults, the convenient instrument fit easily in "every other weekender's valise."[79] The 'ukulele occupied such a vital position in American youth culture that a journalist reporting from Paris during World War I observed that "the average American high school girl, who must have her ukelele, would not feel at home in France, for the ukelele is unknown here."[80] In response to this fad, Tin Pan Alley publishers began a practice that has shaped the look of sheet music in America to the present day by adding 'ukulele chord symbols above the harmonic changes, sometimes accompanied by instructions for tuning the instrument and interpreting the symbols. Although tablature systems were common in steel guitar instruction books of the era, the introduction of such four-string 'ukulele chord symbols preceded the now familiar six-string guitar tabs that later began appearing in the pages of sheet music. By the latter 1910s, it thus became commonplace for sheet music covers to advertise a "ukulele accompaniment," "ukulele chords," or "ukulele instructions," regardless of whether the song possessed a Hawaiian lyrical theme.

For music that was intended to evoke the atmosphere of Hawai'i, Tin Pan Alley songwriters developed a series of stock musical devices to imitate the sound of the 'ukulele and the steel guitar, including rolled piano chords to mimic strumming 'ukuleles; glissandi to imitate the sliding of the steel guitar; and grace note pickups to suggest the effect of plucked strings. Composers also tried to approximate the sound of Hawaiian music by introducing new performance markings. In addition to populating the score of "Hawaiian Dreams" (1915) with grace notes, Herbert Marple advised pianists to play "a la steel guitar"; his follow-up tune, "Hawaiian Twilight," contained more explicit instructions: "Strike accented notes a trifle in advance of chords to which they are tied." To make the most of these developments, marketing slogans such as "Steel Guitar Effect" began to grace covers of Hawaiian-related sheet music. Seattle's Echo Music, the publishers of "My Hawaii" (1917), went further, promising that the release had been "especially adapted to the ukulele and steel guitar"; advertisements for the song "A Vision of Hawaii" (1917) assured consumers that "the way the music is arranged makes you think you hear a Ukelele and a Steel Guitar playing at one time." Not content with selling copies of the sheet music of "Hawaiian Kisses" (1925), its publisher, Uke-Trades, used the song's cover to advertise the availability of an instructional record by May Singhi Breen, who billed herself as "The Ukulele Lady." Customers who were unmoved by Breen's guarantee to "Learn to Play the Ukulele in Six Minutes" could turn to the back page, which advertised folios for players of all ages, including "Kiddy Ukes" by E. B. Marks. Even the most time-honored Hawaiian song was not safe from tinkering by U.S. publishers. Seidel Music sought to distinguish its 1915 release of "Aloha 'Oe" by adding a special piano chorus intended to imitate the 'ukulele, as a detailed publisher's note makes clear (figure 6).

By the start of the Roaring Twenties, the 'ukulele and the steel guitar had begun to make inroads into the worlds of jazz, blues, and country. Though these instruments had their deepest effect on American popular music, the sound of the 'ukulele also influenced American art music in the form of Aaron Copland's *Ukelele Serenade* (1926), one of his Two Pieces for Violin and Piano. Written for the violinist Samuel Dushkin, who premiered the

FIGURE 6.   Special chorus, Queen Lili'uokalani (composer), J. Russel Robinson (arranger of special chorus), "Aloha 'Oe." Published by Seidel Music (1915). Courtesy of the Music Library, University of Michigan, Ann Arbor.

piece in Paris with Copland at the piano, this brief, jazzy duet contains a number of novelty effects, some of which evoke the sound of Hawaiian music. Copland exploits the violin's ability to imitate vocal and steel guitar portamento techniques by rapidly sliding up and down the finger board, and he includes performance markings that instruct the pianist to play rolled chords "like a ukelele."[81] As Copland later described, this experimental piece "begins with quarter tones meant to achieve a blues effect, while arpeggiated chords in the right hand of the piano part simulate a ukelele sound. Later in the piece, the roles are reversed, with pizzicato quadruple violin stoppings representing the ukelele. The bar lines for the two instruments do not necessarily coincide."[82] As a result, its off-kilter, bitonal swing sounds like modernist bluegrass cooked up by the jazz violinist Stéphane Grappelli and Charles Ives. The years that followed brought forth equally memorable encounters with the 'ukulele, whether strummed by Josephine Baker onstage or in the studio, used as a bohemian prop by the beret-wearing Buster Keaton in *Steamboat Bill, Jr.* (1928), or played by Marilyn Monroe in *Some Like It Hot* (1959) to help establish the film's 1929 setting.

"HAWAIIAN MUSIC UNIVERSALLY POPULAR"

> Let the Pathephone transport you as quickly as the enchanted
> carpet in the Arabian Nights to dreamy, beautiful Hawaii.
>
> Pathephone phonograph advertisement (1917)

The level of America's enthusiasm for recorded Hawaiian music was captured by the lead article of the September 1916 issue of *Edison Phonograph
Monthly*, a promotional magazine that kept Edison dealers and avid collec-
tors up to date on the latest releases and industry news. Titled "Hawaiian
Music Universally Popular," this piece conveys the U.S. recording industry's astonishment at how suddenly this music had become fashionable:

> Two years ago what did the public know about Hawaiian Music, Ukule-
> les, Hula Hula Dances? Since then Hawaiian music and American ver-
> sions of it have taken the United States by storm. Many New York
> restaurants have Ukulele players to entertain their guests, theatre or-
> chestra leaders are programming Hawaiian music, vaudeville artists are
> introducing it into their performance, and even the motion picture pro-
> ducers are reflecting the music and customs of Hawaii by filming stories
> of this Pacific island that has been brought into such prominence by the
> originality and fascination of its music and the instrument upon which
> it is played.[83]

The article goes on to claim that "the biggest popular hits of this season are
all Hawaiian songs and the demand for records of these is widespread and
insistent," a declaration that may be taken with a grain of salt, since it accompanies Edison's list of the most recent Hawaiian recordings available for
purchase.[84] But that was not the only company to fan the marketing flames
for Hawaiian music; active competitors included Columbia and Victor, the
latter of which began releasing Hawaiian recordings on a monthly basis in
late 1915.[85] Sheet music firms also attempted to profit from this trend by arranging to have their songs publicized through the medium of phonograph
recordings. On the cover of "Hawaiian Twilight" (1920), Vandersloot Music
proudly announced that the song had been released on thirteen different
recording labels and was also available on piano rolls for eleven types of
player pianos.

Backed by major advertising campaigns, recordings of Hawaiian and
Hawaiian-themed music became widely popular across the States by the
mid-1910s to the extent that critics like Theodor Hoeck, who generally dis-
pensed opinions about classical music and music education, chose to address
the Hawaiian phenomenon. According to his July 1916 column, "Phonograph companies report that they have few records that are growing more

rapidly in popular favor than their so-called 'Hawaiian records.' "[86] W. D. Adams, an advocate of Hawaiian trade, attended that year's Victor Talking Machine convention, where he spoke with the many jobbers, or wholesale dealers, of Victor records and phonograph machines. Writing in the *Hawaiian Annual* as an exponent for islanders keen on increasing trade and tourism, Adams pronounced the record to be "the medium through which our music gets its best advertisement."[87] His animated report, cited frequently ever since, continues with unabashed optimism: "Every jobber was unanimous in stating that the Hawaiian records placed on the market the last year had reached larger sales with them than any other popular records. This in itself goes to show that Hawaiian music has a wonderful charm when you consider the thousands upon thousands of people on the mainland who are purchasing talking machine records every month." Whether Hawaiian music actually topped the sales charts in 1916 has not been confirmed, nor is it clear whether definitive sales records survive, but it is true that the Victor company remained extremely devoted to recording Hawaiian music during this period.

One vivid illustration of their level of commitment appears in the form of an advertising booklet entitled "Victor Hawaiian Records," apparently from 1916.[88] Everything about this expensive promotional piece was devoted to marketing the company's Hawaiian catalog of nearly 150 recordings: its colorful cover depicts a hula girl set against a backdrop of palm trees and a volcano; a stenciled palm tree design frames the borders of each page; several introductory pages describe the appeal of Hawaiian music; and a handful of black-and-white photographs portray the company's top Hawaiian recording artists. Victor attempted to live up to its advertising copy—to bring the "music of the Hawaiian people directly to the homes of all music lovers"—by featuring prominent island musicians, including the Hawaiian Quintette, the Toots Paka Troupe, Irene West's Royal Hawaiian Troupe, Pale K. Lua, and Frank Ferera. In addition to older Hawaiian songs and instrumentals, the catalog lists numerous recordings of Hawaiian *hapa haole* songs, including "Honolulu Hula Girl" and "On the Beach at Waikiki," as well as Hawaiian-themed Tin Pan Alley songs, such as Irving Berlin's "My Bird of Paradise." Victor rode this wave into the next year, when its 1917 catalog expanded to 175 Hawaiian titles.[89]

Why was recorded Hawaiian music so popular in the United States? What made it so "wonderfully fascinating," according to the text of the electric signs that Edison used to promote this music? As part of the early growth of the recording age, these phonograph recordings by Hawaiian musicians captured what sheet music could not: the sound of skilled island musicians performing

Hawaiian and Hawaiian-themed music by employing distinctive techniques and creating unusual timbres. Rather than trying in vain to imitate the sound of strummed 'ukulele chords or the sliding glissandi of the steel guitar on a parlor piano, American consumers could figuratively transport themselves across the ocean with a few turns of the Victrola's crank. But these particular advantages of recorded sound do not explain why Hawaiian music achieved such a high level of popularity in comparison with other types of ethnic and international music that were promoted by the U.S. record industry during this era. Undoubtedly, the appeal of these records drew on the tropical allure that attracted American consumers to Tin Pan Alley's Hawaiian-themed sheet music. Commentary from those who produced and consumed these recordings further suggests that they presented a compelling blend of both the exotic and the familiar as well as a paradoxical combination of escapism tinged with melancholy.

It is possible to gain some sense of what American audiences sought, or were bidden to seek, in Hawaiian music by observing the manner in which it was marketed. The text of a promotional brochure for Kekuku's Hawaiian Quintet identifies the group's novelty as one primary source of its appeal: "Hawaiian music by the gifted native singers and players has been a great success in America because it is different. The wistful beauty of the music seems to carry the American audiences across the Pacific to those beautiful islands of the South Seas. . . . The melodious strains of the songs and the accompaniment on native instruments, with the peculiar sliding of the fingers on the strings, is plaintive and fascinating."[90] Likewise, Columbia described how the music captured the "peculiar charm" of the islands, whereas Pathephone pledged to transport its phonograph customers across the Pacific, where "you will feel the spell of the sunny, languorous South Sea Isles, as you listen to the plaintive haunting Hawaiian melodies."[91] The success of these efforts to pitch musical exoticism is borne out in the commentary of numerous fans throughout the United States, in response to an early attempt at mass-market research. In 1921 Thomas Edison's phonograph machine company sent customers a questionnaire that asked them to list their favorite Edison recordings and inquired about what selections they would enjoy hearing in the future.[92] Scores of respondents listed their favorite Hawaiian songs and articulated their rationale for enjoyment. Some of those surveyed, such as Katrine Strump of Galion, Ohio, echoed industry characterizations: "I like Hawaiian music," she explained, "because it is different from the rest."[93] Other respondents expressed similar fondness for the "pecular [sic] whims of the music," "the weird melody of Hawaiian music," "the Wierdness [sic] of the Hawaiian orchestras," and "the distinctive touch of the guitar."[94] Clearly, fans appreciated these recordings for delivering novel entertainment.

At the same time, however, recordings of Hawaiian music contained many musical elements that were already known to American listeners, elements that allowed them to better appreciate the recordings without becoming inundated by musical difference. That many of these U.S.-produced recordings either featured English-language lyrics or were created as solely instrumental numbers made them that more accessible on the continent. Since these recordings often relied on Western musical elements and adapted recognizable forms drawn from church hymns and popular songs, it is not surprising that Edison's customers listened elsewhere in Hawaiian songs for sources of novelty. Consequently, many fans expressed their attraction to the melodic characteristics of Hawaiian music, pointing to its "melodious," "dreamy," and "tuneful" qualities, rather than to the harmonic, rhythmic, or structural aspects of the music. Many consumers were delighted, not overwhelmed, by the special features that characterized Hawaiian recordings, from its falsetto vocals to its distinctive instrumental timbres, such as the twangy melodic swoops of the Hawaiian steel guitar that evoked a vocal quality of its own.

In contrast to the energy of hot jazz or the sensuous rhythms of the tango, Edison phonograph owners appreciated Hawaiian recordings for offering "more quiet music" and enjoyed songs like "Aloha 'Oe," because it "seems so soft from the rest."[95] "I never tire of that music," wrote a Texas customer, who claimed this music as a personal favorite because it was "so soft and sweet."[96] A listener from Colorado found his copy of "Aloha Sunset Land" to be "soothing and restful," and a Nebraskan confided that Hawaiian music delivered an escape from the everyday: "I find a restfulness or a something where one forgets the cares of life."[97] Edison customers across the nation found especially poignant the slower tempos, lingering melodies, and longing vocals. This combination of melancholy and escapism helps explain the responses of the fan who found "Wailana Waltz" attractive because "it is sweet and sad" and the Texas listener who stated, "The plaintive tone of the Hawaiian music is what makes it so charming and popular."[98] Indeed, the sometimes mournful character of these recordings led to the frequent appearance of the word *plaintive* in advertising copy, and the rapidly ascending steel guitar lines and falsetto vocals contributed to what Victor Records characterized as its "crying, haunting quality."[99] According to such promotional language, these recordings promised to deliver touching, emotionally powerful experiences that were imbued with enough exotic flavor to invigorate the listener's imagination.

Although I have not located any Edison surveys completed by phonograph owners living in Hawai'i, it is clear that islanders who supported trade and tourism were thrilled at first by the American craze for Hawaiian music. Filing another report in the *Hawaiian Annual* of 1917, W. D. Adams declared, "Hawaiian music has done more to popularize these islands than anything else that we have done."[100] Just how readily America's interest in Hawaiian music fostered tourism can be seen in the May 1917 pages of *Sunset* magazine, a California-based travel and recreation monthly targeted to consumers who lived near the Pacific Coast. This issue featured a Hawaiian theme, which extended to the highlighted short story, a piquant travelogue, and a piece that retraced the footsteps of Mark Twain's 1866 trip to the islands. The glossy pages contained an array of Hawai'i-based advertisements that enabled prospective tourists to arrange for transportation, book rooms at leading hotels, and reserve tickets on inter-island steamboat tours. *Sunset* readers also learned where they could purchase a "genuine Hawaiian" 'ukulele from a notice placed by a Honolulu music firm that also sold locally produced sheet music and 'ukulele instructional manuals.[101]

Though U.S. interest in Hawaiian culture proved beneficial for the tourist business, local composers and music publishers grew increasingly concerned about the power of the American music industry. By the mid-1910s, islanders had begun to distinguish between "real" Hawaiian music and the "Hawaiian-American popular records" fashioned by Tin Pan Alley, a distinction that led some critics to voice complaints about deceptive, inauthentic, "so-called Hawaiian songs."[102] In response to "Oh, How She Could Yacki Hacki Wicki Wacki Woo," Adams declared: "This song has been published by one of the largest music concerns in the States, and we should be forced by our pride in all things Hawaiian to resent such practices and do our utmost to the end that *real* Hawaiian music shall reach around the earth and that we may not be placed in the ridiculous light that we are [rapidly] approaching through these methods."[103] At the very least, Adams pleaded, perhaps it would not be too much to ask for American songwriters to "make an attempt to find out a few genuine Hawaiian words instead of making them up."[104] Americans occasionally published heartfelt songs containing messages that virtually any Hawaiian could support. Shortly after visiting in 1914, Harry Lauder, a tourist, composed lyrics for "I Love You, Honolulu" (1915), a paean to its splendid natural treasures. More typical of Tin Pan Alley, however, was Charles Klein's description in "Everybody Do the Hula" (1917) of how to perform the dance: "First you take a little side-step / Any kind you know will do / Then, of course, a little wiggle / That's the Honolulu Hula." Because the vast majority of Hawaiian-themed sheet music during the 1910s and 1920s was produced and distributed in the United States, islanders could do little at that point to prevent the propagation of superficial caricatures of Hawaiian culture.

For the members of the Hawaiian Promotion Committee, responding to Tin Pan Alley was less a matter of championing the Hawaiian language or preserving musical traditions and more one of protecting the economic interests of local musicians. Accordingly, the committee issued a proclamation warning that "Hawaiian music, as it is composed and sold here, is Hawaiian music at its best, and no one will have any apologies to make for its quality. But the managers of the East [Coast] have changed much of the spirit of the songs, and Hawaii is not going to benefit by it."[105] Bergstrom Music, the most active local publishing firm, attempted to remain competitive by producing what it advertised as "genuine Hawaiian songs" and "real Hawaiian song hits," including many of Sonny Cunha's *hapa haole* numbers. In spite of such spirited efforts, however, the unrelenting tide of Tin Pan Alley songs and popular recordings from the mainland eventually proved to be overwhelming. Encountering difficulties similar to those faced by 'ukulele manufacturers, local publishing firms faced very long odds in the struggle over the control, production, and dissemination of commercial Hawaiian music.

The interests of Hawaiian record buyers also took a backseat to those of their American counterparts as a result of a shift in U.S. marketing strategies. Initially, recordings of Hawaiian music were targeted as much for Hawaiian audiences as for American consumers—until it became clear that they were selling at a much higher clip in the United States.[106] Consequently, recorded music originally produced to serve the Hawaiian market became a profitable subgenre for the larger American and international market, a process that helped shape their content. As Pekka Gronow points out, the sad irony of the history of commercial Hawaiian music is that, starting in the late 1910s and continuing for several decades, "most recordings of Hawaiian music were made primarily for sale to non-Hawaiians, often by non-Hawaiian artists."[107] Since no record companies of note had established themselves on the islands by that time, the U.S. record industry maintained its hold on hiring artists, choosing repertory, and producing individual recordings. It was not until after World War II that the Hawaiian recording industry gained more solid footing and came to play a central role in the recording and dissemination of Hawaiian music.[108]

From an economic perspective, the profits reaped by American-based companies from sales of Hawaiian sheet music, phonograph recordings, and instruments reflect the colonial relationship that existed between the United States and Hawai'i at the start of the twentieth century. Indeed, it requires a dose of optimism to characterize this encounter as a contested struggle, given such a wide disparity of industrial power. In terms of ethnic and cultural representation, the U.S. music industry dramatically shaped the meaning of "Hawaiian music" for many of its customers through the production of Hawaiian-themed songs. It could even be claimed that in this era Hawaiian music achieved its greatest victories on behalf of the American-friendly business interests that wished to advance island tourism and trade. The experiences of some Hawaiian participants in this musical process offer partial support for such an interpretation. In her work on Hawaiian entertainment culture from the late nineteenth to the mid-twentieth century, Adria Imada argues that hula dancers and their accompanying musical ensembles "played an important ambassadorial role, offering American audiences live exposure to 'Hawaiian-ness' and exposing Hawaiians in the colony to U.S. imperial centers."[109] By staging local performances and touring the States, these cultural emissaries presented a desirable vision of the islands and helped familiarize Americans with Hawaiian culture. Over time, Imada claims, these efforts became integral to mediating the transformation of Hawai'i from an independent kingdom into an American colonial possession that served as both a military output and a tourist destination. Those who spread Hawaiian music, however, were not helpless pawns in larger political gambits; Imada maintains that this process offered them some degree of agency. "Hula practitioners," she writes, "were neither duped by colonialism or tourism nor wholly willing to accept those conditions of domination. Tourist entertainment, even while objectifying and commodifying its practitioners, did not doom them."[110]

These sentiments may be amplified further by looking to the select group of Hawaiian-born recording artists who helped popularize Hawaiian sounds around the world. In contrast to U.S. performers like Al Jolson, whose recordings rarely attempt to replicate Hawaiian musical practices, many island virtuosos possessed distinctive skills, whether they involved how to get the most out of the 'ukulele or how to inflect their vocals appropriately. Since the profits from these recordings flowed to U.S. record labels—as was also the case for most releases by American performers of this era—Hawaiian recording artists generally profited more from the attendant publicity in the course of establishing their performance careers. Yet some of the most fortunate were able not only to make a living, enjoying aesthetic and economic success, but also to gain international fame. Their recordings now symbolize the long-term artistic survival of these musical pioneers, but they were produced by musicians who had to juggle a variety of industry pressures and audience demands, to pitch their familiarity with

Hawaiian musical culture to the American businessmen who ran the music industry. Thanks to numerous CD reissues and musical digitization projects, recordings by these early artists continue to preserve their musical voices, memories, and struggles.

As the market for Hawaiian recordings grew during the late 1910s and early 1920s, some of the most talented performers became renowned as studio recording artists. One of the most prolific musicians during this era was the steel guitarist Frank Ferera (1885–1951).[111] Born to a Honolulu family of Portuguese descent, Palakiko Ferreira traveled in his late teens to the States, where he adopted the stage name Frank Ferera. He married Helen Louise Greenus, a ʻukulele player and guitarist from Seattle, and together the pair formed a popular vaudeville act. They made their recording debut in July 1915, and the following year landed their first hit with "Drowsy Waters," which exceeded 300,000 copies in print, or nearly twenty times the amount of a typical release of that era.[112] For the next several years the duo continued to produce recordings, perform in clubs and hotels, and make the rounds on the vaudeville circuit. They became especially well known for the melodic clarity of their guitar playing, delivering "charming, always polished, but never flashy performances."[113] After his wife's untimely passing in 1919, Ferera recorded with Anthony Franchini, and then John Paaluhi; he also played in large ensembles and became a talented accompanist. According to some accounts, Ferera recorded more sides than any other guitarist, Hawaiian or otherwise, from 1915 to 1925; other sources estimate that he played on over two thousand records in the course of a career that lasted less than two decades. In the process, Ferera became one of the leading exponents of Hawaiian music, popularizing the sound of the Hawaiian steel guitar among audiences around the world.

Once he was given the opportunity to enter the recording studio, Ferera's profile increased dramatically. In December 1916 his picture was featured on the cover of the *Edison Phonograph Monthly* above the caption "Noted Hawaiian Guitar Player." Early Edison recordings bring out the singing, vocal quality of his approach to playing the steel guitar, which featured characteristic Hawaiian techniques such as glissando slides and melodies plucked out in the high register. As his fame increased, photographs of Ferera, the "Hawaiian Guitar Virtuoso," also landed on sheet music covers, including "Hawaiianola" (1921) and "Honolulu Honey" (1921) (figure 7). The placement of Ferera's photograph with one of his partners on "Honolulu Honey"—beside a larger tropical scene filled with island imagery and a hula girl playing a ʻukulele—suggests how all musicians employed by the major U.S. record companies were subject to commercial demands, marketing

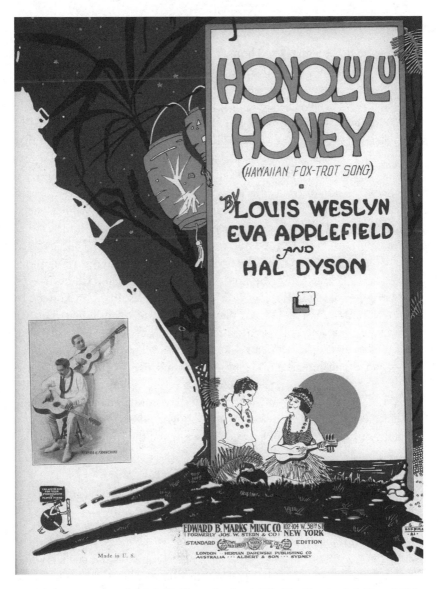

FIGURE 7. Cover art by S. S. Hoffman for Louis Weslyn, Eva Applefield, and Hal Dyson, "Honolulu Honey." Published by Edward B. Marks (1921). Courtesy of the Music Library, University of Michigan, Ann Arbor.

concerns, and popular taste. Though Ferera released many recordings of music from Hawai'i, including medleys of traditional songs and hulas, he also tailored his repertory to American listeners, who did not demand faithful renditions of Hawaiian music. Thus, he released both early *hapa haole* tunes such as Cunha's "Hapa Haole Hula Girl" and Hawaiian-themed Tin Pan Alley songs, including "Yaddie Kaddie Kiddie Kaddie Koo." For that matter, his 1915 Victor recording debut with Helen Louise featured a version of Stephen Foster's "Old Kentucky Home"; later that year they recorded a version of Irving Berlin's "My Bird of Paradise." Ferera freely crossed genre boundaries throughout his recording career, which ended during the Great Depression in 1933. Not only did he record with the sweet jazz bandleader Paul Whiteman, country singer Vernon Dalhart, and vaudevillian Eddie Cantor, but he also tried his own hand at recording tunes as diverse as "O Sole Mio," "St. Louis Blues," and "La Paloma," the age-old Spanish song that Jelly Roll Morton would later play for Alan Lomax. In this fashion, Hawaiian performers played a variety of key roles in America's musical life: spreading the sounds, techniques, and timbres of Hawaiian music; contributing to the craze for Tin Pan Alley's Hawaiian-themed songs; and establishing their own productive and diverse musical careers in the States. Some flourishing performers like Ferera became integrated fully into the American popular music scene, yet they simultaneously had to seek a balance between two worlds, serving as individual emblems of the musical and cultural contestation between Hawai'i and the United States.

CONTEMPORARY SOUNDS OF PARADISE

The remainder of the twentieth century saw a continuing series of interactions and collisions between the musical cultures of Hawai'i and the United States. In some cases Hawaiian links have been highly visible, such as when American popular musicians and movie stars have picked up the 'ukulele to accompany their tropical adventures. Bing Crosby did so as part of the island film excursion *Waikiki Wedding* (Paramount, 1937), the film that introduced his popular version of the song "Sweet Leilani." Accompanied by Lani McIntyre and His Hawaiians, Crosby's rendition was the best-selling American record since the stock market crash of 1929, topping the charts for more than two months and also prompting the sales of tens of millions of copies of sheet music. Its composer, Harry Owens, the Nebraska-born musical director at Honolulu's Royal Hawaiian Hotel, became the first songwriter to win an Oscar as both composer and lyricist; Crosby went on to record upwards of forty Hawaiian or Hawaiian-themed songs. Elvis Presley later followed in Crosby's footsteps when he grabbed a 'ukulele for his role in the film *Blue Hawaii* (Paramount, 1961). Hawaiian influences have also shaped American music in ways not always so evident. For instance, Jimmie Rodgers, one of the early stars of country music, integrated the Hawaiian steel guitar into recordings such as "Everybody Does It in Hawaii" (1929), and the appeal of this sound helped lead to the invention of the pedal steel guitar, which has played an iconic role in various strains of country music.

Over the last eighty years, the dynamics of the musical relationship between Hawai'i and the United States have changed considerably. The distance between the two has been shortened by the introduction of flight service, beginning in the late 1930s, which helped establish the islands as a premiere tourist destination. In 1941 the Japanese attack on Pearl Harbor forever cemented and memorialized the islands' ties with the United States military, and political bonds were formalized further in 1959, when Hawai'i became the fiftieth state. Over this entire period, the U.S. film and television industry has presented a running stream of Hawaiian images, ranging from its multiple versions of *Bird of Paradise* to surfing pictures like the recent *Blue Crush* (Imagine Entertainment, 2002). Likewise, whatever their faults in terms of representation, the individual renderings of Hawai'i in television shows such as *Hawaii Five-O, Magnum, P.I.,* and *Baywatch Hawaii* all have made island life seem less foreign to U.S. viewers. One side effect of such increased familiarity has been that Hawaiian music seems less novel today. I believe this is one reason that mainland interest in Hawaiian-themed music has faded in intensity since midcentury, a decline that also can be traced to the effects of the attack on Pearl Harbor, which put a damper on thinking of Hawai'i primarily as an exotic land of fantasy, and to the ever-shifting nature of popular taste.

Notions about defining Hawaiian music have also changed in response to what George Kanahele has termed the Hawaiian Music Renaissance, a revival of interest in indigenous musical culture that took place on the islands beginning in the 1960s.[114] Self-consciously political, this social and cultural movement enabled Hawaiian musicians to regain substantial control over the production, distribution, representation, and direction of Hawaiian music.[115] Consequently, the music scene in Hawai'i remains very lively today, populated by those who seek to preserve indigenous practices, entertainers who cater to the tourist market, and musicians who often merge older Hawaiian musical practices with contemporary developments. It remains difficult, of course, to identify the roots of these various musical styles, which contain the remnants of several centuries of cultural contestation. As a result, explains

Amy Stillman, "much of the Hawaiian music currently performed and recorded can be regarded simultaneously as an ethnic tradition and as a branch of American popular music."[116] Not surprisingly, the islands continue to spawn the creation of new cross-cultural genres, including Jawaiian music, which merges Jamaican rhythms with Hawaiian melodies, and Hawaiian-language hip-hop.[117]

Today's Hawaiian musicians are actively questioning the future of Hawaiian music and its relationship to American musical culture. One of the most prominent is Jake Shimabukuro, a native of Hawai'i and a fourth-generation Japanese American who carries on the tradition of virtuoso 'ukulele performance while redefining notions of how to play the instrument. Shimabukuro has achieved a level of fame far beyond most aspiring musicians': he signed with Epic Records in 2002 and is currently represented by the William Morris talent agency. In certain respects, he follows in the footsteps of musicians like Sonny Cunha, Frank Ferera, and, more recently, the late Israel Kamakawiwo'ole, by working with both Hawaiian and American popular traditions.[118] Although his most recent album, *Gently Weeps* (2006), pleased traditionalists by featuring solo acoustic instrumentals, he has also run his 'ukulele through various effects boxes to experiment with distortion, echo, delays, and other timbral effects more characteristic of an electric guitarist like Jimi Hendrix. Just as strikingly, his music defies genre boundaries at every turn. The five CDs and two DVDs he has released to date contain instrumental versions of European classical pieces, gospel numbers, American popular favorites, and Hawaiian songs as well as original compositions that draw variously from bluegrass, funk, flamenco, jazz, rock, and heavy metal.

In some circles, Shimabukuro's reception demonstrates how Hawaiian music still carries with it expectations of novelty. On 16 July 2006 Shimabukuro performed in downtown Detroit as part of a free weekend festival titled "Concert of Colors: Metro Detroit's 14th Annual Diversity Festival." For the first time this musical celebration of diversity and difference, featuring a variety of genres performed mainly by musicians of color, was held at a venue normally dedicated to classical music. Shimabukuro appeared on the grand stage of Orchestra Hall, a beautifully restored and acoustically pristine two-thousand-seat auditorium that serves as the home of the Detroit Symphony Orchestra. Programmed as the opening act on the closing Sunday afternoon of the festival, Shimabukuro was unfamiliar to many in the audience, save a small but vocal group of fans seated in the front rows. For that matter, the local radio DJ who served as stage announcer failed to pronounce his name properly, despite the assistance of an index card, and then chuckled a bit about press clippings that drew musical comparisons to Hendrix. Unfazed by this stumbling introduction, Shimabukuro calmly sat down with his four-string 'ukulele and rattled off the first few bars of Hendrix's "Purple Haze," before laughingly announcing that he would be playing acoustic numbers, amplified but without additional electronic effects, during this solo performance. Though he has become more renowned for using unconventional timbres and 'ukulele pyrotechnics, Shimakuburo also makes much of the soft and sweet sounds that attracted American audiences to recorded Hawaiian music in the 1920s. On this afternoon, the thirty-year-old instrumentalist explored tender harmonics as part of his opening number, a cover of the standard "Over the Rainbow," and performed sensitive renditions of Schubert's "Ave Maria" and the Beatles' "Here, There, and Everywhere." Offering a better display of his revisionist attitude toward the 'ukulele, his version of "While My Guitar Gently Weeps" shifted in the midst of a spirited solo from classical harmonic progressions to the power chords of classic rock. His original compositions demonstrated a similar range, moving between cool, breezy numbers and virtuosic showstoppers. What gave the crowd-pleasers extra dramatic punch were his frequent references to a variety of guitar traditions, including the flamenco runs that fill his Latin-inspired "Let's Dance" and the fret-board-tapping technique pioneered by the heavy metal guitarist Eddie Van Halen and featured by Shimabukuro on "Dragon." The highlight of the show took place in the midst of an extended improvisation during "Orange World," a bluegrass-tinged original inspired by his time spent touring with Béla Fleck. Responding to an increasingly vocal crowd, Shimabukuro extended the tune by several choruses, relishing the sharp picking of a twenty-first-century hoedown, before dramatically throwing in a reference to the opening lick of "Dueling Banjos" from the film soundtrack of *Deliverance* (Warner Bros., 1972). Won over by show's end, the stage announcer gave Shimabukuro a healthy embrace and graciously convinced him to play several encores.

In addition to proving that a contemporary Hawaiian musician could entertain a mixed crowd of somewhat skeptical midwesterners, Shimabukuro's performance had much to say about the nature of Hawaiian music today. Gauging simply from his choice of repertory and his interest in recent commercial genres, his music might be read as a sign of capitulation to the overwhelming influence of American popular music. Indeed, though he has garnered much local acclaim, winning multiple Nä Hökü Hanohano (The Stars of Distinction) Awards, the island equivalent of the Grammy Awards, he has also received criticism for pushing too far away from convention. At the same time, Shimabukuro works against stereotypical perceptions of Hawaiian performers by embracing an extremely wide range of musical genres while retaining his facility to play traditional Hawaiian songs. In the process he demonstrates how notions of American (and British and Viennese) music are subject to transformation by an island performer. Conscious of his role in revising notions over the definition of Hawaiian music, Shimabukuro acknowledged the point through some light banter with the Detroit audience by holding up his instrument and explaining that some listeners ask him whether he uses a "real" 'ukulele. He answered yes, gently strumming a simple chord progression to evoke the sound of the Hawaiian entertainer Don Ho, but he then explained that growing up with so much music influenced him to experiment in new directions. Rather than identifying Shimabukuro strictly as an example of Hawaiian capitulation or island rebellion, his music makes the most of the relationship that keeps these two cultural impulses in tension.

Trying to identify a boundary between Hawaiian music and American music, however, may not be as critical at this juncture for a performer like Jake Shimabukuro, a U.S. citizen who has experienced both musical cultures, and more, from childhood. As the expression of a Hawaiian American artist, his performance can thus be heard not only for what it symbolizes about an ethnic musical tradition but also for the portrait it offers of the changing nature of American music. Most visibly, by appearing as a representative of an ethnic minority community within a larger multicultural festival, Shimabukuro embodied the increasing diversity of the nation's musical culture. Though the festival itself may have temporarily dislodged the symphonic tenants of Orchestra Hall, Shimabukuro's mix of repertory placed classical and popular pieces on the same ground; his adaptation of classical guitar techniques to the 'ukulele suggested a similar overlap between the two realms, a tactic that has become habitual on his albums as well. If one were to define the state of American musical culture strictly by the nature of this single performance, it would be characterized by a diversity of repertory, genres, traditions, and musical approaches that cross geographical and temporal boundaries. But this was not a form of diversity ignorant of power relationships, for these varied musical influences were called on by a single performer who consciously adapted and mixed each of them for a variety of artistic purposes.

Jake Shimabukuro struggles to define the future of Hawaiian music and of American music, but his career also indicates how the cross-cultural equation has changed in orientation since Hawai'i became a state in 1959. Today's islanders continue to face long-standing challenges involving the effects of militarization, development, and tourism. The situation has become even more complicated as Hawai'i has become increasingly popular as a tourist destination and a site for foreign investment. Hawaiian musicians—especially young Japanese Americans like Shimabukuro—have achieved enormous popularity in Japan, which has required him to strike a balance between his Hawaiian home and his enthusiastic fan following in Japan. One explanation for Shimabukuro's overseas success derives from his involvement with the 2004 Hawaiian Tourism Japan campaign, for which he served as a goodwill ambassador and to which he contributed a theme song that was used in all radio and television advertisements. Thus, he has become one of the spokesmen helping propel a new epoch of Hawaiian tourism, this time for visitors arriving from Asia. Although the subtitle of this chapter points to the way Hawaiian music has functioned in the American musical imagination, Shimabukuro's budding career indicates not only how contemporary Hawaiian musicians fuel their own creative imaginations with music from across the seas but also how these sounds of paradise attract the musical imaginations of listeners from across the globe.

Conclusion

*American Music at the Turn
of a New Century*

Characterizing American music as a diverse collection of hybrid or creolized forms may have the ring of a postmodern assessment, seemingly ready-made to apply to a contemporary musician like Jake Shimabukuro. Though such a depiction of America's musical life remains equally relevant today, the main musical figures in *Struggling to Define a Nation* together demonstrate how plural and fragmented the stylistic influences on American music in the early twentieth century always were. Indeed, this complex interplay of styles and identities produced a set of distinctly American musical traditions that in certain cases have turned out to be even more influential and enduring than simultaneous attempts by concert music composers to create an American sound. For this reason, it has been essential to look beyond Charles Ives's early experiments with ragtime and gospel hymns to examine concurrent developments in American popular music from early jazz to Tin Pan Alley songs. Likewise, the varied musical currents of this period have made it necessary to adopt a conceptual model of race and ethnicity that expands far beyond black-and-white terms. Taken collectively, the episodes in this book reveal how it is possible to embrace the diversity of American music while recognizing that this diversity arises through the efforts of individuals and communities with different and contradictory perspectives on America. Each of the primary figures in this book is distinctly positioned—whether by class, race, or ethnicity; with respect to experiences of urbanization, migration, immigration, and colonization; and according to differential relations of power. Indeed, we have seen how issues of power mattered so much in this era that numerous individuals, including most Chinese immigrants and many Hawaiian Islanders, were unable to participate fully in defining the musical nation. I believe that American music, as a result of such differing perspectives and opportunities, can be understood best as a series of conflicts or clashes between diverse, and often opposing, musical identities. Rather than symbolizing like-minded communities joining as one, it is these individual sites of cultural debate that constitute the dynamic, contested nature of American musical life.

As the twenty-first century unfolds, debates about American identity and American music continue to occupy contemporary musical life and to reshape today's institutions. Commencing with their 2005 competition, the Pulitzer Prize Board announced major revisions to the official guidelines that govern their prestigious annual prize in music. Professing a "strong desire to consider and honor the full range of distinguished American musical compositions," the awards committee sought to encourage a more expansive range of entries, "from the contemporary classical symphony to jazz, opera, choral, musical theater, movie scores and other forms of musical excellence."[1] Entrants are no longer required to enclose a written score but instead may submit a recording of any new composition that has premiered in live performance or that has been released during the previous year. This announcement by an organization formerly almost exclusively concerned with the world of concert music can be seen as a response to several key transformations in music making over the past century: the spread of recorded music across the globe; technological advances that allow composers to create notated or nonnotated works in the studio, on the computer, or without traditional instruments; and the growth in critical regard for an expansive array of musical expression. Though some might say these changes were long overdue, that one of the organizations dedicated to rewarding American artistic achievement modified its views on what deserves such recognition indicates the persistence of cultural debate over defining American music.

As a broad spectrum of voices has gained entry into American musical life over the past century, the scope of cultural debate as expressed in music has become increasingly difficult to categorize. The continued willingness of contemporary musicians to take a stand in their work about the direction of the nation suggests that future scholars will have ample motivation to study the relationship between music and cultural contestation. It is not as if composers in the concert music world have abandoned this project. High-profile operas that premiered in 2005 proved the contrary by taking on historical subjects whose lingering effects remain unsettled today: John Adams's *Doctor Atomic* deals with the unresolved tensions surrounding the test of the first atomic bomb, whereas Richard Danielpour's *Margaret Garner* traces the title character's tortuous struggles under the oppression of slavery. Nor have these composers severed ties with the American musical past. On multiple occasions Adams has turned to the music of Charles Ives, most famously by quoting the lone trumpet call from *The Unanswered Question* as part of *On the Transmigration of Souls* (2002), the elegy he wrote in response to the tragedy of 11 September 2001.[2] Danielpour incorporates spirituals, gospel, and jazz in his orchestral score for *Margaret Garner*, recalling in spirit the stimulating musical mix that energizes Ives's *Four Ragtime Dances*.

Sentiments of dissent, however, are delivered on a far more frequent basis by today's popular musicians, especially those identified with genres that historically prize acts of rebellion, insubordination, and social activism. What is most striking, perhaps as a natural result of trying to stay relevant to current consumers, is how often these oppositional messages are directed toward the contemporary political landscape rather than to earlier moments in the nation's history. The musical inclination to join ongoing debates becomes particularly acute during times of national crisis and dialogue, such as the period following the 2003 decision by the United States to go to war with Iraq. As one clear consequence, supporters of the peace movement were able to find consolation and support in dozens of antiwar songs released by popular artists, including Bruce Springsteen, R.E.M., Jane's Addiction, Sonic Youth, Le Tigre, Pearl Jam, Ozomatli, the Beastie Boys, Eminem, Jurassic 5, the Roots, and Missy Elliott. With their album *American Idiot* (2004), which bashed the Bush administration and bemoaned life in a media-saturated society, the pop-punk band Green Day rode the strategy of envisioning an alternative nation to critical and commercial heights, winning a Grammy Award for Best Rock Album and achieving multiplatinum sales. One could look as well to recent hip-hop, whether Talib Kweli's socially conscious approach to mounting a cultural revolution in *The Beautiful Struggle* (2004), Chan's attempt in *Part of the Nation* (2004) to carve himself a place in both America and the hip-hop nation by offering takes from the perspective of a Korean American rapper, or the latest release by the group most responsible for grafting politics onto the music of hip-hop, Public Enemy's *Rebirth of a Nation* (2006), which rips and twists the title from D. W. Griffith's 1915 film as a metaphor for the group's ongoing call for social justice.

I do not mean to suggest by this cursory survey that any of the above genres necessarily leans toward the left, nor do I wish to argue that the effect of cultural debate can be found only in music that assails or disrupts the status quo. On the contrary, as we have seen in examples such as Armstrong's "Gully Low Blues" and Berlin's "My Bird of Paradise," the process of struggling to define a nation does not always lead to results that sonically resemble a clash of conflicting or disruptive forces. Today we need look no further than the song "Our America" (2005), a collaboration by the country duo Big & Rich, country singer Gretchen Wilson, and country rapper Cowboy Troy, who dubs his eclectic blend of country, hip-hop, rock, Tex-Mex music, and fiddle tunes "hick-hop." One might expect a group of musicians hailing from such different musical backgrounds to produce unconventional results, perhaps something along the lines of "Nuestro Himno," the controversial Spanish-language reinterpretation of the National Anthem that would appear ten months later. This was not the case, however, even though the two songs do share something very significant in common: "Our America" also presents a new interpretation of "The Star-Spangled Banner." Unlike "Nuestro Himno," however, "Our America" prompted neither sustained outcry nor congressional debate; instead, the song made an appearance on the country charts and was used as the soundtrack for a commercial by an American automobile manufacturer. The song's reception as a symbol of all-American affirmation can be attributed to its faithful rendition of the English lyrics, to the achingly earnest delivery supplied by Big & Rich and Wilson, and to the nature of the group's artistic enhancements. The song begins with a short preamble, during which Big & Rich and Cowboy Troy recite quotations drawn from the Declaration of Independence, the U.S. Constitution, and Martin Luther King Jr.'s "I Have a Dream" speech. Following this lofty introduction, the country trio sings the anthem while Cowboy Troy raps between their phrases. This exchange might have turned blasphemous in other hands, but Troy's contribution supplies the patriotic icing for a celebration of the nation, as his rapped passages give a full rendition of the U.S. Pledge of Allegiance.

Though "Our America" does not contain any audible measure of social protest, its support for the nation, as expressed through an unwavering tribute to the flag and the republic for which it stands, offers material just as ripe for analysis as "Nuestro Himno." Even though the two songs seemingly stand at opposite poles, they both represent compelling products of cultural debate in American music, however differently articulated. A similar methodological stance toward "Our America" thus might explore whether the song was intended or received as a patriotic show of support for U.S. government policies or for anti-immigration advocates, or whether the driving cultural tensions here center around the use of overtly American symbols by the advertising world. In terms of its musical design, "Our America" constructs its message of unity—in which black and white, male and female, stand as one—by bringing together varied styles of music but mediating and softening their sonic differences. Rather than highlighting musical disparities or improvising new lyrics, Troy's rapped pledge accentuates its points without treading on or grabbing the spotlight from the sung anthem. Accordingly, the song channels the spirit of hope and optimism associated with Martin Luther King Jr. by quoting only the first six words of his speech ("I have a dream that someday . . .") while avoiding any specific mention of social critique or injustice. These images of harmony and unity, as so often happens, gain much of their power by omission.

Contemporary musical life and the corresponding terms of cultural debate continue to change in response to various influential developments, from the effects of globalization and transnational corporate culture to the birth of the digital age and the spread of the Internet. In response, some recent cultural theorists have suggested that we have entered an age of postnationalism, an era distinguished less by competition between nations and more by the spread of multinational corporations and the increased volatility of cross-cultural clashes.[3] Today's artists are busy crafting musical responses to these transformations; Ani DiFranco, for example, has for nearly two decades been producing music that addresses the promises and failings of America and that laments the corporate imprint on contemporary culture. Rather than struggling explicitly to define a nation in an increasingly global society, other musicians have turned their attention toward forming local communities, establishing ties across national borders, or building virtual networks in cyberspace, strategies that require equally flexible responses from the scholarly community. It thus remains unclear in the long term whether a new analytical paradigm will be necessary to address music in a postnational age. Nevertheless, as much as these musical innovations will serve in their own local or global ways to help define this nation—and others as well—it seems unwise to underestimate the power of American nationalism, especially in the present era, replete with military action and patriotic discourse. The current status of the United States, with its vast economic, cultural, and military resources, makes it all the more important for us to keep our eyes and ears attuned to it.

By concentrating on issues of power in the study of American music, I have not intended to craft a story of American exceptionalism. Indeed, one of the greatest historiographical challenges proposed by this book derives from the powerful international influences on music in the United States, which suggest how scholars continually must look outward and embrace a transnational perspective when studying American music. Yet, though a similar method might be applied productively to any era or musical tradition, it seems particularly applicable for understanding the music of a nation that historically has defended free speech and the open circulation of ideas, which practices and experiments with such wide-ranging musical traditions, and whose diverse population has devoted so much of its energy and resources to its creation. If we try to envision the contours of studying musical life in America as told through the lens of cultural debate, how might such a larger history proceed? In this book I have tried to explain how defining America and American music has been shaped and challenged along the lines of geography, genre, region, race, ethnicity, and more; however, I recognize that it may prove equally fruitful to expand, transform, or alter these parameters of inquiry. Because of the litany of potential subjects, the greatest challenge involves selection of material, not detection. Subsequent work on American music in the early twentieth century thus could expand on any of the musical figures who make brief appearances in these pages, or turn to other significant artists, such as William Grant Still and the Carter Family. A more expansive chronological study might extend from William Billings to Madonna to view how individual music makers from different eras have struggled to define the nation. While exploring the interaction between music and cultural contestation enables a richer understanding of music that explicitly addresses an era's key social tensions—such as Marvin Gaye's album *What's Going On* or the American musical *Show Boat*—this method can be equally useful for analyzing music that does not so openly broadcast its agenda. As a third option, this stance might be applied to the history of American musical genres. If we are to judge from the bitter outcry that greeted the initial sounds of ragtime, jazz, bebop, and rock and roll, or from the more recent controversies surrounding free jazz, electronic music, disco, heavy metal, minimalism, and rap, it appears possible to frame these contested moments in America's musical history not as a hit parade of new genres, but as a series of challenges to the musical establishment, often to the political establishment as well.

I freely acknowledge, however, that no single analytical method can address all significant musical questions, and that there are certain types of formal and aesthetic issues for which this methodological approach may not be fully up to the task. Ironically, such constraints derive in part from one of the greatest joys that music offers: its ability to provide comfort and liberation from the cultural conflicts and contradictions that surround us. After all, when we hear the soaring majesty of our favorite soprano or thrill to the electric pulse of the latest dance hit, sometimes the last thing we wish to consider involves the political impetus behind or ramifications of its existence. Along these lines, Josh Kun describes a range of listening positions that form what he calls an "audiotopia," in which "music functions like a possible utopia for the listener . . . a space that we can enter into, encounter, move around in, inhabit, be safe in, learn from."[4] As such, music can offer us the opportunity to confront the forces that surround us without necessitating a firm resolution. One might argue that music becomes valuable as a source of comfort specifically because it helps listeners make it through a life fraught with strife, and that it gains this ability precisely by masking its relationship to the instruments of power from which we may wish to escape. Perhaps music would be less necessary in a world without social and cultural conflicts, but I contend that the power of much music derives from how vigorously it engages with the conflicts it hopes to transcend. In the end, of course, regardless of the amount of consolation that music provides, cultural conflict will never disappear. Consequently, I remain convinced that without keeping relations of power firmly in mind, no history of American music, and no history of music, can be complete.

Notes

INTRODUCTION

1. For more on this process, see Albert Boime, *The Unveiling of the National Icons: A Plea for Patriotic Iconoclasm in a Nationalist Era* (New York: Cambridge University Press, 1998).

2. Joyce Howard Price, "President Supports Anthem in English; Spanish Version Called 'An Insult,'" *Washington Times*, 29 April 2006, sec. A, 1.

3. Richard Crawford, "H. Wiley Hitchcock and American Music," in *A Celebration of American Music: Words and Music in Honor of H. Wiley Hitchcock*, ed. Richard Crawford, R. Allen Lott, and Carol J. Oja (Ann Arbor: University of Michigan Press, 1990), 7. Surprisingly few have written on this historiographical topic in detail; key studies include H. Wiley Hitchcock, "Americans on American Music," *College Music Symposium* 8 (Fall 1968): 131–42; Robert Stevenson, *Philosophies of American Music History* (Washington, D.C.: Published for the Library of Congress by the Louis Charles Elson Memorial Fund, 1970); Irving Lowens, *Music in America and American Music* (Brooklyn: Institute for Studies in American Music, 1978); and Richard Crawford, *The American Musical Landscape* (Berkeley: University of California Press, 1993).

4. Lowens, *Music in America and American Music.*

5. Kyle Gann, *American Music in the Twentieth Century* (New York: Schirmer Books, 1997), xiv–xv.

6. Carol J. Oja, *Making Music Modern: New York in the 1920s* (New York: Oxford University Press, 2000).

7. John Tasker Howard, *Our American Music: Three Hundred Years of It* (New York: Thomas Y. Crowell, 1931). The fourth and final revision of Howard's book was published in 1965.

8. Gary E. Clarke, *Essays on American Music* (Westport, Conn.: Greenwood Press, 1977); Alan Howard Levy, *Musical Nationalism: American Composers' Search for Identity* (Westport, Conn.: Greenwood Press, 1983); Barbara L.

Tischler, *An American Music: The Search for an American Musical Identity* (New York: Oxford University Press, 1986).

9. Gilbert Chase, *America's Music: From the Pilgrims to the Present* (Urbana: University of Illinois Press, 1955).

10. H. Wiley Hitchcock, *Music in the United States: A Historical Introduction* (Englewood Cliffs, N.J.: Prentice-Hall, 1969). A broad embrace also characterizes the four volumes of *The New Grove Dictionary of American Music,* ed. H. Wiley Hitchcock and Stanley Sadie (New York: Grove's Dictionaries of Music, 1986).

11. Charles Hamm, *Music in the New World* (New York: W. W. Norton, 1983).

12. Richard Crawford, *America's Musical Life: A History* (New York: W. W. Norton, 2001).

13. Richard Crawford, "Music," in *Encyclopedia of the United States in the Twentieth Century,* ed. Stanley I. Kutler (New York: Charles Scribner's Sons, 1996), 1610.

14. David Nicholls, ed., *The Cambridge History of American Music* (Cambridge: Cambridge University Press, 1998), xiii.

15. George Lipsitz, "High Culture and Hierarchy," review of *Highbrow/Low brow: The Emergence of Cultural Hierarchy in America,* by Lawrence W. Levine, *American Quarterly* 43, no. 3 (1991): 521, 523.

16. Josh Kun, *Audiotopia: Music, Race, and America* (Berkeley: University of California Press, 2005), 17.

17. Theodor W. Adorno, *Essays on Music,* ed. Richard Leppert; trans. Susan H. Gillespie (Berkeley: University of California Press, 2002).

18. Susan McClary, *Feminine Endings: Music, Gender, and Sexuality* (Minneapolis: University of Minnesota Press, 1991), 28.

19. Roy Shuker, *Understanding Popular Music,* 2nd ed. (New York: Routledge, 1994), 239.

20. LeRoi Jones (Amiri Baraka), *Blues People: Negro Music in White America* (New York: William Morrow, 1963).

21. Tricia Rose, *Black Noise: Rap Music and Black Culture in Contemporary America* (Hanover, N.H.: Wesleyan University Press, 1994), xiii, 19.

22. McClary, *Feminine Endings,* 26.

23. Robert Walser, ed., *Keeping Time: Readings in Jazz History* (New York: Oxford University Press, 1999), viii.

24. Robert Walser, *Running with the Devil: Power, Gender, and Madness in Heavy Metal Music* (Hanover, N.H.: Wesleyan University Press, 1993).

25. David Ake, *Jazz Cultures* (Berkeley: University of California Press, 2001).

26. M. M. Bakhtin, *Speech Genres and Other Late Essays* (Austin: University of Texas Press, 1986).

27. Charles E. Ives, *Essays Before a Sonata and Other Writings,* ed. Howard Boatwright (New York: W. W. Norton, 1962), 94.

28. Michael V. Pisani, *Imagining Native America in Music* (New Haven: Yale University Press, 2005), 8.

1. CHARLES IVES'S *FOUR RAGTIME DANCES* AND "TRUE AMERICAN MUSIC"

1. Valuable accounts of ragtime reception are provided by Edward Berlin, *Ragtime: A Musical and Cultural History* (Berkeley: University of California Press, 1980), 32–60, and by Neil Leonard, "The Reactions to Ragtime," in *Ragtime: Its History, Composers and Music*, ed. John Edward Hasse (New York: Schirmer Books, 1980), 102–16.

2. Hiram Moderwell, "Ragtime," *New Republic*, 16 October 1915, 286, as quoted by Daniel Gregory Mason, *Contemporary Composers* (New York: Macmillan, 1918), 247.

3. Bigelow Ives, interviewed in Vivian Perlis, *Charles Ives Remembered: An Oral History* (New Haven: Yale University Press, 1974), 82.

4. Charles E. Ives, *Memos*, ed. John Kirkpatrick (New York: W. W. Norton, 1972), 130.

5. Jan Swafford, *Charles Ives: A Life with Music* (New York: W. W. Norton, 1996), 131.

6. Ives, *Memos*, 57.

7. Lawrence Kramer, "Powers of Blackness: Africanist Discourse in Modern Concert Music," *Black Music Research Journal* 16, no. 1 (Spring 1996): 53.

8. Ibid., 57–58.

9. J. Peter Burkholder, *All Made of Tunes: Charles Ives and the Uses of Musical Borrowing* (New Haven: Yale University Press, 1995), 417.

10. Larry Starr, *A Union of Diversities: Style in the Music of Charles Ives* (New York: Schirmer Books, 1992).

11. The score is published as Charles E. Ives, *Ragtime Dances: Set of Four Ragtime Dances*, ed. James B. Sinclair (New York: Peer International, 1990).

12. Ives, *Memos*, 56–57. It is conceivable that Ives encountered the music during his visit to the 1893 World's Columbian Exposition in Chicago, at which early ragtime musicians are said to have performed outside the main exhibition grounds.

13. William J. Schafer and Johannes Riedel, *The Art of Ragtime: Form and Meaning of an Original Black American Art* (Baton Rouge: Louisiana State University Press, 1973), 9.

14. Berlin, *Ragtime*, 123.

15. Ives, *Memos*, 56.

16. Ives, *Essays Before a Sonata*, 94.

17. Ragtime syncopations also appear in early works by Erik Satie that were written around this time, including *La Mort de Monsieur Mouche* (1900), *La Diva de l'Empire* (1904), and *La Transatlantique* (1904) (Steven Moore Whiting, *Satie the Bohemian* [Oxford: Clarendon Press, 1999], 257–59, 305–12).

Henry F. Gilbert's *Comedy Overture on Negro Themes* (1906) also concludes with a ragtime passage.

18. Clayton W. Henderson, *The Charles Ives Tunebook* (Warren, Mich: Harmonie Park Press, 1990), 92; Burkholder, *All Made of Tunes*, 424.

19. J. Peter Burkholder discusses the influence of abolitionist ideals on Ives in his book *Charles Ives: The Ideas behind the Music* (New Haven: Yale University Press, 1985), 34–35.

20. For more on Brooks, see Ives, *Memos*, 53, 250–52.

21. Ives, *Essays Before a Sonata*, 183. Burkholder recounts a similar tale: "In the first printing of *The Anti-Abolitionist Riots*, Ives's grandfather was mistakenly identified as an anti-abolitionist, an error that angered Ives so much that he corrected it with exclamation marks on his own printed copies of the piece" (Burkholder, *Charles Ives*, 127).

22. Perlis, *Charles Ives Remembered*, 77.

23. Ibid., 59.

24. Swafford, *Charles Ives*, 458.

25. Thornton Hagert, "Band and Orchestral Ragtime," in Hasse, *Ragtime*, 268–84.

26. Ives, *Memos*, 56–57.

27. Ives, untitled postface to "A Set of Pieces for Theatre or Chamber Orchestra," *New Music* 5, no. 2 (January 1932): 24. *Ictus* is a Latin term that here refers to the pulse of the downbeat.

28. For a comprehensive listing of sources and dates, see James Sinclair's preface and "General Editorial Remarks" in Ives, *Four Ragtime Dances*, iii–v, and his entry on *Four Ragtime Dances* in James Sinclair, *A Descriptive Catalogue of the Music of Charles Ives* (New Haven: Yale University Press, 1999), 115–19. Sinclair's complete critical commentary is on file at the John Herrick Jackson Music Library, Yale University. The dates I give here are from Sinclair's and Ives's (not always consistent) estimates. In his works list, compiled around 1935, Ives recalls "about a dozen" ragtime dances or pieces, which he dates "about 1900–1911" (Ives, *Memos*, 150). Several years earlier, in the text of *Memos* (ca. 1932), he offered a more precise estimate: "I started and wrote so many of these ragtime dances, all of them a great deal the same, around 1902 and 1904" (ibid., 69).

The dating of Ives's works, however, remains problematic. Gayle Sherwood's analyses of the surviving sketches related to *Four Ragtime Dances* suggest later dates (ca. 1912–14) than either Ives's or Sinclair's. For more on her approach, which focuses on Ives's handwriting and music paper analyses, see Gayle Sherwood, "Questions and Veracities: Reassessing the Chronology of Ives's Choral Works," *Musical Quarterly* 78 (1994): 429–47. Further commentary can be found in Sherwood, "The Choral Works of Charles Ives: Chronology, Style, Reception" (Ph.D. diss., Yale University, 1995).

29. Most sources for these pieces have been lost (Sinclair, *Descriptive Catalogue*, 119–20).

30. Ibid., 115–19.

31. For a comprehensive list of works related to the ragtime dances, see Sinclair's preface to Ives, *Ragtime Dances*, iii–iv.

32. Ives, *Memos*, 92. Also see Sinclair, *Descriptive Catalogue*, 114–15.

33. Ives, *Memos*, 92.

34. Ibid., 119.

35. Sinclair's catalog entry indicates that the primary fragment was probably intended for Ives's unfinished *Three Ragtime Dances*. According to Sherwood, partial scores survive from as early as 1904, but the primary remaining sources date from approximately 1912–14.

36. These three hymns are reprinted in Henderson, *The Charles Ives Tunebook*, 19–20, 31–32, 58.

37. Dennis Marshall, "Charles Ives's Quotations: Manner or Substance?" *Perspectives of New Music* 6, no. 2 (Spring–Summer 1968): 45–56.

38. Burkholder, *All Made of Tunes*, 213.

39. Judith Tick, "Ragtime and the Music of Charles Ives," *Current Musicology* 18 (1974): 105–13.

40. Ives, *Memos*, 57.

41. Ibid.

42. Tick, "Ragtime and the Music of Charles Ives," 112.

43. Ives's quotation of "Happy Day" has been interpreted as a reference to the Tin Pan Alley song "How Dry I Am," composed by Will B. Johnstone and Tom A. Johnstone. Although this may have shaped subsequent perceptions, it had no bearing on Ives's original intentions: "How Dry I Am" developed from the music of "Happy Day" as a response to Prohibition and was featured in the Broadway show *Up in the Clouds* (1922), more than two decades after Ives began to work with the original hymn.

44. Edward A. Berlin, *Reflections and Research on Ragtime* (Brooklyn: Institute for Studies in American Music, 1987), 3.

45. I thank Denise Von Glahn for her thoughts on this material.

46. Marshall, "Charles Ives's Quotations," 46.

47. For an overview of ragtime orchestration, including representative excerpts from stock arrangements, see Hagert, "Band and Orchestral Ragtime."

48. Burkholder, *Charles Ives*, 84–85.

49. Ives, *Memos*, 92.

50. The first movement of the Third Violin Sonata shares the only other comparable form of cumulative setting (Burkholder, *All Made of Tunes*, 137, 206).

51. Ives, *Memos*, 119.

52. Ibid., 119–20.

53. Swafford, *Charles Ives*, 165.

54. Burkholder, *Charles Ives*, 85.

55. Lawrence Kramer, "Powers of Blackness," 53.

56. The context for this sentence can be found in the epigraph to this chapter.

57. For various positions on the debate surrounding Ives's self-presentation, see Maynard Solomon, "Charles Ives: Some Questions of Veracity," *Journal of the American Musicological Society* 50, no. 3 (1987): 443–70; J. Peter Burkholder,

"Charles Ives and His Fathers: A Response to Maynard Solomon," *Institute for Studies in American Music Newsletter* 18, no. 1 (1988): 8–11; Carol Baron, "Dating Charles Ives's Music: Facts and Fictions," *Perspectives of New Music* 28 (1990): 20–56; Sherwood, "Questions and Veracities."

58. Ives, *Memos*, 69, 75.

59. Moderwell, "Ragtime," as quoted by Mason, *Contemporary Composers*, 247–48.

60. Ivan Narodny, "The Birth Processes of Ragtime," *Musical America*, 29 March 1913, 27, as quoted in Schafer and Riedel, *The Art of Ragtime*, 40.

61. Frank Rossiter, "The 'Genteel Tradition' in American Music," *Journal of American Culture* 4, no. 4 (1981): 114; Rossiter, *Charles Ives and His America* (New York: Liveright, 1975), 261, 369n96.

62. Mason, *Contemporary Composers*, 270–71.

63. Ives, *Essays Before a Sonata*, 78–79.

64. Ibid., 80.

65. Burkholder, *Charles Ives*, 14.

66. Ives, *Essays Before a Sonata*, 80.

67. Ives, *Memos*, 52.

68. Ibid., 53–54.

69. According to Judith Tick, "Ives's various writings about music present the most extraordinary use of gendered aesthetics in the public testimony of an American composer" (Judith Tick, "Charles Ives and Gender Ideology," in *Musicology and Difference: Gender and Sexuality in Music Scholarship*, ed. Ruth A. Solie [Berkeley: University of California Press, 1993], 83). Ives's capacity for producing gendered rhetoric also spawned a doctoral thesis by Patrick Kenneth Fairfield, "Representations of Gender and Sexuality in the Music and Writings of Charles Ives" (Ph.D. diss., Brandeis University, 2000).

70. Lawrence Kramer, *Classical Music and Postmodern Knowledge* (Berkeley: University of California Press, 1995), 181. As Kramer points out, Charles Hamm expands on these notions in his comments to Peter Winkler, published as "Interviews," *Review of Popular Music* 7 (July 1985): 8–10.

71. Burkholder, *All Made of Tunes*, 423. To be more specific, "Ives achieves a kind of musical autobiography, telling of his own experiences and those of people like him. He is an American, indeed a white Anglo-Saxon old-family Protestant from the northeast, a member of a particular class and clan born and raised in a smallish city, and it is his particular experience that he tells us about" (422).

72. Ives, untitled postface to "A Set of Pieces for Theatre or Chamber Orchestra," 24.

73. Ives, *Essays Before a Sonata*, 94.

74. Kramer, "Powers of Blackness," 58.

75. Swafford, *Charles Ives*, 165.

76. Kramer, "Powers of Blackness," 53.

77. Henry Cowell and Sidney Cowell, *Charles Ives and His Music*, rev. ed. (New York: Oxford University Press, 1969), 106.

78. Kun, *Audiotopia*, 21.

79. Larry Starr, *A Union of Diversities*, 15; his emphasis.

80. For a discussion of how these composers, and forty more, incorporated ragtime, see Lawrence A. Wilson, "Ragtime: Its Roots, Style and Influence on Twentieth-Century Music" (D.Mus. diss., Indiana University, 1981). Andrew Buchman offers a comparison with Stravinsky in "Ives and Stravinsky: Two Angles on 'the German Stem,' " in *Charles Ives and the Classical Tradition*, ed. Geoffrey Block and J. Peter Burkholder (New Haven: Yale University Pres, 1996), 131–49.

81. With a tempo marking of *allegro burlesco*, "Clowns" is one of six "Sketches of American Fun" that Powell packaged together in a suite, *At the Fair*.

82. See, Sinclair, *Descriptive Catalogue*, 102–4.

83. Denise Von Glahn, "Musikalische Stadlandschaft: Central Park in the Dark" ("The Sylvan in the City: *Central Park in the Dark*"), *Muzik-Konzepte* 123 (January 2004): 89–108.

84. See the composer's "Note" on the final unnumbered page in Charles E. Ives, *Central Park in the Dark*, ed. Jacques-Louis Monod (Hillsdale, N.Y.: Boelke-Bomart, 1973).

85. Ives also experimented with "Hello! Ma Baby" in his composition Study No. 23 (ca. 1912–14).

86. Ives, "Note," in *Central Park in the Dark*.

2. JELLY ROLL MORTON AND THE SPANISH TINGE

1. Martin Williams makes this observation in the booklet that accompanies the revised edition of *The Smithsonian Collection of Classic Jazz* (Smithsonian Collection, RD 033, 1987), 37.

2. Alan Lomax, *Mister Jelly Roll: The Fortunes of Jelly Roll Morton, New Orleans Creole and "Inventor of Jazz,"* updated, with a new afterword, by Lawrence Gushee (Berkeley: University of California Press, 2001), ix.

3. This quotation appears in the preface to *Ben Harney's Rag Time Instructor*, arr. Theodore H. Northrup (Chicago: Sol Bloom, 1897), cited in Berlin, *Ragtime*, 121.

4. Christopher Washburne also framed the development of jazz in these terms in "Armstrong and Ellington Do the 'Rhumba': The Case for Jazz as a Transnational and Global Music," paper presented at the annual meeting of the American Musicological Society, Houston, November 2003.

5. For a range of perspectives on Creole culture and early jazz, see the opening chapter of Ake, *Jazz Cultures;* James Lincoln Collier, *Jazz: The American Theme Song* (New York: Oxford University Press, 1993), 183–224; Thomas Fiehrer, "From Quadrille to Stomp: The Creole Origins of Jazz," *Popular Music* 10, no. 1 (1991): 21–38; and Lawrence Gushee, "The Nineteenth-Century Origins of Jazz," *Black Music Research Journal* 14, no. 1 (1994): 1–24.

6. Ake, *Jazz Cultures*, 13.

7. Lomax, *Mister Jelly Roll*, 221.

8. George Guesnon, interviewed in William Russell, comp., *"Oh, Mister Jelly": A Jelly Roll Morton Scrapbook* (Copenhagen: JazzMedia, 1999), 106–12.

9. Upon meeting Danny Barker, a New Orleans guitarist, Morton gave him the nickname "Hometown" (Barker, "Jelly Roll Morton in New York," in Martin T. Williams, ed., *Jazz Panorama: From the Pages of the Jazz Review* [New York: Crowell-Collier Press, 1962], 16).

10. Charles Edward Smith, interviewed in Russell, *Oh, Mister Jelly*, 95.

11. Barney Bigard, *With Louis and the Duke: The Autobiography of a Jazz Clarinetist*, ed. Barry Martyn (New York: Oxford University Press, 1986), 5.

12. This comment appears in an interview of Guesnon in Bill Russell, *New Orleans Style*, ed. Barry Martyn and Mike Hazeldine (New Orleans: Jazzology Press, 1994), 75.

13. Gwendolyn Midlo Hall, *Africans in Colonial Louisiana: The Development of Afro-Creole Culture in the Eighteenth Century* (Baton Rouge: Louisiana State University Press, 1992), 157; her emphasis.

14. Lomax, an Assistant Curator for the Archive of the American Folk Song Division at the Library of Congress (LoC), used these interviews as the basis for *Mister Jelly Roll*, which was published first in 1950 and later updated in 2001. The LoC holds the original audiotapes of these interviews, but Morton's comments also can be heard on many of the commercial releases of these recordings, including *Jelly Roll Morton: The Complete Library of Congress Recordings* (Rounder CDROUN1888, 2005). A transcript of the Morton-Lomax interviews is also available on the Monrovia Sound Studio Web site, www.doctorjazz.freeserve.co.uk/ (accessed 15 December 2007). In this chapter I draw on these interviews and, where noted, incorporate quotations from *Mister Jelly Roll*.

15. Morton interview with Lomax, LoC, 1938.

16. Ibid.

17. Bruce Carr, Dionisio Preciado, and Robert Stevenson, "Iradier, Sebastián de," in *Grove Music Online*, ed. Laura Macy, www.grovemusic.com (accessed 15 December 2007).

18. Roberts first published *The Latin Tinge* in 1979; a second edition was published on its twentieth anniversary: John Storm Roberts, *The Latin Tinge: The Impact of Latin American Music on the United States*, 2nd ed. (New York: Oxford University Press, 1999). The significance of this phrase can be traced in subsequent publications that extend the study of the Latin tinge into the nineteenth century: Louise Stein, "Before the Latin Tinge: Spanish Music and the 'Spanish Idiom' in the United States, 1778–1940," in *Spain in America: The Origins of Hispanism in the United States*, ed. Richard L. Kagan (Urbana: University of Illinois Press, 2002), 193–245; Robert Stevenson, "The Latin Tinge, 1800–1900," *Inter-American Music Review* 2, no. 2 (1980): 73–101; and Alfred Lemmon, "New Orleans Popular Sheet Music Imprints: The Latin Tinge prior to 1900," *Southern Quarterly* 27, no. 2 (1989): 41–58.

19. Among many books on this topic, see John Storm Roberts, *Latin Jazz: The First of the Fusions, 1880s to Today* (New York: Schirmer Books, 1999); Ed

Morales, *The Latin Beat: The Rhythms and Roots of Latin Music from Bossa Nova to Salsa and Beyond* (Cambridge, Mass.: Da Capo Press, 2003); and Raúl A. Fernández, *From Afro-Cuban Rhythms to Latin Jazz* (Berkeley: University of California Press, 2006).

20. Recent biographies include Phil Pastras, *Dead Man Blues: Jelly Roll Morton Way Out West* (Berkeley: University of California Press, 2001), and Howard Reich and William Gaines, *Jelly's Blues: The Life, Music, and Redemption of Jelly Roll Morton* (Cambridge, Mass.: Da Capo Press, 2003).

21. This comment by Andy González appears in his foreword to Raúl Fernández, *Latin Jazz: The Perfect Combination* (San Francisco: Chronicle Books, 2002), 9.

22. After writing liner notes for the Riverside reissue (1957) of the Library of Congress recordings, Martin Williams reprinted and partially revised his Morton commentary in several books, the last of which was *Jazz Changes* (New York: Oxford University Press, 1992).

23. Mark Tucker, "Jazz," in *Grove Music Online*, www.grovemusic.com (accessed 15 December 2007).

24. Martin Williams, *Jazz Changes*, 141. Alan Lomax concurred about this perception of the Spanish tinge, stating, "I don't think [Morton] restricted it at all to [a] particular kind of rhythmic pattern that he used in his composition." Lomax made these comments at a Jelly Roll Morton Symposium held at Dixon Hall, Tulane University, on 7 May 1982. See the typescript (reel 2, p. 25) in the collection at the William Ransom Hogan Archive of New Orleans Jazz, Tulane University. Similarly, Don Locke has identified a "Morton lilt," a rhythmic approach that gives the sense that "even in works where no direct tango rhythms can be detailed there is a suggestion of something of that nature" (Don Locke, "Jelly Roll Morton, the Library of Congress Recordings," *Jazz Journal* 13, no. 1 [1960]: 17).

25. Ernest Borneman published three articles on this topic: "Creole Echoes," *Jazz Review* 2, no. 8 (September 1959): 13–15; "Creole Echoes: Part II," *Jazz Review* 2, no. 10 (November 1959): 26–27; and "Jazz and the Creole Tradition," *Jazzforschung* 1 (1969): 99–112. The Borneman quotation is from "Creole Echoes," 14. The Fiehrer is from "From Quadrille to Stomp," 21.

26. Christopher Washburne, "The Clave of Jazz: A Caribbean Contribution to the Rhythmic Foundation of an African-American Music," *Black Music Research Journal* 17, no. 1 (1997): 68–69. For additional musical examples that reflect this influence, see Pamela Smith, "Caribbean Influences on Early New Orleans Jazz" (M.A. thesis, Tulane University, 1986).

27. Morton interview with Lomax, 1938.

28. Lomax, *Mister Jelly Roll*, 3–4. A similar account, first published in the *Record Changer* (March–April 1944) as "A Fragment of an Autobiography," is reproduced in Russell, *Oh, Mister Jelly*, 37–41.

29. Lomax, *Mister Jelly Roll*, 3. Lawrence Gushee's valuable afterword to *Mister Jelly Roll* outlines Morton's family background in detail.

30. For an overview of this era in New Orleans history, see Washburne, "The Clave of Jazz," 61–66.

31. Jack Stewart, "The Mexican Band Legend: Myth, Reality, and Musical Impact, a Preliminary Investigation," *Jazz Archivist: A Newsletter of the William Ransom Hogan Jazz Archive* 6, no. 2 (1991): 1–14.

32. Roberts, *Latin Jazz*, 14.

33. The original quotation is from Eleanor Hague, ed., *Spanish-American Folk-Songs* (1917; reprint, New York: Kraus Reprint Co., 1969), 21n1, and is cited by Stein, "Before the Latin Tinge," 197n25.

34. Lomax, *Mister Jelly Roll*, 6.

35. "Chink" Martin (Martin Abraham Sr.) grew up speaking Spanish as a result of his mother's Filipina background, and he took guitar lessons from a "Mexican professor," Francisco Quinones, before switching to bass and tuba. Interviewed by William Russell, Martin recalled how the northeastern section of the French Quarter at the turn of the century was populated mainly by "Mexicans, Puerto Ricans, and Spanish" who "had been there for years." This interview is part of the Oral History Collection at the William Ransom Hogan (WRH) Archive of New Orleans Jazz, Tulane University.

36. Lomax, *Mister Jelly Roll*, 62.

37. Tom Albert, Frank Amacker, Manuel Manetta, and "Chink" Martin are among the musicians who mention playing these numbers during the early years of jazz in their interviews with William Russell (WRH Archive). Also see William Russell, "Albert Nicholas Talks about Jelly Roll: Part II of an Interview," *Second Line* 30 (Spring 1978): 3–10, and Alden Ashforth and Lawrence Gushee, "An Interview with Joe Darensbourg," *Footnote* 15, no. 3 (February–March 1984): 6–9.

38. Russell, *New Orleans Style*, 23.

39. Williams, *Jazz Changes*, 143.

40. In one of his interviews with Lomax, Morton credits a mentor, Frank Richards, for help with correcting and polishing the final version of the piece.

41. Morton interview with Lomax, 1938.

42. Recordings of Morton's "New Orleans Joys," along with dozens of other tunes, are available online at the Red Hot Jazz Archive Web site, www .redhotjazz.com/jellyroll.html (accessed 15 December 2007). See James Dapogny's transcription of Morton's 1923 performance (Gennett 5486, mx 11538) in his edition of Morton's piano solos (Jelly Roll Morton, *Ferdinand "Jelly Roll" Morton: The Collected Piano Music*, ed. James Dapogny [Washington, D.C.: Smithsonian Institution Press, 1982], 39–47).

43. I thank David Lasocki for suggesting this interpretive angle.

44. Gunther Schuller, *Early Jazz: Its Roots and Development* (New York: Oxford University Press, 1968), 172.

45. Jairo Moreno, "Bauzá—Gillespie—Latin/Jazz: Difference, Modernity, and the Black Caribbean," *South Atlantic Quarterly* 103, no. 1 (Winter 2004): 99.

46. Williams, *Jazz Changes*, 143.

47. Ibid., 149.

48. Peter Narváez, "The Influences of Hispanic Music Cultures on African-American Blues Musicians," *Black Music Research Journal* 14 (1994): 220.

49. Morton titled several pieces after places near New Orleans, naming "Shreveport" after a nearby city, "Ponchatrain" [*sic*] after Lake Pontchartrain, and "Milenberg Joys" [*sic*] after a lakeside dance resort in the town of Milneburg. None of these is marked by an overt Spanish musical tinge. Likewise, in one of his last compositions, "My Home Is in a Southern Town" (1938), he chose not to employ a Spanish tinge, perhaps owing to the song's generalized nostalgia about growing up in the South.

50. Dapogny in Morton, *Ferdinand "Jelly Roll" Morton*, 293.

51. According to James Dapogny, "Thornton Hagert of Vernacular Music Research has discovered that *The Crave*, like Sidney Bechet's *Egyptian Fantasy*, is partly derived from Abe Oleman's *Egyptia*, which was published in 1911 in Chicago by Will Rossiter, Morton's first publisher" (Morton, *Ferdinand "Jelly Roll" Morton*, 473).

52. Pastras dates the piece around 1918 (*Dead Man Blues*, 84). For more details on "The Crave," see Tom Stoddard, *Jazz on the Barbary Coast* (Chigwell, Essex: Storyville Publications, 1982), 34–35.

53. Dapogny in Morton, *Ferdinand "Jelly Roll" Morton*, 473.

54. Morton's 1939 studio version for General uses an AABCC form, but the extended version he performed for Alan Lomax the previous year stretches it out to an AABBACC form.

55. Williams, *Jazz Changes*, 144.

56. Morton interview with Lomax, 1938.

57. A recent collection of essays treats the international spread of jazz as a process that went hand in hand with political, economic, and social developments around the globe; see E. Taylor Atkins, ed., *Jazz Planet* (Jackson: University Press of Mississippi, 2003).

58. Octave Crosby, Charles Love, Manuel Manetta, and Jasper Taylor are among those who worked as jazz musicians in Mexico (WRH Archive).

59. Narváez, "The Influences of Hispanic Music Cultures," 208.

60. Morton's recording was released as "Tia Juana (Tee Wana)," a variant of the original title. The land where the city of Tijuana grew once served as a cattle ranch known as Rancho de Tia Juana. Though the abbreviated term was in use by the late nineteenth century, the song's title makes clear that plenty of prospective American consumers were still unfamiliar with the spelling and pronunciation of Tijuana.

61. Pastras, *Dead Man Blues*, 135.

62. Morton took note of this resemblance, as he later told Floyd Levin. When asked about the final section of "Jelly Roll Blues," the chorus that is grounded by the *tresillo* bass, Morton claimed, according to Levin, that "it was something on the order of the Charleston, but 'it came out before the Charleston did'" (Roy Carew, "Roy Carew's New Orleans Recollections," in Russell, *Oh, Mister Jelly*, 29).

63. Pastras, *Dead Man Blues*, 135.

64. Ibid.

65. The tune was issued by Gennett as "Mamamita," apparently because of a typographical error.

66. Omer Simeon, interviewed in Russell, *Oh, Mister Jelly,* 359.

67. Lomax, *Mister Jelly Roll,* 177. Morton also named his song "Sweet Anita Mine" after Gonzales.

68. Paul Howard, interviewed in Russell, *Oh, Mister Jelly,* 563.

69. Floyd Levin, *Classic Jazz: A Personal View of the Music and the Musicians.* (Berkeley: University of California Press, 2000), 119.

70. Pastras, *Dead Man Blues,* 73.

71. John Spikes, interviewed in Russell, *Oh, Mister Jelly,* 552; Paul Barnes, interviewed ibid., 463. Throughout *Dead Man Blues* Pastras devotes attention to Creole religious practices and voodoo rituals as they may have applied to Morton and several figures in his life.

72. Marili Morden, interviewed in Russell, *Oh, Mister Jelly,* 542.

73. For the full lyrics, see Pastras, *Dead Man Blues,* 59.

74. *Jelly Roll Morton: The Piano Rolls* (Nonesuch, 79363–2, 1997) contains recordings of Morton's piano rolls as realized by Artis Wodehouse, with the assistance of digital technology.

75. William Russell, "Albert Nicholas Talks about Jelly Roll," *Second Line* 30 (Winter 1978): 36.

76. Preston Jackson, interviewed in Russell, *Oh, Mister Jelly,* 383.

77. Barker, "Jelly Roll Morton in New York," 17.

78. Those who knew Jelly Roll Morton provide mixed testimony on his racial politics. His Creole partner Mabel Bertrand told Alan Lomax that "Jelly Roll didn't like Negroes. He always said they would mess up your business. And Negroes didn't like him. I guess they were jealous" (Lomax, *Mister Jelly Roll,* 208–10). Likewise, Lee Collins, a trumpet player from New Orleans, claimed that Morton was "very prejudiced and liked nothing but Creoles" (Lee Collins, as told to Mary Collins, *"Oh, Didn't He Ramble": The Life Story of Lee Collins* [Urbana: University of Illinois Press, 1974], 37).

In contrast, John Spikes, who produced the first jazz record by a nonwhite (black and Creole) group, countered that Jelly Roll "was fair to all races, to everybody. He was a Creole, but he also had darker colored members in his band, too" (John Spikes, interviewed in Russell, *Oh, Mister Jelly,* 552). Danny Barker shared this impression: "I cannot recall one time when Jelly ever mentioned racial prejudice and discrimination . . . not once did he brag that he was a Creole as most of the light-colored downtown musicians would do" (Danny Barker, A *Life in Jazz,* ed. Alyn Shipton [New York: Oxford University Press, 1986], 122).

79. Lomax, *Mister Jelly Roll,* 194.

80. See Baby Dodds, as told to Larry Gara, *The Baby Dodds Story* (Los Angeles: Contemporary Press, 1959), 74.

81. Ibid., 73–74.

82. Omer Simeon, "Mostly about Morton" in *Selections from the Gutter: Jazz Portraits from "The Jazz Record,"* ed. Art Hodes and Chadwick Hansen (Berkeley: University of California Press, 1977), 93.

83. Nicholas considered "Panama" a standard for early New Orleans musicians (Russell, "Albert Nicholas Talks about Jelly Roll: Part II," 9); George Brunies and Lee Collins shared the same impression (WHA Archive). In addition to composing "Panama," William Tyers experimented with Latin rhythms in "Trocha: A Cuban Dance" (1896) and "Maori: A Samoan Dance" (1908).

84. The original source is Edward Kennedy "Duke" Ellington, "Music Is 'Tops' to You and Me . . . And Swing Is a Part of It," *Tops* (1938): 14–18. This article has been republished as " 'Duke' Ellington Explains Swing," in Walser, *Keeping Time*, 106–10.

85. W. C. Handy, *Father of the Blues: An Autobiography*, ed. Arna Bontemps (New York: Macmillan, 1941), 51–53, 97–98.

86. Locke, "Jelly Roll Morton, the Library of Congress Recordings," 16.

87. Carew, "New Orleans Recollections" in Russell, *Oh, Mister Jelly*, 29.

88. Whitney Balliett, *Jelly Roll, Jabbo, and Fats: Nineteen Portraits in Jazz* (New York: Oxford University Press, 1983), 25–26.

89. Morton interview with Lomax, 1938.

90. Williams, *Jazz Changes*, 143–44; his emphasis.

91. Richard Hadlock, "Morton's Library of Congress Albums," *Jazz: A Quarterly of American Music* 2 (1959): 134.

92. Paul Gilroy, *The Black Atlantic: Modernity and Double Consciousness* (Cambridge: Harvard University Press, 1993).

93. In addition to the aforementioned studies by Morales, Narváez, and Roberts, see Roy Brewer, "The Use of Habanera Rhythm in Rockabilly Music," *American Music* 17, no. 3 (1999): 300–317; George H. Lewis, "Ghosts, Ragged but Beautiful: Influences of Mexican Music on American Country-Western and Rock 'n' Roll," *Popular Music and Society* 15, no. 4 (Winter 1991): 85–103; and Alexander Stewart, " 'Funky Drummer': New Orleans, James Brown and the Rhythmic Transformation of American Popular Music," *Popular Music* 19, no. 3 (2000): 293–318.

3. LOUIS ARMSTRONG AND THE GREAT MIGRATION

1. Scott DeVeaux, "Constructing the Jazz Tradition: Jazz Historiography," *Black American Literature Forum* 25 no. 3 (1991): 525–60.

2. Recent collections include: George O. Carney, ed., *The Sounds of People and Places: A Geography of American Music from Country to Classical and Blues to Bop*, 4th ed. (Lanham, Md.: Rowman and Littlefield, 2003); Andrew Leyshon, David Matless, and George Revill, eds., *The Place of Music* (New York: Guilford Press, 1998); and Martin Stokes, ed., *Ethnicity, Identity, and Music: The Musical Construction of Place* (Providence, R.I.: Berg, 1994).

3. Denise Von Glahn, *The Sounds of Place: Music and the American Cultural Landscape* (Boston: Northeastern University Press, 2003); Murray Forman, *The 'Hood Comes First: Race, Space, and Place in Rap and Hip-Hop* (Middletown, Conn.: Wesleyan University Press, 2002).

4. Thomas Brothers, *Louis Armstrong's New Orleans* (New York: W. W. Norton, 2006).

5. William Howland Kenney, *Chicago Jazz: A Cultural History, 1904–1930* (New York: Oxford University Press, 1993). Thomas J. Hennessey's work on jazz in Chicago and New York provides wider context; see his *From Jazz to Swing: African American Jazz Musicians and Their Music, 1890–1935* (Detroit: Wayne State University Press, 1994), chaps. 2, 4.

6. Andrew Berish, "Swinging Transcontinental: Modernity, Race, and Place in American Dance Band Music, 1930–1946" (Ph.D. diss., University of California, Los Angeles, 2006), 37; his emphasis.

7. Brian Cameron Harker, "The Early Musical Development of Louis Armstrong, 1901–1928" (Ph.D. diss., Columbia University, 1997).

8. Guthrie P. Ramsey Jr., *Race Music: Black Cultures from Bebop to Hip-Hop* (Berkeley: University of California Press, 2003).

9. Charles Keil, *Urban Blues* (Chicago: University of Chicago Press, 1966), 66. Also see William Barlow, *"Looking Up at Down": The Emergence of Blues Culture* (Philadelphia: Temple University Press, 1989).

10. Roger Randolph House, " 'Keys to the Highway': William 'Big Bill' Broonzy and the Chicago Blues in the Era of the Great Migration" (Ph.D. diss., Boston University, 1999), 110.

11. Burton W. Peretti, *The Creation of Jazz; Music, Race, and Culture in Urban America* (Urbana: University of Illinois Press, 1992), 43.

12. Jones, *Blues People*, 96.

13. Sidney Bechet, *Treat It Gentle* (1960; reprint, New York: Da Capo Press, 1975), 115.

14. Langston Hughes, *The Big Sea: An Autobiography* (1940; reprint, New York: Hill and Wang, 1963), 23.

15. James R. Grossman, *Land of Hope: Chicago, Black Southerners, and the Great Migration* (Chicago: University of Chicago Press, 1989), 79.

16. Ibid., 4.

17. James R. Grossman, "Blowing the Trumpet: The *Chicago Defender* and Black Migration during World War I," *Illinois Historical Journal* 78, no. 2 (Summer 1985): 84.

18. House, "Keys to the Highway," 82.

19. Michael W. Harris, *The Rise of Gospel Blues: The Music of Thomas Andrew Dorsey in the Urban Church* (New York: Oxford University Press, 1992), 47.

20. Timothy Michael Kalil, "The Role of the Great Migration of African Americans to Chicago in the Development of Traditional Black Gospel Piano by Thomas A. Dorsey, circa 1930" (Ph.D. diss., Kent State University, 1993), 79.

21. Nat Shapiro and Nat Hentoff, eds., *Hear Me Talkin' to Ya: The Story of Jazz as Told by the Men Who Made It* (1955; reprint, New York: Dover, 1966), 112.

22. St. Clair Drake and Horace R. Cayton, *Black Metropolis: A Study of Negro Life in a Northern City*, rev. ed., 2 vols. (New York: Harper and Row, 1962), 1:78.

23. Quoted in Kathy J. Ogren, *The Jazz Revolution: Twenties America & the Meaning of Jazz* (New York: Oxford University Press, 1989), 52.

24. Shapiro and Hentoff, *Hear Me Talkin' to Ya*, 91.

25. Mahalia Jackson, with Evan McLeod Wylie, *Movin' On Up* (New York: Hawthorn Books, 1966), 46.

26. Gary Giddins, *Satchmo* (New York: Da Capo Press, 1992), 76.

27. Jackson, *Movin' On Up*, 41.

28. Milt Hinton and David G. Berger, *Bass Line: The Stories and Photographs of Milt Hinton* (Philadelphia: Temple University Press, 1988), 9.

29. Stanley Dance, *The World of Earl Hines* (New York: Charles Scribner's Sons, 1977), 187.

30. Louis Armstrong, *Satchmo: My Life in New Orleans* (1954; reprint, New York: Signet, 1955), 191.

31. Tim Brooks recovers much of the early history of African American participation in the record business in his book *Lost Sounds: Blacks and the Birth of the Recording Industry, 1890–1919* (Urbana: University of Illinois Press, 2004).

32. Though the term came to symbolize the perpetuation of racial segregation in the music industry, at the time it was coined "race records" balanced the needs of the African American community, whose members employed terms such as "the Race" and "race pride" to sustain themselves as a group, and those of the primarily white-run record industry, which was reluctant to embrace and advertise "Negro records." The most complete study on this subject remains Ronald Clifford Foreman Jr., "Jazz and Race Records, 1920–32: Their Origins and Their Significance for the Record Industry and Society" (Ph.D. diss., University of Illinois, 1968).

33. Clarence Williams is quoted in Lawrence W. Levine, *Black Culture and Black Consciousness: Afro-American Folk Thought from Slavery to Freedom* (New York: Oxford University Press, 1977), 226.

34. Jackson, *Movin' On Up*, 29, 36.

35. Rex Stewart, *Boy Meets Horn*, ed. Claire P. Gordon (Ann Arbor: University of Michigan Press, 1991), 72.

36. Jeff Todd Titon, *Early Downhome Blues: A Musical and Cultural Analysis* (Urbana: University of Illinois Press, 1977), 205–7.

37. "Gully Low Blues" was recorded on 14 May 1927 and released as OKeh 8474 (mx. W 80877-D) on the flip side of "Wild Man Blues."

38. For the initial figures, see Robert M. W. Dixon and John Godrich, *Recording the Blues* (London: Studio Vista, 1970), 19–60. Titon offers higher estimates in *Early Downhome Blues*, 205.

39. Armstrong, *Satchmo*, 161.

40. Garvin Bushell, as told to Mark Tucker, *Jazz from the Beginning* (Ann Arbor: University of Michigan Press, 1988), 1.

41. Burton W. Peretti, *Jazz in American Culture* (Chicago: Ivan R. Dee, 1997), 47.

42. Phyl Garland, *The Sound of Soul* (Chicago: Henry Regnery Company, 1969), 90.

43. Kenney, *Chicago Jazz*, 121–31.

44. Dixon and Godrich, *Recording the Blues*, 16.

45. Francis Davis, *The History of the Blues* (New York: Hyperion, 1995), 62.

46. Shapiro and Hentoff, *Hear Me Talkin' to Ya*, 109.

47. Laurence Bergreen's biography and its appendix of Armstrong's recordings by Darrell K. Fennell provide a useful time line for this period (Bergreen, *Louis Armstrong: An Extravagant Life* [New York: Broadway Books, 1997], 292, 502–4).

48. Sonic clarity would become even more apparent over the next few years with the introduction of new electric phonograph players. Andre Millard discusses the Victor Orthophonic in *America on Record: A History of Recorded Sound* (New York: Cambridge University Press, 1995), 143.

49. Armstrong scholars and musicians offer conflicting interpretations of the tune's "original" derivation. James Lincoln Collier's assertion that the melody was based on "I Wish I Could Shimmy Like My Sister Kate," which Armstrong claimed to have written and sold to Clarence Williams, seems unlikely. The tunes share the same key and similar harmonies, but the two melodies are quite distinct. More convincingly, Collier suggests that these polished gestures may have constituted a set piece that Armstrong had developed over time (James Lincoln Collier, *Louis Armstrong: An American Genius* [New York: Oxford University Press, 1983], 183). Laurence Bergreen provides a more suggestive interpretation, linking the melody of "Gully Low Blues" to "Louis's freewheeling adaptation of an old New Orleans tune played by bands when they were victorious in a cutting contest" (Bergreen, *Louis Armstrong*, 293). Although these musical examples seem to share the same proclamation of power, Bergreen's surrounding commentary is flawed (for example, "S. O. L. Blues," to which he refers in this section, was not released for more than a decade) and not fully documented. The drummer on the session, Baby Dodds, recalled the tune from his earlier apprenticeship with King Oliver ("Louis had a number called *Gully Low*"), a period that meshes with the lyrics in light of Armstrong's arrival in Chicago (Dodds, *The Baby Dodds Story*, 36). Armstrong does not appear to have commented on the song's provenance in his writings. In his vocal introduction to the 1957 rerecording of "Gully Low Blues," he simply refers to it as a "song I wrote." The multidisc set containing this quotation was released as *Satchmo: A Musical Autobiography of Louis Armstrong* (Decca Records, DXM-155, 1957).

50. One account of the usage of "gully low," cited by Brian Harker, can be found in William Russell and Stephen W. Smith, "New Orleans Music," in *Jazzmen*, ed. Frederick Ramsey Jr. and Charles Edward Smith (New York: Harcourt Brace, 1939), 12.

51. OKeh advertisement, *Chicago Defender*, 16 July 1927, sec. 1, 7.

52. Clarence Major, *Juba to Jive: A Dictionary of African-American Slang* (New York: Viking, 1994), 216.

53. Hugues Panassié, *Louis Armstrong* (New York: Charles Scribner's Sons, 1971), 75.

54. Hennessey, *From Jazz to Swing,* 30.

55. Brian Harker has made this same point, and his valuable commentary has informed my work. We diverge to some degree when it comes to interpretation. Harker considers "tentative insertions of northern musical traditions into the Hot Five recordings" in tunes like "Gully Low Blues" to represent Armstrong's ambivalence about combining the musical traditions of New Orleans with those of Chicago and New York, but I hear them as increasingly confident statements proclaiming his individuality (Harker, "The Early Musical Development of Louis Armstrong," 342–43).

56. Armstrong referred to his "country boy" background throughout his life. This anecdote appears in his autobiography *Satchmo* (230).

57. Big Bill Broonzy and Yannick Bruynoghe, *Big Bill Blues: William Broonzy's Story as Told to Yannick Bruynoghe,* rev. ed. (New York: Oak Publications, 1964), 89.

58. James N. Gregory, *The Southern Diaspora: How the Great Migrations of Black and White Southerners Transformed America* (Chapel Hill: University of North Carolina Press, 2005), 123.

59. These comments by Armstrong are part of "The Goffin Notebooks," one of the personal manuscripts and letters compiled in Armstrong, *Louis Armstrong, in His Own Words: Selected Writings,* ed. Thomas Brothers (New York: Oxford University Press, 1999), 86. Armstrong identifies King Oliver as the source of these comments ("The Armstrong Story," in *Louis Armstrong, in His Own Words,* 64). Punctuation as in original.

60. Armstrong, "The Armstrong Story," 61; his emphasis.

61. Ibid.; his emphasis.

62. Bergreen, *Louis Armstrong,* 177–90; James L. Dickerson, *Just for a Thrill: Lil Hardin Armstrong, First Lady of Jazz* (New York: Cooper Square Press, 2002).

63. Looking several decades into his past, Armstrong's spoken introduction to the 1957 release of "Gully Low Blues" conflates this with another song. He recalls it as "the first one done under my banner [as a leader]" and describes Johnny Dodds's fear of speaking into the microphone. Other sources, including his 1951 *Esquire* article, "Jazz on a High Note," reprinted in *Louis Armstrong, in His Own Words,* confirm that this tale concerned the earlier recording of "Gut Bucket Blues."

64. Harker, "The Early Musical Development of Louis Armstrong," 254–57.

65. According to Mezz Mezzrow, Armstrong's vocals on "Heebie Jeebies" (1925) became so popular in Chicago that "you would hear cats greeting each other with Louis' riffs when they met around town—*I got the heebies,* one would yell out, and the other would answer *I got the jeebies,* and the next minute they were scatting in each other's face." See Mezzrow's memoirs, written with Bernard Wolfe, *Really the Blues* (1946; reprint, London: Flamingo, 1993), 120.

66. Armstrong frequently returned to this technique, performing multiple vocal roles in a single recording and turning to overdubbing after the advent of

multitrack recording (Benjamin Givan, "Louis Armstrong's Vocal Recordings," *Musical Quarterly* 87, no. 2 [2004]: 188–218).

67. "High C" refers to the high note at the conventional upper limit of the trumpet. Since cornets and trumpets during this era were B-flat instruments, this high note sounded as a high B-flat, but would be notated as C and commonly called "high C." Since ex. 10 is transcribed for B-flat trumpet, the high C's notated here thus sound as high B-flat. This example has been adapted with a number of alterations from Lee Castle's transcription in Ronny Schiff, ed., *Louis Armstrong: A Jazz Master* (New York: MCA Music Publishing, 1961), 10–11.

68. The rips themselves are fairly smooth, since Armstrong developed a technique employing half-valve glissandos after he began playing with bands in Chicago and New York (Harker, "The Early Musical Development of Louis Armstrong," 333–34).

69. The third episode of Ken Burns's documentary *Jazz* (2000) uses this solo to underscore the narrator Keith David's description of Armstrong's trumpet playing: "Musicians everywhere bought Henderson's records just to hear Armstrong and shook their heads in disbelief at the power in which he played." Though the anachronistic use of this performance to characterize Armstrong's time with Henderson's band may be historically inaccurate, the choice well reflects the music's potency.

70. Skeptical trumpet players accused Armstrong of fraud and even ran tests on his trumpet (Bill Crow, *Jazz Anecdotes: Second Time Around* [New York: Oxford University Press, 2005], 236).

71. When time was not an issue, he did exactly that. Recordings in this era were limited by technology to around three minutes, but during his performances Armstrong often played dozens of choruses. Awestruck musicians tell anecdotes about tunes in which he played more than a hundred high C's and then jumped up to high F as a finale (ibid., 102, 236).

72. Collier, *Louis Armstrong*, 83; Harker, "The Early Musical Development of Louis Armstrong," 375.

73. I thank Paul Machlin for pointing out a number of similarities between Armstrong's trumpet solo on "Gully Low Blues" and his concluding solo on "West End Blues."

74. Hugues Panassié reports being told Armstrong was using "a King Oliver idea" on this track (Panassié, *Louis Armstrong,* 75). The jazz scholar Jeffrey Magee has brought another notable example to my attention: "Lonesome Journey Blues," a twelve-bar blues recorded by Thomas Morris Past Jazz Masters in April 1923 and by Fletcher Henderson's band that December. One of the choruses of Morris's cornet solo features short, high bursts and falling octaves, played over a short duration and compressed range, and his playing influenced Howard Scott in Henderson's band and perhaps Armstrong as well.

75. I thank Deane Root for pointing me in this direction. For more on the teleological drive of Armstrong's live performances as part of an examination of the coherence of his strategy toward taking solos, see Brian Harker, " 'Telling

a Story': Louis Armstrong and Coherence in Early Jazz," *Current Musicology* 63 (Fall 1997): 46–83.

76. Schuller, *Early Jazz*, 107.

77. The paper's main music critic, Dave Peyton, who led an orchestra of his own, favored upstanding, middle-class, orchestral music over what he considered more base forms of jazz. For a more detailed treatment, see Lawrence Schenbeck, "Music, Gender and 'Uplift' in the *Chicago Defender, 1927–1937*," *Musical Quarterly* 81, no. 3 (Fall 1997): 344–70.

78. Armstrong's comments, written in 1969, appear in "Louis Armstrong + The Jewish Family in New Orleans, La., the Year of 1907" in *Louis Armstrong, in His Own Words*, 9; his emphasis.

79. Dance, *The World of Earl Hines*, 166.

80. Brothers, introduction to *Louis Armstrong, in His Own Words*, xx; his emphasis.

81. Bechet, *Treat It Gentle*, 116

82. Shapiro and Hentoff, *Hear Me Talkin' to Ya*, 78.

83. Armstrong, "The Armstrong Story," 53.

84. Peretti, *The Creation of Jazz*, 45. Peretti derives some of these figures from John Chilton, *Who's Who of Jazz: Storyville to Swing Street*, 3rd rev. ed. (New York: Da Capo, 1985).

85. Kenney, *Chicago Jazz*, 35.

86. Barker, *A Life in Jazz*, 42.

87. Nat Hentoff, "Roy Eldridge," in *The Jazz Makers*, ed. Nat Shapiro and Nat Hentoff (New York: Grove Press, 1957), 301.

88. Robert O'Meally, liner notes to *Louis Armstrong: The Complete Hot Five and Hot Seven Recordings* (Columbia/Legacy 63527, 2000), 74.

89. Armstrong, "Jazz on a High Note," 131. Blues singers in subsequent decades used the word *barbecue* as slang for an attractive female (Major, *Juba to Jive*, 22).

90. Harker, "The Early Musical Development of Louis Armstrong," 339–41.

91. Dixon and Godrich, *Recording the Blues*, 22.

92. Gerald Early, *Tuxedo Junction: Essays on American Culture* (New York: Ecco Press, 1989), 295.

93. Stewart, *Boy Meets Horn*, 89. For similar stories about Armstrong's influence as a recording artist and fashion plate, see Buck Clayton, assisted by Nancy Miller Elliott, *Buck Clayton's Jazz World* (New York: Oxford University Press, 1987), 36.

94. Armstrong, "The Armstrong Story," 74.

95. Kenney, *Chicago Jazz*, 38. A gilet is a waistcoat worn under a man's tuxedo. Many of Armstrong's promotional materials are reproduced in Giddins, *Satchmo*.

96. Shapiro and Hentoff, *Hear Me Talkin' to Ya*, 109.

97. OKeh advertisement, *Chicago Defender*, 23 July 1927, sec. 1, 7.

98. Krin Gabbard, "Signifyin(g) the Phallus: *Mo' Better Blues* and Representations of the Jazz Trumpet," in *Representing Jazz*, ed. Krin Gabbard (Durham: Duke University Press, 1995), 108.

99. Farah Jasmine Griffin, *"Who Set You Flowin'?" The African-American Migration Narrative* (New York: Oxford University Press, 1995).

100. O'Meally, liner notes to *Louis Armstrong,* 61; his emphasis.

101. Elijah Wald, *Escaping the Delta: Robert Johnson and the Invention of the Blues* (New York: Amistad, 2004), 97.

102. Interview of Fred Smith in Timuel D. Black Jr., *Bridges of Memory: Chicago's First Wave of Black Migration* (Evanston: Northwestern University Press, 2003), 44.

103. Hughes, *The Big Sea,* 33.

104. Jacqueline Najuma Stewart, *Migrating to the Movies: Cinema and Black Urban Modernity* (Berkeley: University of California Press, 2005), 250.

105. Hazel V. Carby, "It Jus Be's Dat Way Sometime: The Sexual Politics of Women's Blues" in *The Jazz Cadence of American Culture,* ed. Robert G. O'Meally (New York: Columbia University Press, 1998), 474. This article was initially published in *Radical America* 20, no. 4 (1986): 9–24.

106. Madhu Dubey, "Narration and Migration: Jazz and Vernacular Theories of Black Women's Fiction," *American Literary History* 10, no. 2 (Summer 1998): 294.

107. Richard B. Wright, *Black Boy: A Record of Childhood and Youth* (New York: Harper and Brothers, 1937), 228.

108. For further examples, see Harker, "The Early Musical Development of Louis Armstrong," 340.

109. For extensive discussions of the influence of New Orleans on Armstrong, see Brothers, *Louis Armstrong's New Orleans,* and Harker, "The Early Musical Development of Louis Armstrong."

110. William Howland Kenney, *Jazz on the River* (Chicago: University of Chicago Press, 2005), 64.

111. Armstrong, "Jazz on a High Note," 132–35.

112. Giddins, *Satchmo,* 42. Also see Larry L. King, "Everybody's Louie," *Harper's,* November 1967, 69.

113. "Armstrong, "Jazz on a High Note," 128.

114. Gregory, *The Southern Diaspora,* 123.

115. Grossman, *Land of Hope,* 155.

116. Hinton, *Bass Line,* 37.

117. Broonzy, *Big Bill Blues,* 68.

118. Ramsey, *Race Music,* 29.

119. Harker, "The Early Musical Development of Louis Armstrong," 343–45.

120. Ibid., 339.

121. Kenney, *Jazz on the River,* 82–85.

122. Jackson, *Movin' On Up,* 51.

123. Early, *Tuxedo Junction,* 295.

124. "S. O. L. Blues" was first released in 1940 (W 81126-B; Columbia 35661).

125. Shapiro and Hentoff, *Hear Me Talkin' to Ya,* 110.

4. CHINATOWN, WHOSE CHINATOWN?

1. Hoyt's play, *A Trip to Chinatown; or, An Idyl of San Francisco,* is reprinted in *Favorite American Plays of the Nineteenth Century,* ed. Barrett H. Clark (Princeton: Princeton University Press, 1943). It is also available online by subscription through ProQuest in *American Drama: 1714–1915.*

2. Music and Arts Programs of America distributes a four-CD set of these concerts: *Carousel of American Music: The Fabled 24 September 1940 San Francisco Concerts* (CD–4971, 1997). Liner notes by David A. Banks provide a useful overview of the events leading up to the concert.

3. "ASCAP: Music's Hall of Fame Lives at Fair," *San Francisco Chronicle,* 25 September 1940, 1.

4. *Carousel of American Music* includes the audio of Buck's spoken remarks.

5. In his obituary, Schwartz was memorialized by the *Los Angeles Times* as the "composer of 'Chinatown' and other popular melodies" (*Los Angeles Times,* 2 December 1956, sec. 1, 3).

6. The 1910 sheet music edition stresses this point with the subtitle "(Dreamy Chinatown)."

7. Several collections offer introductions to the musical study of race and representation: Jonathan Bellman, ed., *The Exotic in Western Music* (Boston: Northeastern University Press, 1998); Georgina Born and David Hesmondhalgh, eds., *Western Music and Its Others: Difference, Representation, and Appropriation in Music* (Berkeley: University of California Press, 2000); and Ronald Radano and Philip V. Bohlman, eds., *Music and the Racial Imagination* (Chicago: University of Chicago Press, 2000). A number of journals have also devoted entire issues to the intersections of race and music, including *Nineteenth-Century Music Review* 3, no. 1 (2006).

8. For instance, see Jeffrey Magee, "Irving Berlin's 'Blue Skies': Ethnic Affiliations and Musical Transformations," *Musical Quarterly* 84, no. 4 (2000): 537–80.

9. Ralph P. Locke, "Constructing the Oriental 'Other': Saint Saëns's *Samson et Dalila,*" *Cambridge Opera Journal* 3 (1991): 261–302; Philip Brett, "Eros and Orientalism in Britten's Operas," in *Queering the Pitch: The New Gay and Lesbian Musicology,* ed. Philip Brett, Elizabeth Wood, and Gary C. Thomas (New York: Routledge, 1994), 235–56; Matthew Head, *Orientalism, Masquerade and Mozart's Turkish Music* (London: Royal Musical Association, 2000); Ralph P. Locke, "Beyond the Exotic: How 'Eastern' Is *Aida?*" *Cambridge Opera Journal* 17 (2005): 105–39.

10. Pertinent studies include Ellie Hisama, "Postcolonialism on the Make: The Music of John Mellencamp, David Bowie, and John Zorn," *Popular Music* 12, no. 2 (1993): 91–104; Aline Scott-Maxwell, "Oriental Exoticism in 1920s Australian Popular Music," *Perfect Beat* 3, no. 3 (1997): 28–57; Philip Hayward, ed., *Widening the Horizon: Exoticism in Post-War Popular Music* (Blooming-

ton: Indiana University Press, 1999); W. Anthony Sheppard, *Extreme Exoticism: Japan in the American Musical Imagination* (forthcoming).

11. Studies that address representations of Chinatown and of Asian Americans are quite useful for understanding orientalist Tin Pan Alley songs. In particular, see Anthony W. Lee, *Picturing Chinatown: Art and Orientalism in San Francisco* (Berkeley: University of California Press, 2001); James S. Moy, *Marginal Sights: Staging the Chinese in America* (Iowa City: University of Iowa Press, 1993); and Robert G. Lee, *Orientals: Asian Americans in Popular Culture* (Philadelphia: Temple University Press, 1999).

12. Ronald Radano and Philip Bohlman define "racial imagination" as the "shifting matrix of ideological constructions of difference associated with body type and color that have emerged as part of the discourse network of modernity." See their essay "Introduction: Music and Race, Their Past, Their Presence," in their *Music and the Racial Imagination,* 5.

13. Judy Tsou, "Gendering Race: Stereotypes of Chinese Americans in Popular Sheet Music," *repercussions* 6, no. 2 (1997): 25–62.

14. Michael Omi and Howard Winant, *Racial Formation in the United States: From the 1960s to the 1990s* (New York: Routledge, 1994). The use of music to define America along sociocultural, racial, or ethnic lines was by no means confined to Asian American representation. Born and Hesmondhalgh discuss the musical practice of what they term "subject or internal colonialism" in their essay "Introduction: On Difference, Representation, and Appropriation in Music," in their *Western Music and Its Others,* 10.

15. Born and Hesmondhalgh, "Introduction," 46. In tracing the context of a song's creation as well as its subsequent history, I am following what Jeffrey Magee has termed the "song profile" in his essay "Irving Berlin's 'Blue Skies,'" 537–38.

16. Anti-Chinese immigration policy began with the Page Law in 1875, which restricted the flow of Chinese female immigrants, and extended to all Chinese laborers in 1882. In 1943 the U.S. government began to allow a trickle of Chinese immigration and enacted major reforms in the 1965 Immigration Act.

17. For a comprehensive treatment of Chinese representation on the musical stage in this period, see Krystyn R. Moon, *Yellowface: Creating the Chinese in American Popular Music and Performance, 1850s–1920s* (New Brunswick: Rutgers University Press, 2005).

18. Bret Harte and Mark Twain, *Ah Sin, a Dramatic Work,* ed. Frederick Anderson (San Francisco: Book Club of California, 1961).

19. In addition to Moy's *Marginal Sights,* Anthony Lee's *Picturing Chinatown,* and Robert Lee's *Orientals,* see Gina Marchetti, *Romance and the "Yellow Peril": Race, Sex, and Discursive Strategies in Hollywood Fiction* (Berkeley: University of California Press, 1993).

20. Henry Yu, *Thinking Orientals: Migration, Contact, and Exoticism in Modern America* (New York: Oxford University Press, 2001), 175.

21. William Brown Meloney, "Slumming in New York's Chinatown," *Munsey's Magazine,* September 1909, 818–30.

22. The popularity of opium introduced into English terms such as *pipe dream*, or opium-induced fantasy, and *yen*, or craving, which derived from the Cantonese *in yan* (opium craving) (Jan Lin, *Reconstructing Chinatown* [Minneapolis: University of Minnesota Press, 1998], 175).

23. Ivan Light, "From Vice District to Tourist Attraction: The Moral Career of American Chinatowns, 1880–1940," *Pacific Historical Review* 43, no. 3 (1974): 367–94.

24. Gerald Bordman suggests that though the show was billed as a musical comedy, it more closely resembled a revue (Bordman, *American Musical Theatre: A Chronicle,* 2nd ed. [New York: Oxford University Press, 1992], 257). The show's subtitle—"a more or less incoherent resume of current events, theatrical and otherwise"—provides additional support for his claim.

25. The theater program also invites audience members to purchase Asian rugs at A. A. Vantine's, "The Oriental Store," and to dine at Chas. Sing Low, a "first class Chinese restaurant." The American Memory Web site (http://memory.loc.gov) reproduces the program as part of *American Variety Stage: Vaudeville and Popular Entertainment, 1870–1920* (accessed 15 December 2007).

26. Adolph Klauber, "New Show at Casino Is Big and Lively," *New York Times,* 19 July 1910, 7.

27. "Vaudeville Reviews of the Week: Casino," *New York Clipper,* 28 July 1910, 581.

28. "Plays of the Week," *New York Dramatic Mirror,* 30 July 1910, 10; "Some Good Songs in Casino Summer Show," *New York World,* 19 July 1910, 5.

29. Although the rationale for its incorporation remains unclear, historians concur that the song was interpolated into *Up and Down Broadway* during its 1910 Broadway run. Most sources cite 1910 as its date of composition, although David Ewen's claim that it was published in 1906 appears to be supported by a reprint edition held in the collection of the Paramount Theater in Oakland, California. I thank Judy Tsou for bringing this source to my attention. Ewen lists the 1906 date in *American Popular Songs: From the Revolutionary War to the Present* (New York, Random House, 1966), 66.

30. Tsou, "Gendering Race," 58.

31. Charles Hamm, *Irving Berlin: Songs from the Melting Pot: The Formative Years, 1907–1914* (New York: Oxford University Press, 1997), 29–30.

32. For a broad overview of musical orientalist techniques, see Derek Scott, *From the Erotic to the Demonic: On Critical Musicology* (New York: Oxford University Press, 2003), 155–78.

33. Hamm outlines these typical characteristics of Tin Pan Alley songs (*Irving Berlin,* 15).

34. Douglas Gilbert, *Lost Chords: The Diverting Story of American Popular Songs* (Garden City, N.Y.: Doubleday, Doran, 1942), 319.

35. Charles Hamm fleshes out these points in *Irving Berlin* (30–32), citing this quotation (31) from Armond Fields and L. Marc Fields, *From the Bowery to Broadway: Lew Fields and the Roots of American Popular Theater* (New York: Oxford University Press, 1993), 52.

36. Jerome's nineteenth-century musical counterparts occasionally set lyrics that demonized the Chinese to traditional Irish tunes (Tsou, "Gendering Race," 30–31).

37. For a discussion of how musical representations of the Irish changed over several generations, in large part because of increased participation in the music industry by recent Irish immigrants, see William H. A. Williams, *'Twas Only an Irishman's Dream: The Image of Ireland and the Irish in American Popular Song Lyrics, 1800–1920* (Urbana: University of Illinois Press, 1996).

38. Born and Hesmondhalgh, "Introduction," 35–36; their emphasis.

39. Lisa Lowe, "The International within the National: American Studies and Asian American Critique," *Cultural Critique* 40 (1998): 29–48.

40. *Up and Down Broadway* is now best remembered for presenting Irving Berlin in his Broadway debut. In a small role, the twenty-two-year-old Berlin and his partner, Ted Snyder, performed two of Berlin's songs: an ethnic novelty tune, "Sweet Italian Love," and "Oh, That Beautiful Rag."

41. Klauber, "New Show at Casino," 7. Ads for the show printed enthusiastic blurbs from a number of reviews: *New York World*, 24 July 1910, sec. M, 3.

42. "Some Good Songs in Casino Summer Show," 5.

43. The atmosphere of the times was captured by a tribute of sorts to pre-quake Chinatown staged by the city of San Francisco as part of the 1915 Panama-Pacific International Exposition. Entitled "Underground Chinatown," the exhibit featured actors in squalid surroundings portraying opium addicts, criminal assassins, gamblers, and prostitutes (Lee, *Picturing Chinatown*, 167).

44. The other two recordings were released by Prince's Orchestra and by the duo of Grace Kerns and John Barnes Wells (Joel Whitburn, *Pop Memories, 1890–1954: The History of American Popular Music* [Menomonee Falls, Wis.: Record Research, 1986]).

45. Moon, *Yellowface*, 158.

46. The available evidence suggests that Remick came out with the new edition some time after 1910, most likely in 1914 or early 1915. The original 1910 edition shares the same generic cover as other tunes from *Up and Down Broadway*, whereas the new edition makes no mention of the show or any of the performers who recorded it in 1915. Remick also published "operatic" and "popular" vocal editions, as well as arrangements for band, dance band, and even solo accordion.

47. David Jasen, *Tin Pan Alley* (New York: Donald I. Fine, 1988), 48.

48. For more information on Cooney, see her entry in *Who's Who In America: A Biographical Dictionary of Notable Living Men and Women*, vol. 26 (Chicago: Marquis, 1950). Reproductions of a few of her paintings can be found in Lolita L. W. Flockhart, *Art and Artists in New Jersey* (Somerville, N.J.: C. P. Hoagland, 1938), and Paul E. Sternberg, *Paintings by American Women: Selections from the Collection of Louise and Alan Sellars* (Marietta, Ga.: Louise and Alan Sellars Collection of Art by American Women, 1989).

49. Huping Ling, *Surviving on Gold Mountain: A History of Chinese American Women and Their Lives* (Albany: State University of New York Press, 1998), 115.

50. W. Anthony Sheppard, "Cinematic Realism, Reflexivity and the American 'Madame Butterfly' Narratives," *Cambridge Opera Journal* 17, no. 1 (2005): 66.

51. Otto Mensink supports this claim with dozens of examples in "Traditional Japanese Musical Genres and Instruments: Their Illustration in Woodblock Prints," in *The Ear Catches the Eye: Music in Japanese Prints* (Leiden, The Netherlands: Hotei Publishing, 2000), 13–20.

52. Bannister Merwin advised New Yorkers on how to appreciate these inexpensive, widely available works of art in "The Vogue of Japanese Color-Prints," *Munsey's Magazine*, August 1909, 650–59. A few months later, the critic Paul Rosenfeld published one of his earliest articles on the influence of Japanese art on James Whistler: "Whistler and Japanese Art," *Yale Literary Magazine* 75 (November 1909): 55–61.

53. Chase's interest in Japan fills his set of "kimono pictures," which portray kimono-clad figures in a Japanese style. The series includes *Mother and Child* (1886), *The Blue Kimono* (1888), *Back of a Nude* (1888), *The Japanese Print* (ca. 1888), *Making Her Toilet* (1889), *The Grey Kimono* (1901), *The Red Box* (ca. 1901), *Alice in Shinnecock Studio* (1909), and *The Flame* (1913). For reproductions of selected prints, see Katherine Metcalf Roof, *The Life and Art of William Merritt Chase* (New York: Charles Scribner's Sons, 1917). Other contemporary artists who were influenced by Japanese themes and techniques include Louis Rhead, Charles Hovey Pepper, Helen Hyde, and Mary Cassatt.

54. The *Newburgh (N.Y.) News* published Jerome's obituary on Monday, 27 June 1932.

55. E. M. Wickes, *Writing the Popular Song* (Springfield, Mass.: Home Correspondence School, 1916), 34. Sigmund Spaeth offers similar praise in *A History of Popular Music in America* (London: Phoenix House, 1948), 331–32.

56. Moy, *Marginal Sights*, 10–11.

57. Schwartz continued along the same lines without Jerome, writing the piano instrumentals "Chinese Fox Trot," "Chinese One-Step," and "Chinese Waltz," all in 1915, and the music for "Beautiful Girls Are Like Opium" (1920) and "Damn Clever, These Chinese" (1924).

58. Jack Burton, *The Blue Book of Tin Pan Alley: A Human Interest Anthology of American Popular Music* (Watkins Glen, N.Y.: Century House, 1950), 119; and Spaeth, *History of Popular Music in America*, 332.

59. Isaac Goldberg, *Tin Pan Alley: A Chronicle of the American Popular Music Racket* (New York: John Day Company, 1930), 213, 231.

60. Edward B. Marks, *They All Sang: From Tony Pastor to Rudy Vallée* (New York: Viking, 1934), 177.

61. Although Irving Berlin began his career as a singing waiter in a saloon located in New York's Chinatown and later published several of Jerome and Schwartz's songs, he did not compose his own songs about life in the district; however, he did write several songs that feature jokes about Chinese customs and language, including "From Here to Shanghai" (1917) and "Chinese Firecrackers" (1920).

62. Eve Unsell's "Ching Ching Chinaman" (1923) and Gene Rodemich and Larry Conley's "Shanghai Shuffle" (1924) also contain references to Jerome's lyrics.

63. Ellie M. Hisama, *Gendering Musical Modernism: The Music of Ruth Crawford, Marion Bauer, and Miriam Gideon* (New York: Cambridge University Press, 2001), 98.

64. In addition to detailing the opium-related aspects of "China Dreams" and "Down in Chinatown" (1920), Judy Tsou mentions a few earlier pieces of sheet music that base their imagery on opium, including "Sang Lee" (1878) and "Hop-Hop Hippety Hop" (1903) (Tsou, "Gendering Race," 38, 44, 58).

65. Abel Green, *Inside Stuff on How to Write Popular Songs* (New York: Paul Whiteman Publications, 1927), 12.

66. Artis Wodehouse, "Tracing Gershwin's Piano Rolls," in *The Gershwin Style: New Looks at the Music of George Gershwin*, ed. Wayne Schneider (New York: Oxford University Press, 1999), 217.

67. For a detailed study of how such influences shaped Gershwin's music, see Ryan Raul Banagale, "An American in Chinatown: Asian Representation in the Music of George Gershwin" (M.A. thesis, University of Washington, 2004).

68. Erno Rapée, *Encyclopedia of Music for Pictures* (1925; reprint, New York: Arno Press, 1970), 140–45.

69. Daniel Goldmark, *Tunes for 'Toons: Music and the Hollywood Cartoon* (Berkeley: University of California Press, 2006), 33.

70. Barker, A *Life in Jazz*, 39–40.

71. Ibid., 40.

72. Robert Lawson, *At That Time* (New York: Viking, 1947), 43–44.

73. Thornton Hagert describes the use of "Chinatown, My Chinatown" for dancing the one-step in his liner notes to *Come and Trip It: Instrumental Dance Music, 1780s–1920s* (1978), which is available on CD as part of the Recorded Anthology of American Music (New World Records 80293–2, 1994).

74. Stewart, *Boy Meets Horn*, 114.

75. Schuller, *Early Jazz*, 275.

76. Stanley Dance, *The World of Swing* (New York: Charles Scribner's Sons, 1974), 71.

77. Handy, *Father of the Blues*, 288.

78. The jazz critic Matt Glaser comments on Armstrong's speedy version at the opening of "The True Welcome," the fourth episode of the documentary *Jazz* (2000) by Ken Burns.

79. Though he fondly recalled trips to New Orleans' Chinese district and did not frequently express hostility toward Asians, Armstrong joked about the way Chinese people spoke, describing their attempts to cook "lead beans and lice" (Armstrong, *Louis Armstrong, In His Own Words*, 5–6).

80. Three years after producing *Chinatown My Chinatown*, the Fleischer studio used Armstrong's rendition in a 1932 Betty Boop cartoon, *I'll be Glad When You're Dead, You Rascal You*, to add excitement to a jungle chase that ends in a volcanic eruption. Since this feature contains no Chinese bashing,

Fleischer apparently felt Armstrong's version had detached itself from the original; yet he still used it to mark racial difference through parallels between jungle primitivism and black jazz musicians.

81. Gilbert, *Lost Chords,* 319.

82. Richard Crawford and Jeffrey Magee list twenty-five recordings of the song between 1928 and 1941 in *Jazz Standards on Record, 1900–1942: A Core Repertory* (Chicago: Center for Black Music Research, Columbia College Chicago, 1992), 14. This figure grows after tallying recordings by popular dance bands and pop singers of this period.

83. Aware of their admiration, Armstrong dedicated his performance of the song "to the musicians" in his first London appearance (Bergreen, *Louis Armstrong,* 353).

84. Nat Hentoff, "Roy Eldridge," 301–2.

85. The trumpet players Taft Jordan and Dud Bascomb recall the influence of Armstrong's rendition in Dance, *The World of Swing,* 84, 194–96.

86. Bordman, *American Musical Theatre,* 258.

87. *Remick Hits through the Years* (New York: Remick Music Corp., 1951).

88. Michael Freedland, *Jolson* (New York: Stein and Day, 1972), 233.

89. The Chinese American Data Center maintains a Web site (http://members.aol.com/chineseusa) that presents these census results in a user-friendly format (accessed 15 December 2007).

90. Hsaing-shui Chen, *Chinatown No More: Taiwan Immigrants in Contemporary New York* (Ithaca: Cornell University Press, 1992); Lin, *Reconstructing Chinatown;* Scott K. Wong and Sucheng Chan, eds., *Claiming America: Constructing Chinese American Identities during the Exclusion Era* (Philadelphia: Temple University Press, 1998).

91. Recent examples include Karen Shimakawa, *National Abjection: The Asian American Body Onstage* (Durham: Duke University Press, 2002), and Josephine Ding Lee, *Performing Asian America: Race and Ethnicity on the Contemporary Stage* (Philadelphia: Temple University Press, 1997).

92. Ronald Riddle, *Flying Dragons, Flowing Streams: Music in the Life of San Francisco's Chinese* (Westport, Conn.: Greenwood Press, 1983). Also see Moon, *Yellowface;* Nancy Yunhwa Rao, "Songs of the Exclusion Era: New York Chinatown's Opera Theaters in the 1920s," *American Music* 20, no. 4 (2002): 399–444; Mina Yang, "Orientalism and the Music of Asian Immigrant Communities in California, 1924–1945," *American Music* 19, no. 4 (2001): 385–416; Deborah Wong, *Speak It Louder: Asian American Making Music* (New York: Routledge, 2004).

93. Hisama, "Postcolonialism on the Make."

94. The Department of Theater Arts at the University of California at Los Angeles staged *Ah Sin* at Royce Hall, the largest auditorium on campus, 11–14 April 1962. An article from the *UCLA Daily Bruin,* dated 9 April, promoted the title character as "an excellent laundry man, perfect house servant, but lies, steals, and is addicted to opium smoking," and the white student actor who portrayed him wore yellowface: slanting his eyes, wearing a braid, and blacking out

a front tooth. The paper's review on 13 April made no mention of the show's racial politics, proclaiming it equal parts "Genius and Invention."

95. A staged reading of the show (book by Roger Alford, music and lyrics by Hal Stephens) was held at the Page-Walker Arts and History Center in Cary, North Carolina, on 3 February 2001.

96. Thomas S. Hischak, *The American Musical Theatre Song Encyclopedia* (Westport, Conn.: Greenwood Press, 1995), 49–50; my emphasis.

97. In *Everyone Says I Love You,* three Halloween trick-or-treaters—dressed in Chinese-style costumes, peasant hats, and Asian eye makeup—appear at the sound of a gong, bow to each other following Japanese custom, and sing a chorus of "Chinatown, My Chinatown," arranged by Dick Hyman. Allen also uses the tune near the opening of *Radio Days* (Orion Pictures, 1987).

98. The *Mafia* game is published by Gathering of Developers.

99. As of 15 December 2007, customers of amazon.com could choose from more than two hundred CDs and box sets that feature recorded versions of "Chinatown, My Chinatown."

100. Their CD *Swingin' Stampede* (1998) is distributed by Hightone Records (HCDS094).

101. *Oriental Illusions* (1995) is distributed by Memphis Archives (MA 7018).

102. K. Scott Wong, "Chinatown: Conflicting Images, Contested Terrain," *MELUS* 20, no. 1 (1995): 3–15.

103. Moon, *Yellowface,* 8.

104. David Henry Hwang, "A New Musical by Rodgers and Hwang," *New York Times,* 13 October 2002, Arts and Leisure sec., 1, 16.

105. Ben Brantley, "New Coat of Paint for Old Pagoda," *New York Times,* 18 October 2002, sec. B, 1, 24. David H. Lewis defends the original production at greater length in his book *Flower Drum Songs: The Story of Two Musicals* (Jefferson, N.C.; McFarland, 2006).

106. Richard Zoglin, "Not Just Chop Suey: *Flower Drum Song* Gets a Nifty Broadway Tune-Up," *Time,* 28 October 2002, 63.

5. SOUNDS OF PARADISE

1. Some exceptions can be found in songs written in response to the exotic dancers who performed at the 1893 World's Columbia Exposition in Chicago and in the wake of the premiere of *Salome* at the Metropolitan Opera in 1907. See Larry Hamberlin, "Visions of Salome: The Femme Fatale in American Popular Songs before 1920," *Journal of the American Musicological Society* 59, no. 3 (2006): 631–96.

2. Elizabeth Tatar addresses this historiographical challenge in "Introduction: What Is Hawaiian Music?" in *Hawaiian Music and Musicians: An Illustrated History,* ed. George S. Kanahele (Honolulu: University Press of Hawaii, 1979), xxiii–xxx.

3. Amy K. Stillman, "Published Hawaiian Songbooks," *Notes* 44, no. 2 (1987): 221–39.

4. Keith Emmons has archived more than one thousand images of Hawaiian-related sheet music covers from the 1870s to the 1940s on the *Hawaiian and Tropical Vintage Sheet Music Image Archive* (www.hulapages.com; accessed 15 December 2007).

5. Stillman, "Published Hawaiian Songbooks," 221.

6. Along similar lines, I rely in my original text in this chapter on the Hawaiian-language spelling for Hawai'i and 'ukulele by preserving the okina ('), a phonetic symbol that indicates a glottal stop. For all previously published song titles, lyrics, and secondary sources, I adopt the English-language spelling, which removes the okina from each word. The okina is not used for "Hawaiian," since it is an English-language word for which the Hawaiian language uses a different grammatical construction.

7. I would like to thank Amy Ku'uleialoha Stillman for generously sharing her expertise in Hawaiian music and allowing me access to her collection of rare source materials, including various clippings, sound recordings, and early record catalogs. For a representative example of how her work has been recovering the rich history of Hawaiian music largely on the basis of internal Hawaiian perspectives, see Amy Ku'uleialoha Stillman, "Of the People Who Love the Land: Vernacular History in the Poetry of Modern Hawaiian Hula," *Amerasia Journal* 28, no. 3 (2002): 85–108.

8. Gilles de Van, "Fin de Siècle Exoticism and the Meaning of the Far Away," trans. William Ashbrook, *Opera Quarterly* 11, no. 3 (1995): 77.

9. Such cultural exchanges were initiated long before Hawaiian musical ensembles began to tour the United States, as documented in James Revell Carr, "In the Wake of John Kanaka: Musical Interactions between Euro-American Sailors and Pacific Islanders, 1600–1900" (Ph.D. diss., University of California, Santa Barbara, 2006).

10. Fifty-five are collected in Lili'uokalani, *The Queen's Songbook, Her Majesty Queen Lili'uokalani*, ed. Barbara Barnard Smith, text and music notation by Dorothy Kahananui Gillett (Honolulu: Hui Hanai, 1999).

11. For more details on the U.S. premiere, see Patrick Hennessey, "Launching a Classic: *Aloha 'Oe* and the Royal Hawaiian Band Tour of 1883," *Journal of Band Research* 37, no. 1 (2001): 29–44.

12. Stephen Kinzer, *Overthrow: America's Century of Regime Change from Hawaii to Iraq* (New York: Times Books, 2006), 9.

13. The American Memory Web site at the Library of Congress includes a digital collection, "Traveling Culture: Circuit Chautauqua in the Twentieth Century," which contains publicity brochures and advertisements for thousands of traveling performers, including dozens of Hawaiian musicians and groups. See http://memory.loc.gov/ammem/award98/iauhtml/tccchome.html (accessed 15 December 2007).

14. Private communication with Malcolm Rockwell, 26 September 2005. Rockwell is now compiling what promises to be a landmark discography, *Hawaiian and Hawaiian Guitar Records, 1890–1960*.

15. Pekka Gronow, "Ethnic Recordings: An Introduction," in *Ethnic Recordings in America: A Neglected Heritage* (Washington, D.C.: American Folklife

Center, Library of Congress, 1982), 14. Rockwell adds that even though each of these releases was stamped with the label "Recorded in Hawaii," this claim has yet to be confirmed.

16. Tim Gracyk, with Frank Hoffman, *Popular American Recording Pioneers, 1895–1925* (New York: Haworth Press, 2000), 119.

17. Tony Todaro, *The Golden Years of Hawaiian Entertainment, 1874–1974* (Honolulu: Tony Todaro Publishing, 1974), 97.

18. Records maintained by the registrar's office at Yale Law School list Cunha as attending from 1898 to 1900, but he did not complete his studies or receive a law degree.

19. "Hapa Haole Songs," in Kanahele, *Hawaiian Music and Musicians,* 106–7.

20. For further details on the characteristics of modern hula, see Stillman, "Of the People Who Love the Land," 88–90.

21. The Hawaiian phrases at the end of the two stanzas shown in ex. 15 (mm. 16–18) translate loosely as "She sleeps a lot, how's about you?" and "She doesn't get upset, even though the shells are hot."

22. "Premiere of Tully Play Set for Local Theater," *Los Angeles Times,* 11 March 1928, sec. C, 28.

23. Christopher B. Balme, "Selling the Bird: Richard Walton Tully's *The Bird of Paradise* and the Dynamics of Theatrical Commodification," *Theatre Journal* 57 (2005): 1.

24. "Coming to the Theaters," *Washington Post,* 27 April 1916, 12.

25. Helen M. Morosco and Leonard Paul Dugger, *The Oracle of Broadway* (Caldwell, Idaho: Caxton Printers, 1944), 190.

26. "Picturesque Contrast in Play of Hawaii," *New York World,* 9 January 1912, 10.

27. In 1912 Grace Altman Fendler filed a lawsuit charging that *The Bird of Paradise* had been plagiarized from her play *In Hawaii,* which she had shown to Oliver Morosco the year before. After a series of well-publicized court battles, the New York Court of Appeals finally decided in favor of Morosco in 1930, ruling that Tully's scenario for *The Bird of Paradise* was original, even though it included similar details. Balme discusses this case in greater detail in "Selling the Bird," 8–9.

28. "Premiere of Tully Play Set for Local Theater."

29. Edwin Schallert, "Drama," *Los Angeles Times,* 6 January 1920, sec. 3, 4.

30. J. C. Furnas, *Anatomy of Paradise: Hawaii and the Islands of the South Seas* (New York: William Sloane Associates, 1937), 413–14.

31. " 'Bird of Paradise' Has Scenic Beauty," *New York Times,* 9 January 1912, 8.

32. Julian Johnson, "Paradise Bird at the Belasco," *Los Angeles Times,* 12 September 1911, sec. 2, 5.

33. " 'Bird of Paradise' Has Scenic Beauty," 8.

34. Metcalfe, "Drama: New York Result of Captain Cook's Travels," *Life,* 18 January 1912, 168–69.

35. "Picturesque Contrast in Play of Hawaii"; unsigned review of *The Bird of Paradise, New York Clipper,* 20 January 1912, 9.

36. Elizabeth Anna Semple, "The Bird of Paradise," *Overland Monthly* 59, no. 4 (1912): 384; "Los Angeles and Music," *Los Angeles Times,* 21 February 1916, sec. 2, 4.

37. "Coming to the Theaters."

38. K.G., "Belasco—'The Bird of Paradise,'" *Washington Post,* 24 December 1912, 5.

39. Henry Christeen Warnack, "Atmosphere and Natives," *Los Angeles Times,* 3 October 1913, sec. 3, 4.

40. Frank P. Morse, "The Music-Coated Drama," *Washington Post,* 30 April 1916, sec. MT, 2.

41. "New Hawaiian Records," *Talking Machine World* 8, no. 3 (15 March 1912): 36.

42. When the Hawaiian Quintette entered the studio, E. K. Rose replaced A. Kiwaia as a member of the group. One of the more widely available tracks, their 1913 rendition of "Aiaihea (Hula Shouting Song)," can be heard on *Music from the New York Stage, 1890–1920* (Pearl 9053, 1993).

43. "Laurette Taylor Confesses: Actress Discusses Her Hawaiian Role and Tells of Her Ambitions," *New York Times,* 14 January 1912, sec. 10, 6.

44. For a detailed discussion of Tin Pan Alley's "Butterfly songs," see Larry Hamberlin, "American Popular Songs on Operatic Topics, 1901–1921" (Ph.D. diss., Brandeis University, 2004), 215–325.

45. DeSoto Brown, Anne Ellett, and Gary Giemza view the ways in which similar imagery has been harnessed to market island culture in *Hawaii Recalls: Selling Romance to America: Nostalgic Images of the Hawaiian Islands, 1910–1950* (Honolulu: Editions Limited, 1982).

46. Jane C. Desmond, *Staging Tourism: Bodies on Display from Waikiki to Sea World* (Chicago: University of Chicago Press, 1999).

47. For more on the development of the hula girl, see Aeko Sereno, "Images of the Hula Dancer and 'Hula Girl': 1778–1960" (Ph.D. diss., University of Hawai'i, 1990).

48. Desmond, *Staging Tourism,* 72.

49. Adria Imada, "Aloha America: Hawaiian Entertainment and Cultural Politics in the United States Empire" (Ph.D. diss., New York University, 2003), 85–99.

50. Albert P. Taylor, "Hawaii: The Best-Known Building at the Panama-Pacific Exposition, 1915," in *Hawaiian Almanac and Annual for 1916* (Honolulu: Thos. G. Thrum, 1915), 149.

51. Frank Morton Todd, *The Story of the Exposition,* 5 vols. (New York: G. P. Putnam's Sons, 1921), 3:326.

52. Ben Macomber, *The Jewel City: Its Planning and Achievement; Its Architecture, Sculpture, Symbolism, and Music; Its Gardens, Palaces, and Exhibits* (San Francisco: John H. Williams, 1915), 177.

53. A comprehensive description of the Hawaiian building, accompanied by several photographs, can be found in Todd, *The Story of the Exposition,* 3:322–26.

54. Adria L. Imada, "Hawaiians on Tour: Hula Circuits through the American Empire," *American Quarterly* 56, no. 1 (March 2004): 117; John King and Jim Tranquada, "A New History of the Origins and Development of the 'Ukulele, 1838–1915," *Hawaiian Journal of History* 37 (2003): 22.

55. "Philippines and Hawaii May Be Proud of Their Exhibits," *San Francisco Chronicle*, 21 February 1915, special section, unnumbered.

56. Albert P. Taylor, "Hawaii at Panama International Exposition," in *Hawaiian Almanac and Annual for 1915* (Honolulu: Thos. G. Thrum, 1914), 75.

57. "George E. K. Awai Fueled the Hawaiian Music Craze in 1915," *HaʻIlono Mele* 3, no. 9 (1977): 5–6.

58. Taylor, "Hawaii: The Best-Known Building," 147.

59. "Dancing and Music Mark Celebration of Islanders," *San Francisco Chronicle*, 12 June 1915, 5. For further details on the advance planning for the pageant, see "Charm of Hawaii Will Pervade Exposition," *San Francisco Chronicle*, 11 June 1915, 5.

60. Todd, *The Story of the Exposition*, 3:69.

61. W. D. Adams, "The Popularity of Hawaiian Music and Musical Instruments," in *Hawaiian Annual, 1917* (Honolulu: Thos. G. Thrum, 1916), 142.

62. "On the Beach at Waikiki," Bergstrom Music, 1915.

63. Hamberlin, "American Popular Songs on Operatic Topics," 317.

64. Spaeth, *A History of Popular Music in America*, 399–400.

65. Berlin wrote lyrics for two additional Hawaiian-themed songs, "The Hawaiian Blues" and "The Sad Hawaiian Blues," but apparently they were never set to music (Robert Kimball and Linda Emmet, eds., *The Complete Lyrics of Irving Berlin* [New York: Knopf, 2001], 178–79).

66. Quoting "Aloha 'Oe" became fairly common in songs of this era, such as "Dreamy Hawaiian Eyes" (1921) and "In Honolulu by the Sea" (1925).

67. According to Amy Stillman's ongoing research, "Yaaka Hula Hickey Dula" has been recorded by at least sixty artists.

68. Thomas R. Ybarra, "Hawaii," *New York Times*, 22 October 1916, sec. SM, 19.

69. "Publishing and Hawaiian Music," in Kanahele, *Hawaiian Music and Musicians*, 309.

70. Active publishers in this field, such as Sherman, Clay of San Francisco, appended plenty of extra material about Hawaiian music to sheet music publications, including notices about additional Hawaiian songs and instructional manuals for the 'ukulele and steel guitar.

71. Madeira is a Portuguese archipelago located west of Morocco. For more on the origins of the 'ukulele, see King and Tranquada, "A New History of the Origins and Development of the 'Ukulele."

72. Geo. J. Birkel Co., advertisement, *Los Angeles Times*, 13 July 1907, sec. 2, 1.

73. Geo. J. Birkel Co., advertisement, *Los Angeles Times*, 18 September 1913, sec. 2, 1.

74. King and Tranquada, "A New History of the Origins and Development of the 'Ukulele," 22.

75. Southern California Music Co., advertisement, *Los Angeles Times*, 31 July 1914, 13.

76. Adams, "The Popularity of Hawaiian Music and Musical Instruments," 145.

77. Virgil Jordan, "The Yarn of the Ukulele," *Everybody's Magazine*, March 1917, 334; King and Tranquada, "A New History of the Origins and Development of the 'Ukulele," 22.

78. "Hawaiians Are Angry," *New York Times*, 19 September 1915, 10.

79. Jordan, "The Yarn of the Ukulele," 334.

80. "Ignorance Is Bliss," *Stars and Stripes* (France), 22 February 1918, 2.

81. Aaron Copland, *Ukelele Serenade: Violin and Piano* (New York: Boosey and Hawkes, 1968).

82. Aaron Copland and Vivian Perlis, *Copland: 1900 through 1942* (New York: St. Martin's Press, 1984), 126.

83. "Hawaiian Music Universally Popular," *Edison Phonograph Monthly* 14, no. 9 (September 1916): 3.

84. "Songs of Hawaii and Other Popular Numbers Feature October List," *Edison Phonograph Monthly* 14, no. 9 (September 1916): 12.

85. Gracyk, *Popular American Recording Pioneers*, 121.

86. Theodor Hoeck, "The New and Popular Hawaiian Music: What Makes It Different and What Instruments Produce It," *Delineator* (July 1916): 20.

87. Adams, "The Popularity of Hawaiian Music and Musical Instruments," 142.

88. Held in the private collection of Amy Stillman, this twelve-page pamphlet contains what appears to be a publication date of "6–10–16."

89. "Hawaiian Music Recordings," in *Encyclopedia of Recorded Sound in the United States*, ed. Guy A. Marco (New York: Garland Publishing, 1993), 313–14.

90. "Kekuku's Hawaiian Quintet," "Traveling Culture" (undated), American Memory Web site at the Library of Congress (http://sdrcdata.lib.uiowa.edu/libsdrc/details.jsp?id=kekuku/1).

91. "New Hawaiian Records"; Pathé Frères, "Take a Trip to HONOLULU via the Pathephone" (advertisement), *Los Angeles Times*, 4 March 1917, sec. II, 2.

92. Hundreds of completed responses to these questionnaires, originally distributed by Thomas A. Edison, Inc., in 1921, are held in the collection of the University of Michigan Music Library, Ann Arbor.

93. Katrine Stump, Galion, Ohio, Edison survey, undated (presumably early 1921).

94. Elmer Siegfried, Ogilvie, Minnesota, Edison survey, 18 February 1921; J. H. King, Alliance, Nebraska, Edison survey, 26 January 1921; Mrs. John M. Winton, Kansas City, Missouri, Edison survey, 28 March 1921; Alice I. Lora, Bluffton, Ohio, Edison survey, 13 January 1921.

95. Unsigned, undated response to Edison survey, Dahlby, Minnesota; Laura Haberman, Marshall, Missouri, Edison survey, 8 January 1921.

96. G. M. Vicars, Meridian, Texas, Edison survey, 14 January 1921.

97. R. J. Donley, Burnt Mill, Colorado, Edison survey, 27 January 1921; G. P. Cook, Alvo, Nebraska, Edison survey, 27 January 1921.

98. Unsigned, undated response to Edison survey; Mrs. M. B. Hutchinson, Cuero, Texas, Edison survey, 17 February 1921.

99. Gracyk, *Popular American Recording Pioneers,* 121.

100. Adams, "The Popularity of Hawaiian Music and Musical Instruments," 146.

101. This large advertising spread for Hawaiian products can be found in *Sunset* for May 1917 on pages 94–95.

102. "Hawaiian Music Universally Popular," 3.

103. Adams, "The Popularity of Hawaiian Music and Musical Instruments," 144; his emphasis.

104. Ibid.

105. Jordan, "The Yarn of the Ukulele," 334.

106. Gronow, "Ethnic Recordings," 14.

107. Ibid., 15.

108. Jerry Hopkins, "Record Industry in Hawaii," in Kanahele, *Hawaiian Music and Musicians,* 325–34.

109. Imada, "Aloha America," viii.

110. Ibid., 17–18.

111. For further discussion of Ferera's career, from which much of this brief account is drawn, see Gracyk, *Popular American Recording Pioneers,* 118–27.

112. Tim Brooks, *The Columbia Master Book Discography,* 4 vols. (Westport, Conn: Greenwood Press, 1999), 1:24.

113. Gracyk, *Popular American Recording Pioneers,* 120.

114. Kanahele also helped accomplish these goals through his work with the Hawaiian Music Foundation and his editorship of the encyclopedic *Hawaiian Music and Musicians.*

115. Amy Kuʻuleialoha Stillman, "Hawaiian Hula Competitions: Event, Repertoire, Performance, Tradition," *Journal of the American Folklore Society* 109, no. 434 (1996): 357–80; George H. Lewis, "Da Kine Sounds: The Function of Music as Social Protest in the New Hawaiian Renaissance," *American Music* 2, no. 2 (1984): 38–52.

116. Stillman, "Published Hawaiian Songbooks," 221.

117. Andrew N. Weintraub, "Jawaiian Music and Local Cultural Identity in Hawaiʻi," in *Sound Alliances: Indigenous Peoples, Cultural Politics and Popular Music in the Pacific,* ed. Philip Hayward (London: Cassell, 1998), 78–88; Fay Yokomizo Akindes, "Sudden Rush: *Na Mele Paleoleo* (Hawaiian Rap) as Liberatory Discourse," *Discourse* 23, no. 1 (2001): 82–98.

118. For further information about the contemporary musical scene in Hawaiʻi, see Amy Kuʻuleialoha Stillman, "Hula Hits, Local Music and Local Charts: Some Dynamics of Popular Hawaiian Music," in Hayward, *Sound Alliances,* 89–103.

CONCLUSION

1. The original press release is archived on the Pulitzer Prize Web site (www
.pulitzer.org/EntryForms/musicchanges.pdf; accessed 15 December 2007).

2. In *My Father Knew Charles Ives* (2003) Adams explores memories of
growing up, like Ives, with a musically inclined father in New England. This orchestral composition, recalling in its design Ives's *Three Places in New England,*
incorporates minimalist passages of the sort for which Adams is known alongside echoes of brass bands and big band jazz that he remembered hearing as a
child.

3. John Carlos Rowe, "Post-Nationalism, Globalism, and the New American
Studies," *Cultural Critique* 40 (Fall 1998): 11–28.

4. Kun, *Audiotopia*, 2.

Bibliography

ARCHIVES

Archive of Popular American Music, UCLA Library Performing Arts Special Collections, UCLA Library, University of California, Los Angeles.
Billy Rose Theatre Collection, New York Public Library for the Performing Arts.
California History Room, California State Library, Sacramento.
Hawaiian Collection, Hamilton Library, University of Hawai'i at Manoa.
Lilly Library, University of Indiana, Bloomington.
Music Library, University of Michigan, Ann Arbor.
William Ransom Hogan Archive of New Orleans Jazz, Tulane University, New Orleans.
Williams Research Center, the Historic New Orleans Collection, New Orleans.

WEB SITES

American Memory, Library of Congress, http://memory.loc.gov.
Cylinder Preservation and Digitization Project, Donald C. Davidson Library, University of California, Santa Barbara, http://cylinders.library.ucsb.edu.
Hawaiian and Tropical Vintage Sheet Music Image Archive, www.hulapages .com.
Historic American Sheet Music, Rare Book, Manuscript, and Special Collections Library, Duke University, Durham, N.C., http://scriptorium.lib.duke.edu/ sheetmusic.
Lester S. Levy Collection of Sheet Music, Special Collections at the Sheridan Libraries of the Johns Hopkins University, Baltimore, http://levysheetmusic .mse.jhu.edu.

MUSIC SCORES

Ben Harney's Rag Time Instructor. Arranged by Theodore H. Northrup. Chicago: Sol Bloom, 1897.

Copland, Aaron. *Ukelele Serenade: Violin and Piano.* New York: Boosey and Hawkes, 1968.

Ives, Charles E. *Central Park in the Dark.* Edited by Jacques-Louis Monod. Hillsdale, N.Y.: Boelke-Bomart, 1973.

———. *Ragtime Dances: Set of Four Ragtime Dances.* Edited by James B. Sinclair. New York: Peer International, 1990.

———. "A Set of Pieces for Theatre or Chamber Orchestra." *New Music* 5, no. 2 (January 1932).

Morton, Jelly Roll. *Ferdinand "Jelly Roll" Morton: The Collected Piano Music.* Edited by James Dapogny. Washington, D.C.: Smithsonian Institution Press, 1982.

Remick Hits through the Years. New York: Remick Music Corp., 1951.

Schiff, Ronny, ed. *Louis Armstrong: A Jazz Master.* New York: MCA Music Publishing, 1961.

RECORDINGS

Armstrong, Louis. *Louis Armstrong: The Complete Hot Five and Hot Seven Recordings.* Columbia/Legacy 63527, 2000.

———. *Satchmo: A Musical Autobiography of Louis Armstrong.* Decca Records DXM-155, 1957.

Carousel of American Music: The Fabled 24 September 1940 San Francisco Concerts. Liner notes by David A. Banks. Music and Arts Programs of America CD–4971, 1997.

Morton, Jelly Roll. *Jelly Roll Morton: The Complete Library of Congress Recordings.* Rounder CDROUN1888, 2005.

———. *Jelly Roll Morton: The Piano Rolls.* As realized by Artis Wodehouse. Nonesuch 79363–2, 1997.

Music from the New York Stage, 1890–1920. Pearl 9053, 1993.

The Smithsonian Collection of Classic Jazz. Liner notes by Martin Williams. Smithsonian Collection, RD 033 (1987).

BOOKS, ARTICLES, AND UNPUBLISHED WORKS

Adams, W. D. "The Popularity of Hawaiian Music and Musical Instruments." In *Hawaiian Annual, 1917,* 142–46. Honolulu: Thos. G. Thrum, 1916.

Adorno, Theodor W. *Essays on Music.* Selected, with introduction, commentary, and notes by Richard Leppert; translated by Susan H. Gillespie. Berkeley: University of California Press, 2002.

Ake, David. *Jazz Cultures.* Berkeley: University of California Press, 2001.

Akindes, Fay Yokomizo. "Sudden Rush: *Na Mele Paleoleo* (Hawaiian Rap) as Liberatory Discourse." *Discourse* 23, no. 1 (2001): 82–98.

Armstrong, Louis. *Louis Armstrong, in His Own Words: Selected Writings.* Edited by Thomas Brothers. New York: Oxford University Press, 1999.

———. *Satchmo: My Life in New Orleans.* 1954. Reprint, New York: Signet, 1955.

"ASCAP: Music's Hall of Fame Lives at Fair." *San Francisco Chronicle,* 25 September 1940, 1, 12.

Ashforth, Alden, and Lawrence Gushee. "An Interview with Joe Darensbourg." *Footnote* 15, no. 3 (February–March 1984): 6–9.

Atkins, E. Taylor, ed. *Jazz Planet.* Jackson: University Press of Mississippi, 2003.

Bakhtin, M. M. *Speech Genres and Other Late Essays.* Austin: University of Texas Press, 1986.

Balliett, Whitney. *Jelly Roll, Jabbo, and Fats: Nineteen Portraits in Jazz.* New York: Oxford University Press, 1983.

Balme, Christopher B. "Selling the Bird: Richard Walton Tully's *The Bird of Paradise* and the Dynamics of Theatrical Commodification." *Theatre Journal* 57 (2005): 1–20.

Banagale, Ryan Raul. "An American in Chinatown: Asian Representation in the Music of George Gershwin." M.A. thesis, University of Washington, 2004.

Barker, Danny. "Jelly Roll Morton in New York." In *Jazz Panorama: From the Pages of the Jazz Review,* edited by Martin T. Williams, 13–20. New York: Crowell-Collier Press, 1962.

———. *A Life in Jazz.* Edited by Alyn Shipton. New York: Oxford University Press, 1986.

Barlow, William. *"Looking Up at Down": The Emergence of Blues Culture.* Philadelphia: Temple University Press, 1989.

Baron, Carol. "Dating Charles Ives's Music: Facts and Fictions." *Perspectives of New Music* 28 (1990): 20–56.

Bechet, Sidney. *Treat It Gentle.* 1960. Reprint, New York: Da Capo Press, 1975.

Bellman, Jonathan, ed. *The Exotic in Western Music.* Boston: Northeastern University Press, 1998.

Bergreen, Laurence. *Louis Armstrong: An Extravagant Life.* New York: Broadway Books, 1997.

Berish, Andrew. "Swinging Transcontinental: Modernity, Race, and Place in American Dance Band Music, 1930–1946." Ph.D. diss., University of California, Los Angeles, 2006.

Berlin, Edward. *Ragtime: A Musical and Cultural History.* Berkeley: University of California Press, 1980.

———. *Reflections and Research on Ragtime.* Brooklyn: Institute for Studies in American Music, 1987.

Bigard, Barney. *With Louis and the Duke: The Autobiography of a Jazz Clarinetist.* Edited by Barry Martyn. New York: Oxford University Press, 1986.

" 'Bird of Paradise' Has Scenic Beauty." *New York Times,* 9 January 1912, 8.

Black, Timuel D., Jr. *Bridges of Memory: Chicago's First Wave of Black Migration*. Evanston: Northwestern University Press, 2003.

Boime, Albert. *The Unveiling of the National Icons: A Plea for Patriotic Iconoclasm in a Nationalist Era*. New York: Cambridge University Press, 1998.

Bordman, Gerald. *American Musical Theatre: A Chronicle*. 2nd ed. New York: Oxford University Press, 1992.

Born, Georgina, and David Hesmondhalgh, eds. *Western Music and Its Others: Difference, Representation, and Appropriation in Music*. Berkeley: University of California Press, 2000.

Borneman, Ernest. "Creole Echoes." *Jazz Review* 2, no. 8 (September 1959): 13–15.

———. "Creole Echoes: Part II." *Jazz Review* 2, no. 10 (November 1959): 26–27.

———. "Jazz and the Creole Tradition." *Jazzforschung* 1 (1969): 99–112.

Brantley, Ben. "New Coat of Paint for Old Pagoda." *New York Times*, 18 October 2002, sec. B, 1, 24.

Brett, Philip. "Eros and Orientalism in Britten's Operas." In *Queering the Pitch: The New Gay and Lesbian Musicology*, edited by Philip Brett, Elizabeth Wood, and Gary C. Thomas, 235–56. New York: Routledge, 1994.

Brewer, Roy. "The Use of Habanera Rhythm in Rockabilly Music." *American Music* 17, no. 3 (1999): 300–317.

Brooks, Tim. *The Columbia Master Book Discography*. 4 vols. Westport, Conn.: Greenwood Press, 1999.

———. *Lost Sounds: Blacks and the Birth of the Recording Industry, 1890–1919*. Urbana: University of Illinois Press, 2004.

Broonzy, Big Bill, and Yannick Bruynoghe. *Big Bill Blues: William Broonzy's Story as Told to Yannick Bruynoghe*. Rev. ed. New York: Oak Publications, 1964.

Brothers, Thomas. *Louis Armstrong's New Orleans*. New York: W. W. Norton, 2006.

Brown, DeSoto, Anne Ellett, and Gary Giemza. *Hawaii Recalls: Selling Romance to America: Nostalgic Images of the Hawaiian Islands, 1910–1950*. Honolulu: Editions Limited, 1982.

Buchman, Andrew. "Ives and Stravinsky: Two Angles on 'the German Stem.'" In *Charles Ives and the Classical Tradition*, edited by Geoffrey Block and J. Peter Burkholder, 131–49. New Haven: Yale University Press, 1996.

Burkholder, J. Peter. *All Made of Tunes: Charles Ives and the Uses of Musical Borrowing*. New Haven: Yale University Press, 1995.

———. "Charles Ives and His Fathers: A Response to Maynard Solomon." *Institute for Studies in American Music Newsletter* 18, no. 1 (1988): 8–11.

———. *Charles Ives: The Ideas behind the Music*. New Haven: Yale University Press, 1985.

Burton, Jack. *The Blue Book of Tin Pan Alley: A Human Interest Anthology of American Popular Music*. Watkins Glen, N.Y.: Century House, 1950.

Bushell, Garvin, as told to Mark Tucker. *Jazz from the Beginning*. Ann Arbor: University of Michigan Press, 1988.

Carby, Hazel V. "It Jus Be's Dat Way Sometime: The Sexual Politics of Women's Blues." In *The Jazz Cadence of American Culture,* edited by Robert G. O'Meally, 469–83. New York: Columbia University Press, 1998.

Carney, George O. *The Sounds of People and Places: A Geography of American Music from Country to Classical and Blues to Bop.* 4th ed. Lanham, Md.: Rowman and Littlefield, 2003.

Carr, Bruce, Dionisio Preciado, and Robert Stevenson. "Iradier, Sebastián de." In *Grove Music Online,* edited by Laura Macy. www.grovemusic.com (accessed 15 December 2006).

Carr, James Revell. "In the Wake of John Kanaka: Musical Interactions between Euro-American Sailors and Pacific Islanders, 1600–1900." Ph.D. diss., University of California, Santa Barbara, 2006.

"Charm of Hawaii Will Pervade Exposition." *San Francisco Chronicle,* 11 June 1915, 5.

Chase, Gilbert. *America's Music: From the Pilgrims to the Present.* Urbana: University of Illinois Press, 1955.

Chen, Hsaing-shui. *Chinatown No More: Taiwan Immigrants in Contemporary New York.* Ithaca: Cornell University Press, 1992.

Chilton, John. *Who's Who of Jazz: Storyville to Swing Street.* 3rd rev. ed. New York: Da Capo Press, 1985.

Clark, Barrett H., ed. *Favorite American Plays of the Nineteenth Century.* Princeton: Princeton University Press, 1943.

Clarke, Gary E. *Essays on American Music.* Westport, Conn.: Greenwood Press, 1977.

Clayton, Buck, assisted by Nancy Miller Elliott. *Buck Clayton's Jazz World.* New York: Oxford University Press, 1987.

Collier, James Lincoln. *Jazz: The American Theme Song.* New York: Oxford University Press, 1993.

———. *Louis Armstrong: An American Genius.* New York: Oxford University Press, 1983.

Collins, Lee, as told to Mary Collins. *"Oh, Didn't He Ramble": The Life Story of Lee Collins.* Urbana: University of Illinois Press, 1974.

"Coming to the Theaters." *Washington Post,* 27 April 1916, 12.

Copland, Aaron, and Vivian Perlis. *Copland: 1900 through 1942.* New York: St. Martin's Press, 1984.

Cowell, Henry, and Sidney Cowell. *Charles Ives and His Music.* Rev. ed. New York: Oxford University Press, 1969.

Crawford, Richard. *The American Musical Landscape.* Berkeley: University of California Press, 1993.

———. *America's Musical Life: A History.* New York: W. W. Norton, 2001.

———. "H. Wiley Hitchcock and American Music." In *A Celebration of American Music: Words and Music in Honor of H. Wiley Hitchcock,* edited by Richard Crawford, R. Allen Lott, and Carol J. Oja, 3–9. Ann Arbor: University of Michigan Press, 1990.

————. "Music." In *Encyclopedia of the United States in the Twentieth Century,* edited by Stanley I. Kutler, 1609–34. New York: Charles Scribner's Sons, 1996.

Crawford, Richard, and Jeffrey Magee. *Jazz Standards on Record, 1900–1942: A Core Repertory.* Chicago: Center for Black Music Research, Columbia College Chicago, 1992.

Crow, Bill. *Jazz Anecdotes: Second Time Around.* New York: Oxford University Press, 2005.

Dance, Stanley. *The World of Earl Hines.* New York: Charles Scribner's Sons, 1977.

————. *The World of Swing.* New York: Charles Scribner's Sons, 1974.

"Dancing and Music Mark Celebration of Islanders." *San Francisco Chronicle,* 12 June 1915, 5.

Davis, Francis. *The History of the Blues.* New York: Hyperion, 1995.

Desmond, Jane C. *Staging Tourism: Bodies on Display from Waikiki to Sea World.* Chicago: University of Chicago Press, 1999.

DeVeaux, Scott. "Constructing the Jazz Tradition: Jazz Historiography." *Black American Literature Forum* 25 no. 3 (1991): 525–60.

Dickerson, James L. *Just for a Thrill: Lil Hardin Armstrong, First Lady of Jazz.* New York: Cooper Square Press, 2002.

Dixon, M. W., and John Godrich, *Recording the Blues.* London: Studio Vista, 1970.

Dodds, Baby, as told to Larry Gara. *The Baby Dodds Story.* Los Angeles: Contemporary Press, 1959.

Drake, St. Clair, and Horace R. Cayton. *Black Metropolis: A Study of Negro Life in a Northern City.* Rev. ed. 2 vols. New York: Harper and Row, 1962.

Dubey, Madhu. "Narration and Migration: Jazz and Vernacular Theories of Black Women's Fiction." *American Literary History* 10, no. 2 (Summer 1998): 291–316.

Early, Gerald. *Tuxedo Junction: Essays on American Culture.* New York: Ecco Press, 1989.

Ewen, David. *American Popular Songs: From the Revolutionary War to the Present.* New York: Random House, 1966.

Fairfield, Patrick Kenneth. "Representations of Gender and Sexuality in the Music and Writings of Charles Ives." Ph.D. diss., Brandeis University, 2000.

Fernández, Raúl A. *From Afro-Cuban Rhythms to Latin Jazz.* Berkeley: University of California Press, 2006.

Fiehrer, Thomas. "From Quadrille to Stomp: The Creole Origins of Jazz." *Popular Music* 10, no. 1 (1991): 21–38.

Fields, Armond, and L. Marc Fields. *From the Bowery to Broadway: Lew Fields and the Roots of American Popular Theater.* New York: Oxford University Press, 1993.

Flockhart, Lolita L. W. *Art and Artists in New Jersey.* Somerville, N.J.: C. P. Hoagland Company, 1938.

Foreman, Ronald Clifford, Jr. "Jazz and Race Records, 1920–32: Their Origins and Their Significance for the Record Industry and Society." Ph.D. diss., University of Illinois, 1968.

Forman, Murray. *The 'Hood Comes First: Race, Space, and Place in Rap and Hip-Hop.* Middletown, Conn.: Wesleyan University Press, 2002.

Freedland, Michael. *Jolson.* New York: Stein and Day, 1972.

Furnas, J. C. *Anatomy of Paradise: Hawaii and the Islands of the South Seas.* New York: William Sloane Associates, 1937.

G., K. "Belasco—'The Bird of Paradise.'" *Washington Post,* 24 December 1912, 5.

Gabbard, Krin. "Signifyin(g) the Phallus: *Mo' Better Blues* and Representations of the Jazz Trumpet." In *Representing Jazz,* edited by Krin Gabbard, 104–30. Durham: Duke University Press, 1995.

Gann, Kyle. *American Music in the Twentieth Century.* New York: Schirmer Books, 1997.

Garland, Phyl. *The Sound of Soul.* Chicago: Henry Regnery Company, 1969.

Garrett, Charles Hiroshi. "Struggling to Define a Nation: American Music in the Twentieth Century." Ph.D. diss., University of California, Los Angeles, 2004.

Geo. J. Birkel Company. Advertisement. *Los Angeles Times,* 13 July 1907, sec. 2, 1.

Geo. J. Birkel Company. Advertisement. *Los Angeles Times,* 18 September 1913, sec. 2, 1.

"George E. K. Awai Fueled the Hawaiian Music Craze in 1915." *Ha'Ilono Mele* 3, no. 9 (1977): 5–6.

Giddins, Gary. *Satchmo.* New York: Da Capo Press, 1992.

Gilbert, Douglas. *Lost Chords: The Diverting Story of American Popular Songs.* Garden City, N.Y.: Doubleday, Doran, 1942.

Gilroy, Paul. *The Black Atlantic: Modernity and Double Consciousness.* Cambridge: Harvard University Press, 1993.

Givan, Benjamin. "Louis Armstrong's Vocal Recordings." *Musical Quarterly* 87, no. 2 (2004): 188–218.

Goldberg, Isaac. *Tin Pan Alley: A Chronicle of the American Popular Music Racket.* New York: John Day Company, 1930.

Goldmark, Daniel. *Tunes for 'Toons: Music and the Hollywood Cartoon.* Berkeley: University of California Press, 2006.

Gonzáles, Andy. Foreword to *Latin Jazz: The Perfect Combination,* by Raúl Fernándes. San Francisco: Chronicle Books, 2002.

Gracyk, Tim, with Frank Hoffman. *Popular American Recording Pioneers, 1895–1925.* New York: Haworth Press, 2000.

Green, Abel. *Inside Stuff on How to Write Popular Songs.* New York: Paul Whiteman Publications, 1927.

Gregory, James N. *The Southern Diaspora: How the Great Migrations of Black and White Southerners Transformed America.* Chapel Hill: University of North Carolina Press, 2005.

Griffin, Farah Jasmine. *"Who Set You Flowin'?" The African-American Migration Narrative.* New York: Oxford University Press, 1995.

Gronow, Pekka. "Ethnic Recordings: An Introduction." In *Ethnic Recordings in America: A Neglected Heritage,* 1–31. Washington, D.C.: American Folklife Center, Library of Congress, 1982.

Grossman, James R. "Blowing the Trumpet: The *Chicago Defender* and Black Migration during World War I." *Illinois Historical Journal* 78, no. 2 (Summer 1985): 82–96.

———. *Land of Hope: Chicago, Black Southerners, and the Great Migration.* Chicago: University of Chicago Press, 1989.

Gushee, Lawrence. "The Nineteenth-Century Origins of Jazz." *Black Music Research Journal* 14, no. 1 (1994): 1–24.

Hadlock, Richard. "Morton's Library of Congress Albums." *Jazz: A Quarterly of American Music* 2 (1959): 133–37.

Hagert, Thornton. "Band and Orchestral Ragtime." In *Ragtime: Its History, Composers and Music,* edited by John Edward Hasse, 268–84. New York: Schirmer Books, 1980.

———. Liner notes for *Come and Trip It: Instrumental Dance Music, 1780s–1920s.* Recorded Anthology of American Music. New World Records 80293–2, 1994.

Hague, Eleanor, ed. *Spanish-American Folk-Songs.* 1917. Reprint, New York: Kraus Reprint Co., 1969.

Hall, Gwendolyn Midlo. *Africans in Colonial Louisiana: The Development of Afro-Creole Culture in the Eighteenth Century.* Baton Rouge: Louisiana State University Press, 1992.

Hamberlin, Larry. "American Popular Songs on Operatic Topics, 1901–1921." Ph.D. diss., Brandeis University, 2004.

———. "Visions of Salome: The Femme Fatale in American Popular Songs before 1920." *Journal of the American Musicological Society* 59, no. 3 (2006): 631–96.

Hamm, Charles. *Irving Berlin: Songs from the Melting Pot: The Formative Years, 1907–1914.* New York: Oxford University Press, 1997.

———. *Music in the New World.* New York: W. W. Norton, 1983.

Hamm, Charles, and Peter Winkler. "Interviews." *Review of Popular Music* 7 (July 1985): 8–10.

Handy, W. C. *Father of the Blues: An Autobiography.* Edited by Arna Bontemps. New York: Macmillan, 1941.

"Hapa Haole Songs." In *Hawaiian Music and Musicians,* edited by George Kanahele, 106–7. Honolulu: University Press of Hawaii, 1979.

Harker, Brian Cameron. "The Early Musical Development of Louis Armstrong, 1901–1928." Ph.D. diss., Columbia University, 1997.

———. "'Telling a Story': Louis Armstrong and Coherence in Early Jazz." *Current Musicology* 63 (Fall 1997): 46–83.

Harris, Michael W. *The Rise of Gospel Blues: The Music of Thomas Andrew Dorsey in the Urban Church.* New York: Oxford University Press, 1992.

Harte, Bret, and Mark Twain. *Ah Sin, a Dramatic Work.* Edited by Frederick Anderson. San Francisco: Book Club of California, 1961.

"Hawaiian Music Recordings." In *Encyclopedia of Recorded Sound in the United States,* edited by Guy A. Marco, 313–14. New York: Garland Publishing, 1993.

"Hawaiian Music Universally Popular." *Edison Phonograph Monthly* 14, no. 9 (September 1916): 3–4.

"Hawaiians Are Angry." *New York Times,* 19 September 1915, 10.

Hayward, Philip, ed. *Widening the Horizon: Exoticism in Post-War Popular Music.* Bloomington: Indiana University Press, 1999.

Head, Matthew. *Orientalism, Masquerade and Mozart's Turkish Music.* London: Royal Musical Association, 2000.

Henderson, Clayton W. *The Charles Ives Tunebook.* Warren, Mich.: Harmonie Park Press, 1990.

Hennessey, Patrick. "Launching a Classic: *Aloha 'Oe* and the Royal Hawaiian Band Tour of 1883." *Journal of Band Research* 37, no. 1 (2001): 29–44.

Hennessey, Thomas J. *From Jazz to Swing: African American Jazz Musicians and Their Music, 1890–1935.* Detroit: Wayne State University Press, 1994.

Hentoff, Nat. "Roy Eldridge." In *The Jazz Makers,* edited by Nat Shapiro and Nat Hentoff, 297–315. New York: Grove Press, 1957.

Hinton, Milt, and David G. Berger. *Bass Line: The Stories and Photographs of Milt Hinton.* Philadelphia: Temple University Press, 1988.

Hisama, Ellie M. *Gendering Musical Modernism: The Music of Ruth Crawford, Marion Bauer, and Miriam Gideon.* New York: Cambridge University Press, 2001.

———. "Postcolonialism on the Make: The Music of John Mellencamp, David Bowie, and John Zorn." *Popular Music* 12, no. 2 (1993): 91–104.

Hischak, Thomas S. *The American Musical Theatre Song Encyclopedia.* Westport, Conn.: Greenwood Press, 1995.

Hitchcock, H. Wiley. "Americans on American Music." *College Music Symposium* 8 (Fall 1968): 131–42.

———. *Music in the United States: A Historical Introduction.* Englewood Cliffs, N.J.: Prentice-Hall, 1969.

Hitchcock, H. Wiley, and Stanley Sadie, eds. *The New Grove Dictionary of American Music.* 4 vols. New York: Grove's Dictionaries of Music, 1986.

Hoeck, Theodor. "The New and Popular Hawaiian Music: What Makes It Different and What Instruments Produce It." *Delineator* (July 1916): 20.

Hopkins, Jerry. "Record Industry in Hawaii." In *Hawaiian Music and Musicians: An Illustrated History,* edited by George S. Kanahele, 325–34. Honolulu: University Press of Hawaii, 1979.

House, Roger Randolph. " 'Keys to the Highway': William 'Big Bill' Broonzy and the Chicago Blues in the Era of the Great Migration." Ph.D. diss., Boston University, 1999.

Howard, John Tasker. *Our American Music: Three Hundred Years of It.* New York: Thomas Y. Crowell, 1931.

Hughes, Langston. *The Big Sea: An Autobiography.* 1940. Reprint, New York: Hill and Wang, 1963.

Hwang, David Henry. "A New Musical by Rodgers and Hwang." *New York Times,* 13 October 2002, Arts and Leisure sec., 1, 16.

"Ignorance Is Bliss." *Stars and Stripes* (France), 22 February 1918, 2.

Imada, Adria L. "Aloha America: Hawaiian Entertainment and Cultural Politics in the United States Empire." Ph.D. diss., New York University, 2003.

———. "Hawaiians on Tour: Hula Circuits through the American Empire." *American Quarterly* 56, no. 1 (March 2004): 111–49.

Ives, Charles E. *Essays Before a Sonata and Other Writings.* Edited by Howard Boatwright. New York: W. W. Norton, 1962.

———. *Memos.* Edited by John Kirkpatrick. New York: W. W. Norton, 1972.

Jackson, Mahalia, with Evan McLeod Wylie. *Movin' On Up.* New York: Hawthorn Books, 1966.

Jasen, David. *Tin Pan Alley.* New York: Donald I. Fine, 1988.

Johnson, Julian. "Paradise Bird at the Belasco." *Los Angeles Times,* 12 September 1911, sec. 2, 5.

Jones, LeRoi (Amiri Baraka). *Blues People: Negro Music in White America.* New York: William Morrow, 1963.

Jordan, Virgil. "The Yarn of the Ukulele." *Everybody's Magazine,* March 1917, 334–36.

Kalil, Timothy Michael. "The Role of the Great Migration of African Americans to Chicago in the Development of Traditional Black Gospel Piano by Thomas A. Dorsey, circa 1930." Ph.D. diss., Kent State University, 1993.

Kanahele, George S., ed. *Hawaiian Music and Musicians: An Illustrated History.* Honolulu: University Press of Hawaii, 1979.

Keil, Charles. *Urban Blues.* Chicago: University of Chicago Press, 1966.

Kenney, William Howland. *Chicago Jazz: A Cultural History, 1904–1930.* New York: Oxford University Press, 1993.

———. *Jazz on the River.* Chicago: University of Chicago Press, 2005.

Kimball, Robert, and Linda Emmet, eds. *The Complete Lyrics of Irving Berlin.* New York: Knopf, 2001.

King, John, and Jim Tranquada. "A New History of the Origins and Development of the 'Ukulele, 1838–1915." *Hawaiian Journal of History* 37 (2003): 1–32.

King, Larry L. "Everybody's Louie." *Harper's,* November 1967, 61–69.

Kinzer, Stephen. *Overthrow: America's Century of Regime Change from Hawaii to Iraq.* New York: Times Books, 2006.

Klauber, Adolph. "New Show at Casino Is Big and Lively." *New York Times,* 19 July 1910, 7.

Kramer, Lawrence. *Classical Music and Postmodern Knowledge.* Berkeley: University of California Press, 1995.

———. "Powers of Blackness: Africanist Discourse in Modern Concert Music." *Black Music Research Journal* 16, no. 1 (Spring 1996): 53–70.

Kun, Josh. *Audiotopia: Music, Race, and America.* Berkeley: University of California Press, 2005.

"Laurette Taylor Confesses: Actress Discusses Her Hawaiian Role and Tells of Her Ambitions." *New York Times,* 14 January 1912, sec. 10, 6.

Lawson, Robert. *At That Time.* New York: Viking, 1947.

Lee, Anthony W. *Picturing Chinatown: Art and Orientalism in San Francisco.* Berkeley: University of California Press, 2001.

Lee, Josephine Ding. *Performing Asian America: Race and Ethnicity on the Contemporary Stage.* Philadelphia: Temple University Press, 1997.

Lee, Robert G. *Orientals: Asian Americans in Popular Culture.* Philadelphia: Temple University Press, 1999.

Lemmon, Alfred. "New Orleans Popular Sheet Music Imprints: The Latin Tinge prior to 1900." *Southern Quarterly* 27, no. 2 (1989): 41–58.

Leonard, Neil. "The Reactions to Ragtime." In *Ragtime: Its History, Composers and Music,* edited by John Edward Hasse, 102–16. New York: Schirmer Books, 1980.

Levin, Floyd. *Classic Jazz: A Personal View of the Music and the Musicians.* Berkeley: University of California Press, 2000.

Levine, Lawrence W. *Black Culture and Black Consciousness: Afro-American Folk Thought from Slavery to Freedom.* New York: Oxford University Press, 1977.

Levy, Alan Howard. *Musical Nationalism: American Composers' Search for Identity.* Westport, Conn.: Greenwood Press, 1983.

Lewis, David H. *Flower Drum Songs: The Story of Two Musicals.* Jefferson, N.C.: McFarland, 2006.

Lewis, George H. "Da Kine Sounds: The Function of Music as Social Protest in the New Hawaiian Renaissance." *American Music* 2, no. 2 (1984): 38–52.

———. "Ghosts, Ragged but Beautiful: Influences of Mexican Music on American Country-Western and Rock 'n' Roll." *Popular Music and Society* 15, no. 4 (Winter 1991): 85–103.

Leyshon, Andrew, David Matless, and George Revill, eds. *The Place of Music.* New York: Guilford Press, 1998.

Light, Ivan. "From Vice District to Tourist Attraction: The Moral Career of American Chinatowns, 1880–1940." *Pacific Historical Review* 43, no. 3 (1974): 367–94.

Lili'uokalani, Queen of Hawai'i. *The Queen's Songbook, Her Majesty Queen Lili'uokalani.* Edited by Barbara Barnard Smith. Text and music notation by Dorothy Kahananui Gillett. Honolulu: Hui Hanai, 1999.

Lin, Jan. *Reconstructing Chinatown.* Minneapolis: University of Minnesota Press, 1998.

Ling, Huping. *Surviving on Gold Mountain: A History of Chinese American Women and Their Lives.* Albany: State University of New York Press, 1998.

Lipsitz, George. "High Culture and Hierarchy." Review of *Highbrow/Lowbrow: The Emergence of Cultural Hierarchy in America,* by Lawrence W. Levine. *American Quarterly* 43, no. 3 (1991): 518–24.

Locke, Don. "Jelly Roll Morton, the Library of Congress Recordings." *Jazz Journal* 13, no. 1 (1960): 15–18.

Locke, Ralph P. "Beyond the Exotic: How 'Eastern' Is *Aida*?" *Cambridge Opera Journal* 17 (2005): 105–39.

————. "Constructing the Oriental 'Other': Saint Saëns's *Samson et Dalila*." *Cambridge Opera Journal* 3 (1991): 261–302.

Lomax, Alan. *Mister Jelly Roll: The Fortunes of Jelly Roll Morton, New Orleans Creole and "Inventor of Jazz."* Updated, with a new afterword, by Lawrence Gushee. Berkeley: University of California Press, 2001.

"Los Angeles and Music." *Los Angeles Times*, 21 February 1916, sec. 2, 4.

Lowe, Lisa. "The International within the National: American Studies and Asian American Critique." *Cultural Critique* 40 (1998): 29–48.

Lowens, Irving. *Music in America and American Music*. Brooklyn: Institute for Studies in American Music, 1978.

Macomber, Ben. *The Jewel City: Its Planning and Achievement; Its Architecture, Sculpture, Symbolism, and Music; Its Gardens, Palaces, and Exhibits*. San Francisco: John H. Williams, 1915.

Magee, Jeffrey. "Irving Berlin's 'Blue Skies': Ethnic Affiliations and Musical Transformations." *Musical Quarterly* 84, no. 4 (2000): 537–80.

Major, Clarence. *Juba to Jive: A Dictionary of African-American Slang*. New York: Viking, 1994.

Marchetti, Gina. *Romance and the "Yellow Peril": Race, Sex, and Discursive Strategies in Hollywood Fiction*. Berkeley: University of California Press, 1993.

Marks, Edward B. *They All Sang: From Tony Pastor to Rudy Vallée*. New York: Viking, 1934.

Marshall, Dennis. "Charles Ives's Quotations: Manner or Substance?" *Perspectives of New Music* 6, no. 2 (Spring–Summer 1968): 45–56.

Mason, Daniel Gregory. *Contemporary Composers*. New York: Macmillan, 1918.

McClary, Susan. *Feminine Endings: Music, Gender, and Sexuality*. Minnesota: University of Minnesota Press, 1991.

McKirahan, Jr., Richard D. *Philosophy before Socrates: An Introduction with Texts and Commentary*. Indianapolis: Hackett, 1994.

Meloney, William Brown. "Slumming in New York's Chinatown." *Munsey's Magazine*, September 1909, 818–30.

Mensink, Otto. "Traditional Japanese Musical Genres and Instruments: Their Illustration in Woodblock Prints." In *The Ear Catches the Eye: Music in Japanese Prints*, 13–20. Leiden, The Netherlands: Hotei Publishing, 2000.

Merwin, Bannister. "The Vogue of Japanese Color-Prints." *Munsey's Magazine*, August 1909, 650–59.

Metcalfe. "Drama: New York Result of Captain Cook's Travels." *Life*, 18 January 1912, 168–69.

Mezzrow, Mezz, with Bernard Wolfe. *Really the Blues*. 1946. Reprint, London: Flamingo, 1993.

Millard, Andre. *America on Record: A History of Recorded Sound*. New York: Cambridge University Press, 1995.

Moon, Krystyn R. *Yellowface: Creating the Chinese in American Popular Music and Performance, 1850s–1920s*. New Brunswick: Rutgers University Press, 2005.

Morales, Ed. *The Latin Beat: The Rhythms and Roots of Latin Music from Bossa Nova to Salsa and Beyond.* Cambridge, Mass.: Da Capo Press, 2003.

Moreno, Jairo. "Bauzá—Gillespie—Latin/Jazz: Difference, Modernity, and the Black Caribbean." *South Atlantic Quarterly* 103, no. 1 (Winter 2004): 81–99.

Morosco, Helen M., and Leonard Paul Dugger. *The Oracle of Broadway.* Caldwell, Idaho: Caxton Printers, 1944.

Morse, Frank P. "The Music-Coated Drama." *Washington Post,* 30 April 1916, sec. MT, 2.

Moy, James S. *Marginal Sights: Staging the Chinese in America.* Iowa City: University of Iowa Press, 1993.

Narváez, Peter. "The Influences of Hispanic Music Cultures on African-American Blues Musicians." *Black Music Research Journal* 14 (1994): 203–24.

"New Hawaiian Records." *Talking Machine World* 8, no. 3 (15 March 1912): 36.

Nicholls, David, ed. *The Cambridge History of American Music.* Cambridge: Cambridge University Press, 1998.

Ogren, Kathy J. *The Jazz Revolution: Twenties America & the Meaning of Jazz.* New York: Oxford University Press, 1989.

Oja, Carol J. *Making Music Modern: New York in the 1920s.* New York: Oxford University Press, 2000.

Omi, Michael, and Howard Winant. *Racial Formation in the United States: From the 1960s to the 1990s.* New York: Routledge, 1994.

Panassié, Hugues. *Louis Armstrong.* New York: Charles Scribner's Sons, 1971.

Pastras, Phil. *Dead Man Blues: Jelly Roll Morton Way Out West.* Berkeley: University of California Press, 2001.

Pathé Frères. "Take a Trip to HONOLULU via the Pathephone" (advertisement). *Los Angeles Times,* 4 March 1917, sec. II, 2.

Peretti, Burton W. *The Creation of Jazz; Music, Race, and Culture in Urban America.* Chicago: University of Illinois Press, 1992.

———. *Jazz in American Culture.* Chicago: Ivan R. Dee, 1997.

Perlis, Vivian. *Charles Ives Remembered: An Oral History.* New Haven: Yale University Press, 1974.

"Philippines and Hawaii May Be Proud of Their Exhibits," *San Francisco Chronicle,* 21 February 1915, special section, unnumbered.

"Picturesque Contrast in Play of Hawaii." *New York World,* 9 January 1912, 10.

Pisani, Michael V. *Imagining Native America in Music.* New Haven: Yale University Press, 2005.

"Plays of the Week." *New York Dramatic Mirror,* 30 July 1910, 10.

"Premiere of Tully Play Set for Local Theater." *Los Angeles Times,* 11 March 1928, sec. C, 28.

Price, Joyce Howard. "President Supports Anthem in English; Spanish Version Called 'An Insult.' " *Washington Times,* 29 April 2006, sec. A, 1.

"Publishing and Hawaiian Music." In *Hawaiian Music and Musicians: An Illustrated History,* edited by George S. Kanahele, 308–11. Honolulu: University Press of Hawaii, 1979.

Radano, Ronald, and Philip V. Bohlman, eds. *Music and the Racial Imagination*. Chicago: University of Chicago Press, 2000.

Ramsey, Guthrie P., Jr. *Race Music: Black Cultures from Bebop to Hip-Hop*. Berkeley: University of California Press, 2003.

Rao, Nancy Yunhwa. "Songs of the Exclusion Era: New York Chinatown's Opera Theaters in the 1920s." *American Music* 20, no. 4 (2002): 399–444.

Rapée, Erno. *Encyclopedia of Music for Pictures*. 1925. Reprint, New York: Arno Press, 1970.

Reich, Howard, and William Gaines. *Jelly's Blues: The Life, Music, and Redemption of Jelly Roll Morton*. Cambridge, Mass.: Da Capo Press, 2003.

Riddle, Ronald. *Flying Dragons, Flowing Streams: Music in the Life of San Francisco's Chinese*. Westport, Conn.: Greenwood Press, 1983.

Roberts, John Storm. *Latin Jazz: The First of the Fusions, 1880s to Today*. New York: Schirmer Books, 1999.

———. *The Latin Tinge: The Impact of Latin American Music on the United States*. 2nd ed. New York: Oxford University Press, 1999.

Roof, Katherine Metcalf. *The Life and Art of William Merritt Chase*. New York: Charles Scribner's Sons, 1917.

Rose, Tricia. *Black Noise: Rap Music and Black Culture in Contemporary America*. Hanover, N.H.: Wesleyan University Press, 1994.

Rosenfeld, Paul. "Whistler and Japanese Art." *Yale Literary Magazine* 75 (1909): 55–61.

Rossiter, Frank R. *Charles Ives and His America*. New York: Liveright, 1975.

———. "The 'Genteel Tradition' in American Music." *Journal of American Culture* 4, no. 4 (1981): 107–15.

Rowe, John Carlos. "Post-Nationalism, Globalism, and the New American Studies." *Cultural Critique* 40 (Fall 1998): 11–28.

Russell, Bill. *New Orleans Style*. Edited by Barry Martyn and Mike Hazeldine. New Orleans: Jazzology Press, 1994.

Russell, William. "Albert Nicholas Talks about Jelly Roll." *Second Line* 30 (Winter 1978): 34–39.

———. "Albert Nicholas Talks about Jelly Roll: Part II of an Interview." *Second Line* 30 (Spring 1978): 3–10.

———, comp. *"Oh, Mister Jelly": A Jelly Roll Morton Scrapbook*. Copenhagen: JazzMedia, 1999.

Russell, William, and Stephen W. Smith. "New Orleans Music." In *Jazzmen*, edited by Frederick Ramsey Jr. and Charles Edward Smith, 7–37. New York: Harcourt Brace, 1939.

Schafer, William J., and Johannes Riedel. *The Art of Ragtime: Form and Meaning of an Original Black American Art*. Baton Rouge: Louisiana State University Press, 1973.

Schallert, Edwin. "Drama." *Los Angeles Times*, 6 January 1920, sec. 3, 4.

Schenbeck, Lawrence. "Music, Gender and 'Uplift' in the *Chicago Defender*, 1927–1937." *Musical Quarterly* 81, no. 3 (Fall 1997): 344–70.

Schuller, Gunther. *Early Jazz: Its Roots and Development.* New York: Oxford University Press, 1968.

Scott, Derek. *From the Erotic to the Demonic: On Critical Musicology* (New York: Oxford University Press, 2003).

Scott-Maxwell, Aline. "Oriental Exoticism in 1920s Australian Popular Music." *Perfect Beat* 3, no. 3 (1997): 28–57.

Semple, Elizabeth Anna. "The Bird of Paradise." *Overland Monthly* 59, no. 4 (1912): 381–85.

Sereno, Aeko. "Images of the Hula Dancer and 'Hula Girl': 1778–1960." Ph.D. diss., University of Hawai'i, 1990.

Shapiro, Nat, and Nat Hentoff, eds. *Hear Me Talkin' to Ya: The Story of Jazz as Told by the Men Who Made It.* 1955. Reprint, New York: Dover, 1966.

Sheppard, W. Anthony. "Cinematic Realism, Reflexivity and the American 'Madame Butterfly' Narratives." *Cambridge Opera Journal* 17, no. 1 (2005): 59–93.

———. *Extreme Exoticism: Japan in the American Musical Imagination* (forthcoming).

Sherwood, Gayle. "The Choral Works of Charles Ives: Chronology, Style, Reception." Ph.D. diss., Yale University, 1995.

———. "Questions and Veracities: Reassessing the Chronology of Ives's Choral Works." *Musical Quarterly* 78 (1994): 429–47.

Shimakawa, Karen. *National Abjection: The Asian American Body Onstage.* Durham: Duke University Press, 2002.

Shuker, Roy. *Understanding Popular Music,* 2nd ed. New York: Routledge, 1994.

Simeon, Omer. "Mostly about Morton." In *Selections from the Gutter: Jazz Portraits from "The Jazz Record,"* edited by Art Hodes and Chadwick Hansen, 92–93. Berkeley: University of California Press, 1977.

Sinclair, James. *A Descriptive Catalogue of the Music of Charles Ives.* New Haven: Yale University Press, 1999.

Smith, Pamela. "Caribbean Influences on Early New Orleans Jazz." M.A. thesis, Tulane University, 1986.

Solomon, Maynard. "Charles Ives: Some Questions of Veracity." *Journal of the American Musicological Society* 50, no. 3 (1987): 443–70.

"Some Good Songs in Casino Summer Show." *New York World,* 19 July 1910, 5.

"Songs of Hawaii and Other Popular Numbers Feature October List." *Edison Phonograph Monthly* 14, no. 9 (September 1916): 12.

Southern California Music Company. Advertisement. *Los Angeles Times,* 31 July 1914, 13.

Spaeth, Sigmund. *A History of Popular Music in America.* London: Phoenix House, 1948.

Starr, Larry. *A Union of Diversities: Style in the Music of Charles Ives.* New York: Schirmer Books, 1992.

Stein, Louise. "Before the Latin Tinge: Spanish Music and the 'Spanish Idiom' in the United States, 1778–1940." In *Spain in America: The Origins of His-*

panism in the United States, edited by Richard L. Kagan, 193–245. Urbana: University of Illinois Press, 2002.

Sternberg, Paul E. *Paintings by American Women: Selections from the Collection of Louise and Alan Sellars.* Marietta, Ga.: Louise and Alan Sellars Collection of Art by American Women, 1989.

Stevenson, Robert. "The Latin Tinge, 1800–1900." *Inter-American Music Review* 2, no. 2 (1980): 73–101.

———. *Philosophies of American Music History.* Washington, D.C.: Published for the Library of Congress by the Louis Charles Elson Memorial Fund, 1970.

Stewart, Alexander. " 'Funky Drummer': New Orleans, James Brown and the Rhythmic Transformation of American Popular Music." *Popular Music* 19, no. 3 (2000): 293–318.

Stewart, Jack. "The Mexican Band Legend: Myth, Reality, and Musical Impact, a Preliminary Investigation." *Jazz Archivist: A Newsletter of the William Ransom Hogan Jazz Archive* 6, no. 2 (1991): 1–14.

Stewart, Jacqueline Najuma. *Migrating to the Movies: Cinema and Black Urban Modernity.* Berkeley: University of California Press, 2005.

Stewart, Rex. *Boy Meets Horn.* Edited by Claire P. Gordon. Ann Arbor: University of Michigan Press, 1991.

Stillman, Amy Kuʻuleialoha. "Hawaiian Hula Competitions: Event, Repertoire, Performance, Tradition." *Journal of the American Folklore Society* 109, no. 434 (1996): 357–80.

———. "Hula Hits, Local Music and Local Charts: Some Dynamics of Popular Hawaiian Music." In *Sound Alliances: Indigenous Peoples, Cultural Politics and Popular Music in the Pacific,* edited by Philip Hayward, 89–103. London: Cassell, 1998.

———. "Of the People Who Love the Land: Vernacular History in the Poetry of Modern Hawaiian Hula." *Amerasia Journal* 28, no. 3 (2002): 85–108.

———. "Published Hawaiian Songbooks." *Notes* 44, no. 2 (1987): 221–39.

Stoddard, Tom. *Jazz on the Barbary Coast.* Chigwell, Essex: Storyville Publications, 1982.

Stokes, Martin, ed. *Ethnicity, Identity, and Music: The Musical Construction of Place.* Providence, R.I.: Berg, 1994.

Swafford, Jan. *Charles Ives: A Life with Music.* New York: W. W. Norton, 1996.

Tatar, Elizabeth. "Introduction: What Is Hawaiian Music?" In *Hawaiian Music and Musicians: An Illustrated History,* edited by George S. Kanahele, xxiii–xxx. Honolulu: University Press of Hawaii, 1979.

Taylor, Albert Pierce. "Hawaii at Panama International Exposition." In *Hawaiian Almanac and Annual for 1915,* 74–80. Honolulu: Thos. G. Thrum, 1914.

———. "Hawaii: The Best-Known Building at the Panama-Pacific Exposition, 1915." In *Hawaiian Almanac and Annual for 1916,* 147–50. Honolulu: Thos. G. Thrum, 1915.

Tick, Judith. "Charles Ives and Gender Ideology." In *Musicology and Difference: Gender and Sexuality in Music Scholarship,* edited by Ruth A. Solie, 83–106. Berkeley: University of California Press, 1993.

———. "Ragtime and the Music of Charles Ives." *Current Musicology* 18 (1974): 105–13.

Tischler, Barbara L. *An American Music: The Search for an American Musical Identity.* New York: Oxford University Press, 1986.

Titon, Jeff Todd. *Early Downhome Blues: A Musical and Cultural Analysis.* Urbana: University of Illinois Press, 1977.

Todaro, Tony. *The Golden Years of Hawaiian Entertainment, 1874–1974.* Honolulu: Tony Todaro Publishing, 1974.

Todd, Frank Morton. *The Story of the Exposition.* 5 vols. New York: G. P. Putnam's Sons, 1921.

Tsou, Judy. "Gendering Race: Stereotypes of Chinese Americans in Popular Sheet Music." *repercussions* 6, no. 2 (1997): 25–62.

Tucker, Mark. "Jazz." In *Grove Music Online*, edited by Laura Macy. www.grovemusic.com (accessed 15 December 2007).

Unsigned review of *The Bird of Paradise. New York Clipper*, 20 January 1912, 9.

Van, Gilles de. "Fin de Siècle Exoticism and the Meaning of the Far Away." Translated by William Ashbrook. *Opera Quarterly* 11, no. 3 (1995): 77–94.

"Vaudeville Reviews of the Week: Casino." *New York Clipper*, 28 July 1910, 581.

Von Glahn, Denise. "Musikalische Stadlandschaft: Central Park in the Dark" ("The Sylvan in the City: *Central Park in the Dark*"). *Muzik-Konzepte* 123 (January 2004): 89–108.

———. *The Sounds of Place: Music and the American Cultural Landscape.* Boston: Northeastern University Press, 2003.

Wald, Elijah. *Escaping the Delta: Robert Johnson and the Invention of the Blues.* New York: Amistad, 2004.

Walser, Robert, ed. *Keeping Time: Readings in Jazz History.* New York: Oxford University Press, 1999.

———. *Running with the Devil: Power, Gender, and Madness in Heavy Metal Music.* Hanover, N.H.: Wesleyan University Press, 1993.

Warnack, Henry Christeen. "Atmosphere and Natives." *Los Angeles Times*, 3 October 1913, sec. 3, 4.

Washburne, Christopher. "Armstrong and Ellington Do the 'Rhumba': The Case for Jazz as a Transnational and Global Music." Paper presented at the annual meeting of the American Musicological Society, Houston, November 2003.

———. "The Clave of Jazz: A Caribbean Contribution to the Rhythmic Foundation of an African-American Music." *Black Music Research Journal* 17, no. 1 (1997): 59–80.

Weintraub, Andrew N. "Jawaiian Music and Local Cultural Identity in Hawai'i." In *Sound Alliances: Indigenous Peoples, Cultural Politics and Popular Music in the Pacific*, edited by Philip Hayward, 78–88. London: Cassell, 1998.

Whitburn, Joel. *Pop Memories, 1890–1954: The History of American Popular Music.* Menomonee Falls, Wis.: Record Research, 1986.

Whiting, Steven Moore. *Satie the Bohemian.* Oxford: Clarendon Press, 1999.

Wickes, E. M. *Writing the Popular Song.* Springfield, Mass.: Home Correspondence School, 1916.

Williams, Martin. *Jazz Changes.* New York: Oxford University Press, 1992.
———, ed. *Jazz Panorama: From the Pages of the Jazz Review.* New York: Crowell-Collier Press, 1962.
Williams, William H. A., *'Twas Only an Irishman's Dream: The Image of Ireland and the Irish in American Popular Song Lyrics, 1800–1920.* Urbana: University of Illinois Press, 1996.
Wilson, Lawrence A. "Ragtime: Its Roots, Style and Influence on Twentieth-Century Music." D.Mus. diss., Indiana University, 1981.
Wodehouse, Artis. "Tracing Gershwin's Piano Rolls." In *The Gershwin Style: New Looks at the Music of George Gershwin,* ed. Wayne Schneider, 209–24. New York: Oxford University Press, 1999.
Wong, Deborah. *Speak It Louder: Asian Americans Making Music.* New York: Routledge, 2004.
Wong, K. Scott. "Chinatown: Conflicting Images, Contested Terrain." *MELUS* 20, no. 1 (1995): 3–15.
Wong, K. Scott, and Sucheng Chan, eds. *Claiming America: Constructing Chinese American Identities during the Exclusion Era.* Philadelphia: Temple University Press, 1998.
Wright, Richard B. *Black Boy: A Record of Childhood and Youth.* New York: Harper and Brothers, 1937.
Yang, Mina. "Orientalism and the Music of Asian Immigrant Communities in California, 1924–1945." *American Music* 19, no. 4 (2001): 385–416.
Ybarra, Thomas R. "Hawaii." *New York Times,* 22 October 1916, sec. SM, 19.
Yu, Henry. *Thinking Orientals: Migration, Contact, and Exoticism in Modern America.* New York: Oxford University Press, 2001.
Zoglin, Richard. "Not Just Chop Suey: *Flower Drum Song* Gets a Nifty Broadway Tune-Up." *Time,* 28 October 2002, 63.

Index

Blues," 56, 75–76; "Fickle Fay
Creep," 56; "Jelly Roll Blues," 56,
63–68, 77, 233n62; "La Paloma," 52;
"Mama 'Nita," 56; "Mama's Got a
Baby," 56, 76; "Mamamita," 56,
233n65; "Mamanita," 56, 70, 73, 75,
77, 81; "Mamanita Blues," 56, 73;
"Milenberg Joys," 233n49; "Maple
Leaf Rag," 48–49, 52, 56; "My
Home Is in a Southern Town,"
233n49; "New Orleans Blues," 52,
56, 58–65, 70, 77, 81, 232n42; "New
Orleans Joys" (*see* Morton, "New
Orleans Blues"); *New Orleans
Memories*, 78; "Original Jelly-Roll
Blues," 56–57, 76; *The Spanish
Tinge* (Morton), 78; "Soap Suds,"
56, 71; "Sweet Anita Mine," 56,
234n67; "The Pearls," 56–57,
69–70; "Tia Juana (Tee Wanna),"
56, 70–73, 81, 233n60; "Wolverine
Blues," 72
Moy, James, 144
"Mr. Dooley," 144
Munsey's Magazine, 130
Murphy, Stanley, 187
Murray, Billy, 139, 153
Museum of Chinese in the Americas,
162
music: and national identity, 3–6, 11,
14–15, 18, 143; and place, 84–85
"My Dreamy China Lady," 148, 150
"My Gal From Honolulu," 171
"My Hawaii," 197
"My Hawaiian Maid," 176
"My Honey Lou," 187
"My Honolulu Bride," 187
My Honolulu Girl, 179
"My Honolulu Lady," 172
"My Honolulu Lulu," 187–88
"My Hula Lula Girl," 165–66
"My Rose of Waikiki," 187
"My Waikiki Ukulele Girl," 187
"My Yellow Jacket Girl," 158

"Nagasaki," 154
Nä Hökü Hanohano Awards, 211

"Nani Na Pua Ko'olau," 171
Narváez, Peter, 63, 75
"Nashville Woman's Blues," 112
Nesbitt, John, 154–55
New Orleans, 56–58, 63
"New Orleans Stomp," 111
Nicholas, Albert, 75–76, 235n83
Nicholls, David: *The Cambridge History of American Music*, 7
Nicholson, Jack, 160
"Night in Hawaii," 185–86
Noble, Johnny, 176
"Nuestro Himno," 1–4, 218; and
American identity, 3–4; and immigration rights, 2–4; interpretations
of, 2–3; origin of, 1; and "The
Star-Spangled Banner," 1, 3

O'Meally, Robert, 105, 107
"Oh, How She Could Yacki Hacki
Wicki Wacki Woo (That's Love in
Honolu)," 187, 203
Oja, Carol, 6
OKeh Records, 90–91, 93, 95, 102, 106,
117–20
okina, 251n6
"Old Hundred," 29
"Old Kentucky Home," 208
Oliver Ditson Co., 171
Oliver, Joe "King," 76, 89–90, 97, 104,
111–12, 114, 238n49, 240n74
Omi, Michael, 127
"Ona Ona," 186
"One-Two-Three-Four," 181, 190
"On the Beach at Waikiki," 176,
186–87 190–91, 200, 254n62
opium, 124, 130–32, 137–38, 245n22,
248n64
"Opium Dreams," 160
Orchestra Hall, 210, 212
Oriental Illusions (Memphis
Archives), 126, 161–62
orientalism, 125–27, 149
Ory, Kid, 91, 106, 117, 127
"O Sole Mio," 208
"Our America," 218
"Over There," 4

steel guitar, 15, 168, 179–80, 185, 197,
    200, 254n70, 254n71; glissando on,
    197–98
Stewart, Jacqueline, 109
Stewart, Rex, 90, 106, 154
Still, William Grant, 123, 220
Stillman, Amy Ku'uleialoha, 169, 210,
    251n7
Stop! Look! Listen! (Dillingham), 189,
    191
Story, Chick, 148–49
Stover, Dr. G. H., 186
Stravinsky, Igor, 46
Strong, Jimmy, 114
Strump, Katrine, 201
Sunset, 203
Sunset Café, 114
Swafford Jan, 23, 36, 42
"Sweet Leilani," 208
"Sweet Luana," 181

Tampa Red, 112
Tan, Amy, 159
Tangerine (Shubert), 179
tango, 49, 53–54
Tatum, Art, 127
Taylor, Deems, 123
Taylor, Laurette, 181
Teagarden, Jack, 127
Ten Eyke, Melissa, 131
"Texas Moaner Blues," 112
theater orchestra, 23–26, 29–30, 36
"They're All Good American Names,"
    145
Thomas, John, 94
Thomas, Walter "Foots," 78
Thomson, Virgil, 45
"Tia Juana," 70–71
Tick, Judith, 27, 228n69
Tijuana, 69–71
Tin Pan Alley, 12, 15, 21, 23, 41, 46, 72,
    115, 121–52, 158–60, 162, 164–76,
    181–83, 185–97, 200–204
Tizol, Juan, 77
Tommy Dorsey and His Orchestra,
    126
Toots Paka Troupe, 200

tresillo, 49, 53–54, 59–60, 64–66, 68,
    71–73, 75, 78–79, 233n62
Trevi, Glori, 1
Trip to Chinatown, A (Hoyt), 121–22,
    243n1
"Trocha: A Cuban Dance," 235
Tsou, Judy, 127, 130, 142
Tucker, Mark, 53
Tully, Richard Walton, 177–81
Twain, Mark, 129, 160, 203
Tyers, William H., 57, 76, 235n83

"Ua Like No A Like," 186
Uke-Trades, 197
'ukulele, 15, 165, 168, 170, 185,
    195–99, 200–201, 203, 205–12,
    251n6, 254n70; chord symbols,
    197
Ulric, Lenore, 181
Understanding Popular Music
    (Shuker), 9
Up and Down Broadway, 131, 133,
    139, 152–53, 156, 163, 245n24,
    245n25, 245n29, 246n40, 246n46
Up in the Clouds, 227n43
Urban Box Office, 2
U.S. Bureau of Education, 3
U.S. Constitution, 218
U.S. national anthem. *See*
    "Star-Spangled Banner"

Van, Gilles de, 170
Van Halen, Eddie, 211
Vandersloot Music, 199
Variety, 192
Vaughan, Sarah, 124, 127
Victor Orthophonic, 93, 238n48
Victor Records, 114, 173, 180,
    199–200, 202, 208
Victrola, 90, 201
Vietnam War, 4
"A Vision of Hawaii," 197
Von Glahn, Denise, 46
Von Tilzer, Albert, 187, 192

Waikiki Beach, 186, 190
"Waikiki Blues," 187

Text: 10/13 Aldus
Display: Aldus
Compositor: Binghamton Valley Composition, LLC
Printer and binder: Thomson-Shore, Inc.